Personal Conflict Management

Personal Conflict Management, 2nd edition details the common causes of conflict, summarizes the theories that explain why conflict happens, presents strategies for managing conflict, and invites consideration of the risks of leaving conflict unsettled. The book balances information about conflict with specific skills and tools to transform these difficult encounters, and explores how gender, race, culture, generation, power, emotional intelligence, and trust affect how individuals perceive conflict and choose conflict tactics. Detailed attention is given to the role of listening and both competitive and cooperative negotiation tactics. Separate chapters explain how to deal with bullies and conflict via social media. The book caps off its exploration of interpersonal conflict with chapters that: provide tools to analyze one's conflicts and better choose strategic responses; examine the role of anger and apology during conflict; explore mediation technique; and evaluate how conflict occurs in different situations such as family, intimacy, work, and social media.

Suzanne McCorkle is an Emerita Professor of Public Policy and Administration, as well as Director of Conflict Management Studies at Boise State University.

Melanie J. Reese is Dispute Resolution Coordinator for the Idaho Department of Education and Professor Emerita at Boise State University.

Personal Conflict Management

Theory and Practice

2nd edition

Suzanne McCorkle
Melanie J. Reese

Routledge
Taylor & Francis Group

NEW YORK AND LONDON

This edition published 2018
by Routledge
711 Third Avenue, New York, NY 10017

and by Routledge
2 Park Square, Milton Park, Abingdon, Oxon, OX14 4RN

Routledge is an imprint of the Taylor & Francis Group, an informa business

First Published 2010 Pearson Education, Inc.

Library of Congress Cataloging-in-Publication Data
Names: McCorkle, Suzanne, author. | Reese, Melanie, author.
Title: Personal conflict management : theory and practice / Suzanne
   McCorkle, Melanie J. Reese.
Description: 2nd edition. | New York : Routledge, 2017. | Revised edition of the
   authors'
Identifiers: LCCN 2017018431 | ISBN 9781138210981 (hardback) | ISBN
   9781138210998 (pbk.) | ISBN 9781315453811 (ebook)
Subjects: LCSH: Conflict management. | Problem solving. | Interpersonal
   relations.
Classification: LCC HM1126 .M396 2017 | DDC 303.6/9—dc23
LC record available at https://lccn.loc.gov/2017018431

ISBN: 978-1-138-21098-1 (hbk)
ISBN: 978-1-138-21099-8 (pbk)
ISBN: 978-1-315-45381-1 (ebk)

Typeset in Joanna MT
by Apex CoVantage, LLC

Visit the eResource: www.routledge.com/9781138210998

Contents

Toolbox Resources

Cases

Preface

In our combined 50-plus years of teaching conflict management, mediation, and related course-work, we have used many resources. We found that over the years our conceptualization of an interpersonal conflict course differed from what was available in existing textbooks.

Specifically, we were interested in demonstrating the value of collaborative models for resolving conflict and the necessity and benefits in understanding competitive approaches. Our experience as mediators and organizational facilitators also influenced much of our curriculum and expanded our conceptualization of conflict management.

Finally, having taught a course in conflict management at three different universities, we discovered the value of differing approaches to interpersonal conflict: some instructors focus entirely on interpersonal conflict theory, others combine theory and application, and many transition from interpersonal conflict to other settings. Our aim was to create and to represent innovations in curriculum and cutting-edge concepts arising from research. In the 2nd edition, we expanded more on the area of conflict in intimate relationships and added a focus on conflict within the worlds of social media.

We believe that a text should be accessible and inviting to the students. Toward that end, we have included many examples, case studies, and application exercises. At the beginning of each chapter, vocabulary terms and chapter objectives identify key concepts for students to master. As we field-tested the book, we found the discussion questions within the chapters were helpful guides for classroom interaction. They also enhance students' ability to integrate the concepts with their lives. Our goal is to support an interactive environment that optimizes opportunities for learning.

In the 2nd edition, we also updated exercises, case analyses, and project/essay suggestions at the end of each chapter to provide a focus for class or group discussion, as well as potential topics for student assignments.

Acquiring conflict management knowledge and skill is beneficial to students, regardless of their major. We want to make this course enjoyable and thought-provoking for students and instructors. We would love to hear back from you about ways to improve the course or suggestions for making this material more meaningful.

Suzanne McCorkle and Melanie Reese

Acknowledgments

We would like to thank all those who assisted in the creation of this book. In particular, we thank our students, whose comments inspired many of the cases and who helped field-test the chapters. We also thank the many instructors who have provided comments to enlighten the 2nd edition. We thank our editor, Laura Briskman, and copyeditor, Christina Tang-Bernas, and all of the publication team at Routledge.

Section I

The Nature of Interpersonal Conflict and Its Causes

Even though we cannot change others, we are not powerless in the face of conflict. *Personal Conflict Management, 2nd edition* explores the dynamic world of interpersonal conflict management. Conflict managers can develop more successful relationships and better reach career goals than those who do not cope well with conflict.

Successful conflict management stands on a three-part foundation of knowledge, attitudes, and skills. First, the competent conflict manager must have knowledge about conflict theory, causes, patterns, and tactics. Second, the best conflict managers embrace the productive and creative energy of conflict. Finally, flexible conflict managers develop a toolbox of skills to engage in competitive conflict (when one must) and cooperative conflict (when one can). Although it may take two to tango, it only takes one person to create the opportunity to change a conflict. One person, with knowledge, skill, and the right attitude, can enhance the probability of transforming an unproductive conflict into opportunities for everyone. No set of skills can promise to resolve every conflict, but we can guarantee one trend: Many conflicts will not improve on their own.

Section I begins with an examination of the nature of interpersonal conflict and how it differs from other communication contexts. The section continues with a discussion of the dominant theories that guide the study of interpersonal conflict, the contrast between competitive and cooperative approaches to interpersonal conflict, an elaboration of conflict causes, and how sex/gender, race, culture, generation, power, trust, and humor affect the choices people make during conflict.

Chapter 1

Conflict in Everyday Life

Vocabulary

Argument	Interpersonal conflict
Barnlund's six views	Intrapersonal communication
Choice point	Intrapersonal conflict
Connotative meaning	Latent conflict
Denotative meaning	Process goals
Deutsch's crude law on social relationships	Pseudo-conflict
Face goals	Relationship goal
Interdependence	Substantive goals

Objectives

After reading the chapter, you should be able to:

1.   Identify the components in the definition of interpersonal conflict
2.   Explore the role of perception in communication and conflict
3.   Differentiate between interpersonal conflict, argument, and negotiation
4.   Explain why conflict is an inherent and crucial part of the human condition
5.   Explain how the seven assumptions affect the choices made by conflict scholars

What Is Interpersonal Conflict?

Interpersonal conflict *is a struggle among a small number of interdependent people (usually two) arising from perceived interference with goal achievement.* Interpersonal conflict occurs when one person perceives that another person is blocking an important goal.

The definition of interpersonal conflict recognizes that conflict is both internal and external. Internally, when an individual feels a struggle between personal goals and someone else's actions, conflict is germinated. The external dimension of interpersonal conflict manifests in how one acts. In other words, the internal feeling of struggle affects how one *behaves* externally. Even though the conflict may not be an obvious topic of conversation, communication is different than before the conflict germinated because of a feeling of inner disequilibrium.

Most individuals have experienced the instinct that something is wrong when talking with a friend or acquaintance. Even though no discussions have occurred about the topic of concern and no obvious conflict strategies have been applied, a conflict is being expressed through the nuances of nonverbal communication—perhaps a look of disagreement or eye rolling when a topic someone would rather avoid is brought up. One person may know there is a conflict and the other does not. For example, there may be a general sense of tension at work between coworkers that others observe, but the workers themselves aren't consciously aware of their behaviors. At other times, there is no doubt that a conflict exists. Direct expression of conflict can take many forms—some productive such as starting cooperative problem solving and some less so, for example yelling and calling each other names. A discussion of each part of the definition of interpersonal conflict will highlight its important elements.

Interpersonal Conflict Is a Struggle

The term "struggle," popularized by Keltner (1987) as it relates to interpersonal conflict, is an apt description of how conflict differs from casual disagreements, mild differences, or intellectual argument. Not all differences rise to the level of interpersonal conflict. An interpersonal conflict is hallmarked by a feeling of struggle, meaning participants in an interpersonal conflict are invested in the outcome. In casual disagreements, mild differences, or intellectual arguments, the participants have less investment in the outcome. They even might argue as a type of entertainment. Two friends may call each other "pig," "stupid," "brat," or even profane names in a ritual of good-natured banter. What might be fighting words in another context is a type of bonding for these friends. Sports fans may argue passionately about which quarterback is the all-time best as a type of entertainment and a way to practice their command of statistics, facts, and sports trivia. The conversation, unless it takes a negative turn and becomes personal, is not an interpersonal conflict.

Sometimes a conversation that starts as a casual disagreement can transition into an interpersonal conflict. For example, Jake is deeply invested in a perception of himself as a sports expert who loves his Denver Broncos. When his sports expertise is questioned, even playfully, he may see the challenger as interfering with his role as a defender of his team. If his self-image is challenged, Jake may become defensive. To be an interpersonal conflict, the participants must feel invested in the outcome—emotionally and/or relationally.

Interpersonal Conflict

Interpersonal conflict is a struggle among a small number of interdependent people (usually two) arising from perceived interference with goal achievement.

Interpersonal Conflict Occurs Among a Small Number of People

The minimum number is two. The maximum number is open but limited to a number less than when group dynamics begin to alter communicative processes. Group communication contains many of the characteristics of a two-person conversation, but it also includes unique dynamics such as group leadership, the possibility that everyone may not talk to every other person, or specialized role development (see Chapter 16). Although this book examines interpersonal conflict in a variety of settings (friendship, family, and work), the primary focus is the dynamic interplay of two individuals.

Even though **intrapersonal conflicts**—purely internal struggle about one's goals—do occur, they are not the primary interest of this book. Psychologists are interested in internal states and may focus on conflict completely within the self. The feeling that two of one's cherished goals are in conflict is not unusual. A person may believe that exercise is important to long-term health and have a goal of staying fit, yet spend free time playing Clash of Clans online. Internal conversations, called **intrapersonal communication**, might have the "internal athlete" chewing out the "couch potato" in a tussle among competing goals.

CASE 1.1

Let's Switch Jobs

Rachel and Beth are coworkers. Beth has been working for the company for over three years. Rachel was hired as part-time help about a year ago. Both work at the front desk as receptionists. Every morning when Rachel arrives there is a pile of customer service requests, files to be processed, and appointments that need to be scheduled. When Beth comes in, she goes to the back room to help other coworkers with general filing.

It is June 29, and the end of the month is the busiest time in the company. Rachel is stressing that she won't get through all the customer requests by the end of the day, which could really be bad for some of the customers. Rachel enters the back office to ask Beth if she will help at the front desk. As Rachel enters the back room, she sees Beth shopping on the Internet for new flip-flops.

Rachel:	"Beth, could you help me up front? I don't think I'm going to get through all the paperwork by the end of the day."
Beth:	"I can't right now. I'm waiting for Brent to get off the phone to help me lift boxes in the filing room."

Disgusted, Rachel walks to the front desk where she continues to slog through the customer service requests. After a while, the FedEx truck arrives to drop off a pile of mail and boxes. One of the packages is addressed to Beth from Eddie Bauer. Rachel gets up and goes to the back room to hand out what FedEx has delivered. She saves Beth's delivery for last.

Rachel:	"Beth, you have a delivery."
Beth:	"Really, who from?"
Rachel:	"Eddie Bauer."
Beth:	"Oh, awesome! I ordered my husband a nice lunch box to take to work."
Rachel:	"It must be nice to have the time to shop while you're at work. Is that all you ever do back here?"
Beth:	"I only shop when I have some downtime."
Rachel:	"Well, you want to switch places for a while? I'd love to be paid to shop on the Internet!"

Rachel drops the package onto the floor and stomps back to the front desk. Beth glares at her as she walks away.

DISCUSSION QUESTION • 1.1

How is conflict expressed by Rachel in Case 1.1?

How people react to conflict makes all the difference. In Case 1.1, Beth may be clueless that a problem even exists. Rachel avoids talking with Beth about job expectations, but she becomes angry when her expectations aren't met. Avoidance, overreaction, and lashing out can turn a minor disagreement into a full-blown conflict.

Interpersonal Conflict Requires at Least a Minimal Amount of Interdependence

Interdependence can be understood as the level to which people need each other to attain their goals. Few goals can be achieved in complete isolation. Students cannot get A's in a class without someone to evaluate their work; teachers and students are interdependent. Bosses need employees to complete tasks, and employees need bosses to write paychecks: They are interdependent.

DISCUSSION QUESTION • 1.2

Are strangers waiting for a bus interdependent? If so, how? If not, what would have to change for them to become interdependent in a significant way?

Interdependence is tied inextricably to perceptions of goal interference. If one person doesn't need another to reach a goal, there is no interdependence and no reason to care. Without some perceived interdependence, there is no reason to engage in conflict.

Some authors claim that interdependence must be significant and urgent for interpersonal conflict to exist. Lulofs and Cahn (2000) distinguish between conflict, disagreements, bickering, and aggression on the basis of interdependence. They assert: (1) People perceive they have different means or seek different outcomes, (2) they realize the conflict could negatively impact the relationship if not addressed, and (3) there is a sense of urgency. Although urgency affects intensity, within the definition in this book, the parties to a conflict must have mutual dependency only to the extent that one party thinks the other is interfering with goal achievement. What moves conflict to be fully expressed or not is the individuals' weighing of the importance of their relationship to the importance of the goal interference.

CASE 1.2

The Coffee Conundrum

Archer and Miles decided to have a coffee before their next class, which sometimes is a real snoozer. In line, they ribbed each other about their coffee choices. Archer said that Miles' tall latte order was a wimpy choice; Miles retorted that Archer's plain coffee was just sad, at least he could order a manly espresso. Archer responded that his coffee was a Jamaican Arabica blend from the Blue Mountain region that didn't need to be diluted with hot milk.

As they picked up their brews from the barista, Archer accidentally jostled Miles, and some of his latte sloshed onto his shirt. Archer laughed and said, "That's the best use for a latte

I've seen yet. Maybe that shirt will have a clean spot now." The two attractive coeds in line behind them, who also were in their next class, snickered.

Interdependence exists in Case 1.2, The Coffee Conundrum. Archer and Miles are in the same class and friends enough to share a coffee. They enjoy good-natured banter together. If the coffee line experience occurred among two individuals who had no other contact and who might never see each other again, Miles may or may not feel the same urge to escalate the event to a conflict. Does this mean that strangers cannot have an interpersonal conflict? No. Even if Miles and Archer have no long-term relationship, either party may be offended enough at the other's behavior to create a perception of interference with self-image goals, particularly if the conversation was observed by others. A perception of important goal interference might lead to escalation of the situation—elevating it to a fully expressed interpersonal conflict. Long-term relationships are not a requirement for interpersonal conflict to occur. Conflicts require a minimal amount of interdependence—just enough to allow a perception of interference with goals.

Conflict Includes Interference With Goal Achievement

Every individual has goals. These goals may be profound or simple. Goals relate to tangible resources (**substantive goals**), how things should be done (**process goals**), who the parties are to each other (**relationship goals**), or one's sense of self-worth, pride, self-respect, or power (**face goals**). For example, in the Coffee Conundrum Case, everyone in line had the same initial substantive goal—get some coffee. Archer and Miles also were enjoying some nonconsequential banter about the merits of coffee, meeting relationship goals. There is no conflict so far. The potential for a conflict emerges when the coffee is spilled and Archer makes fun of the accidental spill. At that moment, a **choice point** exists—a moment when how one responds can change the entire direction of a relationship. Miles can laugh it off and make some comment about Archer's clumsiness, or he can take offense. If Miles feels embarrassed because the women observing the incident laughed at him, his self-esteem goals might be threatened. When his self-esteem goals are threatened, he may initiate a more serious conflict with Archer in an attempt to get even. Goals, a key construct in understanding the nature of conflict, are discussed in more depth in Chapter 4.

CASE 1.3

Daryl's Time-Bound Friendship

Back in high school, Mark was a good friend. Years later, we still see each other sometimes and go to a football game or do something together, but we don't hang out every day.

This is the way I see it. I wanted to change myself when I moved out of my mom's house. I want to marry and have a good life someday, so I need a good job and to make something of myself in the world.

Mark doesn't feel the same way. Mark is still doing the same things we did as kids. It's like he's locked in a time warp or something. He still looks at me and sees me as I was years ago. His opinions haven't changed much. He acts like we are still buddies in school who don't have any other responsibilities. He just wants to party every time we get together, and he spends every dollar he has on beer or his car. When I say I have to go to work and save money, Mark tells me to not be so serious and says I'm becoming a stuck-up college nerd. I think that if I hadn't known Mark all these years, I'd never choose him as a friend now.

DISCUSSION QUESTION • 1.3

Which of the four goal types is most evident in Case 1.3, "Daryl's Time-Bound Friendship"?

Conflict Is Perceived

The word *perceived* is critical to our understanding of interpersonal conflict. The act of communication is not an exact transference of meaning from one person to another. To the contrary, the meaning of any message or act is interpreted by the receiver of the message. Words carry different meanings for different individuals. The **denotative meaning** (dictionary definition) of a word is different from the **connotative meaning** (personal association for a word). For a teenager, the word "Snapchat" may be positively associated with the freedom to communicate with friends via videos and photos. For a parent, the word "Snapchat" may be negatively associated with a time-wasting activity that probably involves behaviors they wouldn't approve of—after all, the photos on Snapchat disappear after you look at them. While the denotation of Snapchat would be same for parent and teen, their connotations of Snapchat change depending on how each perceives the technology.

Other aspects of how communication works also compound the difficulties in communicating effectively. Messages are perceived differently than intended more often than we think. An inconsequential act in one person's mind can be perceived as an intentional slight by another person. One way of explaining how these interpretation mismatches occur is through Barnlund's concept of the six people in every two-person conversation.

Barnlund (1970), in his classic analysis of interpersonal communication, proposed that every conversation between two people really involves six views:

1.   How you view yourself
2.   How you view the other person
3.   How you believe the other person views you
4.   How the other person views himself or herself
5.   How the other person views you
6.   How the other person believes you view her or him

The interplay among **Barnlund's six views** provides fertile ground for interpersonal conflict. Mack may see himself as the workplace clown who makes everyone happy by telling jokes. He may believe that others see him as a good person who is well-intentioned when he jokes around. Mack thinks Maria is too serious and needs to loosen up a little and not work so hard, so he drops by her area every day to bring a little cheer into her life. Maria actually may view Mack as an insensitive sexist because he wastes work time telling inappropriate and sexually charged jokes. She sees herself as a professional who has a sense of humor but not for jokes that put down people, particularly women. Maria thinks Mack views her as inferior or as a sex object because of the jokes he tells about women. The interplay among the six views in a simple communicative encounter highlights two aspects of communication: How one is perceived can vary, and communication is not always received the way it was intended. With all the many ways messages can go astray, it is amazing that more conflicts do not erupt.

DISCUSSION QUESTION • 1.4

Discuss Barnlund's six views in Case 1.2, The Coffee Conundrum.

Conflict occurs whenever one party *perceives* the other person is standing between him or her and the attainment of an important goal. When the perception of goal interference is not activated, the conversation may be bantering or mild disagreement without rising to the level where interpersonal conflict manifests.

Perception is tricky business and, unless telepathy is achieved, requires skillful vigilance during conflict. What each individual perceives is her or his reality. An objective observer may study individuals and conclude that two people have different goals and are, in fact, interfering with each other's goal achievement—but the participants don't yet perceive it. In this scenario, interpersonal conflict does not yet exist; it is **latent conflict**. Conversely, two individuals may be embroiled in conflict when no goal interference objectively exists or is intended. The goal interference is based on miscommunication or inaccurate perceptions of another person's intentions. Some scholars label these events **pseudo-conflicts**, yet the struggles that ensue are just as hurtful and time consuming as objectively "real" differences. When perceived goal interference occurs, the conflict occurs. As Folger, Poole, and Stutman (2013) comment, "Regardless of whether incompatibility actually exists, if the parties believe incompatibility exists, then conditions are ripe for conflict" (p. 4).

> **KEY 1.1**
>
> Others rarely see us as we see ourselves.

Interpersonal Conflict Is Different From Argument

You may be surprised to learn that skillful arguing does not equate to skillful conflict management. To the contrary, stern dedication to logic may contribute to the creation of considerable interpersonal conflict. Someone who tells an angry coworker not "to be so emotional" is valuing rationality over feelings and probably makes their conflict bigger. **Argument** is a rational weighing of facts and evidence using the rules of logic (Herrick, 2015). Argument can be played by a set of formal rules like those used by an academic debate team.

Everyday arguments don't have a formal rule book, but share the idea of preferring logic over emotion. Arguments need not be emotional or even about topics that the debaters particularly care about. Some people just like to argue. Members of a college debate team research and argue both sides of an issue with equal vigor. Those who love argument will find something to disagree about no matter the topic. They enjoy the tussle of logic. The antiseptic purity of logic may work well when both parties value it equally, but it won't work with those who lead with their heart rather than their head. For more emotional individuals, rational responses that deny the legitimacy of feelings will make the conflict worse.

While interpersonal conflict and argument are not synonymous terms, there is considerable overlap between the process of personal conflict management and the process of negotiation. Negotiation, whether formal or informal, is the method used to resolve many differences, and is the focus of Chapter 9.

Seven Assumptions About Interpersonal Conflict

Now that we know what interpersonal conflict is, the next question is: How do communication scholars approach its study? Several general assumptions affect how interpersonal conflict is researched and the recommendations made for conflict managers.

First, *conflict is an inevitable and integral part of life.* As the author of *The Coward's Guide to Conflict* remarks, conflict is inescapable: "We can run, but we cannot hide! We can sprint, jog, scream, deny, avoid, and make any other desperate attempt to get away from conflict, but we cannot make conflict disappear from our lives. Conflict is a part of life. And, like it or not, you will have to deal with it in some way" (Ursiny, 2003, p. xvii). Knowing that conflict is an integral part of the human experience, scholars examine the attitudes, knowledge, analytical abilities, and skills that differentiate productive from destructive conflict experiences. Studying conflict is crucial because it is a part of everyday life. After studying interpersonal conflict, you may discover more choices are available to you than you previously thought.

Second, *conflict can be invigorating.* Some people find it so exciting that they constantly stir things up to create conflict. Conflict can be invigorating in both good and hurtful ways. Protracted negative conflict literally can make a person ill (Glendinning, 2001; Laschinger & Nosko, 2015; Wickham, Williamson, Beard, Kobayashi, & Hirst, 2016). Conversely, safely managed conflict can stimulate creativity or renew an at-risk relationship. Conflict can lead to personal and societal change.

The range of skills, attitudes, and assumptions that individuals bring to everyday problems underscores the fact that people do not have one uniform experience of conflict. Some individuals fear conflict; others seem to thrive on it. Yet research indicates that when asked to recall past conflicts, respondents almost uniformly talk about events that were negative and painful (McCorkle & Mills, 1992; Zweibel, Goldstein, Manwaring, & Marks, 2008). Even though personal experiences of conflict differ and people tend to view conflict as negative, the facts summarized in Table 1.1 make the study of conflict important.

Third, *overuse of any one strategy is a weakness.* People who only know one response to a conflict situation continue to reuse the same strategies and tactics—even when those behaviors do not have desirable outcomes. Studying interpersonal conflict helps an individual gain the capacity to analyze the nature of conflict, build an understanding of the available choices, and develop a repertoire of skills suitable to many different conflict situations.

Fourth, *we need more than one set of negotiation skills.* Americans live in a culture in which cooperative and competitive conflict management systems exist side by side. Persons aware of only one conflict perspective—cooperative or competitive—lack the knowledge and skills to be effective when conflict arises with a person operating in the opposite system. Competent conflict managers know how these two systems differ and how to bargain from strength in any situation. We provide strategies to approach conflict productively when competition is necessary and techniques to collaborate when cooperation is desirable. Knowledge of both cooperative and competitive approaches will help you navigate through confusing conflict situations with skill and confidence.

Fifth, *the cost of poorly managed conflict in relationships is high.* "By 2 years of age, children are highly familiar with conflict interchanges, and by the age of 4, they are veteran observers of, and participants in, family conflicts" (Stein & Albro, 2001, p. 115). Children learn about conflict management from many sources, including parental modeling. For intimate partners, the quality and type of communication during conflict is related to relationship satisfaction and long-term commitment

TABLE 1.1 Seven Assumptions About Interpersonal Conflict

Conflict is an inevitable and integral part of life.
Conflict can be invigorating.
Overusing any one strategy is a weakness.
We need more than one set of negotiation skills.
The cost to relationships of poorly managed conflict is high.
Lack of conflict management skills is correlated with increased abuse.
The cost of poorly managed conflicts at work is severe.

(Leggett, Roberts-Pittman, Byczek, & Morse, 2012). Other effects of unregulated conflict in relationships include loss of friendship or intimacy, avoidance, stress, illness, decreased self-confidence, relationship breakup/divorce, and sometimes violence. The ability to maintain important relationships is improved through the study of interpersonal conflict. Simply put, conflict management is part of the work of maintaining a personal or intimate relationship (Mansson, 2014).

Sixth, *the cost of poorly managed conflict to employers and employees is severe.* The Dana Measure of Financial Cost of Conflict itemizes the hidden costs of workplace conflict, including the monetary value of wasted time, lost opportunity, lower motivation, decreased productivity, absenteeism, conflict-incited theft, and illness. Dana (2003) concluded that even a relatively simple conflict among employees that consumes two hours per week of a manager's time can have direct costs of $30,000 to a business. A classic formula estimates that managers spend as much as 20 percent of their total time dealing with conflict (Marin, Sherblom, & Shipps, 1994). A study specific to the construction industry estimated the average on-the-job interpersonal conflict depletes 5.25 hours of work time at an average cost of $10,948 per issue (Brockman, 2014). An increasingly diverse workplace exposes employees, sometimes for the first time, to other social, racial, ethnic, or religious groups—enhancing opportunities for misunderstandings that may grow into conflicts.

Bullying (discussed in Chapter 11) probably is the most under-recognized kind of workplace conflict and stress (Boucaut, 2003). An annual workplace bullying survey found 27 percent of Americans faced abusive conduct at work and another 21 percent witnessed bullying at work (Namie, Christensen, & Phillips, 2014). Effects of conflict or bullying in organizations may include lack of productivity, stress, absenteeism, health issues, decreased self-confidence, poor work relationships, customer service erosion, increased turnover, a tarnished company reputation, legal actions, and sometimes violence. Studying interpersonal conflict is important to protect yourself as an employee and to encourage workplace productivity as a supervisor.

Lastly, *a lack of conflict management skills is correlated to increased verbal and physical aggression* (Olson, 2002). Although aggression and violence are complex phenomenon, acquiring conflict management skills provides alternatives to abusive behaviors. Many people act aggressively because they feel they have no other options to get their needs met. Acquiring skills in conflict management broadens choices and is instrumental in reducing violence and aggression.

DISCUSSION QUESTION • 1.5

Which of the assumptions about the study of conflict is most important to you personally at this stage of your life? Which of the five benefits do you most wish to have?

Developing a strong understanding of conflict is critical because the financial and personal costs are too high if we do not. Unmanaged and unproductive conflict affects our families, our friendships, and our livelihoods. Equipped with the right attitude, knowledge, and skills, interpersonal conflicts can be approached with less fear, more confidence, and better outcomes.

Beneficial Aspects of Interpersonal Conflict

There are also numerous advantages to the better management of interpersonal conflict that merit attention (summarized in Table 1.2). First, *knowledge of how to manage conflict and the ability to solve problems is a source of power.* Organizations value people who can solve problems. Bloomberg's 2015 annual survey of recruiters found businesses want but have difficulty finding applicants with communication skills, strategic thinking abilities, leadership skills, and creative problem-solving (Levy & Rodkin,

TABLE 1.2 Beneficial Aspects of Studying Conflict

Managing conflicts productively is a source of personal power.
Managing conflicts saves money.
Managing conflicts builds confidence.
Conflict managers create personal standards and ethics.
Managing conflicts creates opportunity.

2016). Many employers would rather hire someone who communicates well, knows how to manage conflict, and solves problems than someone who only has technical knowledge. Supervisors who manage conflict successfully avoid the inefficiencies of unproductive conflict.

Second, *conflict management saves money*. U.S. companies that use internal dispute resolution systems or professional managers of internal company disputes, called ombudsmen, claim up to 90 percent of employee disputes are settled quickly—reducing long appeals, wrongful termination lawsuits, and other productivity losses (Saleh, 2003; Wexler & Zimmerman, 2000). If conflict causes workplace turnover, actual and peripheral monetary costs are incurred, including costs of recruitment, opportunity lost while positions are unfilled, training costs, overall stress on workgroups when positions are vacant, and so forth.

DISCUSSION QUESTION • 1.6

Deutsch's crude law of social relationships suggests that your behaviors will lead others to behave in similar ways. That is, what goes around comes around. Have you experienced situations in which negative attitudes bred more negative attitudes or productive and positive behaviors led others to be more productive and positive?

Third, studying *conflict management can build personal confidence and competence*. In the personal realm, the successful management of conflict offers similar advantages as those in the world of work. Ursiny (2003) asserts that dealing with conflict productively may lead to better relationships, increased confidence, less anger, less depression, greater respect for others, increased intimacy, career enhancements, less fear, and a greater sense of personal strength. Skilled conflict managers develop a greater sense of confidence when conflict arises and know that they have choices in how to respond, which is an improvement over the helpless, trapped, or out-of-control feelings that some experience during conflict.

Fourth, *competent conflict managers set personal standards of ethics*. As Canary and Lakey (2013) explain, when you think strategically about managing conflict, you also have to take ethics into consideration. It isn't enough to just have a deep understanding of conflict and a robust toolbox of skills. A conflict manager also must decide which strategies he or she feels are appropriate in a given situation and when the boundaries of personal or social ethics would say: "That strategy of conflict management is too repugnant for me to use."

Finally, *conflict management creates opportunity*. The issues raised during conflict present individuals with choice points—not only in how to communicate and what tactics will be chosen, but also in what the future will become. We can assess if goals should be changed or determine what a relationship should be like in the future. These and other important choices arise in conflict and create forks in the road of a relationship. Morton Deutsch (2014) explains these crossroads through his **crude law of social relationships**, which posits: "The characteristic processes and effects elicited by a given type of social relationship also tend to elicit that type of social relationship, and a typical effect tends to induce the other typical effects of that relationship" (p. 12). In other words, the choices we make in communication are often reciprocated and played back to us by the other. Our actions create our future. Clearly, conflict management is an integral skill for making people's lives better.

Summary

Interpersonal conflict is defined as a struggle among a small number of interdependent people stemming from perceived goal interference. Argument and mild disagreement do not fit the definition. Goals can be substantive, relationship, face, or process focused. The definition of interpersonal conflict is based in the individual who perceives goal interference and, subsequently, alters his or her behavior.

Although each person may experience interpersonal conflict differently, seven general assumptions of conflict apply to everyone: (1) conflict is inevitable, (2) conflict can be invigorating, (3) overuse of any one conflict strategy is a weakness, (4) cooperative and competitive conflict perspectives exist in modern life, (5) the cost of poorly managed conflict on relationships is high, (6) lack of conflict management skills is related to verbal and physical aggression, and (7) the cost of poorly managed conflict at work also is substantial. Unmanaged conflict can affect virtually all aspects of life in a negative way.

The choices we make in choosing conflict strategies may have a reciprocal effect on others according to Deutsch's crude law on social relationships. Becoming a competent conflict manager has many benefits, including (1) managing conflicts productively is a source of personal power, (2) managing conflicts saves money, (3) managing conflicts builds confidence, (4) conflict managers create personal standards and ethics, and (5) managing conflicts creates opportunity.

Chapter Resources

Exercises

1. In groups, select two people willing to talk about their first impressions of each other. As they discuss their first impressions, diagram their experience using Barnlund's six views.
2. As a group, discuss instances during past encounters where misperception or lack of communication played a role in the conflict.
3. How would you answer the questions posed in the following:

    "I have frequent conflict with my friends and spouse; is there something wrong with me?"
    "I just ignore conflicts whenever they come up; is that a good strategy?"
    "Why do I always feel like I'm the one who lost, even when I get my way?"
    "I like to keep things stirred up because it helps me feel alive; is that wrong?"
    "I don't like conflict, so I let the other person have his or her way; is there a problem with that?"

Journal/Essay Topics

1. What disagreement from your past had the greatest impression on you? Describe the conflict and then compare what occurred to the definition of interpersonal conflict. According to the definition of conflict in the text, is your example an interpersonal conflict?

2. Select a recent interpersonal conflict you experienced. Describe the conflict using Barnlund's six views.
3. Provide an example of how Deutsch's crude law on social relationships has played out in real life.

Research Topics

1. Consult textbooks or journal articles to learn more about group or organizational conflict. Write a paper that describes how group or organizational conflict differs from interpersonal conflict.
2. Compare the definition of conflict in this text to other definitions of conflict. How are the definitions different? What common threads run through all of the definitions?

Mastery Case

Examine the Mastery Mini-Cases. Mark each item as: **Clearly** a conflict using the definition of interpersonal conflict, **Not** a conflict using the definition, or **Maybe** a conflict. State the reasoning behind your classification of each case.

1. You are waiting to get your free tickets to a concert on campus. Four students arrive and get in line while thanking the person ahead of you for saving a place for them. You are very annoyed.
2. You have been planning for months to go home with your roommate over the holiday break and visit his family. One day, your roommate says you should "find something else to do over break because I'm going skiing with some friends." You can't believe he said this and hotly reply, "Hey, we've been planning our trip for months. If you switch out now because you got a better deal, you are a scumbag."
3. You are house-training your puppy. He is far enough along to know what you want him to do, but he gets mad when you are gone all day and urinates on the kitchen floor.
4. A newly married couple differs on what to do with their money. He wants to save and invest to build wealth and buy items only when enough cash is saved to make the purchase. She wants to borrow money and get a new plasma television right now. They have the same conversation several nights in a row. After the last episode, he sleeps on the couch.
5. Two members of the debate team argue for and against changing national policies based on the effects of climate change.
6. You trip over an uneven sidewalk in front of the student union center and break your ankle. You are trying to decide whether to sue the university for damages.
7. Your sister keeps texting you about how crummy her car is. You realize that the reason she told you about her car problems was because she wanted to borrow your car again. You don't want to lend it to her, so you actively avoid answering her texts or going places she might be for the next week.
8. Your professor makes a comment that people of "your generation," as a whole, are less patriotic than her generation. You are offended and tell your friend about it.

References

Barnlund, D. C. (1970). A transactional model of communication. In K. K. Sereno & D. Mortenson (Eds.), *Foundations of communication theory* (pp. 83–102). New York: Harper & Row.

Boucaut, R. (2003). Workplace bullying: Overcoming organizational barriers and the way ahead. In W. J. Pammer & J. Killian (Eds.), *Handbook of conflict management* (pp. 148–168). New York: Marcel Dekker.

Brockman, J. L. (2014). Interpersonal conflict in construction: Cost, cause, and consequence. *Journal of Construction Engineering & Management, 40*(2), 1–12.

Canary, D. J., & Lakey, S. (2013). *Strategic conflict*. New York: Routledge.

Dana, D. (2003). Retaliatory cycles: Introducing the elements of conflict. In J. Gordon (Ed.), *Pfeiffer's classic activities for managing conflict at work* (pp. 167–172). New York: Wiley.

Deutsch, M. (2014). Cooperation, competition and conflict. In P. T. Coleman, M. Deutsch, & E. C. Marcus (Eds.), *The handbook of conflict resolution: Theory and practice* (3rd ed., pp. 3–28). San Francisco: Jossey-Bass.

Folger, J. P., Poole, M. S., & Stutman, R. K. (2013). *Working through conflict* (7th ed.). Boston: Pearson.

Glendinning, P. M. (2001). Workplace bullying: Curing the cancer of the American workforce. *Public Personnel Management, 30*(3), 269–287.

Herrick, J. A. (2015). *The history and theory of rhetoric* (5th ed.). New York: Routledge.

Keltner, J. W. (1987). *Mediation: Toward a civilized system of dispute resolution*. Anandale, VA: Speech Communication Association.

Laschinger, H. K., & Nosko, A. (2015). Exposure to workplace bullying and post-traumatic stress disorder symptomology: The role of protective psychological resources. *Journal of Nursing Management, 23*, 252–262.

Leggett, D. G., Roberts-Pittman, B., Byczek, S., & Morse, D. T. (2012). Cooperation, conflict, and martial satisfaction: Bridging theory, research, and practice. *Journal of Individual Psychology, 68*(2), 182–199.

Levy, F., & Rodkin, J. (2016). *The Bloomberg job skills report 2016: What recruiters want*. Bloomberg.com. Accessed 4 July 2016.

Lulofs, R. S., & Cahn, D. D. (2000). *Conflict: From theory to action* (2nd ed.). Boston: Allyn & Bacon.

Mansson, D. H. (2014). Trust as a mediator between affection and relational maintenance in the grandparent-grandchild relationship. *Southern Communication Journal, 79*(3), 180–200.

Marin, M. J., Sherblom, J. C., & Shipps, T. E. (1994). Contextual influences on nurses' conflict management strategies. *Western Journal of Communication, 58*(3), 201–228.

McCorkle, S., & Mills, J. L. (1992). Rowboat in a hurricane: Metaphors of interpersonal conflict management. *Communication Reports, 5*(2), 57–66.

Namie, G., Christensen, D., & Phillips, D. (2014). *WBI U.S. workplace bullying survey*. Workplacebullying.org. Accessed 4 July 2016.

Olson, L. N. (2002). "As ugly and painful as it was, it was effective": Individuals' unique assessment of communication competence during aggressive conflict episodes. *Communication Studies, 53*(2), 171–188.

Saleh, D. N. (2003). This employee benefit pays off—the ombudsman. *Accounting Today, 17*(20), 8–9.

Stein, N. L., & Albro, E. R. (2001). The origins and nature of arguments: Studies in conflict understanding, emotion, and negotiation. *Discourse Processes, 32*(2–3), 113–133.

Ursiny, T. (2003). *The coward's guide to conflict*. Naperville, IL: Sourcebook.

Wexler, J. A., & Zimmerman, P. (2000). In-house resolution of employment disputes. *CPA Journal, 70*(12), 62–64.

Wickham, R. E., Williamson, R. E., Beard, C. L., Kobayashi, L. B., & Hirst, T. W. (2016). Authenticity attenuates the negative effects of interpersonal conflict on daily well-being. *Journal of Research in Personality, 60*, 56–62.

Zweibel, E. B., Goldstein, R., Manwaring, J. A., & Marks, M. B. (2008). What sticks: How medical residents and academic health care faculty transfer conflict resolution training from the workshop to the workplace. *Conflict Resolution Quarterly, 25*(3), 321–350.

Chapter 2

Conflict Management Theories

Vocabulary

Approach-approach conflict

Approach-avoid conflict

Attribution error

Attribution theory

Avoid-avoid conflict

Connotative

Constructive conflict

Constructivism

Denotative

Destructive conflict

Exchange theory

External attribution

Field theory

Game theory

Interaction theory

Interdependence

Internal attribution

Mechanical process

Mixed-motive situation

Nature

Negative interdependence

Nurture

Positive interdependence

Prisoner's Dilemma

Psychodynamic theory

Self-serving bias

Social exchange theory

Symbols

Systems theory

Theories

Transactional process

Objectives

After reading the chapter, you should be able to:

1. Understand the historical background of conflict theories
2. Differentiate between nature and nurture theories
3. Differentiate between constructive and destructive conflict
4. Explain attribution theory as it applies to conflict management

The Purpose of Theory

In the middle of a conflict, have you ever wondered, "Am I the only person this happens to? What is going on here? Why are we at odds?" Be assured: Conflict definitely happens to everyone! Friends who discuss conflicts find they have similar experiences. When patterns emerge, people wonder why. Speculation about why things occur is a theory-creating activity.

CASE 2.1

Liam and Olivia's Happy Holiday

When Liam and I were married, we moved away from home to go to college. After two years, we were able to get enough money to go home for Christmas for a week. On Christmas Eve, we were at my in-laws'. My sister-in-law wanted me to look at some pictures of her niece. I was so tired; I said I would look at them tomorrow. She threw the pictures across the room and said, "Liam, I need to talk to you now!" I knew this could not be good. An hour later, Liam came back upstairs and we left.

In the car, I asked what the scene was all about. He said that his mother and sister wanted him to divorce me. I was shocked and couldn't understand why they didn't like me. Liam said he didn't want a divorce, but I needed to be more involved with his family. I told him his family should be more considerate of my needs. As we drove to my sister's house, we both got angrier and started to pick at each other's faults. By the time we reached my sister's house, we were both fuming in silence. This incident started an argument that went on for two years every time we visited his family. Finally, we stopped going to visit his family together.

Generally speaking, **theories** are not facts but rather tentative explanations for observed behaviors. They provide rich tools for analyzing conflict. Conflict managers use theory to provide insight into the root causes of conflict, identify patterns in interactions, and provide hints for how best to proceed toward a positive outcome.

Most theories applied to dispute resolution originally were developed in some other context and have since been adapted to interpersonal conflict. The scientific study of interpersonal conflict management began after World War II with the first interpersonal conflict textbooks emerging in the 1970s. Table 2.1 summarizes the types of questions asked by conflict theorists and researchers.

TABLE 2.1 Questions for Conflict Theorists and Researchers

1. What determines if a conflict becomes destructive or constructive?
2. Does culture, age, sex, or status impact conflict or negotiations?
3. What tactics work better than others during interpersonal conflict?
4. What is the difference between effective communication and communication that leads to misunderstandings?
5. What helps individuals keep focused on their goals rather than being distracted by unexpected emotions (anger, anxiety, or wounded pride)?
6. How do the individuals in a conflict use power to influence each other?
7. What role does personality play in conflict?

Source: Adapted from Deutsch (2000a)

This chapter examines some of the many theories about the process of conflict. These theories, in turn, affect the recommendations made by practitioners on how to improve communication and better manage conflict.

Nature Versus Nurture

Since humans began to ask "why?" a debate has ensued about whether behavior is learned (**nurture**) or determined by biology (**nature**). Geneticists, biologists, psychologists, and social scientists, among many others, generally support the primacy of one side or the other in the nature-versus-nurture debate. Do genetics, chemical balances, hormones, brain functioning, and other innate factors cause us to behave in certain ways (nature), or are we born into this world as a blank slate to be written on by our environment (nurture)?

If the consensus among scholars were that people behaved in conflicts entirely based on their genetic predisposition or entirely based on chemical and/or hormonal influences, there would be little need for classes in conflict management. The means to influence conflict behavior would be gene therapy, drugs, or hormone suppression/injection. For example, if all men are equally prone to aggression because of testosterone and all women equally prone to passivity due to estrogen, then violence in the world could only be altered by changing everyone's chemical balance. Why learn new communication skills if behavior is hardwired?

Those in the nurture camp believe that most behavior comes from interaction with the environment. People learn conflict behaviors from parents, peers, mass media, social media, and culture. Theorists from the nurture viewpoint consider humans to be a mostly blank slate at birth (or earlier), written on by their surroundings. The strongest influences on behavior happen after birth.

DISCUSSION QUESTION • 2.1

What personal experiences or observations lead you to believe that behaviors are caused by either nature or nurture? Do you believe any conflict management behaviors could be caused solely by biological or genetic influences?

Some scholars argue for a combined approach—a bit of biology blended with some social learning and environmental influences. For example, researchers determined that in some situations, genetics, chemical balances, or hormones may prompt some tendencies toward aggressive behavior, but the influence is not strong enough to explain why some people are much more aggressive than others.

In Case 2.1, Olivia discovers she is not fitting into Liam's family. A "nature" explanation might argue that part of the problem is that Liam's family is genetically or biologically programmed to behave differently than those from Olivia's genetic background. However, to attribute all explanations to biology would be to ignore social relationships and the influence of culture. Conversely, social scientists have developed theories that might explain this conflict by saying Olivia grew up in a family that had different rules, based on fundamentally different values and goals than Liam's family—and those differences are causing the conflict.

Most researchers recognize that neither side of the nature/nurture debate can explain all behavior. Subsequently, multiple theories abound to explain conflict.

Communication Theory

Before we focus specifically on conflict management theories, we will examine the nature of communication. Early theorists, such as Shannon and Weaver (1949), represented communication as a

mechanical process—as if communication were like a machine with discrete parts that functioned in preset sequences. Implicit in a mechanical model is the idea that communication occurs in a series of one-way messages. Person A talks and is the message sender to Person B. In turn, Person B talks and becomes the sender, making Person A the new receiver. In a **mechanical model of communication**, meaning resides in the message. Communication is like an old-style intercom system—you can talk or you can listen, but you can't do both at the same time.

In the 1960s, theorists such as Watzlawick, Beavin, and Jackson (1967) rejected the mechanical approach and proposed that communication is a complex **transactional process** that occurs continuously and simultaneously. While one person talks, the other person is listening and reacting nonverbally. Both individuals are communicating simultaneously because each is giving feedback to the other. When Liam's sister threw the pictures across the room, everyone's reactions were instantly obvious without a switch having to be turned to say "your turn to communicate now." Additionally, the transactional view posits that communication is ongoing, meaning that one "cannot *not* communicate." Even refusing to participate in a discussion is an act of communication. When Liam and Olivia stopped talking to each other, their silence still was communicating volumes of hurt, anger, and frustration.

Meanings are in people is another truism for modern communication scholars. Words and gestures have no inherent meanings. Meanings must be interpreted by those who perceive them. There is no connection between most words and their meanings. The words *smart phone* refer to a portable communication device. Because humans invent words, the smart phone could just as well have been labeled a telephone without a cord (TWC) or a "buzzer." Words are **symbols** to which humans attach meaning.

To make matters more complex, words have **denotative** and **connotative** meanings (as discussed in Chapter 1). For Liam's sisters, in Case 2.1, being more involved meant (connotatively) looking at pictures of babies, helping with cooking, and creating a sisterly friendship. For Olivia, being involved meant showing up during holidays. Because their connotative meanings were different, their expectations were not met.

DISCUSSION QUESTION • 2.2

Describe a conversation where people were using the same words but attaching different connotative meanings.

Theories Influencing Conflict Management Studies

Early Ideas About Conflict

The earliest theories of dispute management focused on the most visible and dramatic aspects of conflict. They shared a common view of life as a struggle that often led to aggression and violence. Darwin theorized that life progresses based on competition among species, implying that aggressive competition is an inherent part of survival. Marx's social theory saw inevitable struggles for resources between classes that would simmer and then erupt in violent revolution against the rich. Freud's **psychodynamic theory** conceived an internal struggle between the id and the superego (see Deutsch, 2000a; Lulofs & Cahn, 2000). Early theorists suggested that psychologically, socially, or genetically, people were driven by aggression. Later theorists such as Lewin began to divert from this assumption.

Field theory was proposed by Lewin and others in the pre–World War II era of 1920 to 1940. Lewin suggested that within any system there are forces that drive conflicts and forces that restrain conflicts. Deutsch (2000a) explained that these forces create tensions leading to three basic types of conflict. When there are two choices of equal positive value, an **approach-approach conflict** exists. For example, in a company downsizing employees, one individual might be given the choice of taking a promotion at the same location (which is seen as desirable) or moving to another state (where the individual has close relatives and friends). When there are two choices of equal negative value, an **avoid-avoid conflict** emerges. In this situation, an employee would be forced to choose between being downsized or a demotion to a job he or she considers less valuable. When there are opposing negative and positive values, an **approach-avoid conflict** is created. An employee might be given a promotion, but only if he or she moves to a detested location. A field theorist would look at Liam and Olivia in Case 2.1 and speculate that Olivia's holidays were an avoid-avoid conflict: She could offend Liam's family by not going to holiday dinners, or she could offend them by not acting "the right way" when she did attend.

DISCUSSION QUESTION • 2.3

Describe a time when you felt torn by an approach-avoid or an avoid-avoid conflict.

Post–World War II Influences on Conflict Theory

Game theory evolved in the 1940s as a mathematical way to calculate projected gains and losses while playing games to simulate human choice making. Social scientists adapted game theory to the idea that people in a conflict are interdependent and exhibit a mix of cooperative and competitive impulses. Game theory is particularly useful when studying negotiation.

Game theory works well in areas where resources and choices are limited (Deutsch, 2000a; Schelling, 1960). It can involve sophisticated mathematical analysis and is useful to detect the structure and rules for behaviors that operate in existing relationships and organizations (Jost & Weitzel, 2007). Its limitation is the assumption that people in conflicts always act rationally and predictably.

The **prisoner's dilemma** illustrates a classic situation explored by game theorists. Bertha and Rosie are caught outside a convenience store after it is robbed. The police try to get a confession to convict at least one on a more serious charge. The suspects are separated, and each is told the same thing: "If you testify that the other person did the crime, you will get a lesser sentence." If both confess, however, there is no deal and both will be prosecuted to the full extent of the law. If one confesses and implicates her partner, but the other does not confess, the betrayer gets a deal from the prosecutor and the betrayed gets three years in prison. If they both stay silent, they get only one year in prison each. Table 2.2 details their choices and possible outcomes. Given the odds, in a totally rational world, both should stay silent, but often they don't. Game theorists would explain that people assess their personal probability of a positive outcome based on what they think the other person will do.

The gambling game of Texas Hold 'Em illustrates the limits of game theory. Like many card games, each individual is competing to see who wins based on the relative rank order of the hands. In a purely rational world, each player would assess the statistical probability of the cards being the

TABLE 2.2 The Prisoner's Dilemma

		Rosie the Robber	
		Rosie Stays Silent	Rosie Confesses
Bertha the Burglar	Bertha Stays Silent	Both serve 1 year	Rosie goes free
Bertha serves 3 years
	Bertha Confesses	Rosie serves 3 years
Bertha goes free	Both go to jail for 2 years

winning combination and would bet accordingly. If that were all that occurred, poker would be predictable—and boring. What makes poker exciting is the unknown. In Texas Hold 'Em, people bluff—they lie and put on fake expressions to fool their opponents. Even though a player knows his or her cards probably are not the best at the gaming table, a gambler may pretend to be strong and induce others to throw away their "winning" hands. Because people don't always play by the rational rules, predicting their behavior is challenging.

Constructive and Destructive Conflict

The concept of **constructive** versus **destructive conflict** was developed from field theory in the 1940s and still is used today. Deutsch's theory of constructive and destructive conflict identified two core concepts in scholarly thinking about conflict management. First, people's goals are **interdependent**—meaning the probability of one's goal attainment is linked to the probability of the other's goal attainment. If the connection is positive, each person's goals are moving in the same direction; if one attains his or her goals, so will the other person (**positive interdependence**). Goals can be positively linked for many reasons, such as liking the other person, sharing resources, common group membership, common values, culture, common enemies, or division of labor. If the connection is negative, attainment of one person's goals means that the other will not attain his or her goals. **Negative interdependence** of goals can result from factors such as disliking the other person or a competitive reward structure. As Deutsch (2000b) notes, "If you're positively linked with another, then you sink or swim together; with negative linkage, if the other sinks, you swim, and if the other swims, you sink" (p. 22).

DISCUSSION QUESTION • 2.4

Give examples of areas where you currently are positively interdependent. Give examples of areas where you experienced negative interdependence.

The second dimension is that actions to achieve goals are either effective or bungling (Deutsch, 2000b). The actions that people take to reach their goals can be well-chosen and effective or ill-advised and ineffective. Had the Case 2.1 participants attempted to discuss how Olivia could become a member of the extended family, constructive conflict might have been possible. By demanding that Liam divorce his wife, a negative competitive situation was created. Liam ultimately had to choose between his wife and his family.

Situations often are **mixed motive**: The goals are more or less positive or more or less negatively related and the actions are more or less effective. For example, a salesperson may work in a company that gives cash awards to the employee who sells the most during a month. The situation seems purely competitive. In reality, if the sales staff like each other, motives are mixed—each wants to win the bonus but not to offend coworkers who also are friends.

Deutsch's theory may seem to suggest that only cooperative conflicts can be productive. To the contrary, Deutsch, and other modern theorists, believe that competition also can be productive. He states:

> I do not mean to suggest that competition produces no benefits. Competition is part of everyday life. Acquiring the skills necessary to compete effectively can be of considerable value. Moreover, competition in a cooperative, playful context can be fun. It enables one to enact and experience, in a non-serious setting, symbolic emotional dramas relating to victory and defeat, life and death, power and helplessness, dominance and submission; these dramas have deep personal and cultural roots.
>
> (Deutsch, 2000b, p. 28)

To the extent that competition is sometimes necessary, competent conflict managers must learn how to use traditional negotiation and to "win" when necessary. To the extent that conflict is not always necessary, competent conflict managers must learn to apply cooperative strategies. Chapter 3 delves into cooperative and competitive conflict in more detail.

Attribution Theory

Attribution theory, originating in the 1950s by Heider, explains how people attempt to make sense of the world around them (Manusov & Spitzberg, 2008). As individuals observe the world, they are attributing meaning. Danny sees two of his friends, Jackson and Emma, walking side by side down the street. Both are in committed relationships with other people. Jackson has his arm around Emma's waist as they walk very close together. Attribution theory suggests that Danny will make sense of his observation by attributing meaning to the situation. It is as if the mind asks, "What does this piece of information mean?" The answer often is then treated as if it were truth. Danny might infer that Emma and Jackson are having an affair. In reality, Emma might be unwell, and Jackson is helping her back to her car. If Danny talks to Emma's partner and says Emma is having an affair, he acts on his attribution rather than seeking information to check his assumptions. Attributions about the other person—and the subsequent interpretation of those attributions—often are what drives a conflict.

DISCUSSION QUESTION • 2.5

What attributions have you made recently about people you have met? How do attributions contribute to conflict?

Two types of attributions can be made about behavior: internal or external. **Internal attributions** label behavior as arising from the other person's personality, values, or characteristics. For example, Liam's sister took Olivia's statement that she wanted to look at the pictures later as meaning Olivia was stuck-up, unfriendly, and uncaring (internal to her personality). However, when Olivia didn't look at the pictures, the sister could have interpreted her choice as a result of being tired after a long drive (external or outside of her personality). **Externalizations (external attributions)** assume that the behavior is caused by a situation outside the individual's control. For example, Darla is chairing a meeting and wants to start on time; Jerod walks in 10 minutes late. If Darla attributes Jerod's lateness to his character (internal attribution), she might be wondering if he is being passive-aggressive because she was given the lead on this project and he was not. An external attribution would occur if she sees that Jerod was on a call and thinks it must be with an important client or he would come to the meeting on time

Attribution theorists have noted a behavioral pattern of assigning personality flaws to others' failings while assigning external reasons to one's own faults. Assigning internal or external causation without a factual base is called an **attribution error.** A **self-serving bias** occurs when we assign internal attributions to our successes ("I studied hard and that's why I got an A.") and external factors to our shortcomings ("The teacher doesn't like me, that's why I only got a C−.") In general, we are more complimentary of our own behaviors than we are of others, according to attribution theorists.

KEY 2.1

To avoid unnecessary conflict, ask questions to verify assumptions based on attributions.

In conflict, how one attributes motive to the other person makes a dramatic difference in how one behaves. If a group sees another group as not trustworthy (an internal attribution), they act toward that group with suspicion. Not being trusted may lead to resentment and misjudgments, which creates more defensiveness. Defensiveness, in turn, is seen as a personality flaw in others (internal attribution).

Attribution theory is useful because it raises awareness about how individuals make sense of behaviors. People who are optimists may attribute good in people; pessimists may see the bad. Both might be wrong. Conflict managers must be aware of how attributions affect communication and problem solving.

Exchange Theories

Exchange theories posit that people make relationship choices on a cost-benefit tally system. **Exchange theory** is built on the metaphor of an economic marketplace and assumes that people will make choices that are the most beneficial to them. In other words, an individual might think: If there is profit in it, I will stay in the relationship; if it costs too much, I'm out.

Social exchange theory is another theory that originated in the 1950s. It proposes that people evaluate the costs and rewards of a relationship by the amount of effort required to attain rewards and avoid costs (see West & Turner, 2014). Social exchange theory explains the occasional feeling that another person is too calculating—assessing how he or she can benefit before investing anything in the relationship. When rewards are perceived as too low and someone is viewed as interfering with reward attainment, conflict is likely. Social exchange theory is in action every time you hear someone say, "I broke up with my boyfriend/girlfriend because it just wasn't worth the trouble anymore." One spouse may see constant bickering and high tension as too much of a cost (to personal happiness) and decide to get a divorce. In Case 2.1, if Liam uses exchange theory to judge his relationship, he may break up with Olivia if he feels he is sacrificing more than the overall relationship brings back to him in rewards.

DISCUSSION QUESTION • 2.6

Consider the "economic" language used to describe relationships. "You owe me one." "This isn't worth the hassle." "What's the payoff?" Do you think most relationships really use a social exchange theory model?

It is hard work to sustain a good relationship, which is an investment cost in exchange theory's viewpoint. Relationships also provide a variety of potential rewards—esteem, financial security, intimacy, resource access, and so forth. In a committed relationship where both are going to college, time can be a rare commodity. Time for romance may conflict with time to study. Socializing with a partner's friends may interfere with time to exercise and stay in shape. Going to a movie may be at the cost of lost sleep or a poorly written assignment. Within social exchange theory, each individual calculates the costs and benefits to the relationship and to career ambitions before making choices.

Interaction Theories

Interaction theories focus attention on the communication and interactions among people rather than on the individual. To interaction theorists, conflict management must involve the perspectives of all parties to the conflict, not just one side (Olson & Braithwaite, 2004). **Constructivism**, one type of interaction theory advanced by Delia, states that people create meaning through a series of personal constructs (or schemas) (Delia & Crockett, 1973). Each person's construct of what it means to be friends, patriotic, or a good worker may be significantly different.

Students' constructs of a "good teacher" vary considerably. One student may construct the concept of a good teacher versus a bad teacher based on workload:

Good Teacher	Bad Teacher
Understands I have a life	Thinks only his or her class is important
Assigns little homework	Assigns too much homework
Awards high grades	Grades too hard

A second student may construct the concept of a good teacher versus a bad teacher quite differently, based on outcome:

Good Teacher	Bad Teacher
Motivates me to learn	Doesn't care about my learning
Gives meaningful assignments	Gives busywork assignments
Makes me think and work hard	Grades too easily

A course syllabus is the instructor's attempt to set expectations on what the workload and assignments will be like, so everyone has the same construct of what to expect in the class.

Communication is difficult in the best of times. When people are acting from different constructs or schemas, conflict seems inevitable. According to constructivists, people moderate this difficulty through an agreed-upon social construction—i.e., they talk and create a mutual construct. For example, a constructivist would point out that the individuals who enter into a marriage will almost always have different constructs in at least one area about how the marriage should work. The construct of "an ideal marriage" or "an ideal spouse's behavior" can be quite different, from as simple an idea as who does the household chores to as complicated as how family finances are run.

Only through interaction can individuals work to create a shared meaning, or construct, about important issues. For conflict managers, constructivist theories suggest that the right way to manage conflict is through social creation of meaning, not through an adherence to predetermined absolute and universal truth. To succeed, those in conflict need to create a shared construction of meaning, not only about the issues being negotiated but also about how to behave during conflict. Each individual has a personal construction of what it means to be a good parent, boss, or romantic partner. If personal constructions are not shared with others, conflict occurs because each individual is pushing toward a different ideal.

DISCUSSION QUESTION • 2.7

What is your construct of a good partner or a good friend? Consider those areas where another's construct may differ from yours and identify where conflict could erupt.

Systems Theory

In contrast to theories that focus on processes within the individual, **systems theory** includes all of our relationships and interactions. The most fundamental idea in systems theory is that one cannot understand the whole system just by looking at its composite elements (von Bertalanffy, 1968).

In other words, the system is more than the sum of its parts. Applied to conflict, systems theory suggests one must examine the interaction between the parties over time and in context rather than focusing on just one side or at just one moment in time. For example, a systems theorist would need to know more about Liam and Olivia in Case 2.1 before analyzing their situation: What has occurred in the past during holidays? What are the norms for Liam's family during holidays? What are the norms for Olivia's family of origin during holidays? What type of relationship do Liam and Olivia have? What has the relationship been between Liam and his sisters and between Olivia and the sisters-in-law before this event? Are any cultural influences at play in the system? Only by looking at the entire system could the meaning in a single episode be made clear.

Systems have identities that go beyond their individual parts. Liam's sisters and parents have an identity as a family system. A newcomer, such as Olivia, may unknowingly break the customs in her partner's family, and she can also be seen as an outsider who is a threat to that family system. When threatened, a system moves to enforce its rules or protect its identity—in Liam's case, by asking him to divorce his wife.

DISCUSSION QUESTION • 2.8

Which theory of interpersonal conflict makes the most sense to you? Which theory appeals to you the least?

Summary

A theory is a tentative explanation for behavior. Modern communication theories represent the communication process as more transactional than mechanical. Theories of human behavior tend toward one of two basic ideas: Behaviors result mostly from inherent or biological causes (nature) or behaviors result mostly from culture and context (nurture).

Early conflict management theories, such as psychodynamic and field theory, focused on human aggression and internal psychological states. Later theories, such as game theory, developed an interest in conflict strategies and tactics or, in the case of Deutsch, the components of destructive and constructive outcomes and the nature of interdependence.

Attribution theory explains how individuals perceive others' motives and behaviors, and how we assign internal or external causes to why people act the way they do. Exchange theory, borrowing from an economic model, posits that individuals make decisions based on a cost and reward evaluation. Interaction theories focus on the conflict pair rather than the individual and the means by which meaning is created together. Constructivists examine the mental structures that individuals use to judge behaviors. Finally, systems theory expands awareness to the macro level by looking at the entire context in which conflict is embedded.

Chapter Resources

Exercises

1. Assess a current relationship using exchange theory. What are the benefits of the relationship? What are the costs?
2. Develop a "rule" about how conflict should be managed between teachers and students. Is the rule you created similar to or different from what has occurred in the past when students and teachers disagree?

3. Analyze the film *Why Him?* Which theory best explains the conflict between the dad (played by Bryan Cranston) and the rich fiancé, Laird Mayhew (played by James Franco)?
4. Are there tensions among groups on your campus based on attributions one group makes toward another? For example, do athletes have trouble being accepted into the best work-groups in classes based on an attribution that athletes are not very smart? Do political groups react toward each other based upon unfair attributions?

Journal/Essay Topic

1. Identify a pattern of behavior you are curious about. Which theory in the chapter helps explain what you have observed?

Research Topics

1. Select two theories from the chapter. Review published research to understand more about the two theories. Write a paper that compares the theories' assumptions and the type of research questions that arise from each perspective.
2. Select a theory of conflict not discussed in this chapter, such as standpoint theory, the coordinated management of meaning theory, or narrative theory. What insights about conflict can be gained from the theory you selected?
3. Game theory has a prominent role in a wide variety of films. For example, in *Sherlock Holmes* (a BBC series, 2012), Sherlock and Moriarty engage in a test of game theory in "The Final Problem" episode (See: https://blogs.cornell.edu/info2040/2015/09/18/game-theory-sherlock-holmes-moriarty-the-final-problem/). Choose a movie that highlights game theory and provide an analysis of how the characters make decisions as it relates to the theory. Examples: *The Princess Bride*, *Panic Room*, *Thirteen Days*, *Murder by Numbers* (see others at www.gametheory.net/popular/film.html).

Mastery Case

Examine Mastery Case 2A, "Holly the Hun," using one of the theories in this chapter. Explain how the theory sheds light on this case.

Holly the Hun

Holly worked on the assembly line at the packing plant for five years before she became a manager. The line typically had ten workers, some men and some women. When she first got the promotion, most people were happy for her—except Walter, who thought he had worked for the company longer and deserved the promotion. Time has passed, and now all of the line employees hate her. She used to be friendly with her staff, but now she avoids them. Holly rarely leaves her cubicle near the plant manager's office and frequently is seen having lunch with him. Holly sends e-mail messages instructing the assembly-line workers to follow new procedures. When she does talk to people, she tells people what to do and doesn't seem to listen when anyone else has an idea. She carefully plots interactions with the line workers to maintain control of every minute, so nobody else has a chance to speak much. In discussions among themselves, the line workers say that Holly has a bizarre idea of what supervisors should do and that she thinks she is superior to them now.

Examine Mastery Case 2B, "Homeward Bound," using one of the theories in this chapter. Explain how the theory sheds light on this case.

Homeward Bound

Shannon and Kendrick have a long-term goal of buying an expensive home together someday. Kendrick gets into an elite graduate school where, upon graduation, he can expect to get a high-paying job. Shannon also was accepted to a graduate school, but her program isn't in the same state where Kendrick has been accepted and they don't want to live separately. Kendrick could go to a less prestigious school near Shannon's school. The couple has a decision to make: If they go to Kendrick's school, they will be able to afford a home sooner, but Shannon will have to put off graduate school until after Kendrick finishes his program. Ultimately, going to Kendrick's school will lead to the goal of buying a nice home sooner. Unbeknownst to Kendrick, Shannon has elevated her desire to go to graduate school to a higher level than buying a home sooner.

References

Delia, J. G., & Crockett, W. H. (1973). Social schemas, cognitive complexity, and the learning of social structures. *Journal of Personality*, *41*(3), 413–429.

Deutsch, M. (2000a). Introduction. In M. Deutsch & P. T. Coleman (Eds.), *The handbook of conflict resolution: Theory and practice* (pp. 1–17). San Francisco: Jossey-Bass.

Deutsch, M. (2000b). Cooperation and competition. In M. Deutsch & P. T. Coleman (Eds.), *The handbook of conflict resolution: Theory and practice* (pp. 21–40). San Francisco: Jossey-Bass.

Jost, P. J., & Weitzel, U. (2007). *Strategic conflict management: A game-theoretical introduction*. Cheltenham, UK: Edgar Elgar.

Lulofs, R. S., & Cahn, D. D. (2000). *Conflict: From theory to action* (2nd ed.). Boston: Allyn & Bacon.

Manusov, V., & Spitzberg, B. (2008). Attribution theory: Finding good cause in the search for theory. In D. O. Braithwaite & L. A. Baxter (Eds.), *Engaging theories in interpersonal communication: Multiple perspectives* (pp. 37–50). Thousand Oaks, CA: Sage.

Olson, L. N., & Braithwaite, D. O. (2004). "If you hit me again, I'll hit you back:" Conflict management strategies of individuals experiencing aggression during conflicts. *Communication Studies*, *55*(2), 271–285.

Schelling, T. C. (1960). *The strategy of conflict*. London: Oxford Press.

Shannon, C. E., & Weaver, W. (1949). *The mathematical theory of communication*. Urbana: University of Illinois Press.

von Bertalanffy, L. (1968). *General systems theory: Foundations, development, applications*. New York: George Braziller.

Watzlawick, P., Beavin, J., & Jackson, D. (1967). *The pragmatics of human communication*. New York: Norton.

West, R. L., & Turner, L. H. (2014). *Introducing communication theory: Analysis and application* (5th ed.). New York: McGraw-Hill.

Chapter 3

Competitive and Cooperative Conflict Approaches

Vocabulary

Accommodation

Argumentativeness

Avoidance

Communication climate

Creating value

Defensive climates

"I" statements

Interest-based conflict

Interests

Mixed-motive situation

Mutual gains

Passive aggression

Positions

Supportive climates

Taking value

Universal team approach

Verbal aggression

Worldview

Zero-sum

Objectives

After reading the chapter, you should be able to:

1. Explain the assumptions of competitive and cooperative approaches
2. Discriminate between situations that require competition and those where cooperation might result in better outcomes
3. Explain the four myths of competition
4. Explain the difference between supportive and defensive climates

Generally speaking, there are two approaches to conflict: competition and cooperation. This chapter explores how the assumptions of these two views affect the strategies, tactics, and probable outcomes of interpersonal conflict; examines what happens when the counterparts in a conflict are firmly fixed in opposite views; and illustrates how most conflicts involve both competitive and cooperative aspects.

CASE 3.1

Sibling Rivalry

Sergio and Antoine are brothers. Their parents provided the teens with a car to use, leaving the scheduling up to the two of them to figure out. Sergio, the oldest, drives them both to school and has claimed the car during weekends. Antoine has tried to talk to Sergio about sharing the car more equitably. Sergio says it was his car first and his brother needs to live with it until Sergio moves out next year. Antoine tried again, this time with a schedule in hand that had each of them sharing the driving during the week (even giving Sergio an extra day) and alternating Friday and Saturday nights each weekend. Sergio responded by laughing at Antoine and told him, "Get over it already."

Antoine came up with a new plan. He drew up a list of all of the items that belonged to him that Sergio regularly borrows. The list included clothes, sporting equipment, and interactive games. Antoine also listed ways he had helped Sergio in the past with chores, homework, and occasionally lending him money. He also wrote down the few times he had covered for Sergio when he's come in after curfew. For his second negotiation attempt, Antoine presented Sergio with the lists he'd created and said, "Look, bro, if you want to be completely independent from each other, that certainly would have some benefits for me. But I'd rather continue to help each other out and share stuff. So, now about that car schedule . . ."

The previous chapter discussed theories that researchers propose to explain how people enact conflict. This chapter examines how a larger worldview affects the choices an individual makes during a conflict. A **worldview** is an overarching set of beliefs about how the world works and one's place in it. Is the world a dog-eat-dog place where one must fight to get ahead (the competition worldview)? Or, is the world a place where people can work together peacefully (the cooperative worldview)? Or, is the world some combination of competitive and cooperative impulses?

To help differentiate between the competitive and cooperative worldviews, the discussion in this chapter will begin with what the competitive and cooperative worldviews look like when applied in extreme ways. As you read the section on competition, remember that competition is not all bad. Chapter 9 will illustrate how to compete using reasonable tactics that avoid the downsides of the extremely competitive worldview.

> If it doesn't matter who wins or loses, then why do they keep score?
>
> —Football coach, Vincent Lombardi

The Competitive World

Individuals steeped in the competitive paradigm believe there are only three choices in conflict: win, lose, or draw. Table 3.1 presents some of the assumptions brought to conflict by those with a competitive versus a cooperative approach. For diehard competitors, winning is tied inextricably to ego—the *best* player wins. In an extreme competitive view, the goal is to win, and only one person can win at a time. If you win, you get everything and I lose. Resources in the competitive world often are viewed as **zero-sum**, meaning there is a finite amount of something, and any part

TABLE 3.1 Assumptions About Conflict

Extreme Competitive Worldview	Extreme Cooperative Worldview
• Winning is the goal	• Meeting needs of all parties while maintaining a relationship is the goal
• Zero-sum resources	• Expandable resources
• Position focused	• Interest focused
• View *other* as the opponent	• View the *issue* as the opponent

of it you get takes away the percentage I can achieve. For example, there is one piece of pizza left and two people want it. When one person takes it, the amount is reduced to zero (making pizza a zero-sum resource).

If the "opponent" in conflict is equally powerful and skilled, compromise to achieve a tie is an acceptable outcome. Going for a draw makes the situation even. The compromise splits the difference so both win (or lose) equally (Withers, 2002). In the extreme, the competitive view is driven by fear of losing. Because extreme competitors often only look at one issue at a time, creativity in finding solutions is a challenge.

Competitive conflict sometimes is initiated by a perception that one party has a right to seek compliance from another person as a type of entitlement. The feeling that one person's goal is more important than another person's goal can grow from any number of ideas. A boss might perceive the authority of his or her job title means all subordinates must automatically comply with the boss' every wish. Some people might see their social status as the reason to overlook the goals of persons of presumed lower status. Feelings of status superiority can be as simple as an older sibling thinking a younger sibling always comes second, to the more complex and damaging feelings that one gender, social status, race, or ethnicity is superior to another. In other cases, the drive to competition simply is a need to feel "right" in a specific situation. Hullett and Tamborini (2001) explain, "The perception of high rights involves the perception that the actor is justified in seeking compliance. . . . Of course, having the right to seek compliance does not necessarily mean that the target will see the situation in the same way and thus not resist the attempt" (p. 4). In other words, competition gives rise to more competition.

McLaughlin posits four types of resistance strategies by those who see a compliance demand as unjust: stating one will not comply, managing self-identity by attacking the other's authority, presenting reasons for noncompliance, and entering into bargaining about the request (cited in Hullett & Tamborini, 2001). For example, at bedtime a child may assert, "I will not go to bed" (non-negotiation). The rebellious child may bluster to a babysitter, "You are not the boss of me" (attack the other's authority). If the father is putting a child to bed, the boy may say, "Mom lets me stay up later on weekends" (justification for noncompliance). After not succeeding at other strategies, a child may switch to the last strategy and say, "I'll be good if you let me stay up" (negotiation).

Inherent at the extreme edge of the competitive view is the role of loser. Losers receive fewer resources, may be left with less power, be one down in the relationship, or suffer loss of face. When complying, they may choose strategies of **avoidance** (removing oneself from the controversy), **passive aggression** (begrudging compliance, perhaps with a plan to get even), or **accommodation** (submission). Losers may develop a convenient temporary amnesia and forget to take actions that benefit the winner, or comply with surly indifference.

DISCUSSION QUESTION • 3.1

What does it mean to be "one up" or "one down" in a relationship? How can having someone being "one down" affect a relationship in the short and long term?

Those who are about to lose a conflict that deeply threatens a cherished goal may apply extreme strategies, such as severing the relationship or threatening violence. Those in stable relationships who lose small conflicts may retaliate in other ways. Cedric and Jasmine may differ over a simple issue like what movie to see on Friday night. Cedric may prevail, saying, "Since I am paying for the tickets, I get to decide." The situation is a classic win/lose scenario. If Jasmine decides she doesn't like being the loser, she may take actions to ensure Cedric doesn't have a good time at "his" movie. She might stall so they miss the beginning of the film and get bad seats, talk during the most important parts of the movie, or insist they leave early. Because she doesn't like the role of loser, Jasmine turns the win/lose outcome into a lose/lose situation.

At its extreme, classic tactics of competition include verbal aggressiveness and argumentativeness. **Argumentativeness** is defending one's positions and attacking the other party's positions. Stein and Albro (2001) note that although winning for one's side is the general goal of argument, some arguments are to determine who is the dominant individual in the situation, group, or relationship. If the argument is a battle for dominance, it has entered the realm of personal conflict.

Verbal aggression attacks others and their positions (Rogan & La France, 2003). Name-calling, sneering tones, and demeaning evaluative statements are tactics of verbal aggression. These tactics subvert the esteem of the other person and usually create a face conflict. Even if the initial conflict was about something else, it now is about pride or self-image. (You can read more about face conflict in Chapter 4.)

As we mentioned earlier, the competitive approach sees power as a zero-sum resource—believing that there is a finite amount of power to go around. Bacharach and Lawler (1986) analyzed the fallacies in that perspective. First, it is a fallacy that power only can be developed by withholding resources to make the other person dependent. Power is based on a connection with the other party where one person has something that the other desires. From a profoundly competitive drive, power is gained by making someone more dependent or blocking his or her ability to acquire a desired goal. Although people can go to extremes, as in spousal abuse where money and contact with other people are withheld to create absolute dependence, the effort to sustain negative dependence typically is not proportionate to the payoff. A secretary who unnecessarily is miserly with office supplies tries to get power by creating scarcity. The ill-will created through this strategy probably outweighs the benefits.

DISCUSSION QUESTION • 3.2

What lessons about competition did you learn as a child (such as "losing builds character" or "it doesn't matter if you win or lose, it's how you play the game.")? What did these lessons teach you about winning and losing, cooperating and competing?

Second, it is a fallacy to view coercion as a rightful entitlement of the powerful. Firstborns may give orders to their younger siblings because they believe an older child automatically has authority, as in Case 3.1, "Sibling Rivalry." One spouse may coerce a desired behavior in a partner by withdrawing intimacy. Instead of complying, the partner may also pull away in an attempt to balance power. In this kind of spiral of negative action and reaction, the couple grows further apart. Reducing intimacy also reduces the interdependence of the couple, and a spurned partner may look elsewhere for affection. An interesting aside is the paradox of coercive power: Overusing coercive power often leads to the decreased effectiveness of that source of power. A teen who constantly has his car taken away as a punishment for breaking house rules may learn self-reliance by using the bus system or making new friends who have cars, thereby denying his parents that source of power.

DISCUSSION QUESTION • 3.3

Give examples of how coercion by a boss or a parent actually reduced that person's power.

Kohn (1986), a critic of the competitive influence, claims North Americans are socialized to believe in the universal virtues of competition based on four assumptions that actually are myths. Myth 1 states *competition is an unavoidable part of human nature*. The success of cooperative and mutual gains systems seems to belie that assumption, as do anthropological studies of collaborative cultures such as the Zuni Indians, which are much less competitive than European-American culture.

CASE 3.2

Your Call

On a foggy night, a navy ship suddenly sees a blip appear on its radar screen. A story is told where the following conversation occurred (Seymour, 1997):

Navy Ship: "Unknown radar contact. Alter your course 10 degrees."
Reply: "Alter your course 10 degrees south."
Navy Ship: "Alter your course 10 degrees north. This is the captain in command."
Reply: "Alter your course 10 degrees south. I am a seaman second class."
Navy Ship: "I order you to change course immediately. We are a battleship."
Reply: "We are a lighthouse. Your call."

Myth 2 claims that *competition encourages people to do their best, and without competition, mediocrity would rule*. Kohn believes that energy, creativity, and wealth are wasted through unnecessary competition. Modern management theories that encourage cooperation are transforming the workplace. In education, competitive grading systems assume that if only two students can receive an A in a class of thirty, the best students will rise to the top of the academic heap. Competitive grading systems deter collaboration, study groups, or other ventures that might help all students learn the course concepts more effectively. Sometimes competition helps people build their skills, but not always.

Myth 3 asserts that *competitive games are the best way to have a good time*. This probably is true for the few individuals who excel and win. In contrast, those who cannot win at games typically drop out. Melanie loves the game cribbage and almost always wins. She really enjoys the game; her friends who always lose do not enjoy it. They now refuse to play with her. Similarly, individuals who know they cannot win a bonus in a competitive salary schedule may slack off because they know the reward is unattainable.

Myth 4 proposes that *competition builds character*. Although competition may help build positive self-esteem in some individuals, in an unbalanced environment the opposite effect probably occurs for those who are habitual losers. Critics argue that cooperation provides more room for success and is a better promoter of healthy self-esteem.

DISCUSSION QUESTION • 3.4

Do Kohn's four myths match up with your life experiences? Provide examples from school, work, family, and/or personal relationships that show these myths in action.

While we have been illustrating the extreme view of competition, remember that competition exists along a continuum. Most people influenced by North American or European-based cultures were socialized to compete to one extent or another. Although loving competition too much may not be good, knowledge of competitive systems and how to bargain competitively is a necessary life skill. Benefits to competition include stimulating positive emotions for those who prefer the style, ensuring a share of available resources when resources are scarce, and motivating high performance. Chapter 9 presents productive strategies for competitive bargaining.

At its best, competition is an appropriate response to genuine scarce resources and is manifested through strategies that do not rely on verbal aggression and personal attacks. For those higher on the competitiveness scale, it may be an exciting pastime. If conflict is a dance, the competitive dance "is usually not the waltz but the aggressive and spicy tango" (Cohen, 2003, p. 435). At its worst, however, competitors can adopt a win-at-all-costs view or a belief that the ultimate goal is to prevent the other from winning.

The Cooperative Approach

The cooperative approach, sometimes called a mutual gains perspective or interest-based bargaining, seeks creative and innovative solutions that maximally meet the needs of all parties. **Mutual gains** encompass the concept that the goals of all parties in a conflict might be met if creative strategies are applied to the problem. The term **interest-based conflict** arises from a focus on the underlying needs (**interests**) of each of the parties rather than on their surface demands (**positions**). At the extreme, those holding a mutual gains view believe that people were born to cooperate. They believe all conflicts can be settled in ways that maximize each person's needs. Those at the extreme edge of the mutual gains worldview believe every problem has a creative solution that doesn't require competition. Those totally committed to the cooperative worldview may naively believe that if people just keep talking, they can eventually work out even the most intractable problems.

When approached strategically, the mutual gains worldview has attractive strategic benefits. A business theorist early in the twentieth century, Mary Parker Follett, popularized looking beyond the surface of competitive aspects of an issue. She tells a story of two sisters squabbling over one orange. The mother suggested they split the orange and each take half—a traditional compromise solution to split the difference. "They both refused this compromise, so the mother asked them what they needed the orange for. One sister needed the orange to make juice, and half an orange was hardly enough. The other needed the orange for a cake she was baking and needed the entire peel. Of course, the clever mother helped the two daughters see that they could both be satisfied. One got the peel, the other got the fruit" (Withers, 2002). Mutual gains bargainers live in a world of abundance dominated by potential. Contrary to the competitive assumption that the other is the opponent, those who take an interest-based approach shift the focus to the problem as the obstacle to be overcome. Once the extreme assumptions of competitive conflict are breached, more creative solutions become possible.

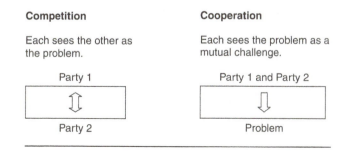

FIGURE 3.1 Competitive and Cooperative Approaches

Interests Versus Positions

One of the features distinguishing competitive and cooperative worldviews is a focus on positions versus a focus on interests. **Positions** are demands, proposed solutions, or other fixed outcome statements. Taking a position is like standing on top of the hill and daring others to force you to come down. When parents and their college freshman daughter are considering where she will live and who will pay for college expenses, the discussion can easily become stuck in positions. Saying to one's parents, "I am going to live in an apartment with my boyfriend at college, and there is nothing you can do about it," is a position. The parent's response, "No you are going to live at home, and we will not pay for you shacking up with that boy!" is also a position. Conflicts played out at the level of positions fall into the classic competitive worldview. When a negotiation or conflict starts and stays with fixed positions, it is challenging to find a solution all parties will find acceptable. Those who start negotiation with an unyielding position find compromising or thinking creatively difficult. Changing one's mind is perceived as backing down, creating a loss of face.

Interests are needs. Each position has underlying interests that may be obscured or unexpressed. Beneath the demand to live off campus may be an array of unexpressed interests: a desire for independence, a need for a quiet space to study, concerns about being socially isolated from college life, distaste for daily commuting, or fear of seeing a boyfriend less often. Likewise, the parents who say "No" and make their own positional demand that the daughter remain in the home during all of her college years have unexpressed interests: fear for their child's safety or consequences of "bad" life choices, lack of money, or sadness that children eventually will make their own way in the world. As long as positions are competitively exchanged, the outcome probably will be influenced more by power than by a genuine seeking of a solution aimed to maximize the needs of all parties.

While competitive conflict operates in a world of positions, the mutual gains worldview always looks for the interests in a situation. Cooperative conflict managers use techniques to look below the positions for the underlying interests. Someone with an interest-based perspective will begin the conversation with a discussion of needs rather than a statement of position. Their thinking is that with less ego and face involved in defending positions, a mutually acceptable solution becomes more possible.

DISCUSSION QUESTION • 3.5

What are the positions of the parties in Case 3.1? What interests might underlie each of the positions?

The key difference between competitive and cooperative approaches is how conflict is framed. Competitors focus on self-centered concerns and goals. Cooperators focus on the processes that can lead to positive outcomes for both. Katz and Block (2000) believe people with outcome goals are focused on their positions—the outcome they want. People focused on process goals are interested in a strategy leading to a successful conflict resolution.

Individuals focused on process goals are thought to be more invested in the interaction and more likely to take risks. They are more interested in a variety of solutions. In contrast, outcome-focused individuals are more personally invested in one particular solution, may not use good problem-solving skills, can be rigid in their thinking, and see the inability to achieve desired positions as a personal failing. Because achieving all of one's goals in every conflict is unlikely, outcome-oriented goals lead to less satisfaction with conflict.

Which Approach to Conflict Is Best?

Each worldview has strengths and weaknesses. Each worldview, at extreme, may be unsustainable in the long term. A weakness of the interest-based view can be the naive belief that a creative outcome always is possible. A weakness of the competitive worldview is when focused on winning, other important goals may be lost.

KEY 3.1

Competent conflict managers are skilled at both competitive and mutual gains conflict.

A competent conflict manager avoids the extremes of either worldview and adopts the skills of cooperation and competition strategically. Although individuals in conflict do have more choices than may seem apparent at first glance, not all situations respond to creative problem solving. If after numerous attempts, the other person simply will not engage in cooperative conflict management, ethical competition may be required to achieve important goals. Perhaps the resources in the situation genuinely are scarce and worth competing for—one promotion or one bonus. In these cases, having cooperative tunnel vision is just as limiting as overzealous competitiveness. In Case 3.1, Antoine probably would have continued to hit a wall in trying to engage in collaboration with his brother. However, by adopting a competitive stance and showing he was willing to play "hardball," he was able to move Sergio into interest-based negotiations. Chapter 9 will reveal several strategies to move people stuck in competitive strategies toward more cooperative negotiation.

Extreme competitors may manipulate individuals who put all of their faith in cooperative conflict management. Some pop culture books suggest all conflict can be managed if the individuals simply follow preset steps. Generally speaking, formulaic steps are not effective if the other person doesn't follow the same rule book. As discussed later in Chapter 9, the two processes in bargaining are creating value and taking value. Interest-based conflict managers are adept at **creating value**. They are creative, innovative, and capable of making numerous suggestions for solving a problem. Competitors are masters at **taking value**. Lax and Sebenius (1986) comment, "Value creators see the essence of negotiating as expanding the pie, as pursuing joint gains. This is aided by openness, clear communication, sharing information, creativity, an attitude of joint problem solving, and cultivating common interests. . . . Value claimers, on the other hand, tend to see this drive for joint gain as naive and weak-minded" (p. 32). Competitors may play along while the other is disclosing and creating value. Then they use the information to their advantage and leave the table with the lion's share of resources.

Case 3.1 illustrates one scenario where extreme competition and extreme cooperation meet. Sergio, the competitor, used aggressiveness and persistence in an attempt to wear down cooperative Antoine, whom he viewed as weak. Antoine was frustrated by his lack of success using interest-based tactics. Antoine could have given up and acquiesced to Sergio's demands. Instead, he recognized the clash between the competitive and cooperative approaches and changed to a competitive strategy. After proving that he "understood the game" and was able to compete, Sergio was motivated to change his strategy and engage in problem solving. Antoine was not a pure advocate of the cooperative worldview. He preferred to approach conflict cooperatively but understood that other people don't always feel the same way. So, Antoine learned some non-toxic competitive strategies to keep from being run over by people who only want to use competition.

Like Antoine, successful conflict managers are skilled at both competition and cooperation and can avoid the extremes of either worldview. As stated in Chapter 2, conflict can be a **mixed-motive situation**—open to interest-based creativity but containing some goals that genuinely are in opposition. Employees may sit down together to work out the vacation schedule and have success in bringing creative problem solving to 95 percent of the calendar. The last 5 percent, however, contains sticky issues where several employees want exactly the same days off. The employees need negotiation skills to uphold their goals for the part of the issue that is competitive where resources are scarce and goals are in conflict.

Supportive and Defensive Climates

Communication climates are associated with cooperative and competitive tactics, and can be determined by the extent individuals feel valued by others. Like meteorological climates, communicative climates can be hot and stormy, cold and chilling, or warm and temperate. Gibb (1961) introduced the classic concept of supportive and defensive climates, providing a useful framework to consider how tone affects conflict management. In **defensive climates**, individuals feel threatened and react to others negatively. In **supportive climates**, individuals feel safer and are more likely to engage in productive problem solving and conflict management. Gibb identified dichotomous clusters of behaviors that are likely to produce defensive climates or supportive climates (Table 3.2).

Descriptive language is less likely to cause defensiveness than evaluative language. Many statements beginning with "You are . . ." become negative evaluations about the other person (such as "You are a jerk," "You are not listening," or "You are inconsiderate"). Descriptive statements make *observations* about behaviors, for example: "When you roll your eyes, I don't know what you are thinking." Or, "When I hear derogatory comments about women, I feel uncomfortable." One way to describe rather than evaluate is to use **"I" statements**, which present the description from the perspective of the speaker, such as: "I felt . . .," "I thought . . .," or "I observed . . ." Where *evaluative language* judges and can incite the other to become defensive or to engage in competition, descriptive statements invite cooperation. A good test of whether an attempt at a descriptive statement works is if the listener would be unable to argue with it. For example, Randy said to Sara, "You gave me a dirty look, then stomped off and slammed the door." Sara could argue in response it wasn't a "dirty look," that she doesn't "stomp," and the wind caught the door; she didn't "slam" anything. Randy could

TABLE 3.2 Supportive and Defensive Climates

Supportive Behaviors	Defense-Provoking Behaviors
Description	Evaluation
Problem solving	Control
Spontaneity	Strategy
Empathy	Neutrality
Equality	Superiority
Open-mindedness	Certainty

instead remove the evaluative terms and describe what he observed and felt: "When I asked if you were going out with your friends, you looked at me but didn't answer. I felt in trouble for asking. Then you went to your room, closed the door, and haven't talked to me all evening." Description invites discussion; evaluation invites defensiveness.

DISCUSSION QUESTION • 3.7

How do you react to comments that are phrased with the word *You* as opposed to comments that avoid the word? For example, which phrasing sounds better? "When *you* play your music so loud, I can't get my work done" or "When the music is so loud, I can't get my work done."

Statements that try to *control* someone's behavior prompt more defensiveness than those engaging the other in *problem solving*. A supervisor may notice two employees who are not getting along and order them to "quit bickering and get back to work." An order is less likely to result in the desired behavior than saying, "I've noticed you two are having some challenges working together" (a descriptive statement). "What do the two of you think can be done about that in a way that is good for both of you and the unit as a whole?" (a problem-solving statement). Attempting to control another person elicits competitiveness and resistance; mutual problem solving solicits cooperation.

Car salespeople may be great at engaging people in conversations and getting them to talk about themselves, but these strategies typically are perceived as a manipulative ploy to gain an advantage. Any tactics perceived as a manipulation may garner a defensive reaction. *Spontaneity* means responding to the moment. Asking questions in a genuine attempt to find out how goals are in conflict or inviting the other person to engage in mutual problem solving will build a warmer climate.

In the way Gibb uses the term, *neutrality* carries with it a lack of caring about the other person. George Bernard Shaw commented, "Indifference is the essence of inhumanity." Jodi asks Harrison what he wants to do for their first anniversary. His response is an indifferent, "Whatever." Jodi is left feeling hurt and devalued by Harrison. In contrast, *empathy* shows interest in the other person's needs, goals, or values. The next time a question like that came up, Harrison, who is a quick learner, shows Jodi he values her by acknowledging her message: "I can't believe we've been together a year already." Recognizing that Harrison cares, Jodi presses on with, "I'm thinking that we could go out for a nice dinner to celebrate." Empathetic Harrison does not want to spend money on a dinner, but fortunately for him empathy does not mean the same thing as agreement. He is able to tell Jodi that he is worried about the cost of a big night out, but he agrees they should figure out a way to celebrate, maybe by having a picnic at the park where they first met.

> The opposite of love is not hate, it's indifference. The opposite of art is not ugliness, it's indifference. The opposite of faith is not heresy, it's indifference. And the opposite of life is not death, it's indifference.
>
> —Nobel Prize for Peace winner, Elie Wiesel

A tone of voice that conveys "I am better than you" or "I know more than you" carries an implied superior-to-inferior relationship. *Superiority* triggers defensiveness. Morris and Amelia are a couple nearing retirement. Morris always handles the finances and investments for the couple, and Amelia knows little about the state of their retirement nest egg. Over dinner she broaches the topic of retirement with her husband. He gives her a patronizing gesture and says, "Don't worry your pretty little head about it, dear. I have it under control." Exhibiting superiority can be a competitive tactic to gain advantage. Valuing people regardless of status is more associated with cooperative conflict management. A tone and approach that demonstrates *equality*—or at least less superiority—opens the door to more congenial and less competitive behaviors. Morris could have said, "It's actually quite complicated. I have investments in multiple places to supplement our Social Security. How much do you want to know?" Sharing information is one way of creating more equality in a relationship. Susan is a manager who lets her employees know that she's heard some policy changes are coming down the pike from corporate, although she's not sure what they'll be yet. This disclosure serves to develop trust with her employees. Giving others access to information does not translate into a direct loss of power. In fact, in Susan's case, she gains power in the improved relationship with her staff.

TOOLBOX 3.1 Transforming Defensiveness

For each example, label the type of defensive statement (evaluation, certainty, superiority, neutral, strategy, or control). Rewrite the statement using the opposing supportive strategy (description, open-mindedness, equality, empathy, spontaneity, or problem solving). The first example is illustrated for you.

Defensive Provoking	More Supportive
Example:	
1. "You are a hypocrite." (EVALUATION)	"I'm bothered when you tell me that I should eat more healthily while you're eating junk food for breakfast." (DESCRIPTION)
2. "I don't care. Whatever!"	
3. "We've tried something like that before. It didn't work then, and it won't work now."	
4. "I'm the oldest, so I'm driving."	
5. "You tell me your offer first, and I'll see if I'm still interested."	
6. "You just think everyone should do your work."	
7. "I can't believe you would consider voting for someone like that for president!"	

Gibb's term *certainty* describes those who approach a conversation as if they know all the answers, are dogmatic about their rightness, and downgrade ideas that are contrary to their own. The opposite is *openness* to change and consideration of opposing views. This does not mean that one can't have an opinion, a strong belief, or a favorite solution. Being open is about being willing to consider another perspective. Instead of saying, "That idea won't work," a more open reply might be, "Explain to me how that idea would work. I don't understand." Several years ago, a university held a community improvement conference for religious leaders in the state. Spiritual leaders from a wide range of faith traditions attended, and much of the conference required considerable group work and discussion. Several of the religious leaders came from faith traditions that held their church's beliefs were "the only truth" and viewed others who didn't ascribe to the exact same traditions, history, or core beliefs as wrong. Although the attendees were strong in their individual beliefs and certain in the correctness of their spiritual truths, they did not display certainty in their conversations. Discussions were marked by provisional statements like this: "In our faith, we believe_____. What does your faith believe?" Participant reviews of the conference were consistent in their praise for the welcoming atmosphere and how much they learned—mostly from the other participants. Provisional dialogue is about being willing to hear and explore differing ideas, yet it does not require people to abandon their own.

Competitive conflict and defensive climates often exist side by side. Mutual gains conflict prospers in a more supportive climate. Just as conflicts can be more or less competitive or cooperative (mixed motive), climates can be more or less defensive or supportive. "Friendly" competition can occur in supportive climates. For example, a friendship group may gather to play small-stakes poker. At the end of evening, one player may walk away with the majority of the money (a scarce resource). The situation is competitive but friendly and supportive. Likewise, employers may use competitive rewards to motivate employee performance. In a supportive climate, coworkers can compete without rancor. It is not as likely, however, that cooperative conflict management will prosper in a defensive climate where trust is lacking. You can recognize a defensive climate with unhealthy, negative competition by how you feel—on edge and looking for the next attack. Likewise, you can recognize a supportive climate with mutual gains opportunities by how you feel—safe in expressing your opinions and ideas. Research indicates that a supportive climate can moderate the negative effects of high pressure jobs. For example, emergency room nurses in supportive teams feel much less stress (Johansen & Cadmus, 2016).

Summary

Competition and cooperation are dichotomous approaches that affect attitudes and behaviors during interpersonal conflict. Competitive and cooperative conflict management approaches have advantages and disadvantages, with implications for future relationships and the achievement of goals. The competent conflict manager develops skills for all contingencies and situations.

Competitors envision three possible outcomes: win, lose, or draw. Those who lose in competition may provoke a fourth option: Both parties lose. Competition may entail argumentativeness and aggressiveness. Resources in the competitive view are perceived as zero-sum. There are two fallacies of the competitive approach: (1) Power can only be developed by withholding resources to create dependence, and (2) coercion is a rightful entitlement of the powerful. Kohn proposed four myths that lead to the acceptance of competition: competition is a part of human nature, competition is required to do our best, competitive games are the best way to have a good time, and competition builds character.

The cooperative view holds that mutual gains are the most productive outcomes and the needs of all parties in most conflicts can be met with a little creativity. Instead of focusing on positional demands, cooperative conflict managers seek underlying needs or interests.

A weakness of cooperative conflict management is moving beyond creating value to taking value. Many conflict situations contain motivations for competition and for cooperation: They are mixed-motive situations.

Interpersonal conflicts also occur in climates that are more or less supportive or defensive. Evaluation, control, strategy, neutrality, superiority, and certainty sustain defensive climates. Supportive climates are created through empathy, problem solving, spontaneity, description, equality, and open-mindedness.

Chapter Resources

Exercises

1. Some board games can be converted to a noncompetitive mode by using a **universal team approach**. In games like Trivial Pursuit, no matter how many individuals are playing, select two tokens and put them on the game board. When it is the first token's turn, everyone works together to answer the question. The first token advances or loses its turn depending on whether the team can deduce the answer. When it is the second token's turn, the entire team again answers the question. The game is to race the tokens around the board. The tokens can be tied to some other outcome, such as "If the blue peg wins, we'll have chicken for dinner; if red wins, we'll make spaghetti." In your groups, identify a favorite game. Can the game be converted from a competitive model to a group-based or cooperative model? What would be gained or lost if the game were played noncompetitively?

2. Analyze Case 3.2, "Your Call." Which approach to conflict is each party embracing? How do you know?

3. Have you been employed in a workplace that had a particularly defensive or supportive climate? In Gibb's terms, what kinds of communication characterized the workplace? Did the climate in the workplace affect how conflict occurred?

4. Change the following "You" statements into "I" statements.

    A. "You are so inconsiderate. You never think about my feelings."
    B. "You need to finish one thing before you start another."
    C. "What you need is a good attitude adjustment. You are so negative."
    D. "We wouldn't be having this argument if you would just do what you say you were going to do."

Journal/Essay Topics

1. Write an essay about the approach to conflict you learned as a child. Were you taught to use more competition or cooperation? Give specific examples of how you were taught those lessons.

2. Analyze your reactions to defense-provoking behaviors. Are there specific aspects of Gibb's defensive communication climates that seem to elicit a negative reaction from you?

Research Topics

1. Investigate the writing of Mary Parker Follett. Summarize and evaluate her perspective on conflict.

2. Review the change of management strategy employed by the Sears CEO, Eddie Lampert, and the impact the reliance on a competitive worldview had on the employees and long-term health of the corporation.

Mastery Case 3A

Not in My Space!

Examine what went wrong in this attempt at negotiating a living situation on campus in Mastery Case 3A.

In 2016, a UCLA freshman made national news when trying to negotiate with her new roommates in advance of arriving on campus. She sent them e-mails about her preferences for which bed, desk, and closet she would have use of. When her new roommates didn't respond, she sent them a demand for what she wanted. A series of e-mails ensued, with increasing hostility (https://www.thecut.com/2016/09/ucla-freshman-sends-future-roommate-insane-dramatic-email.html).

References

Bacharach, S. B., & Lawler, E. J. (1986). Power dependence and power paradoxes in bargaining. *Negotiation Journal, 2*(2), 167–174.

Cohen, J. R. (2003). Adversaries? Partners? How about counterparts? On metaphors in the practice and teaching of negotiation and dispute resolution. *Conflict Resolution Quarterly, 20*(4), 433–440.

Gibb, J. (1961). Defensive communication. *Journal of Communication, 11*, 141–168.

Hullett, C. R., & Tamborini, R. (2001). When I'm within my rights: An expectancy-based model of actor evaluative and behavioral responses to compliance-resistance strategies. *Communication Studies, 52*(1), 1–16.

Johansen, M. L., & Cadmus, E. (2016). Conflict management style, supportive work environments and the experience of work stress in emergency nurses. *Journal of Nursing Management, 24*, 211–218.

Katz, T. Y., & Block, C. J. (2000). Process and outcome goal orientation in conflict situations: The importance of framing. In M. Deutsch & P. T. Coleman (Eds.), *The handbook of conflict resolution: Theory and practice* (pp. 279–288). San Francisco: Jossey-Bass.

Kohn, A. (1986). *No contest: The case against competition*. Boston: Houghton Mifflin.

Lax, D. A., & Sebenius, J. K. (1986). *The manager as negotiator: Bargaining for cooperation and competitive gain*. New York: The Free Press.

Rogan, R. G., & La France, B. H. (2003). An examination of the relationship between verbal aggressiveness, conflict management strategies, and conflict interaction goals. *Communication Quarterly, 51*(4), 458–469.

Seymour, D. (1997, March–April). Charting a future for quality in higher education. *About Campus*, 4–10.

Stein, N. L., & Albro, E. R. (2001). The origins and nature of arguments: Studies in conflict understanding, emotion, and negotiation. *Discourse Processes, 32*(2–3), 113–133.

Withers, B. (2002). *The conflict management skills workshop*. New York: AMACOM.

Chapter 4

Causes of Conflict

Vocabulary

Content goals

Expectation management

Expectancy violation theory

Face

Face goals

Flashpoint

Future focus

Goal

Initial goals

In-process goals

Internal rationalizing process

Metacommunication

Process goals

Relationship goals

Retrospective goals

Scarce resources

Self-concept

Self-identity

Self-serving bias

Sense-making

Social learning theory

Substantive goals

Topics

Values

Objectives

After reading the chapter, you should be able to:

1. Differentiate among conflict causes and topics
2. Relate the process of sense-making to conflict flashpoints
3. Understand common causes of conflict
4. Differentiate among types of goals
5. Explain the dynamic nature of goals

CASE 4.1

It's My Money

Aidan and Abigail have been married since starting college and are beginning their first professional jobs. Abigail is a bookkeeper and pays all the family bills. Aidan's new job has a 401(k) plan, and they have been trying to find time to look over his investment choices. Tonight, they are watching television.

Abigail:	"This might be a good time to look at the retirement paperwork and get that done."
Aidan:	"I took care of it."
Abigail:	"What do you mean, you took care of it?"
Aidan:	"I turned it in."
Abigail:	"But we were going to go over it together and talk about it."
Aidan:	"Talk, talk, talk. I took care of it so we don't need to 'talk' about it."
Abigail:	"You always tell me you don't know anything about finance and you just turned in your retirement paperwork? I'm the one who knows about our family budget and finance. What did you set up?"
Aidan:	"I took care of it. I don't have time to talk about this stuff."
Abigail:	"You don't have time. What about having time to pay the rent and buy groceries? What's going to happen if we don't have enough money?"
Aidan:	"You're so dramatic! Don't worry about it. It's my money; I'll do what I want with it."
Abigail:	"It's your money? I can't believe you said that. Maybe we should get separate checkbooks and split all our expenses if that is 'your' retirement?"
Aidan:	"You always have to overreact." He turns up the volume on the television.

In Case 4.1, Aidan and Abigail seem to have the same long-range goal: saving for retirement. Their conversation about retirement planning, however, is less than harmonious. They may not even understand how their conversation turned into conflict.

This chapter explores the causes of conflict. Our discussion is guided by several assumptions: (1) Topics of conflict are not the same as causes of conflict, (2) people's behaviors in conflict are motivated by reasons that make sense to them, (3) conflict behaviors are more learned (nurture) than biological (nature), (4) conflict causes arise from goal interference, (5) goals are dynamic, and (6) effective conflict managers focus on the future more than on past causes. After explaining the assumptions that guide the search for conflict causes and examining the nature of goals in conflict, we conclude with some preliminary skills for goal analysis.

Conflict Topics Are Not Necessarily Conflict Causes

If asked "What caused a conflict?" people respond with topics like money, parenting styles, cleaning the house, or a nasty comment on a social media page. At first glance, Abigail and Aidan's conflict in Case 4.1 seems to be about money, but in reality the conflict is about something else.

Topics are what the conversation was *about* rather than an identification of what gave rise to the conflict—its cause. Confusing a conflict topic with its underlying cause is easy. A **flashpoint** is the event that precipitates a conflict and usually is directly related to the topic, but not necessarily directly connected to the underlying cause. For example, when Simone sees that her roommate Dom has left his stinky pizza boxes all over the living room, she may chastise him verbally the next time they meet. The pizza boxes are not the cause of the conflict. They merely are the stimulus that precipitates a struggle over some other issue—perhaps standards of cleanliness, who cleans the house, or when the house is cleaned. The same conflict could be manifested through several different flashpoints—pizza boxes, shirts left on a chair, or dishes in the sink.

When people have lots of conflict about seemingly different topics, there may be a hidden underlying cause that links all of the disputes. Two employees may clash one day about proper procedure, the next day about whose job it was to deliver a product, and a third day about who should take a weekend shift. All of these topics may be masking the same underlying conflict cause—perhaps hurt feelings or a power struggle. A supervisor who takes conflict topics one at a time may miss the underlying cause and spend time on the wrong problems. The conflict will continue to pop up over and over again in different disguises. Dealing with the topic of the moment does not necessarily address the underlying issue in a conflict. Wise conflict managers remember to look beyond the obvious to see if there is a hidden underlying cause for the difficulty.

Conflict Behaviors Are Motivated by Reasons That Make Sense

The behaviors of people during conflict may seem odd and irrational. Regardless of how it may look to an outsider, those who engage in conflict do so for reasons that make good sense—to them. **Sense-making** is how we weave together knowledge, feelings, intuitions, and backgrounds to make sense of the world. Through sense-making, humans leap from perception, to interpretation, to action.

CASE 4.2

Attribution Errors: Part I

Mason is proud that he bikes and gets exercise while saving the environment from the carbon dioxide that would go into the air if he drove the five miles to work every day. Mason lives in a modern student housing building where smaller private bedrooms are part of the trade-off for larger common areas and exercise rooms. Because he doesn't have much space, Mason sometimes leaves his very expensive bike chained up in an unused corner of the common area.

One morning, when Mason goes to get his bike to go to work, he notices a very large message taped to his bike. The note is so large, he—and all of his roommates—can read it from across the room. The note says: "To the jerk who puts his junk in our common area: Move it or lose it! This is your last warning." The note is fastened on the bike with duct tape that discolors the paint when removed.

Mason has been having trouble with Logan, who is a real slob who never cleans up the shower room. Mason decides to get even with Logan after this latest insult by putting all of Logan's shampoo and shower stuff in the trash and throwing it out.

In Case 4.2, Mason combines his past experiences, biases, and knowledge of his neighbors to make sense of what happened. To Mason, the note writer *intended* to deface his property because of the type of adhesive used. Mason *assumes* Logan left the note and judges him to be a slob, dangerous, and surly. Logan's assumed actions are viewed as intentional—designed to show Mason that he can't be bullied and to cause Mason maximum embarrassment because many people saw the note as they walked by.

CASE 4.2

Attribution Errors: Part II

Tony actually wrote the note and affixed it to Mason's bike, not Logan. Tony has a new friend who he wanted to impress when invited over to the common room. Instead of the evening Tony had planned in his mind, the bike in the corner was the impetus for the entire night's conversation. They spent most of their time talking about cycling. Tony is more of a geek than an athlete and thinks the focus on physical sport made him look bad. He blames the owner of the bike, who never should have left it in the common room.

Assuming there is no rational justification for the other person's behavior is common for those in conflict. However, what does the situation seem like to Tony—the actual writer of the note? Based on his assumption that he has a right to use the common area to his best advantage, Tony's actions make sense—to him. He is reacting from frustration and ruined expectations, which he blames on the bike's presence in the common area.

An objective observer may point to the false assumptions made by Mason and Tony. Both men are acting on incomplete information and a desire to advance personal goals. Like most people caught in the vortex of conflict, Mason and Tony do not take the time to sit back and analyze the situation or to verify their assumptions. Instead, they are applying an **internal rationalizing process**.

Conflicts arise, in part, because individuals do not have the same criteria or standards for what makes sense (the schema discussed in Chapter 2). Factors that influence sense-making include sense of self, attitudes, beliefs, biases, morals, values, philosophies, past experiences, physiological states, gender, age, education, culture, religion/spirituality, prior relationships, knowledge of the subject matter, family upbringing, conflict style, competitiveness versus cooperativeness, and the list could go on.

DISCUSSION QUESTION • 4.1

Identify a conflict you've observed or been a participant in. Choose a behavior you exhibited during the conflict that an outsider might label irrational. Discuss the internal rationalizing process that may have supported your behavior.

Competent conflict managers attempt to view others as acting from reasons that make sense to them, rather than acting from mean-spirited motives. By asking questions, conflict managers try to discover the needs and rationales others bring to conflict situations. Knowing that people view the world through personal sense-making processes helps us understand the value of a basic conflict management tool—expectation management. **Expectation management** includes any communication intended to move two people's views of a situation closer together. Because of past experience, roommates may expect different behaviors from each other, as happened in Case 4.2. Sometimes people retaliate based on what they expected to see rather than what really happened, and conflict erupts. Sometimes individuals expect others will somehow intuit what the right thing is to do (in one individual's perspective). When the expected behaviors don't occur, disappointment and potential conflict follows. Communicating what one expects as soon as possible during times of uncertainty is a powerful tactic to prevent and minimize conflict.

Before leaving the discussion of how individuals make sense of their behaviors, it is necessary to distinguish between creating a rationale for a behavior and behaviors that are illegal, unethical, or unwise. The internal gymnastics that allow simple ethical breaches can grow into thinking that allows cruel or violent behavior. An example of this occurred in your author's neighborhood. Someone has been poisoning dogs by tossing tainted meat into backyards in the middle of the night. The poisoner probably had some reason that makes sense to him or her for these illegal and cruel slayings. Perhaps the person couldn't sleep at night when dogs bark, was bitten by a dog as a child, thinks dogs are dangerous, or wants attention. Standards of a civil society, however, eschew this type of dangerous and extreme response.

Learning the difference between what makes sense "inside oneself" and what makes sense in society is a part of moral development. Internal rationalizations do not justify or excuse poor behavior or violence. Understanding rationalizations, however, can help a conflict manager discover what is preventing productive conflict transformation.

Conflict Behaviors Are Learned

Social learning theory posits that attitudes and behaviors are developed by observing others. Children initially learn how to behave during conflict from their parents and caregivers. Violence in the home is a prominent factor in predicting violent behavior in children when they become adults (Margolin & Gordis, 2004). Later in life, playmates, teachers, the faith community, television, music lyrics, and other media gain influence (Glascock, 2003).

DISCUSSION QUESTION • 4.2

What roles do family and media play in teaching aggressive behavior? What responsibility do individuals have as consumers of media violence? How involved should parents be in monitoring or curtailing their children's exposure to violent music, movies, and games?

Cable entertainment is a haven for verbal aggressiveness. Comedies contain about thirty acts of verbal aggression per hour. Research indicates that exposure to media violence leads to increased aggressiveness, particularly among young males and sensation seekers (Slater, Henry, Swaim, & Anderson, 2003). Violence in music lyrics has been linked to increased aggression (Anderson, Carnagey, & Eubanks, 2003). Video game violence was shown to decrease empathy for others (Funk, Baldacci, Pasold, & Baumgardner, 2004). There are ample places to learn verbal aggression and bad conflict management strategies, including social media (discussed in Chapter 17). Many reality shows create a competitive environment and intentionally select participants who will act badly. Fortunately, media influence can be countered by positive relationships with parents or mentors, constructive peer associations, and turning passive users of media into more analytical observers.

Knowing that conflict behaviors are learned is important to students of conflict management for two reasons. First, learned behaviors can be changed. Changing the patterns formed early in life may not be easy, but it is possible. Second, people have choices to make during conflict. Individuals are not destined to behave in negative and aggressive ways or in positive and cooperative ways. Behaviors are a result of the choices we make.

Goal Interference Causes Conflict

Every individual has goals. A **goal** is a desired condition. Goals may be profound or simple. Goals can include behaviors like quitting smoking; outcomes like earning an "A" in a class; self-image factors like seeing yourself as a tough, independent individual who is not dependent on your parents; image-management factors like wanting others to view you as attractive or competent; or states of being like having a fulfilling relationship with an intimate partner.

Goals always are related to *needs*. An examination of Mayer's (2000) categories of conflict illustrates how conflict types relate to goal interference. Mayer claims there are several common types of conflict, including communication, emotion, value, and structure.

Communication conflicts arise from goal interference about information. Which information is right? What information should be used as criteria for decisions? Is communication adequate? Are we interpreting the data the same way? If a supervisor uses all CAPITALS in an e-mail and the employees are upset because the supervisor "yelled at them," communicative intent may have been misinterpreted. If a couple argues about how much in monthly payments they can afford for a new car and they unknowingly are using a different base for their estimates, a conflict arising from different data may occur. If the same couple knows they are using different data and argue over which number is correct, a conflict about criteria may arise.

> Conflict frequently escalates because people act on the assumption that they have communicated accurately when they have not.
>
> —Conflict author and consultant Mayer (2000, p. 10)

Emotions feed conflict. *Emotional conflicts* center on the experience and expression of feelings. People are not purely rational beings. Feelings matter. The supervisor who sends an e-mail critical of one employee to the entire staff may cause a variety of emotional responses—resentment from the employee who is criticized and fear of similar ridicule from the rest of the staff. The anger of parents when children stay out too late partly is a manifestation of fear that the son or daughter will be hurt. Conflict escalation is fueled by emotions.

Value conflicts pivot around deep-seated beliefs about right and wrong. One person's **values** may not match exactly with the values of a friend, neighbor, or coworker. Couples may conflict over whether to save money (a value of thrift) or go into debt to fund vacations (valuing fun). Employees may hotly contest which music is played in the workplace because of the values associated with particular musical genres—talk radio (with a conservative or liberal leaning), country western, contemporary music, or trap hip hop. Mayer identifies goal interference around values as among the most intransigent of conflicts because self-image and identity are so inextricably tied to personal values. For example, coworkers who are offended by a colleague's music may also be rejecting the values embedded in the music.

Structure conflicts relate to the external framework that surrounds a conflict. Structure includes resources, decision-making processes, time, methods of communication, and setting. The rules or methods of making decisions may be a barrier to goal attainment, or conflicts may arise about the appropriate style for organizing tasks. For example, two competing styles of meeting management may cause distress. One approach is very organized, agenda driven, and task oriented. The other approach focuses on social relationships and is free from structural constraints. Neither style inherently is better than the other, but meetings organized by someone with an opposite style may lead to power struggles over how to run a meeting.

Just as people act in conflicts for reasons that make sense to them, people interpret goal interference (as discussed in Chapter 1) in ways that make sense to them. Tony, in Case 4.2 Part II, had a self-image that he wanted to protect and relationship-building goals that he wanted to advance. The bicycle got in the way of his goal achievement, in his mind. An objective observer would note that the goal could be achieved in other ways, but people who perceive goal interference do not necessarily analyze situations objectively or see all of their choices.

Four Main Goals During Conflict

There are four primary goals that impact interpersonal conflict (Table 4.1). An individual's goals may relate to tangible resources (**content** or **substantive goals**), how things should be done (**process goals**), who the parties are to each other (**relationship goals**), or one's sense of **self-image** (**face goals**). All conflicts will contain perceived interference with one or more of these goals.

Content Goals

Content goals (also called **substantive goals**) include tangible resources or any measurable factor around which desired outcomes can be built. These goals speak to the question: "Do I have control of the resources that I want?" Resources can be basic, such as food, clothing, and warmth. Resources also include items such as money, property, time, and access. When a customer confronts a businessperson to get a refund for a broken product, the issue is about what, if anything, should be done about the broken item. The consumer's goal probably is to get a refund. When roommates clash over what activities should occur in their apartment on Sundays, the issue is about how time and space should be used. Each roommate may have a specific goal around a different activity. When a family of four is given two tickets to a movie they all want to see, the issue is about what to do with two tickets that four people covet.

Scarce resources are the cornerstones of content conflict. A **scarce resource** is anything someone perceives to be in limited supply. The perception of scarcity drives the willingness to enter into conflict to control the resource. The resource can be actually scarce or just perceived as scarce. Two boys were throwing an imaginary baseball back and forth while waiting in a long line. The activity kept the 4- and 8-year-olds entertained until the older boy tired of the game and pantomimed putting the ball in his pocket. The younger child became quite upset and started a fight to get the pretend ball back. Fortunately, Mom found another imaginary ball in her purse. Just as the two boys fought over an imaginary ball, adults sometimes struggle for intangible resources such as self-esteem or love as if they are substantive and in limited supply. The core of sibling rivalry is the view that parental love is limited. When love is viewed as scarce, attention given to one child lessens the amount of attention available to the other child. Perceived scarce resources may overlap with relationship and/or face goals.

TABLE 4.1 Four Primary Goals During Conflict

Content/Substantive goals:	Do I have control of the resources that I need?
Process goals:	Are decisions being made in the way I want? Are we communicating in ways that work for me?
Relationship goals:	What is the nature of our relationship? Am I satisfied with my role and participation in the relationship? Do we want the same type of relationship?
Image/Face goals:	Is my self-image being maintained? Do I need to try to change your self-image?

Actual scarce resources are measurably limited. A cake has only so many slices. Every piece taken away means less left for others. A cake is a zero-sum resource since as portions are removed, the total available will become zero when the last slice is eaten. At work, if only one promotion is available, the resource of promotional advancement is scarce. If more than one person wishes the promotion, anyone else in consideration for the advancement can be seen as hindering goal achievement. Family income is a scarce resource. If there is $500 left each month after budgeted expenses are subtracted from the family's income, then a long list of desires may compete for the few remaining dollars: saving for the future, a vacation, new cell phones; dining out; helping with college expenses; and the list could be endless.

DISCUSSION QUESTION • 4.3

What perceived or actual scarce resources are prominent at this juncture in your life? Do conflicts arise around these scarce resources?

Another twist on content/substantive issues is the tendency to cloak goals with a content-like disguise. A process, face, or relationship goal may be expressed as a content issue. When a couple habitually fights about who does the laundry, one should wonder if the conflict really is about the laundry or about power. Repeated conflicts either have not been managed successfully or are about something other than the visible content. Dana (2005) comments:

> We are propelled into conflict by the appearance of incompatible positions on a substantive issue—I want "A" whereas you want "B." But what *appear* as substantive issues that we believe represent our differences in rational (objective) self-interests are often, in reality, mere facades concealing perceived threats to our underlying emotional needs.
>
> (p. 87)

For example, in Case 4.1, Aidan and Abigail may seem to be contesting over the scarce resource of money, but the conflict probably is more about how decisions are made (process) or Abigail's self-image as a money manager (image/face).

Process Goals

Process goals involve how a person wishes events to unfold, how decisions are made, or how communication occurs. Process goals speak to two types of questions: "Are decisions being made in ways I prefer?" and "Is the type of communication that is occurring what I want to happen?" When Aidan made a decision that affected Abigail and the family's future, she objected to not being included. She felt the decision was made using the wrong process—a unilateral decision rather than an equal discussion. Likewise, when managers tell employees that new procedures are being implemented, the employees may feel a better decision would have been made if their input had been solicited.

When and where to have discussions about important topics also can impact process goals. A partner who brings up a money issue in front of her significant other's parents may be violating an expectation of privacy. Avoiding arguing in front of the children or believing a couple shouldn't "go to bed mad" are examples of process expectations. Expectations can make conflict better or worse, depending on whether all parties have the same expectations. One newly married couple, neither of which was a "morning person," determined after several nasty altercations before 8 A.M. that they just shouldn't talk to each other before having a cup of coffee. Together they determined the best process for communicating—for them.

DISCUSSION QUESTION • 4.4

Conflict managers sometimes arrange to meet in a neutral location to discuss issues. If you were having a conflict with roommates, what location would be neutral? How can location affect the process of a conflict?

Relationship Goals

Relationship goals involve who the parties want to be to each other. Relationship goals speak to these questions: "What is the nature of our relationship?" "Am I satisfied with my role and participation in the relationship?" "Do we want the same type of relationship?"

Friends may have divergent perceptions about what it means to be friends, how often friends should see each other, or what type of personal information friends should exchange. Jealousy arising from different expectations of what is appropriate can affect romantic relationships, friends, and family members. Parents and teens may develop different goals about transitioning from the parent-child roles to being friends. Employees may desire an equal relationship with a supervisor, whereas the supervisor prefers a more formal subordinate-superior relationship. The depth and shape of relationships are not automatic; they are negotiated.

Relationship goals are complex, and they may change. As children age, they struggle to achieve autonomy and increased privacy, creating boundary management issues. When a six-year-old informed his mom that "When I'm seven, I can ride my bicycle wherever I want," she disagreed. Her definition of the relationship includes being a protector of her child, which cannot be done if he's riding his bicycle miles away.

Image/Face Goals

Self-concept is a relatively stable set of perceptions about oneself. Even though self-concept changes throughout life as an individual accumulates experience, at any specific moment in time self-concept is resistant to change.

The concept of **face** is tied to self-concept.

> 'Face' refers to a claimed sense of favorable social self-worth that a person wants others to have of her or him. It is a vulnerable identity-based resource because it can be enhanced or threatened in any uncertain social situation. Situations such as conflict management.
> (Ting-Toomey & Kurogi, 1998, p. 187)

Face can be subdivided into three areas: *Self-face* is one's personal image. *Other-face* relates to awareness, or lack thereof, about the other's image of himself or herself. *Mutual-face* exhibits concern for both parties and/or the image of the relationship (Ting-Toomey, Oetzel, & Yee-Jung, 2001, p. 89).

KEY 4.1

Become aware of your own goals.

One of the assumptions of face theory is that all people are concerned about face in one way or another. Although everyone does not view the same things as problematic, embarrassing personal attacks probably will clash with the target's sense of self (identify/face). Many conflicts are caused

TABLE 4.2 Face Goals

Affirmation of face:	Creating a new self-image
Reaffirmation of face:	Consistently exhibiting a self-image
Saving face:	Acting to correct a tarnished image
Transformation of face:	Changing from one self-image to another
Subversion of face:	Acting to tarnish someone else's self-image

by perceived threats to self-image. Someone who perceives he or she is being verbally attacked, being made to look bad, or facing controlling behaviors may feel emotionally threatened. If one's self-image, autonomy, and/or the ability to feel happy about oneself is attacked, conflict is likely. Many interpersonal conflicts begin with someone defending against a perceived attack. Rogan and La France (2003) claim "conflict is generally deemed to be an inherently face-threatening interactional context" (p. 461).

Face goals are the affirmation, reaffirmation, saving, transformation, or subversion of self or other face (Table 4.2). When meeting new people, individuals *affirm* or create a public image. A new friend might tell a joke to affirm his image as a funny guy. As relationships develop, the personal image is *reaffirmed* through repeated behaviors. Consistently making jokes reaffirms his identity as a funny guy. If he tells a joke that is in poor taste and listeners tell him so, *face saving* may need to occur. He tells an off-color joke in front of his boss, and his boss is offended. He apologizes and doesn't tell that kind of joke to his boss again. As individuals grow and change, *face transformation* may become desirable. He now wants to get a promotion and to be seen as a mature person. He quits telling jokes at work. *Subversion* of face occurs when someone acts to counter the image of another person. A coworker who also wants the promotion may remind coworkers of what a goof the other is, thereby subverting his attempts at transformation of his image from a joker to someone with serious management potential.

DISCUSSION QUESTION • 4.5

Do you have the same face/self-image now as when you first started college? What type of image management kicked in when you first enrolled in higher education?

Face is dynamic because people do not present a single, uniform identity to the outside world. An individual may employ a different aspect of self-identify at work than at home. At work, Marco may be all business, use powerful language, and demand respect. At home, Marco may defer to his partner and exhibit warm and loving mannerisms. Managing multiple identities and goals can be difficult. An account executive who has cultivated a tough, uncompromising image may be embarrassed at social events if work and home identities clash. At a dinner party with colleagues, his partner may expect him to be warm and affectionate, behaviors that contradict his work image.

CASE 4.3

Moving Back Home?

When Bob was young, he thought of himself the way his mother described him: "a good boy." Bob would try to behave to make his mother happy. Sometimes, the other kids would make fun of the clothes Bob's mother chose for him—dress pants with matching button-down shirts and sweaters. Bob was a quiet and polite boy, but not very popular at school.

As Bob became a teenager, he was less interested in what his mother wanted and more interested in what his peers thought. When the family moved to a new town, Bob decided it was time to assert himself. Taking money from his savings account, Bob bought the same types of clothes of the social group he admired. He contemplated several tattoos.

Bob's parents were shocked and disappointed. They lectured him, saying he was ruining his life. Bob was pleased that it was easier to make friends at his new school and didn't pay much attention to his parents.

After graduating from high school, Bob moved out and got a job at the coffee shop near the local college. He got a couple of discrete tattoos and gauged his ears. Although the shop required a dress code of black shirts and pants, Bob would "forget" and wear printed T-shirts about once a week. Bob would imitate his thirty-year-old boss behind his back and call him a stupid mocha-nerd. One day, Bob came to work and his boss said, "I guess I'm not as stupid as you think I am. You're fired."

Out of work and out of money, Bob called his parents to see if he could move back home. They agreed—but only if he cleaned up his look, got a part-time job, and enrolled in college next term. Bob has a decision to make.

DISCUSSION QUESTION • 4.6

What are each party's face goals in Case 4.3, "Moving Back Home?"

Perception Patterns Affect How Goals Are Interpreted

Human behavior research led to several discoveries about how perception works (Adler & Proctor, 2017; Ayoko, Callan, & Hartel, 2003). These findings add to the complexity of identity management.

1. *We judge ourselves more charitably than we judge others.* As stated in Chapter 2, a **self-serving bias** judges the same behavior differently in self than in others: "When she says something evaluative about another friend, it's because she is nasty; when I make critical comments, they are intended to be helpful." An exception is that individuals with low self-esteem may judge themselves more harshly than they judge others. For example, social comparisons of self to others among young Facebook users may be particularly vulnerable to misinterpretation. A young user who sees the beautiful, successful, happy postings on Facebook, may experience a lowering of self-esteem (de Vries & Kuhne, 2015).

2. *We attribute our behaviors to external circumstances and others' behaviors to internal character traits.* "If I am late to work, it is because something important held me up. If you are late to work it is because you are lazy and inconsiderate." Dana (2005) labels these tendencies **wrong reflexes.** Assuming the other is a "bad person" is the wrong reflex. Dana highlights the inflexibility that can result from internal attributions if someone thinks the "conflict is the direct result of your incompetence, ignorance, meanness, or other defect; it can only be resolved if you recognize and correct your defects" (p. 29).

3. **We tend to favor negative impressions of others over positive ones.** We are more influenced by negative than by positive descriptions. A professor who is unkempt and disorganized, even though very knowledgeable and interesting, may be given low evaluations by students. When asked to describe this professor, students might be inclined to highlight the negative attributes over the positive ones.

4. **We are influenced by what is most obvious.** It is not unusual for people to notice what someone is wearing and not notice what the individual is doing.

5. **We cling to first impressions.** On the way to meet a salesperson for lunch, an inconsiderate driver zoomed into a parking space that another driver was waiting for. When entering the restaurant, the client realized the salesperson was the parking space thief. Regardless of how pleasantly the salesperson behaves during lunch, any future relationship is tainted by the negative first impression. Likewise, the first tactics used during conflict may carry a greater impression than those developed later.

6. **We assume that others are similar to us.** When a new employee won't look a superior in the eye, the boss may infer that the employee is shifty, lying, or untrustworthy. If the new employee is from a culture where eye contact with those in a higher social position is impolite, the behavior may be intended as a sign of respect. Judging others by personal or cultural standards is common, yet extremely unfair. Intercultural conflicts sometimes are caused by differing expectations of how communication should unfold and how people should act. For many Westerners, directness is preferred as a means of communication. The act of being direct matches the self-image of decisive, efficient negotiators. In some cultures, indirectness is preferred and matches a value of maintaining harmony and preventing embarrassment (Ma, 1992).

7. **We predict the reactions of other people based on our perceptions of them.** According to **expectancy violation theory**, we anticipate how people will act by looking at the relationship we share, our views of that person, and the situation. Then, how the other person reacts is interpreted and compared to expectations. When expectations are violated, negative reactions and conflict are more likely (Hullett & Tamborini, 2001). In Case 4.1, Abigail expected to be included in the decision and that her knowledge of monetary matters would carry some weight in how her spouse's retirement funds were allocated. When Aidan casually made a decision without her, expectations were violated.

Goals Are Dynamic

It is beneficial to recognize which type of goals is present when seeking to understand a specific conflict. Goals may overlap and change as the conflict evolves, so goal analysis may need to be done more than once. Conflict may begin with one cause and morph into another. There are four primary reasons why goals are dynamic: (1) The goals may have been unconscious or ill-defined at the beginning, (2) individuals are opportunistic and may adapt goals to fit changing circumstances, (3) perceptions may change, and (4) goals may be recast after the conflict episode. The following example illustrates the transitory nature of goals: A woman attempts to return a sweater to the department store because it has a flaw. She does not have a receipt. Her initial goal is to take the sweater back, but she hasn't considered how she would like the reimbursement—a replacement sweater, in-store credit, or refund. Upon seeing the sign that says, "No refunds without a receipt," she determines that the policy is unfair if there is a flaw in the product. She now has the goal to get a cash refund. As she speaks with the customer service representative who is upholding the store policy, she sees him as uncaring and the store as mismanaged. She grudgingly settles for an in-store credit. After she leaves the store with her in-store credit, she writes the CEO of the company to discuss how customer service procedures could be improved, a very different goal

TABLE 4.3 Goals Emerge and Change

Initial goal:	I felt neglected by my girlfriend, so I tried to make her want to be with me by ignoring her.
In-process goal:	Ignoring her wasn't working, so I gave up on that and started acting normally again. I just wanted her to spend more time with me. She broke up with me.
Retrospective goal:	I'll tell friends I wasn't interested in a long-term relationship anyway.
New goal:	I just want a relationship with someone who will spend lots of time with me.

than when she first arrived at the store with the flawed sweater. As conflicts progress, goals shift (Hocker & Wilmot, 2014).

Table 4.3 summarizes the three phases that goals go through during a conflict: initial, in-process, and retrospective. At the beginning, each individual may be aware of **initial goals** or only have a vague notion of what would be a desirable outcome. As a conflict unfolds, goals may be modified as new information is learned or perceptions change. Goals are **in process.** After a conflict episode is completed, individuals look back and may state to self or others a **retrospective goal**—what one "says" the goal was during the conflict. At the end of one conflict episode, expectations may reset to create a new initial goal.

Face goals can be reshaped retrospectively. When the outcome would cause embarrassment, an individual may tell friends that "he really didn't care" or that his real goal was something different. For example, Ashley and Andrew may struggle over who has to clean the bathroom because both individuals dislike the work and think it is beneath them. Their goals are to get the other to do the cleaning (initial goals). Ashley may persuade Andrew that he should do the cleaning this time. As a surprise reward, Ashley makes dinner for him. Andrew may tell his other roommates that his goal all along was to get Ashley to make him dinner (retrospective goal).

Skills to Enhance Goal Analysis and Development

Goals overlap and may not fit entirely into one neat category. Content goals may take on image or face-threatening aspects or give rise to process questions. Process goals may overlap with relationship goals. The complexity of goals can be difficult to unravel. If the goals are not clear, managing the conflict is harder. If a conflict goes on too long, the probability is high that at least one person will become emotionally invested in being right—creating an image/face conflict. One might think, "This has gone on so long, if I back down now I'll look like a real loser."

A group of friends gathers on a rainy weekend afternoon and decides to play Trivial Pursuit. The initial goal is to do something together. The nature of competitive games, however, may activate other goals. One friend may have a goal of proving how smart she is to the rest of the group. Another may want to compete and win to reinforce a self-image as a worthy person. Are the goals in conflict? Perhaps. It depends on how each person pursues accomplishing an individual goal and if one set of behaviors leads another person to perceive interference with goal achievement. For instance, Ellie wants to chat and be with her friends, and she does not pay much attention to the strategy of the game. Devon and Jerome see her behavior as devaluing their goals of winning through competition. Because of the interplay between Ellie, Devon, and Jerome, Molly may decide that she now wants to win to show Devon and Jerome how petty they are. Ellie may decide that if people are going to say mean things to each other, she isn't going to play at all.

DISCUSSION QUESTION • 4.7

Have you been in the middle of a conflict and realized that you don't really want what you're fighting for?

Knowing what you want is an important key to success. Unfortunately, individuals sometimes are not self-aware of goals. Determining "what is it that I am struggling to achieve?" can be challenging. People who are not aware of their goals demand things that do not really meet their needs. When others comply with those demands, everyone is confused and angry when the problem is not resolved. This phenomenon is capsulized in the saying: "Sometimes, you get what you ask for, not what you want."

In conflict, one of the most important skills is becoming conscious of goals by asking yourself, "What do I want to achieve at the end of the conflict?" "If the conflict is settled, what would I need to meet my goals?" or "What is keeping me from accomplishing the goal on my own?" Understanding feelings and the goal interference that give rise to conflict provides greater clarity. With clarity about goals, conflicting parties can work together effectively and efficiently to discover better outcomes. Table 4.4 offers initial skills for goal analysis that are added to in the analysis chapter later in this book.

KEY 4.2

Be aware of the past, but focus on the future.

Helping the other person understand your intentions also is a critical conflict management skill, particularly when defensive reactions occur, the conversation is tense, or the medium of communication reduces important nonverbal cues. Text messages and Snapchat lack the full range of nonverbal cues that help the other party interpret the meaning of messages. A casual note dashed off may elicit a defensive response if it is interpreted as personal criticism. **Metacommunication**, communicating about communication, can help. When asking a difficult question, one might use metacommunication to preempt defensive comments by saying, "I don't mean this question in a bad way . . ." When comments are contextualized with a statement about intention, they are less open to misinterpretation. When a spouse asks her partner to take out the garbage, he may reply, "Sure." After waiting five minutes, she may say, "Fine, I'll take it out myself!" and remove the garbage. Each party had a different interpretation of "when" the garbage should be taken out—immediately or when he got around to it. When he says, "Sure," she might metacommunicate: "By 'sure' do you mean you'll take the garbage out immediately or in a couple of hours? I want to know because it smells, and if you are too busy, I will take it out myself."

TABLE 4.4 Skills to Locate and Discuss Goals

1. Spend time analyzing what you really need.
2. Discuss goals face-to-face when you can.
3. Avoid using casual social media for important goal discussions.
4. Metacommunicate about your goals.
5. Don't get stuck in the ancient past if it keeps you from managing a conflict.

Although understanding the general cause of conflict is important, conflict managers cannot dwell too long on the past. If a conflict has been going on for years, the original cause of the conflict may not really matter anymore.

Knowledge of causes helps determine where the goal inference is located. Different strategies are used when interference is perceived but not actually occurring. For example, the perceived interference could be based on misassumptions, misperceptions, or inadequate information. In those cases, sharing more information might reduce the conflict. If actual goal interference is occurring, knowledge of causes is crucial to understanding which outcome will meet the other's goals. Focusing too much on the past, however, can be counterproductive. In general, productive conflict managers are not particularly concerned with root causes, deep historical background, or every tactical move that occurred over the duration of a conflict. Effective conflict managers need to be **future focused** and move ahead into a different and more productive path. Be aware of the past, but focus on the future.

TOOLBOX 4.1   Identifying Goals

Here are some questions to ask to identify goal interference:

- Have similar conflict episodes happened with this person before? What goals were seen as incompatible during the past conflict?
- What does the other person seem to need from the conflict?
- What might the other person be afraid of losing?
- What combination of goals is the other person working to achieve?
- Are perceived or actual scarce resources a part of the conflict?
- Are hidden goals being masked by other issues?

Summary

Conflict topics are not the same as conflict goals. People may not consciously be aware of their goals or may conceal goals for a variety of reasons. The flashpoint that precipitates a conflict may not be what the conflict really is about. Because of the complexity of goals, people should not jump to conclusions too quickly at the onset of a conflict; circumstances frequently are not what they appear. Similarly, becoming aware of personal goals is a powerful force and a critical skill for competent conflict managers.

Individual conflict behaviors are motivated by reasons that make sense to that person. Sense-making is how one weaves together past experience and knowledge to interpret the world. Sense-making is not a logical activity; instead it is governed by variables such as self-concept, culture, religion, and subject matter knowledge.

Although genetics, hormones, or body chemistry can influence behavior, social learning theory posits that most conflict responses are learned. Many factors influence behaviors—family, culture, media, and friends. Fortunately, conflict participants usually have a choice in how to act so behaviors are not determined solely by one's past.

The cause of conflict is a perception of goal interference, which falls into four main types: content/substantive, process, relationship, and image/face. One's image can be affirmed, reaffirmed, saved, transformed, or subverted. Perceptions of goal interference are further complicated by a series of self-serving biases.

Conflict managers must realize the dynamic nature of goals. Goals change before, during, and after the conflict. Focusing on the future, being aware of one's goals, and meta-communication are key skills in the conflict manager's toolbox.

Chapter Resources

Exercises

1. In the Mastery Case for this chapter, assign the roles of Washington, Smith, and Jones. Roleplay the conversation that would occur between the three roommates. Washington should start the conversation casually and then surprise Jones with the decision that Jones needs to move out. What goals emerge during the role play? Do the goals of any of the individuals change in-process or retrospectively? Has anyone's identity/face been attacked? How do face goals emerge during the role play?
2. Discuss the following situation. Two roommates are conflicting over who has to pay how much for the cable bill when one person ordered the sports channel upgrade without getting explicit agreement in advance from the other roommate. Roleplay the conversation that might occur when the first cable bill arrives with the new charges. Identify the types of goals that emerge during the conversation (process, image/face, content/substantive, or relationship). If a process goal was evident, the conflict would be about how the decision was made; if a relationship goal were evident, the dispute focus would be on: "Do we have the type of relationship where one person can make decisions for the other?" or "Who has the power to make these types of decisions?" If a content goal were most important, it would be about the money; if a face goal were activated, the conflict would be about self-image and not losing esteem (or, if approached negatively, putting the other person down).
3. The cable program *Cheaters* "helps" people who think a loved one is being unfaithful by secretly following the partner and recording any clandestine activities. A hallmark of the show is an emotional confrontation between the heartbroken client and the cheating partner and his or her paramour. Many of those caught cheating blame their partner for the infidelity, claiming the partner somehow "forced" them into cheating. Which concepts from the chapter explain how the one committing the infidelity can blame his or her actions on the faithful partner?

Journal/Essay Topic

1. Identify some of your most important personal goals. Goals can relate to relationships, substantive things, processes, or self-esteem. Categorize the goals by type. Do you think the same goals will predominate throughout your life? What changes might you expect?

Research Topics

1. Explore the concept of "face" and how it is conceptualized in different cultures.
2. Review conflict research from the past two years to determine what conflict topics are most experienced by college students.
3. Review conflict research from the past two years to determine what conflict topics are most experienced by romantic couples.

Mastery Case

In Mastery Case 4A, "The Roommate Revolt," which concepts from this chapter best explain what is occurring?

The Roommate Revolt

Smith, Jones, and Washington are on the college soccer team and decide to be roommates their junior year. Disputes soon erupt over housework. Smith and Washington like the house to be picked up so, in their words, "it doesn't look like a pig sty." Jones isn't as concerned about clutter, as long as things are relatively clean. Smith and Washington made several direct comments to Jones like "Hey, pick up your stuff from the living room because somebody might come over." Jones might pick up a few things, but it doesn't last. Jones rarely does the dishes or any of the "inside" chores, although Jones does take out the trash, pick up the yard, and do any repairs that are needed. Jones had a part-time job for a while but was fired and hasn't looked for another job, which means more time for Jones to hang around the house.

The issue has bubbled beneath the surface for a few weeks. Jones casually mentioned that the rent would be late this month. Washington noticed that Jones has several new games and is planning a ski trip over winter break. Washington and Smith decide that Jones is ducking paying the rent and has to go. They ask Jones to be sure to be home at 6 o'clock that evening so they can talk about a few things. They will demand that Jones move out.

References

Adler, R. B., & Proctor, R. F. (2017). *Looking out, looking in* (15th ed.). Boston: Cengage.
Anderson, C. A., Carnagey, N. L., & Eubanks, J. (2003). Exposure to violent media: The effects of songs with violent lyrics on aggressive thoughts and feelings. *Journal of Personality and Social Psychology, 84*(5), 960–971.
Ayoko, O. B., Callan, V. J., & Hartel, C. E. J. (2003). Workplace conflict, bullying, and counterproductive behaviors. *The International Journal of Organizational Analysis, 11*(4), 283–301.
Dana, D. (2005). *Managing differences: How to build better relationships at work and home.* Prairie Village, KS: MTI Publications.
Funk, J. B., Baldacci, H. B., Pasold, T., & Baumgardner, J. (2004). Violence exposure in real-life, video games, television, movies, and the Internet: Is there desensitization? *Journal of Adolescence, 27*(1), 23–39.
Glascock, J. (2003). Gender, race, and aggression in newer TV networks' primetime programming. *Communication Quarterly, 51*(1), 90–100.
Hocker, J. L., & Wilmot, W. W. (2014). *Interpersonal conflict* (9th ed.). New York: McGraw-Hill.
Hullett, C. R., & Tamborini, R. (2001). When I'm within my rights: An expectancy-based model of actor evaluative and behavioral responses to compliance-resistance strategies. *Communication Studies, 52*(1), 1–16.
Ma, R. (1992). The role of unofficial intermediaries in interpersonal conflicts in the Chinese culture. *Communication Quarterly, 40*(3), 269–278.
Margolin, G., & Gordis, E. B. (2004). Children's exposure to violence in the family and community. *Current Directions in Psychological Science, 13*(4), 152–155.
Mayer, B. (2000). *The dynamics of conflict resolution: A practitioner's guide.* San Francisco: Jossey-Bass.

Rogan, R. G., & La France, B. H. (2003). An examination of the relationship between verbal aggressiveness, conflict management strategies, and conflict interaction goals. *Communication Quarterly, 51*(4), 458–469.

Slater, M. D., Henry, K. L., Swaim, R. C., & Anderson, L. L. (2003). Violent media content and aggressiveness in adolescents: A downward spiral model. *Communication Research, 30*(6), 713–726.

Ting-Toomey, S., & Kurogi, A. (1998). Facework competence in intercultural conflict: An updated face-negotiation theory. *International Journal of Intercultural Relations, 22*(2), 187–225.

Ting-Toomey, S., Oetzel, J. G., & Yee-Jung, K. (2001). Self-construal types and conflict management styles. *Communication Reports, 14*(2), 87–104.

Vries, D. A. de, & Kuhne, R. (2015). Facebook and self-perception: Individual susceptibility to negative social comparison on Facebook. *Personality and Individual Differences, 86*, 217–221.

Chapter 5

How Sex/Gender, Race, Culture, and Generation Affect Conflict

Vocabulary

Accommodation cultural style

Collectivist culture

Cultural socialization

Culture

Discussant cultural style

Dynamic cultural style

Engagement cultural style

Essentializing

Ethnocentric errors

Genderlect

Generational cohort

High- and low-culture context

Individualist cultures

In-group

Privilege

Root culture

Self-construal

Stereotype confirmation

Tag question

Unearned privilege

Variable

Objectives

After reading the chapter, you should be able to:

1. Understand how race, culture, sex/gender, or generation might impact how behaviors are perceived during conflict
2. Differentiate between earned and unearned privilege
3. Critique the collectivism/individualism culture dichotomy
4. Understand how research variables relate to the understanding of conflict management

Life would be more predictable if people were all the same. The variations among individuals that make life interesting also make conflict management more challenging. Because people are different in many ways, 100 percent predictability of how someone will react during a conflict is impossible. However, researchers have isolated several things that consistently affect conflict, providing insight into how conflict begins, why it persists, and how the same issue negotiated with two different people can be completely different experiences.

Researchers try to understand the things that make a difference in how people enact personal conflict. A research **variable** is a specific trait, behavior, or pattern isolated for investigation. For example, biological sex and gender are common variables in social science research to determine if boys and girls or men and women behave in ways that are similar or different.

This chapter explores the known research on several relatively observable personal characteristics affecting conflict. Although numerous other variables could be explored, we focus on those that have received considerable attention through the years and may present enduring challenges for conflict managers: sex/gender, race, culture, and age/generation. Additional non-group-based factors that affect how conflict plays out are discussed in the next chapter, including power, trust, and humor.

Sex/Gender

Considerable research explores potential differences between how women and men experience conflict. This section overviews the research consensus that gender matters (sometimes) during interpersonal conflict. For example, findings indicate men tend to withdraw from conflict more than women and engage in activities that distract from relationship threats. Men engage in more overt aggression, women in more covert aggression, and men have more internal physical reactions to conflict than women (Buysse et al., 2000; Verona, Reed, Curtin, & Pole, 2007).

Gender differences in communication behaviors can affect how each person tends to behave during an interpersonal conflict. For example, self-disclosure can be important to the successful management of a conflict. Meta-analysis on the question of whether men or women disclose more information found that women did disclose more, but the differences were small and changed depending on whether men talked to men, women and men talked together, or women talked to women (Dindia, 2000).

Researchers generally fall into one of two camps when explaining apparent differences between men and women. One camp claims differences are based on nature: genetics, hormones, or other biological/chemical processes, including biological sex. The other perspective argues that differences are due to nurture: influences of upbringing and culture, including the variable of gender identification. Most social science research on males and females in conflict subscribes to "nurture" and social learning theories. Although the research on gender as a learned variable is compelling, some differences may have physiological components. Psychological research indicates that men and women's brains may process conflict information differently, which might be a result of hormonal or other biological causes.

Two competing "nurture" hypotheses arise from gender research (Thimm, Koch, & Schey, 2003). First, the **genderlect** hypothesis posits that women talk in measurably different ways than men and that responses to women's speech are caused by these differences. Central to the genderlect hypothesis is the assumption that a male standard of speech is the norm; women's speech was viewed as abnormal. Genderlect researchers in the 1970s discovered that women habitually used less powerful forms of speech than men—such as permitting interruptions, using qualifying words ("somewhat"), adding softeners ("maybe we should"), and appending **tag questions** ("It's a nice day, isn't it?"). More recent research suggests that although males have a wider repertoire of verbal strategies than women, powerless speech is used by both genders—depending on situations, social status, and power (Thimm et al., 2003). Genderlect researchers highlight a double bind for women who adopt powerful speech patterns. They may be perceived as acting outside the norm of their gender and labeled as pushy and not feminine. Similarly, men who show high sensitivity or speak softly are labeled as indecisive, weak, and not masculine.

DISCUSSION QUESTION • 5.1

How is conflict managed differently at work if the group is all women, all men, or mixed? Are there strategies of conflict management used by women in the workplace that are perceived as inappropriate when used by men?

Research subscribing to the second thread of nurture theory focuses on the claim that gender is learned and part of **cultural socialization**. From this view, "girling" and "boying" of individuals begins at birth (McConnell-Ginet, 2003). Those who greet a newborn baby have difficulty knowing what to say or how to talk if they do not know the child's gender. Whether the baby is "strong and hearty" or "sweet and precious" often depends on the visitor's perception of the infant's gender. Cultural socialization teaches children from birth what is expected from their sex.

Cultural socialization theories contend that social imprinting continues in the school system. Girls and boys historically were treated differently in elementary classrooms and portrayed differently in textbooks. Although textbooks have gradually accepted gender-balanced language and less stereotypical images, "witch" and "mother" were the primary "careers" mentioned for women in children's books before the 1990s. Research also indicated that children did not perceive the generic "he" as including females. To balance the presentation of gender in textbooks, unnecessary gender references were altered, such as writing "mail carrier" rather than "mailman." If sentence structure required a pronoun, "he or she" or the plural was used. To counter those who claimed using "he or she" was silly and pronouns really didn't make a difference, some college textbooks were published using "she" instead of "he" throughout the text (arguing that if the pronoun really didn't matter, nobody should object if "she" was the pronoun). Grade school textbooks have moved slowly to portray women and men in modern, more diverse career roles.

Different treatment of boys and girls reinforced the theory that gender—and gendered conflict management strategies—was learned. Early gender research found that calling out in class, being aggressive, and other behaviors accepted in boys were reprimanded in girls, giving boys advantages in receiving teacher attention. Boys also had more opportunities to use scarce science equipment and learned to take chances in order to succeed (Pipher, 1995). Differences in boy/girl or male/female behavior continue to diverge and solidify as a part of group identity creation. Hence when women in the workplace used powerful and assertive language, which was traditionally reserved for men, they were viewed more negatively. For example, a study of male and female conflict strategies in the workplace found that females used avoidance, cooperative conflict strategies, and problem solving most often, with only 6 percent of women using aggressive tactics. Men used aggression 32 percent of the time (yelling, getting loud, pressuring people), followed by problem solving, with all other strategies far behind (Thimm et al., 2003). Both males and females felt their gendered identity affected their choices of communicative strategies at work.

Research continues to uncover areas where gender affects conflict behaviors. In a bargaining experiment, Kray, Thompson, and Galinsky (2001) found that when told an experiment was to test inherent negotiation ability, women did worse on the task and men did better. The authors suggest that **stereotype confirmation** is a powerful force in bargaining: Individuals adapt their behaviors to fit the prevailing social stereotype that men are good bargainers and women are not. In a second experiment, the authors found when male and female pairs were reminded of social stereotyping, women performed better as bargainers and men performed less well. The researchers theorized that telling women negotiation skill differences were just stereotypes motivated them to do well. Conversely, giving men the message that society expected them to be better negotiators caused stress and pressure to live up to high social expectations, or perhaps men felt so confident that they would "let" the women gain some advantage from a chivalrous sense of fair play. The two studies indicate that the way in which a stereotype is activated—calling it an inherent trait or calling it a social stereotype—affects how individuals react. In another study, men selected control strategies and were more verbally aggressive than women; women were more concerned with relationship goals than were men (Rogan & La France, 2003).

Repeatedly, studies show women do less well in negotiation than men. Eckel, de Oliveira, and Grossman (2008) found several regularities in research results they believed would impact negotiation.

1. Women are more egalitarian and interested in fairness when negotiating than men, even when there is a personal cost.
2. Women are more sensitive to the relationship impact of negotiation strategies and may be more successful in negotiations where the long-term relationship is more important.
3. Women request less and accept less than men during negotiations.
4. Stereotyping of so-called "appropriate" behavior for men and women triggers biases that can adversely affect negotiations.

The body of literature about gender and communication seems to indicate that sometimes gender matters and sometimes it doesn't. What is important to conflict managers is an awareness that stereotypes about gender do exist, and potential differences based on biological differences may exist. If men and women actually do behave differently during interpersonal disputes, the wise conflict manager must be alert and make strategic choices in cross-gender conflict situations. When stereotypes enter the arena, the conflict managers can work to alter perceptions that are based on gender bias or false gender-based expectations.

Race

Just as most researchers agree gendered behaviors derive from sociocultural influences rather than from biology, communicative behaviors of racial groups are seen to arise from historical influences of culture, status, and power rather than from biological imprinting. It is widely acknowledged that initial communication research in the United States used a male, white, upper-class model as the "norm" and labeled all others as different from the norm. Early research tended to cast "differences" as deficits in communicative skills, rather than looking for the strengths in each group's style (Vasques-Scalera, 2002). In other words, if the standard for good communication was European-American, then any other group varying from that norm could unfairly and inaccurately be perceived as dysfunctional. This perspective denied the cultural identity, voice, and unique experiences of many people and gave rise to the African-American communication studies movement (Gilchrist & Jackson, 2012). Similarly, scholars are searching for appropriate research methods and assumptions when studying Latinos (Hidalgo, 1998). Specialized textbooks on race and other resources provide a deeper analysis of interracial communication than we are able to provide in this book (see: Orbe & Harris, 2015).

Persistent and historical racism has a pernicious effect on society in innumerable ways that in turn impact interpersonal conflict management. For example, news programs persist in showing blacks and minorities as perpetrators of violence more than whites (despite the actual proportion of violence in a given community). Researchers link these depictions to social stereotypes of African-Americans as violent and untrustworthy lawbreakers (Dixon, 2008). This research is just one example of the phenomenon where biased behavioral expectations are created from social stereotypes. Bias and stereotypes impede quality conflict management. Conflict managers who have no contact or friends from other racial groups may be more prone to stereotypes, because they lack the experience of positive social contact to offset social bias and systematic racism. One-quarter of whites in a survey of interracial friendships had no interracial friendships. Asians and Hispanics were more likely than blacks or whites to have friends in every racial-ethnic group (Briggs, 2007).

Modern researchers typically apply a diversity standard to their findings—noting differences without evaluating any one group's communicative behaviors as "inherently better" than another. Similarly, the astute conflict manager foregoes prejudgment when selecting an appropriate communication style and conflict management strategy. For example, some researchers find black American men and women have a more assertive and direct style of speaking than white Americans, and black women smile less than white women in formal contexts (Hughes & Baldwin, 2002; Hammer, 2005). As Orbe and Harris (2015) suggest, those who are unaware of these style difference can misattribute the behavior difference. To illustrate, an African-American may assertively challenge someone else's assertion—a behavior that is acceptable with her in-group, but an unexpected behavior in those who have a different style. Because the verbal style is unexpectedly different, social stereotyping or internal attributions may be placed onto the assertive speaker. Studies show young black college women are well aware of these dynamics and use specific communication strategies to change perceptions of their behaviors (Scott, 2013).

The benefits of working to discover and ameliorate potential communication differences across groups are suggested by studies that found interracial couples use communication skills to maintain a successful relationship and build mutually compatible strategies for managing conflict, compared to some same-race couples who use more indirect or mean-spirited strategies (MacNeil & Adamsons, 2014; Seshadri & Knudson-Martin, 2013). Researchers imply many interracial couples grow closer as a way of responding to overt and implicit social disapproval.

Culture

Culture refers to national or ethnic groups who share common assumptions, tendencies, and experiences. Culture is an important variable in conflict because cultural groups have different assumptions and expectations about how conflict should be managed. The term culture also has been applied loosely to any group that develops common experiences. For example, some argue that there are different cultures for women and men, rural and urban, suburban and inner city, young and old, snowboarders and Clash of Clans aficionados, and so forth. In this chapter we focus on the larger cultural issues and will not discuss business culture or social group cultures.

> Almost all peoples believe that their way of thinking about and doing things is the best way. They learn to evaluate other ways of thinking about and doing things as unusual, wrong, or inferior. To question the universality of your own reality or mindset, or to acknowledge that the reality or mindset of other may fundamentally differ from your own is disorienting.
>
> —Kimmel, 2000, p. 457

Because individuals from various cultures have different perceptual filters that shape what is appropriate, intercultural communication is fertile ground for ethnocentric errors. For example, during a group project, Xing Li, an exchange student, did not bring his concerns about the work into the open overtly, but subtly signaled that there was a problem. The group leader, from a European-American culture, accused Xing Li of holding out on the group and being manipulative. From Xing Li's cultural standpoint, he *was* supporting the group. When we interpret others' behaviors based on what we would expect from ourselves, we make an **ethnocentric error**. These errors invite defensiveness, create negativity, and either cause conflict or make conflict more difficult to manage. Building a basic understanding of culture is essential to conflict management competence. Mastering three theories about culture will begin the journey to build culture-competence: high/low cultural context, collectivism/individualism, and cultural conflict style.

High/Low Cultural Context

Nonverbal researcher Hall introduced the notion of high- and low-context culture in *Beyond Culture* (1976). In **low-context cultures**, most of the meaning is in the message. Several languages are low context, and the way the language is structured implies concrete cause-and-effect relationships (e.g., in German, English, and Northern European languages). People in these cultures listen to words more than other communicative nuances. If the meaning is determined more from the context of the message than the words, then the culture is **high context**. High-context language groups use more linguistic imagery or metaphor (e.g., Japanese, Chinese, Arabic, and Mediterranean languages). In these cultures, the nuances of a situation or subtle nonverbal elements may carry more meaning than the words uttered.

For example, Xing Li, from a high-context culture, may have not wanted to confront the group directly, so he shared a proverb one day about a family that didn't check their facts and got into all kinds of trouble. In a high-context culture, the story was an indirect and clear message—everyone should know there is an analogous problem with the workgroup after hearing the story. The low-context leader and group members listened to the story and took it at face value—it was just a story. They missed the indirect and nuanced message.

Collectivism and Individualism

The most popular typology for distinguishing cultures is the notion of *collectivism and individualism*, as seen in Table 5.1. While the characterization is oversimplified, **individualist cultures** value the person's needs and goals first, whereas **collectivist cultures** value the **in-group**'s needs and goals first. During conflict, these preferences are believed to result in differing behaviors. Individualists work assertively and use direct communication to achieve their personal interests; collectivists use indirect communication and defer to the interests of the in-group. Individualists are more confrontational and less sensitive to the other party's needs, interests, or face during conflict; collectivists avoid public confrontation, prefer compromise, and are sensitive to the problems that can arise when someone loses face.

For example, Xing Li in the above story might avoid direct confrontation because it would damage relationships. If the teacher who received the inaccurate report asked, "Which of the group members wrote the section with all the bad data?" Xing Li might not answer or might say something like, "We all worked together on the report." The more culturally individualistic group members might eagerly point out the person whose did the sloppy work.

When Chinese businesspeople interact with their more assertive American counterparts, each person's expectations of what should occur may be violated (Deng & Xu, 2014). Common expectations must be created for everyone about what strategies are appropriate to the specific context for communication in cross-cultural situations.

TABLE 5.1 Individualist and Collectivist Cultures

Individualist Cultures	Collectivist Cultures
United States	Japan
Australia	Russia
Germany	China
Canada	Taiwan
	Korea
	Hong Kong

Deng and Xu's (2014) study found four strategies helped Chinese workers (in China) to manage their American supervisors: (1) off-line talk, such as privately discussing potential areas of disagreement before a meeting; (2) switching modes, including saying something like, "I am doing what the company asks and being constructively confrontational," before making a direct comment that otherwise might hurt a coworker's feelings; (3) supporting arguments with facts to help manage disagreement without seeming to be making personal comments; and (4) turning to a higher authority (talking to the boss) was occasionally used when a conflict seemed unsolvable.

DISCUSSION QUESTION • 5.2

What are the characteristics of your root culture, according to the individualistic/ collectivist framework? Do your personal behaviors fit those predicted in the framework? What are the dangers inherent in making assumptions about others' root cultures and how can we mitigate those dangers?

Contemporary researchers hold that reality is considerably more complicated than the simple dichotomy offered by the individualist and collectivist culture framework (see Ting-Toomey, 2010; Ting-Toomey & Oetzel, 2001). First, not all individuals from a particular geographic area integrate cultural teachings in the same manner or in the same depth. Thinking all persons in a group are alike commits the stereotype of **essentializing**, assuming just because people share some commonality, they all think or act alike and are essentially the same. Essentializing is most apparent at the macro-level, i.e., assuming everyone from an Asian country shares the same cultural values and assumptions.

Second, cultural assumptions, even when integrated by the individual, do not always spin out in ways that seem logical. For example, individualistic cultures are assumed to be more confrontational than collectivist cultures. However, Cai and Fink (2002) found that members of individualistic cultures reported using the avoidance style more than did individuals in collectivist cultures. Also contrary to the basic tenets of the high- and low-context theory is the amount of competitive conflict tactics exhibited among Japanese or Russians. Because rank and status determine one's power and share of resources in socially stratified cultures, competitive tactics to establish one's place in the hierarchy are common (Adair et al., 2004).

A more sophisticated cultural profile looks at several dimensions rather than just collectivism and individualism. France is both high- and low-context (a history of nuanced diplomacy and a contemporary focus on direct problem-solving processes). France is categorized as both egalitarian (through its socialist politics) and hierarchical (interested in status and rank). Russia is categorized as collectivist, yet it also exhibits a competitive "have" and "have-not" social hierarchy. Japan and Brazil are collectivist in conversation and hierarchical in organization. In negotiation studies, individuals from these countries do not behave as predicted by naive cultural categorization. Contrary to what might be expected for an individualistic culture, U.S. negotiators have in common with Brazil a strong preference to share information (where secrecy to gain advantage might be predicted). Russian and Japanese negotiators are more likely than other negotiators to use power negotiation strategies when the model would predict cooperative behaviors (Adair et al., 2004).

Cultural Conflict Management Style

An alternate perspective on cultural conflict describes an individual's predispositions on two variables: how disagreement is expressed during conflict and how emotions are expressed during conflict. Hammer (2002) developed the Intercultural Conflict Style Inventory as a means of assessing intercultural differences. Hammer's research finds two stylistic ways that disagreements are expressed in conflicts—directly or indirectly—and two ways that emotions are managed during conflict—expressively or with restraint (Table 5.2).

According to Hammer (2002), the dimensions of cultural style interact to create four distinct intercultural conflict communication styles: discussant, engagement, accommodation, and dynamic. The styles tend to align with geographic cultural areas. However, an individual within a culture could display a non-normative style.

Discussant cultural style individuals are high in direct expression of conflict and low in showing emotion. These individuals confront conflict directly, are highly verbal, argue, and prefer to hold emotions inside (e.g., Northern Europe, Australia, and the United States). **Engagement cultural style** individuals also are high in direct expression of disagreement, but they differ in preferring more expression of emotion and may be intense, loud, or passionate (e.g., Southern Europe, Cuba, and Russia). **Accommodation cultural style** individuals prefer to express conflict indirectly and to hold emotion inside (e.g., Chinese, Japanese, Native American, Mexican, and Korean). **Dynamic cultural style** individuals prefer high expression of emotion in conflict with indirect expression of the issues. The topic of the conflict will be expressed passionately but vaguely through stories, metaphor, or other indirect strategies (e.g., Kuwait, Iraq, Egypt).

For individuals in each cultural style, the ways in which "competent" conflict management occurs are different. Some express conflict directly and some tacitly; some energetically express emotions, and some strategically withhold emotional information. These differences can be critical. When viewed through the eyes of one's culture, the behaviors of the other person will seem wrong and be open to ethnocentric errors. For instance, Su (2006) found Taiwanese and U.S. accounting students had different views on what constituted unethical accounting practices. For example, Taiwanese accounting students would be more likely than American students to cover up the actions of superiors or coworkers if their behaviors were unethical but not illegal. Communication differences across cultures too often are misinterpreted by those from different cultures as motivated by ill-will, strategic manipulation, or the intent to do harm.

TABLE 5.2 Dimensions of Intercultural Conflict Style

How Conflicts Are Expressed	
Direct	Indirect
Words carry meaning	Meaning in the context
Directly state the problem	Ambiguity, stories, metaphor
Face to face	Intermediaries
Speak one's mind	Withhold criticism to save public face
Highlight differences	Highlight commonalities
Persuade and argue	Indirect to save face
Solution focused	Relationship focused

How Emotions Are Expressed	
Expressive	Restraint
Overtly expressed	Withheld and suppressed
Humor as a tension regulator	Avoid humor
Nonverbals express feelings	Nonverbals hide feelings
Passionate and loud	Soft and constrained
Build trust through joint expression	Build trust through emotional control
Be emotional, then work together	Be calm, then work together

TABLE 5.3 Levels of Cultural Awareness

1. *Cultural chauvinists* know very little about other cultures and have little interest in them.
2. *Ethnocentric* individuals see differences caused by nationality, racial, or religious groupings as a reason to feel superior.
3. *Tolerant* people believe their own culture is best and see differences as caused by understandable differences and as a result of living in different places.
4. *Minimalists* understand differences but trivialize them, believing all people basically are alike.
5. Those who *genuinely understand* know differences are real and many times based on fundamental value differences.

Source: Adapted from Kimmel (2000)

Culture may play an important role in how individuals in conflict perceive each other, how they select strategies, and the styles they prefer. The key word is *may*. When in conflict with a person from a different **root culture** (the cultural group an individual was born and raised in), a sophisticated conflict manager will be alert to the *potential* of cross-cultural variation but would never assume that the individual essentially is like all others in a cultural group. **Self-construal**, or how one views oneself, is a powerful influence in developing communicative styles and sometimes trumps general cultural identity (Gudykunst & Kim, 2003; Kim, Lee, Kim, & Hunter, 2004; Takahashi, Ohara, Antonucci, & Akiyama, 2002). Kimmel's (2000) levels of cultural awareness in Table 5.3 suggest that genuine and deep knowledge of a culture's values is superior to superficial knowledge or stereotypes (see also Kim, 2007).

Age and Generation

Generational cohorts may engage conflict management differently. A **generational cohort** is a group that is influenced by major events and social-cultural changes that affect their worldview. The experiences of different generations in Table 5.4 illustrate the influences and tendencies of the generations coexisting today. Whether these differences will persist and if they are derived from common values of a generational cohort or from the differing goals and experiences of age groups is open to debate (Deal, Altman, & Rogelberg, 2010; Twenge, 2010).

The importance of generational differences during interpersonal conflict is that what feels like the "correct" way of thinking and acting for one generation may be different from the next generation. In a survey by the Society of Human Resource Managers, 69 percent of respondents said intergenerational conflict was an issue in their workplace (SHERM, 2011). For example, Boomers and Net Generation individuals may have different values about work and levels of loyalty to an employer. Goal achievement and **self-identity** tied to success at work are more likely in a Boomer than in someone just entering the workforce, who may see work just as a means to achieve other goals. Xers' primary complaints about work are that management ignores their ideas and does not give them enough recognition (O'Bannon & Dennis, 2001). Xers feel they deserve quick recognition and a place at the decision-making table; Boomers assume recognition should be earned over a long period of time and that employees should be self-motivated. These differences create areas ripe for conflict and misunderstanding. O'Bannon and Dennis (2001) state, "If Boomers fail to recognize and acknowledge the unique issues facing Xers, the result will be a workplace fraught with miscommunication, misunderstandings and harsh feelings, resulting in higher-than-normal turnover ratios and dysfunctional supervisor-employee relationships" (p. 97).

Compared to Gen Xers, Millennials hold work as less central to their lives, and consequently have a different work ethic and less interest in status or salary. Millennials like to be mobile and

TABLE 5.4 The Experiences of Different Generations

Builders/Traditionalists	
Born	1901–1945
Influenced by	The Great Depression and World War II
Tendencies	Cautious about money, willing to work for the common good, disciplined
Weaknesses	May be inflexible and too cautious

Boomers	
Born	1946–1965
Influenced by	Vietnam, civil rights movement, threat of nuclear war, television, rock and roll
Tendencies	Live the good life, self-absorbed, workaholics, confident, willing to take on causes, team sports, optimism
Weaknesses	Think they are "special," will break rules/ethics in own self-interest

Xers	
Born	1966–1977
Influenced by	Divorce, Watergate, MTV, Bill Clinton, Madonna, Beavis and Butt-Head
Tendencies	Distrust government, more open to diversity, work is just a means to an end, independent, comfortable with technology, individual sports
Weaknesses	Pessimistic, personal life trumps work, may seem unmotivated, easily bored

Y-ers	
Born	1977–1986
Influenced by	AIDS, Princess Diana's death, *Challenger* explosion
Tendencies	Ability to multitask and change directions quickly, adaptable, curious, direct, willing to think outside the box
Weaknesses	Impulsive, expect to know, don't expect jobs to last forever so may leave them often, question directions, may seem impertinent or insubordinate, may be distracted easily

Millennials	
Born	1987–2001
Influenced by	Internet, political scandals, cell phones
Tendencies	Comfortable with change, expect to know details, consumer driven, burdened by debt, nonlinear thinking, tolerant, technology savvy, generally optimistic
Weaknesses	Less comfortable in hierarchy, expect to be informed and may not follow well, tends towards narcissism

Source: Adapted from Hicks and Hicks (1999); Lancaster and Stillman (2002); Pew Research (2014); Raines and Hunt (2000)

telling them that the appointment offers lifelong job security might sound like a long prison sentence rather than an enviable benefit. Millennials also want high job satisfaction and work-life balance. Millennials often carry high debt and are under-employed, as they entered the workforce during an economic recession. Based on their generation's values, work benefits and work conditions may be more motivating than mere salary (O'Connor & Raile, 2015).

DISCUSSION QUESTION • 5.3

What generation do you belong to? What influences your generation beyond what is listed in Table 5.4? For example, was your generation molded by President Kennedy's assassination, the Columbine shootings, the attacks on September 11, 2001, or the Great Recession (2008–2010)? What generation does your supervisor or teacher belong to? Give an example of a situation in which generational differences caused conflict or made mutual understanding more difficult.

The assumptions and experiences of different generations can cause distress when parents and children, bosses and subordinates, or age-separated coworkers communicate. Not only may their assumptions and goals be different, but given what we know from attribution theory (see Chapter 2), evaluations of the other age group probably will be less than charitable. Raines and Hunt (2000) studied the perception gap in the workplace between Boomers and Xers. They argue that perceived differences across the generations necessitate three levels of response. Level 1 is acknowledging the difference and letting it go. If the issue is not important, there is little profit in using energy to engage in conflict. Level 2 is changing personal behavior. Adapt to the preferences of the other generation by changing word usage or adopting the style of communication that the other prefers. Level 3 is "using a generational template to talk it over" (p. 46). In level 3, the generational difference is brought to the surface as a point of discussion. For example, Boomers believe in working one's way up the organization and are offended by young Xers who expect fast advancement and who push their agenda forward. A manager who orchestrates a discussion among staff of what it means to work as a team can create an alternative model that all generations can follow.

KEY 5.1

Be aware that sex/gender, race, generation, or culture might affect how people communicate. Being different doesn't mean communication behaviors are wrong.

The Taking of Privilege

One interesting concept developed from gender and race research explores the concept of privilege. A **privilege** is an advantage that others do not have. Some privileges are earned. Students earn the privilege to use the university web portal through their status as a member of the university community. The university president probably has a private parking space earned through the designation of his or her job. An **unearned privilege** is taken as if it is a right based on social status. Those with inherited wealth have access to resources that were not earned: money, good primary education, better credit scores, influential social networks, opportunities to attend prestigious universities, and so on. Those who falsely believe that one group inherently is better than another expect privileges that are unearned. The concept of *whiteness* as an unearned privilege has garnered attention as an enduring issue in society and has been the focus of diversity awareness programs for whites since the 1990s (McIntosh, 1993).

How does unearned privilege impact conflict management? To the extent that race, gender, or any other variable becomes a lens through which the other person is perceived, the variable matters. Competent conflict managers assess the extent to which their tactics and strategies are affected by the taking or giving of unearned privilege.

DISCUSSION QUESTION • 5.4

In what ways are you privileged? Are your privileges earned or unearned? How are you disadvantaged by others' unearned privileges?

Mastering Conflict Management Research

The research to discover what behaviors or characteristics are paired with various perceptions during a conflict is useful for many reasons. We highlight three of them.

First, research provides insight into personal behaviors. You can read the research conducted with people like you and see if that trend is something you've experienced. You may peruse the section on gender and conflict in this book and say, "That is exactly what my experience has been!" or "My experience is not like that at all!" Second, research is useful to understand others' behaviors. Knowledge of the range of normative behavior helps individuals understand possible responses to conflict situations and to avoid the fallacies of thinking that "everyone else must act just like me" or "I'm the only one who feels this way." Third, research—to the extent that patterns of behavior have been identified—offers a way to anticipate how others might behave during conflict. Knowing that when variable X is activated in a conflict, outcome Z has a probability of occurring provides opportunities for thoughtful choice making. In other words, knowing that culture or gender might make a difference in how conflict strategies are selected helps you be aware of that possibility when engaged in cross-gender or cross-cultural conflict.

DISCUSSION QUESTION • 5.5

How can conflict research benefit you personally in your everyday interactions? Which of the reasons why research is useful is the most meaningful to you?

When reading the findings cited in this and other books, remember the limitations of the research process. First, social science research always is limited because of the plethora of things that are occurring simultaneously. No matter how carefully an experiment in human communication is designed, researchers cannot completely control what people feel and think. Unlike pure laboratory experiments where a chemical can be put in a test tube in a precise amount to observe the reaction, humans cannot turn off their thoughts, experiences, or perceptions to isolate just one variable. In addition to the difficulties of isolating variables in human research, the choices people make in one context may be different than the choices they make elsewhere. For example, the conflict styles engaged in at work may be routinely avoided at home. Context matters when looking at human behavior research.

The second caution is about so-called average behaviors. For example, the U.S. census notes that the average age of first marriage has steadily increased and now is the age of 26 years. People who married before the age of 22 or after the age of 30 are not "average" in their marriage behaviors. Move far enough away from the average—marry in your late 30s—and you become an "outlier" in statistical terms. Averages become more complicated when isolating communicative behaviors. Researchers apply powerful levels of mathematics to sort through their data, move beyond averages, and determine if differences discovered in a study are statistically significant or if they might have resulted from chance.

There remains a range of human behavior in any situation that is not represented fully by average or statistical results. For example, one study found that people who are more committed to a relationship are less likely to report thinking about alternatives to the relationship and less likely to feel trapped (Stanley, Markman, & Whitton, 2002). These results suggest commitment is an important variable that may explain why individuals choose different tactics during relationship conflicts—opting to work toward harmony rather than competing for individual goals. But not everyone in the same relationship commitment category reacts in the same way. Social science research result can't have the predictive power of a chemistry experiment. Unlike chemistry, social science research provides trends and averages, not universal laws. So, if you don't exactly fit the norm, don't worry.

The third caution is research may not represent everyone. Because of convenience, research in the social sciences has been conducted primarily on university students who do not represent the full range of human experience. For example, individuals who begin a career before or immediately after high school graduation would systematically be excluded if only university students are used as subjects—as would most elderly and any other group underrepresented on university campuses.

> **DISCUSSION QUESTION • 5.6**
>
> Identify any research findings presented so far in this book or in your class that speak directly to your experience. Do you think the findings apply to everyone who is in your demographic group?

A fourth caution about research is embedded in who asks the questions that guide research. The questions for study tend to be chosen by the interests of the researcher and the results interpreted from the frame of the researcher's culture (see Hidalgo, 1998). When the ranks of researchers were dominated for decades by upper-middle-class white men, few questions were asked from the perspective of women, nonwhites, or the working poor. As the ranks of researchers opened to more socially and racially diverse populations, research increased about communication patterns unique to blacks, Latinos, women, and other underrepresented groups.

Regardless of its limitations, social science research is useful because it aspires to understand and predict human behavior. Research results are helpful to understand which variables are activated when a conflict evolves differently with one person than with another.

However, we do not wish to give the impression that all important research in the social sciences is variable-analytic. Other perspectives guide many critical lines of research into the understanding of human communication and human behavior.

Summary

Researchers have identified several group-identity related factors that affect how people behave during conflict. Sex/gender, race/ethnicity, culture, and generation are discussed.

Genderlect and cultural socialization theories underpin research on biological sex and gender. Genderlect focuses on language differences, and cultural socialization explores how individuals learn socially appropriate gendered behaviors. Perceptions based on sex/gender may create expectations for appropriate behavior that impact conflict management.

Research on race and ethnicity examines many variables, including misassumptions about communication differences and unearned privileges. Perceptions-based stereotyping of race or ethnicity may create expectations for appropriate behavior that impact conflict management.

Culture refers to national or ethnic groups who share common assumptions, tendencies, and experiences. One typology classifies cultures as high- or low-context. Another common typology of cultural behavior contrasts individualistic groups (low-context) with collectivist groups (high-context). A weakness of this typology is essentializing—treating all members of a group as if they are the same. An alternative cultural typology examines two dimensions (how disagreement is expressed and how emotions are expressed) to create four intercultural conflict styles (discussant, engagement, accommodating, and dynamic).

Another variable appearing in much research is age. Generational cohorts perceive events differently enough to create sources of conflict. Conceptions about work, in particular, seem to vary across age groups and are affected by major cultural and social events.

The existence of patterns of behavior is interesting to conflict researchers and has strong implications for competent conflict managers. Isolating characteristics and variables that give rise to certain outcomes or conflict behaviors offers insights into possible entry points for transforming personal conflicts, but must be considered in terms of the limitations inherent in social science research.

Chapter Resources

Exercises

1. A group of coworkers are moving into a newly renovated building. The supervisor says it doesn't matter who gets which office and that the group should decide over lunch. The supervisor is called away just before the meeting starts. Based on the variables discussed in the chapter, how might the discussion play out if some of the workers want the same office and:

    A. All of the workers are female (or male).
    B. One female and one male both want the same large office with a window.
    C. All of the workers but one is from the Boomer generation.
    E. One worker consistently is a top sales earner and another has more seniority but is less productive.

2. In a culturally diverse class, each individual will report on how and when the New Year is celebrated in their homelands. How do these differences/similarities show reflections of what is important in a culture? (adapted from Gerritsen & Verckens, 2006).

3. List all of the countries of origin represented in the class. Reference each country on Hofstede's cultural index (geert-hofstede.com) and create charts for each culture pair. For example, if the countries of origin were United States, Mexico, Japan, and Nigeria, the pairs created on the Hofstede index would be: U.S with Mexico, U.S. with Japan, U.S. with Nigeria, Mexico with Japan, Mexico with Nigeria, and Japan with Nigeria. Discuss the communication challenges that each paired group might experience.

4. What conflict flashpoints are likely among individuals from different age cohorts who are working on a group project together, based on Meister and Willyerd's (2010a) comparison of how generations deal with content?

Traditionalists:	Give me detail in prose writing style
Baby Boomers:	Boil it down for me but give me everything.
Generation X:	Just tell me what I need to know right now.
Millennials:	When I need the information, I'll just get it online.

Research Topics

1. Examine conflict research conducted in the last two years in a communication or psychology peer-reviewed journal. Do gender, race, or class appear as variables in the research studies? If so, what was discovered? What other variables are used in the studies?
2. Investigate the research on "whiteness" and racial identity construction. How does the construction of racial identity impact conflict in particular areas, such as sports, media, sports mascots, politics, or the music industry?
3. Based on the differences across generations, detail several suggestions for communicating with generations other than your own.

Mastery Case

Analyze Mastery Case 5A, "John's Brief Internship." Which concepts from the chapter best explain what is occurring in the case?

John's Brief Internship

John, a 20-year-old college junior, was excited to start an internship at the city museum. John had been in and out of the museum as a patron since he was small. John started his internship full of ideas on how to make the museum experience better for patrons.

One of the supervisors, Mrs. Bean, has worked at the museum for twenty years. Although Mrs. Bean has lots of experience, she tells others what to do more than doing the work herself. She calls John "The Intern" and doesn't seem to know what his name is even after two weeks on the job. She often makes snippy remarks to John and to patrons when they ask questions, implying that if they were truly cultured, they wouldn't need to bother her with questions.

John is tempted to fight for his rights as an employee, but after listening to other workers, it seems like her behavior has been going on for years. Complaints have been filed, but nothing ever seems to happen. Mrs. Bean knows many of the movers and shakers in town and chats with them about plays that are at the performing arts center. John knows it would take lots of energy to fight a battle against Mrs. Bean. John's friends have remarked that he is usually angry when he meets them after work. John finally couldn't take it anymore and approached his supervisor to ask for a different internship placement.

References

Adair, W., Brett, J., Lempereur, A., Okumura, T., Shikhirev, P., Tinsley, C., & Lytle, A. (2004). Culture and negotiation strategy. *Negotiation Journal, 20*(1), 87–111.

Briggs, X. (2007). "Some of My best friends are . . .": Interracial friendships, class, and segregation in America. *City & Community, 6*(4), 263–290.

Buysse, A., De Clercq, A., Verhofstadt, L., Heene, E., Roeyers, H., & Van Oost, P. (2000). Dealing with relational conflict: A picture in milliseconds. *Journal of Social & Personal Relationships, 17*(4–5), 574–597.

Cai, D. A., & Fink, E. L. (2002). Conflict style differences between individualists and collectivists. *Communication Monographs, 69*(1), 67–87.

Deal, J. J., Altman, D. G., & Rogelberg, S. G. (2010). Millennials at work: What we know and what we need to do (if anything). *Journal of Business Psychology, 25*(2), 191–199.

Deng, Y., & Xu, K. (2014). Chinese employees negotiating differing conflict management expectations in a U.S.-based multinational corporation subsidiary in Southwest China. *Management Communication Quarterly, 28*(4), 609–624.

Dindia, K. (2000). Sex differences in self-disclosure, reciprocity of self-disclosure, and self-disclosure and liking: Three meta-analyses reviewed. In S. Petronio (Ed.), *Balancing the secrets of private disclosures* (pp. 21–35). Mahwah, NJ: Erlbaum.

Dixon, T. L. (2008). Who is the victim here? The psychological effects of overrepresenting White victims and Black perpetrators on television news. *Journalism, 9*(5), 582–605.

Eckel, C., de Oliveira, A, C. M., & Grossman, P. J. (2008). Gender and negotiation in the small: Are women (perceived to be) more cooperative than men? *Negotiation Journal, 24,* 429–445.

Gerritsen, M., & Verckens, J. P. (2006). Raising students' intercultural awareness and preparing them for intercultural business (communication) by e-mail. *Business Communication Quarterly, 69*(1), 50–59.

Gilchrist, E. S., & Jackson, R. L. (2012). Articulating the heuristic value of African American communication studies. *The Review of Communication, 12*(3), 237–250.

Gudykunst, W. B., & Kim, Y. Y. (2003). *Communicating with strangers: An approach to intercultural communication.* Boston: McGraw-Hill.

Hall, E. T. (1976). *Beyond culture.* Garden City, NY: Anchor.

Hammer, M. (2002). *Resolving conflict across the cultural divide: Differences in intercultural conflict styles.* Hammer Consulting.

Hammer, M. R. (2005). The intercultural conflict style inventory: A conceptual framework and measure of intercultural conflict resolution approaches. *International Journal of Intercultural Relations, 29,* 675–695.

Hicks, R., & Hicks, K. (1999). *Boomers, Xers, and other strangers: Understanding the generational differences that divide us.* Wheaton, IL: Tyndale House.

Hidalgo, N. M. (1998). Toward a definition of a Latino family research paradigm. *Qualitative Studies in Education, 11*(1), 103–120.

Hughes, P., & Baldwin, J. (2002). Communication and stereotypical impressions. *Howard Journal of Communications, 13*(2), 113, 128.

Kim, M-S. (2007). The four cultures of cultural research. *Communication Monographs, 74*(2), 279–285.

Kim, M-S., Lee, H., Kim, I. D., & Hunter, J. E. (2004). A test of a cultural model of conflict styles. *Journal of Asian Pacific Communication, 14*(2), 197–222.

Kimmel, P. R. (2000). Culture and conflict. In M. Deutsch & P. T. Coleman (Eds.), *The handbook of conflict resolution: Theory and practice* (pp. 453–474). San Francisco: Jossey-Bass.

Kray, L. J., Thompson, L., & Galinsky, A. (2001). Battle of the sexes: Gender stereotype confirmation and reactance in negotiation. *Journal of Personality and Social Psychology, 80*(6), 942–958.

Lancaster, L. C., & Stillman, D. (2002). *When generations collide.* New York: HarperCollins.

MacNeil, T. A., & Adamsons, K. (2014). A bioecological view of interracial/same-race couple conflict. *International Journal of Conflict Management, 25*(3), 243–260.

McConnell-Ginet, S. (2003). "What's in a name?" Social labeling and gender practices. In J. Holmes & M. Meyerhoff (Eds.), *The handbook of language and gender* (pp. 69–97). Boston: Blackwell.

McIntosh, P. (1993). Examining unearned privilege. *Liberal Education, 79*(1), 61–62.

Meister, J. D., & Willyerd, K. (2010a, May). Mentoring millennials. *Harvard Business Review.*

Meister, J. C., & Willyerd, K. (2010b). *The 2020 workplace.* New York: HarperCollins.

O'Bannon, G., & Dennis, D. (2001). Managing our future: The generation X factor. *Public Personnel Management, 30*(1), 95–110.

O'Connor, A., & Raile, A. N. W. (2015). Millennials' "Get a 'real job'": Exploring generational shifts in the colloquialism's characteristics and meanings. *Management Communication Quarterly, 29*(2), 276–290.

Orbe, M. P., & Harris, T. M. (2015). *Interracial communication: Theory into practice* (3rd ed.). Los Angles: Sage.

Pew Research Center. (2014). *Millennials in adulthood*. Pewresearch.org. Accessed 16 August 2016.

Pipher, M. (1995). *Reviving Ophelia: Saving the selves of adolescent girls*. New York: Penguin.

Raines, C., & Hunt, J. (2000). *The Xers & the boomers: From adversaries to allies—a diplomat's guide*. Menlo Park, CA: Crisp Publications.

Rogan, R. G., & La France, B. H. (2003). An examination of the relationship between verbal aggressiveness, conflict management strategies, and conflict interaction goals. *Communication Quarterly, 51*(4), 458–469.

Scott, K. D. (2013). Communication strategies across cultural borders: Dispelling stereotypes, performing competence, and redefining Black womanhood. *Women's Studies in Communication, 36*, 312–329.

Seshadri, G., & Knudson-Martin, C. (2013). How couples manage interracial and intercultural differences: Implications for clinical practice. *Journal of Marital and Family Therapy, 39*(1), 43–58.

Society for Human Resource Management (SHERM). (2011). *SHERM poll: Intergenerational conflict in the workplace*. Shrm.org. Accessed 15 January 2017.

Stanley, S. M., Markman, H. J., & Whitton, S. W. (2002). Communication, conflict, and commitment: Insights on the foundations of relationship success from a national survey. *Family Process, 41*(4), 659–675.

Su, S-H. (2006). Cultural differences in determining the ethical perception and decision-making of future accounting professionals: A comparison between accounting students from Taiwan and the United States. *Journal of American Academy of Business, 9*(1), 147–158.

Takahashi, K., Ohara, N., Antonucci, T., & Akiyama, H. (2002). Commonalities and differences in close relationships among the Americans and Japanese: A comparison by the individualism/collectivism concept. *International Journal of Behavioral Development, 26*(5), 453–465.

Thimm, C., Koch, S. C., & Schey, S. (2003). Competence, cooperation, and conflict in the workplace. In J. Holmes & M. Meyerhoff (Eds.), *The handbook of language and gender* (pp. 528–549). Boston: Blackwell.

Ting-Toomey, S. (2010). Intercultural conflict competence. In W. Cupach, D. Canary, & B. H. Spitzberg (Eds.), *Competence in interpersonal conflict* (2nd ed., pp. 139–162). Long Grove, IL: Waveland.

Ting-Toomey, S., & Oetzel, J. G. (2001). *Managing intercultural conflict effectively*. Thousand Oaks, CA: Sage.

Twenge, J. M. (2010). A review of the empirical evidence on generational differences in work attitudes. *Journal of Business Psychology, 25*, 201–210.

Vasques-Scalera, C. (2002). The diversity framework informing this volume. In J. S. Trent (Ed.), *Included in communication: Learning climates that cultivate racial and ethnic diversity* (p. iv). Washington, DC: AAHE.

Verona, E., Reed, A., Curtin, J. J., & Pole, M. (2007). Gender differences in emotional and overt/covert aggressive responses to stress. *Aggressive Behavior, 33*, 261–271.

Chapter 6

How Power, Trust, and Humor Affect Conflict

Vocabulary

Coercive power

Distributive power

Expert power

Integrative power model

Legitimate power

Power

Power currency

Power management

Referent power

Reward power

Trust

Zero-sum

Objectives

After reading the chapter, you should be able to:

1. Differentiate between distributive and integrative views of power
2. Explain how trust impacts conflict management.
3. Distinguish between helpful and unhelpful humor in conflict situations

Power

> The fundamental concept in social science is power, in the same sense in which energy is the fundamental concept in physics.
>
> —Philosopher Bertrand Russell (1938)

The perception of power, or its absence, is omnipresent in human relationships. Those who perceive they do not have power may be motivated to reach for more power. Too often, both parties in a conflict view the other party as having the most power, leading to an out-of-control spiral of negative power-grabbing tactics.

Power is defined as the ability to have influence or bring about a desired outcome. Coleman (2000) identifies four themes in how power is treated in social science research: (1) Coercion power, or *power over*, is the ability to induce someone to do something they would not otherwise have done. (2) *Power with* is jointly developed, noncoercive, and based on partnership. (3) *Powerlessness* or dependence is a view that correlates rigidity, power struggles, irrationality, and violence among those who feel powerless. (4) *Empowerment, or power to*, is the flip side of powerlessness. Those who are **empowered** feel they have enough power to achieve their goals. An example will illustrate these types of power. Students in a classroom typically accept the designated authority given a professor. In that situation, they perceive that the teacher has *power over* them and can force them to do things they would not do without a mandate, such as read books, write papers, talk about uncomfortable topics, do group projects, and take tests. If a group of students has been ignored by campus leaders, and feels *powerless* to affect change, protests or violence may erupt. If students feel safe in negotiating the usefulness of assignments in a class, they are *empowered*. Students who have voting seats on university promotion and tenure committees have *power with* others.

> "It is critical to bear in mind that power is typically context-dependent and that even the most powerful people are powerless under certain conditions."
> —Coleman, 2000, p. 124.

Distributive Power

Traditional views of power are **distributive**. Power is seen as a fixed resource that can be wielded to gain concessions from others. If the instructor has 95 percent of the power in a class, the students can only have up to 5 percent. Within this perspective, power is **zero-sum**, meaning its parts add up to 100 percent, and taking any of the power pie results in less for others. As portions of a zero-sum item are taken away, eventually none remains (hence the name "zero sum"). In a distributive world, one must scramble for a share of the power pie. Modern views of power conceptualize it as an expandable concept based on relationships and will be discussed later in the Integrative Power section of the chapter.

When power is examined through the distributive model, categorizing where power comes from is relatively simple. Power typologies describe sources of power. French and Raven's classic typology (see Table 6.1) asserted there are five sources of interpersonal power: reward, coercive, legitimate, expert, and referent (Raven & Rubin, 2001). Employers who give performance raises, parents who give or deny praise when their children succeed, or friends who celebrate success with a night out all are exerting **reward power**. In a traditional sense, the person desiring the reward has less power than the individual who controls the giving of the reward. To "earn" the reward, one must comply with the powerful person's wishes.

Bosses who threaten to fire an employee, parents who ground teenagers from using the car for rule-breaking, or teachers who threaten to give pop quizzes if students do not read their assignments are applying **coercive power**. Coercive power threatens retribution if the desired behavior is not forthcoming.

TABLE 6.1 Sources of Traditional Power

Reward power	Control of material or psychological resources
Coercive power	Use of fear and punishment to control behavior
Legitimate power	Position within a hierarchy
Expert power	Knowledge and specialized skills
Referent power	Association with an admired individual
Information power	Knowledge and the ability to explain

A formal title, rank, or office in an organization bestows **legitimate power**. Legitimate power derives from the automatic respect given to the office and a perceived right of officials to lead. Professors, judges, police, managers, and government officials all have the power of positions awarded to them that create a legitimate power base.

Having specialized knowledge, skill, or expertise is the source of **expert power**. Skilled professionals, such as plumbers, protect the exclusivity of their craft by requiring specific training and certifications. Across generations, children may have expertise that parents and grandparents lack when it comes to using new technology.

Referent power arises from valued personality traits in one's self or through association with others. Movie stars and elite athletes demand high salaries when making commercials because the public admires them. Advertisers ride along with the star's referent power, and they hope that the admiration for the star is associated with their product. Supervisors may wield referent power if they are the type of person an employee admires and uses as a role model. Claiming to be the offspring of the governor may or may not yield referent power when trying to talk your way out of getting a speeding ticket.

Information power was added to the typology after its initial creation. Those who know things and can share that information with others in understandable ways develop information power (Elias, 2008; Raven, 2008). Often the person who holds the historical knowledge in an organization has power over those who are more recently hired, despite having less legitimate power.

Individuals in conflict make attributions about the other person's power. These judgments are influenced by cultural norms about power. Powerful people are perceived as having more control of resources. Perceptions of power are based on indicators such as the kind of car driven, clothes worn, or technology used. On campus, a student saw a woman he was working with on a group project driving into the parking garage in her Lexus convertible. He walked over to her and said, "Wow, is that your car?" You could almost see his perception of the Lexus driver changing based on an attribution of status and wealth. An impressive job title, a large office, expensive jewelry, and an address in an exclusive area may be perceived as indicators of power and status. Lack of these indicators may lead to attributions that someone is powerless.

Even if one has power under the French and Raven classification, success is not automatic. At work, for example, expert, referent, and reward power are positively linked to employees' positive feelings, but legitimate power is negatively correlated with good feelings about the supervisor. Use of coercive power actually reduced employees' intentions to work hard or stay with the firm (Zigarmi, Roberts, & Randolph, 2015). In other words, just because one has a form of traditional power doesn't mean that person actually can influence others.

In addition, when reward or coercive power are attempted, three criteria must exist in the mind of the person on the receiving end of the power move for it to be successful. (1) The recipient must believe you have the authority to follow through with the threat/reward. (2) The recipient must believe you have the will to follow through with the threat/reward. (3) The recipient must find a reward to be something desirable and a threat as something to be avoided. The threat of a three-day suspension from work is not effective for someone who would just as soon have time off to go skiing. An offer of a reward of honor at a company banquet may not be desirable to an introvert who would rather have a reward gift card.

KEY 6.1

When one source of power isn't working, cultivate another source.

Situational Power

The ability to influence is not automatically attached to those with property, titles, or status. In reality, power is derived from the perceived connections among the individuals that motivate one individual to give precedence to another. In other words, *power is entirely situational*. Because the student in the above example valued an expensive car, he granted his classmate higher status and power. If one values and respects a title, then power is given to the person who holds the title. Because students generally respect the title "doctor of philosophy" and the university gives faculty the authority to award grades, professors are granted legitimate, expert, and reward power. Each of these sources of power, however, can be removed. Students can neutralize a teacher's power by refusing to comply with instructions during class time or deciding that they no longer care about their final grade. The influence of a manager can be undercut if the CEO ridicules his or her work. The power of the person who owns the only car in a friendship group is diminished when another friend purchases a vehicle.

DISCUSSION QUESTION • 6.1

What are your sources of potential power (see Table 6.1) in various relationships? Do you have a tendency to rely on just one or two sources? Do you use different power sources in different contexts (home or work)?

Integrative Power

The changeability of power based on the connections among individuals and their perceptions of each other is the basis of the **integrative power model**. Contrary to the self-focused applications of distributive power, integrative power models hold that power *always* is based on a line of connection between individuals. Emerson (1962) theorized that:

> The power of person A with person B is equal to how much B is dependent on A. Likewise, the power of B with A is equal to how much A is dependent on B.

For Emerson, the root of power is dependency on another person to reach a goal.

In a traditional distributive view, power is limited. Modern **power currency** perspectives attempt to break the boundary of their distributive roots to offer an expansive view of power. If one's sources of power are weak in a specific relationship, changing to another power source that is more valued by the other party can develop power. For example, during times of economic downturns, employees may not receive raises or additional financial compensation for their work. They may even be asked to pay more for health insurance or expected to take a pay cut. In these instances, bosses no longer have the traditional pay raise reward power at their disposal. Lower-level supervisors need other sources of power to motivate their employees, perhaps creatively using travel monies, special assignments, praise, or other nonmonetary resources as rewards. For example, public managers who often have few monetary resources may use training opportunities or employee recognition programs to motivate employees (McCorkle & Witt, 2014).

The expanded view of power currencies and the integrative power model suggest there are many ways to cultivate power, all based on the unique connections between specific individuals (see Table 6.2).

Power Management

Related to the concept of cultivating power is **power management**. When one or both individuals perceive power as too unbalanced, a redistribution of power may be necessary to set the stage for

TABLE 6.2 Modern Power Currencies

Cooperation
Links to community
Endurance and a reputation for doing what one agrees to do
Cultural traditions
Listening
Networking
Integrity
Patience
Attractiveness
Nuisance ability
Persistence
Public speaking and verbal skills
Languages
Traditional logic and organization ability
People skills
Dependability
Self-esteem
Emotional stability
Ethical sense
Spirituality
Personal self-worth

---

effective conflict management. In other words, sometimes one person in a relationship thinks the other has too much ability to influence decisions. Folger, Poole, and Stutman (2013) conclude, "There is widespread agreement among scholars of conflict that any significant imbalance of power poses a serious threat to constructive conflict resolution" (p. 160). When an employee feels management holds all the power and will not listen, there is little incentive to enter into negotiations. When difficulties arise, an employee may simply quit or rebel through passive-aggressive tactics. If the employer wants to reduce dissatisfaction and turnover, steps may be taken to empower the employees, perhaps by creating feedback systems or problem-solving mechanisms to help employees and supervisors work together. When one partner believes the other has all the power, there is little incentive to work on the relationship. If both want the relationship to continue, the perceptions about power must be adjusted to create an environment where conflicts can be managed productively. Without power management, power struggles lead to inefficient workplace behaviors, a decrease in interpersonal relationships, as well as a tendency to choose destructive tactics.

When power struggles erupt, individuals may attempt to gain or exert more power through coalition building, aggressive tactics, emotional distancing, rumors starting, intentionally annoying behaviors, avoidance of the other person, or personal attacks. For example, if a couple is having a conflict, the one who feels less powerful may try to cultivate power by being emotionally distant. The unconscious logic says: "If I seem to care less about the relationship, then my partner will want to shore up the relationship and I will have more power." In all too many cases, however, both people in the relationship will alternately feel less powerful and enact the same strategy of appearing not to care. Gradually, each one steps away from the relationship more and more, and it becomes harder and harder to manage the initial conflict or rebuild what has been lost.

Awareness of the power structure in a relationship and self-monitoring how one's expressive behaviors affect the power structure is helpful for conflict managers in any setting. For example, one study linked low self-monitoring (always saying what one feels and thinks rather than adapting situationally) to relationship issues (Oyamot, Fuglestad, & Snyder, 2010). Another study found that students who were put in an experimental situation where they were a boss put less attention on their interactions with subordinates, derogated subordinates, and felt self-satisfaction (Georgesen & Harris, 2000)—behaviors which are not conductive to productive conflict management.

When power differences exist in ways that affect the quality of a relationship, power management strategies can be implemented. The goal of **power management** is not to make power exactly equal, but to manage the perception of power in a range where the lower power person no longer feels helpless or manipulated.

Power management strategies by the more powerful individual include the following:

- Allowing the other to be included in decision making
- Listening
- Restraining from power-grabbing moves
- Remaining silent until the other has a chance to express his or her ideas
- Sharing information
- Increasing statements about the connection between the two individuals
- Highlighting the value of the other in the relationship
- Validating the other's concerns or experiences

Leaders who sincerely want to know their workers' ideas have learned to ask for input before expressing their thoughts. Once the powerful individual speaks, others may be unwilling to indicate disagreement or feel that decisions already have been made so why bother with more discussion. In contrast, making statements about the commonalities both parties share enhances a sense of positive interdependence.

Power management strategies of the less powerful individual also can be addressed. Those who feel powerless are vulnerable to defeatist strategies that reinforce weakness and may lead to an acceptance of extreme measures or violence as the only solution. Positive power management can be undertaken by the less powerful individuals in numerous ways. Internally, one focuses on maintaining positive self-esteem and building networks or coalitions to increase power. Externally, when talking to more powerful individuals, it is important to look at issues from their perspective. Analyze the situation to determine the powerful individual's interests and frame your ideas in terms that will make the most sense to the other person. Strategically, capture their attention first with their self-interest, then meld their interests with your own.

> Trust is the glue that holds relationships together.
>
> —Researchers Lewicki & Wiethoff, 2000

Trust

Trust is defined as "an individual's belief in, and willingness to act on the basis of, the words, actions, and decisions of another" (Lewicki & Wiethoff, 2000, p. 87). Trust is best understood through attribution theory. In other words, trust develops from perception and/or experience that a person has trustworthy qualities. When a friend doesn't follow-through with a promise, the attributions made about the lapse will affect overall trust felt toward that friend. If an internal attribution is made ("I guess he's not the kind of person who does what he says he will"), trust is lessened. If an external attribution is made ("I can see that his car was broken, and that's why he didn't pick me up when promised"), then trust may be unaffected. If the friend with the broken car gets another friend to take over the task, trust probably will be enhanced.

When trust is high, behaviors are perceived as stemming from good intentions. When trust is lacking or has been broken, the same behaviors are attributed as manipulative, self-centered, or motivated by ill-will. Lewicki and Wiethoff (2000) conclude that individuals decide how much to trust based on a predisposition to see good or evil in others, psychological orientation, reputation, stereotypes, and actual experiences over time. A study of business relationships similarly showed that trust that was developed before a conflict emerged reduced blaming and negative consequences (Celuch, Bantham, & Kasouf, 2011).

The development and maintenance of trust is an important task for successful conflict managers in any setting. In new relationships, trust is constructed from small bricks into a solid structure. To create trust, individuals can spend time on shared activities, cultivate common interests, find common goals, comment on similar reactions to situation, and build on areas where both stand for the same values (Lewicki & Wiethoff, 2000). When trust is lost, the reconstruction process can be lengthy and difficult.

DISCUSSION QUESTION • 6.2

Have you been in a relationship where trust was lacking or broken? How was communicating with that person different after trust was broken?

TOOLBOX 6.1   Are You Trustworthy?

1. Do you behave consistently and appropriately?
2. Are you reliable?
3. Do you meet deadlines?
4. Do you follow through as promised?
5. Are you clear about deadlines and consequences if they are not met?
6. Do you seek agreement on procedures to evaluate the actions of self and others?
7. If distrust occurs, do you cultivate other ways to exhibit trustworthiness?
8. Do you discuss expectations to increase common awareness rather than assuming everyone has the same expectations?
9. Can you admit your errors?
10. Do you take responsibility for your choices and their outcomes?

Humor

Humor changes its quality depending on when it is used and who uses it (Winterheld, Simpson, & Orina, 2013). Using humor during conflict can be intended to decrease tension, anxiety, or aggression—motives that would seem productive. People who use humor may be trying to lighten the situation. When humor works, it can be a useful communication device.

Humor often is used as a bonding device. Sharing the irony of an unpleasant situation through subtle humor can bring people together. For example, if a supervisor berates an entire work team for a minor infraction, after the boss leaves someone might say: "That was fun." The irony lightens the situation without blaming anyone for the problem. Similarly, good-natured teasing can be a way to politely point out improper behavior without having to make a direct statement (Heiss & Carmack, 2012).

Although humor can be a tension reliever, it also is known as an aggressive weapon. Humor can be used to cloak a personal attack. When confronted about a negative criticism, the speaker may say, "Just kidding," as if to rewrite the history of the remark. Aggressive humor can attack by making someone the butt of a joke. Humor also can be an avoidance tactic to turn attention away from an unwanted topic. Humor can be used to point out social norm breaking or to gain compliance through shaming. Instead of asking a late coworker to get to work on time, a colleague may comment in a joking fashion, "Oh, look who's decided to grace us with her royal presence." Negative humor often is directed by those who feel superior toward those they see as lower in status.

Raven (2008) commented that *hard humor* (sarcasm, ridicule, embarrassment) is a form of coercive power, and *soft humor* (whimsy) can be used to soften bad news. In negotiation, for example, hard humor sometimes is used to put the bargaining opponent on the defensive by ridiculing any small misstatements or retelling a story of past embarrassment. In contrast, flapping one's arms while walking around the room to illustrate profits flying away if a deal is accepted could be a softer, more humorous tactic.

Self-defeating humor is made at one's own expense through self-disparaging comments or doing things that make oneself look foolish. Self-defeating humor is associated with lower self-esteem, conflict avoidance, or overly ingratiating tactics. For example, Darcy, who is a bit overweight, might respond to a question about where to go to lunch by saying, "It's a good idea to take my opinion since I'm clearly someone who has sampled all the options." Consistent use of disparaging humor by conflict managers is discouraged (Winterheld et al., 2013).

A conflict manager's awareness of the type of humor he or she typically uses can be helpful in choosing tactics more strategically. Likewise, it can be helpful to know the type of humor used by others, so one isn't surprised by aggressive humor in the middle of a negotiation. Humor research presents a model with two dimensions: (1) Is the humor directed at the self or toward the other, and (2) is the humor positive or negative (see, for example, Hall, 2010). Table 6.3 presents the types of humor.

Research on humor discovered interesting effects that can be explained using attribution theory. Generally, people do not always credit a well-intended humor user with good intentions (Bippus, 2003). For example, one roommate may crack jokes in a well-intended attempt to reduce tension, and the other roommate may interpret the joking as a personal attack. Furthermore, identical humor attempts can be perceived in many different ways by individual listeners. If the humor is perceived as funny, then the recipient might go along with the tension-relieving intention. If the recipient perceived that the humor was made for mood improvement or to establish common ground, then it might be viewed as productive (an attribution that the humor was used for the benefit of both parties). If the receiver of the humor perceived that the humorist used a joke because of a lack of argumentative skills, it also could be perceived as productive (an attribution that the speaker was self-oriented but not negative). If the receiver perceived that the humor was an attack, hostile, or intended to change the topic, then a negative attribution occurred and the conflict typically escalated.

TABLE 6.3 Types of Humor

Positive
    Self-enhancing humor: a positive outlook about the odd things that happen in life
    Affiliative humor: funny comments that include others' positives
Negative
    Aggressive humor: put-down humor, sarcasm, ill-intended teasing, ridicule, derision
    Self-defeating humor: self-disparagement, amusing others at one's own expense

---

Sources of Conflict Patterns

Where do the patterns discussed in these last two chapters come from? What forces move entire groups of people to act in similar ways? Many social scientists point to social learning for the answer. Partly, we play out scripts written for us by external forces—culture, social media, customs, and rituals. For example, we are taught by role models (real or fictionalized) how to behave when inhabiting specific roles, such as a father, daughter, subordinate, Latina, football player, and so forth. Social roles create expectations and provide an easy model for behavior whether the behavior is sensible and productive during conflict or not. Coleman (2000) comments:

> These social norms establish shared expectations among members of a system, which in most cases came into existence long before the individuals who now respond to them. It argues that we largely act out these preexisting scripts in our institutions and organizations, and that it is these roles, these shared norms and scripts, that dictate our experiences, our expectations, and our responses.
>
> (pp. 119–120)

We often do not know why we make the choices we do unless we engage in purposeful self-analysis.

Perceptions of other individuals affect what one expects and how one behaves. In many situations, none of the variables discussed in these two chapters may seem to matter. In other situations, one or more variables are somehow activated and become crucial. The competent conflict manager is aware of variables that impact how the process of conflict plays out and how the individuals in conflict are perceived.

Summary

Power is the ability to have influence or bring about a desired outcome. It can be perceived as power over others, power with others, powerlessness, or empowerment. In a competitive view, power is perceived as a fixed resource (distributive). In a cooperative view, power is seen as flexible (integrative). French and Raven identified five sources of power: reward, coercion, legitimate, expert, and referent (later adding information as the sixth type). Power also can be viewed as a currency exchange.

Trust is a willingness to act based on another person's words or actions. Behaviors during conflict are perceived differently when trust is high than when trust is low. Similarly, humor is judged differently depending on perception of the speaker's intent. Humor can be an effective means of breaking tension and lightening the mood during conflict, but it can also serve as a damaging expression of underlying issues.

Chapter Resources

Exercises

1. Raven claimed in 1992 that supervisors go through several stages when using power in the workplace: (1) Deciding some goal requires the supervisor to try to influence employees, (2), Assessing the supervisor's power in relationship to the employee and choosing a type of power, (3) Setting the stage to use that type of power, (4) Applying power, and (5) Assessing the effects of the effort.

    In each of the cases below, which sources of French and Raven's power can be used? Analyze how a person might use one source of power using the five steps outlined above.

A. A supervisor needs to get an employee to stop accessing private social media during work time.
B. A business consultant wants to appear credible to a client who comes to her office.
C. A student wants to ask a professor if he can take a test at a later date.
D. Someone wants a roommate to leave so another friend can move in.

2. List several examples where someone of equal status attempted to exert *power over* you or used *coercive power*. For example, you would be attempting a power-over tactic if you said to your roommate: "The next time you clean the bathroom, let me know and I'll buy some more cleaning supplies." The statement assumes the roommate will be the one to do the cleaning task. If the roommate does not disagree with your assumptions, you have successfully exerted the power-over strategy.

3. Which of these definitions of power are more distributive and which are more integrative?

A. "Power is the ability to get things done, to mobilize resources, to get and use whatever it is that a person needs for the goals he or she is attempting to meet" (Rosabeth Moss Kanter).
B. "Power is the ability to act to meet personal needs or a group's objectives" (Donald Klein).
C. "Power is the ability to cause or prevent change. It may be a moving force or a blocking force" (Rollo May).
D. "The processes of power are persuasive, complex and often disguised in our society" (John French and Bertram Raven).

4. Keep a record for two continuous hours of any humor you use or hear. At the end of the session, categorize the humor for the following:

A. Was the humor intended positively or as a means of control?
B. Did the humor imply a superior-inferior relationship?

5. Are there other variables that you believe impact conflict behaviors than those discussed in this chapter or the previous chapter? What other factors might make a difference in how people behave during conflict?

Research Topics

1. Review several resources on trust. How is trust built, broken, and rebuilt?
2. Raven (2008) commented that public signs illustrate all of the types of power. For example, a sign outside your apartment might say, "No dog walking. $50 fine" (coercive power). Alternately, it could use referent power with a bit of humor: "Don't let your dog be a stain on the neighborhood."

Take a picture of a sign on campus or in your neighborhood.

A. Analyze the type of power the sign is attempting.
B. Rewrite the sign to demonstrate other types of power.

Mastery Case

What elements from the chapter shed light on case 6A, Melinda's Not Funny?

Melinda's Not Funny

Melinda works in the dining hall. When customers ask for a portion of the item she is dishing up, she frequently makes humorous comments about food selections, such as:

"Your momma would be sad you're not eating vegetables."
"This meat loaf really looks like dog food today—ha ha."
"You're the only person today to take the spinach; I'll start calling you Popeye."

References

Bippus, A. M. (2003). Humor motives, qualities, and reactions in recalled conflict episodes. *Western Journal of Communication, 67*(4), 413–426.

Celuch, K., Bantham, J. H., & Kasouf, C. J. (2011). The role of trust in buyer-seller conflict management. *Journal of Business Research, 64*(10), 1082–1088.

Coleman, P. T. (2000). Power and conflict. In M. Deutsch & P. T. Coleman (Eds.), *The handbook of conflict resolution: Theory and practice* (pp. 108–130). San Francisco: Jossey-Bass.

Elias, S. (2008). Fifty years of influence in the workplace: The evolution of the French and Raven power taxonomy. *Journal of Management History, 14*(3), 267–283.

Emerson, R. M. (1962). Power-dependence relations. *American Sociological Review, 27*, 31–41.

Folger, J. P., Poole, M. S., & Stutman, R. K. (2013). *Working through conflict* (7th ed.). Boston: Pearson.

Georgesen, J. C., & Harris, M. J. (2000). The balance of power: Interpersonal consequences of differential power and expectancies. *Personality and Social Psychology Bulletin, 26*(10), 1239–1257.

Hall, J. A. (2010). Is it something I said? Sense of humor and partner embarrassment. *Journal of Social and Personal Relationships, 28*(3), 383–405.

Heiss, S. N., & Carmack, H. J. (2012). Knock, knock; who's there? Making sense of organizational entrance through humor. *Management Communication Quarterly, 26*(1), 106–132.

Lewicki, R. J., & Wiethoff, C. (2000). Ethical and unethical bargaining tactics: An empirical study. In C. Menkel-Meadow & M. Wheeler (Eds.), *What's fair: Ethics for negotiators* (pp. 221–220). San Francisco: Jossey-Bass.

McCorkle, S., & Witt, S. L. (2014). *People skills for public managers.* Boston: Routledge.

Oyamot, C. M., Fuglestad, P. T., & Snyder, M. (2010). Balance of power and influence in relationships: The role of self-monitoring. *Journal of Social and Personal Relationships, 27*(1), 23–46.

Raven, B. H. (2008). The bases of power and the power/interaction model of interpersonal influence. *Analysis of Social Issues and Public Policy, 8*(1), 1–22.

Raven, B. H., & Rubin, J. Z. (2008). The interdependence of persons. In S. M. Schmidt, D. Geddes, S. C. Currall, & A. Hochner (Eds.), *Power and negotiation in organizations* (3rd ed.). Dubuque, IA: Kendall/Hunt.

Winterheld, H. A., Simpson, J. A., & Orina, M. M. (2013). It's in the way that you use it: Attachment and the dyadic nature of humor during conflict negotiation in romantic couples. *Personality and Social Psychology Bulletin, 39*(4), 496–508.

Zigarmi, D., Roberts, R. P., & Randolph, W. A. (2015). Employees' perceived use of leader power and implications for affect and work intentions. *Human Resource Development Quarterly, 26*(4), 359–384.

Section II

Conflict Management Skills

Section II presents essential skills in a conflict manager's toolkit. Most people enter conflict with some fears, hopes, and skills learned through experience. Unfortunately, much of our learning about conflict comes from the adversarial and sometimes cruel world of the grade school playground, the middle school quest for identity, and unsavory media examples. Some individuals seem to have learned conflict coping skills from a fictional character who is full of withering sarcasm and hurtful indifference. The competent conflict manager must understand how to restructure unproductive communication.

Training and adding new skills can have a positive impact. A study of doctors and medical personnel found five positive long-term effects of conflict training: (1) a new view of the potential positive aspects of conflict was built, (2) knowing how to analyze conflicts encouraged time to reflect before automatically responding, (3) discovering cooperative and interest-based ways of approaching difficulties was an eye-opener, (4) self-awareness and knowing one's hot buttons built confidence, and (5) learning it's better to listen than to always talk helped reduce tension and allowed problem solving (Zweibel, Goldstein, Manwaring, & Marks, 2008). Chapter 7 presents the most basic skills that competent conflict managers must master: listening, defusing emotions, reframing, and asking questions. With these basics, individuals are prepared to respond skillfully to a variety of conflict situations.

Chapter 8 examines conflict management styles. Knowledge of conflict styles—one's own and the styles of others—helps the conflict manager adapt to different situations and people. Moving away from seeing some conflicts as a clash of personalities and toward viewing them as stylistic differences allow more strategic options for conflict transformation. Understanding and building emotional intelligence enhanced conflict management competence.

Chapter 9 teaches negotiation skills. Productive competitive negotiation techniques are revealed. Methods for interest-based bargaining are presented.

Finally, Chapter 10 delves into a deeper understanding of conflict through sophisticated methods of analysis. Successful deconstruction of conflict provides conflict managers tools to determine optimal strategies.

Chapter 7

Listening and Seeking Information

Vocabulary

Affective event	Frame
Appreciative listening	Hearing
Attitude	Listening
Close-ended questions	Mindfulness
Comprehensive listening	Multitasking
Content paraphrasing	Open-ended questions
Dialogic (relational) listening	Probing questions
Discriminative listening	Reframing
Emotional paraphrase	Selective perception
Empathetic listening	Summarizing
Evaluative (critical) listening	Validating

Objectives

After reading the chapter, you should be able to:

1. Explain the disadvantages of poor listening in competitive and cooperative conflict
2. Contrast the six types of listening and explain which are most useful to conflict managers
3. Apply techniques to defuse emotion and reframe positional statements

Listening is the primary tool for discovering what is happening during interpersonal conflict. Contrary to popular opinion, listening is not automatic. **Hearing** is an automatic, physiological event that occurs for anyone with fully functioning ears. **Listening** requires mental effort to process the stimuli garnered through hearing. It begins with the perception process of attending to a message, organizing the stimuli into something that makes sense, and evaluating its meaning.

For conflict managers, focused listening is essential. First, listening is a way of gathering information. Knowledge of the other party's goals and needs is a prerequisite to productive conflict management. For example, in determining where two neighbors will routinely park their vehicles, one states part of his motivation for buying that house was the view from his window of the apple tree across the street (a goal of relaxing in a pleasant environment). After acquiring that information, the discerning neighbor will assess how the new data does or does not change the conflict. She now knows what is most important to her neighbor. As a cooperative bargainer, she might state that although she would like to park her large truck in front of her neighbor's house because of the extra space on that curb, she would do her best not to block the view of the tree. As a competitive bargainer, she might suggest that if she parked her truck on her neighbor's unused RV parking spot beside his house, she would never have to block his view. Discernment of the other party's interests is helpful when engaging in competitive conflict, and knowing the other's needs is critical to an interest-based approach.

Second, listening is an essential skill because demonstrating empathy creates a connection among individuals. When the conflict partner is framed as a responsible individual rather than an evil opponent, a less caustic range of tactics and strategies can be chosen. For example, communicating care for a neighbor's desire for an unobstructed view opens the door for collaborative discussion. Finally, listening develops power. Having information and knowledge is a basis of power.

CASE 7.1

The Mistake

Gerald was sad to see his last assistant, Marcie, take a promotion within the hospital. She had worked for him for more than ten years, and they had a great synchronicity that made their small unit very efficient and able to serve the needs of their patients. Sometimes it was almost as if they had telepathy. He would ask about a task, and she would just smile and say, "Already done." Marcie often worked late to be sure that medical orders were ready for the next day.

Because Gerald was the senior manager in the medical imaging unit, he conducted the interviews to fill Marcie's vacant position. He selected Paulo, who was a young graduate fresh from school.

Gerald spent extra time in the unit during the first week to be sure that Paulo had the routine down: Schedule the patients, confirm their insurance will pay, let everyone on the team know when patients are coming for the next two days, and order the supplies to do the imaging tests. Sure, there were some nuances to the details of getting things done, but Marcie always sorted things out, so it was assumed that Paulo would figure everything out.

It had been a rough week with training added on top of regular duties, and they had stayed a little late on two days. Gerald stayed particularly late on Thursday to catch up on his weekly reports so he could play golf on Friday afternoon. About 4 P.M. he dropped over to Paulo's station and asked if everything was going well. Paulo said, "No problems."

"Great," said Gerald, "I'm taking off, and I'll see you next week." Paulo, because he had worked overtime on two days that week, left shortly after Gerald.

Gerald arrived as usual on Monday morning ready to work with their typical fifteen to twenty patients a day. He was shocked to see that patients filled the lobby instead of being in the ready room. As soon as he sat down in his small office, three of the technicians crowded into the room, very angry that their equipment wasn't ready and the lobby was full of patients who weren't going to get their tests. It turns out that Paulo, who wasn't scheduled to arrive for another fifteen minutes, left Friday without picking up the supplies for the Monday morning tests. It was going to be a rough day.

The Listening Process

Listening can easily go wrong. Listening is complex and can be conceived in many ways (Gearhart & Bodie, 2011). This chapter introduces the three steps to listening, which will build a basic understanding of how error can creep into the process. The three-listening steps are: attend, organize, and interpret. The *attending step* can be particularly difficult. The mind uses automatic processes to filter the multitudinous data available to the senses to keep from being overwhelmed. A problem arises when too much information is filtered out or there is too much focus on less essential information. While reading this chapter, several things may compete for your attention: People may be talking in the next room, you may be listening to music, your cell may ping indicating a new text message, or thoughts about upcoming plans for the weekend may intrude. To comprehend what is being read, you must tune out extraneous stimuli so they recede into the background while you "attend" to reading. If the conversation in the next room turns to a topic of interest, attention may wander from reading to eavesdropping. If the word "apartment" appears in one of the cases, it could trigger some internal turmoil if you had just broken up with a significant other and need to find a new place to live. Physical pain, hunger, discomfort, and other internal states also are distracters vying for your attention. Without constant vigilance, attention may drift during important encounters. Paying attention takes energy and effort.

DISCUSSION QUESTION • 7.1

What challenges do you face in attending and organizing messages while sitting in class, talking to your friends, or at work?

The belief in **multitasking**, doing more than one thing at a time, seems to be omnipresent in modern life. Unfortunately, neuroscience has discovered the brain really doesn't do more than one thing at a time (Medina, 2015). It just switches rapidly back and forth between tasks. A problem arises when one task becomes more interesting than the other, and the brain changes the proportion of time spent on each task. A simple example shows how so-called multitasking can falter when driving a car. The driver is focused on the road and is driving safely. Then the satellite radio buzzes to indicate a favorite song is playing on another station. The familiar alert tone may move the driver's attention from the road to the radio display. If several favorite songs are on the display, the time spent reading and thinking about which song to pick next can cause a mishap. When talking on a cell while driving, and perhaps fighting with your mother, more and more attention may be drawn to the distressing conversation with less attention given to the road. Accidents often result. That is the reason many U.S. states have banned cell phones while driving.

When conversing with a friend on a cell, you may hear a tap-tap-tap sound in the background (cluing you that the person on the other end of the line probably is playing an electronic game). Multitasking requires switching attention between the conversation with you and the (sometimes) more interesting game. As more attention is given to a tricky game move, the rest of the world fades into the background, i.e., gets filtered out. The pull of personal electronic devices can be strong. We once observed someone giving a formal presentation at a conference who stopped talking when her cell beeped to see who was texting—not a behavior that enhanced her credibility among her professional colleagues.

Listening also can be sidetracked in the next part of the listening process: organizing. In the *organizing step*, the mind takes the incoming data and makes sense of it. The mind compares current information to past knowledge. An accepted truism of perception is that people tend to see and hear what they expect to see and hear. Past experiences create filters through which we perceive the world. When a stranger speaks loudly and with intensity, the veracity of the message is filtered by comparison to one's past experiences with loud and intense people. The message then is categorized as coming from someone who is (fill in the blank with an impression: angry, frustrated, a bully, dangerous, etc.). For example, someone from a culture which values calmness and low speaking tones may miscategorize a loud and impassioned speaker from a culture that values authentic emotions. Because the perception process means information is organized based on what we already know about the world, we are vulnerable to erroneous prejudgments and stereotypes as information is categorized.

KEY 7.1

Listening is the quintessential mark of a competent conflict manager.

After organizing and categorizing the incoming message, the listener then *interprets* it and chooses how to respond. Is the message good or bad? Is someone ignoring me or really didn't hear me ask a question? In the interpretation step, the message is put into context, and decisions are made on how to respond. The meaning of any message lies in the interpretation of the receiver of that message. What goes into our interpretations (cultural biases, past experiences, relational history, beliefs, values, and much more) affects our ability to listen effectively.

The three parts of the listening process work together to create understanding or to distort reality. A tragic example occurred several years ago near Los Angeles. Juliet Qualls, a 19-year-old deaf woman, was using sign language that was observed by members of a gang. The gang members misinterpreted a sign-language gesture as meaning a rival gang and killed her (Lee, 1991). The gang members attended to the message by observing her use of sign language, organized the gesture through their past experiences as belonging in the category of "rival gang sign," and interpreted her use as showing a lack of respect. The consequences were fatal.

The Black Lives Matter campaign was intended, in part, to alert everyone that some police had a predisposition to perceive young black men as threatening and dangerous. A concern raised by the Black Lives Matter proponents is that perceptional errors committed by authorities lead to fatally bad choices. For example, some police seemed to have a predisposition to categorize something held in the hand as a gun instead of as a cell phone. When a conscious or unconscious lens

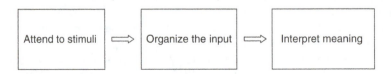

FIGURE 7.1 The Listening Process

says "all members of that group are dangerous," one's perception of any member of that group will be skewed if the initial false assumption is not addressed.

Effective conflict managers challenge themselves to be aware of how they are attending, what is influencing their categorization of information, and how interpretations influence their responses. The effectiveness of the listening process requires constant awareness of each of the three elements: attending, organizing, and interpreting.

> The average person suffers from three delusions: (1) that he is a good driver, (2) that he has a good sense of humor, and (3) that he is a good listener.
>
> —Former president, University of Southern California, Steven Sample

Barriers to Effective Listening

A significant barrier to good listening is created by the listener's attitudes. One attitude stems from the assumption that listening requires no special effort. Thinking no effort is required, individuals put little energy into skill development. Acknowledging that listening can be improved is a necessary first step. A myth about listening states that not talking is being a good listener. Unfortunately, being trained to "be quiet" when someone else is speaking does not necessarily mean the silent person is attending to what is said. Teachers know a good percentage of students who look like they are paying attention to a lecture are actually thinking about something other than the topic of the moment. Table 7.1 summarizes common listening barriers.

Pretending to listen, called *pseudo-listening*, does not qualify as listening. A classic joke illustrates the trap of pretending to listen. The scene starts with the husband reading the newspaper. His wife comes into the room and says, "Does this dress make me look fat?" From behind the paper he replies from habit, "Yes, dear." She is not amused. Pretending to listen and giving fake feedback can be disastrous.

We learn an array of bad listening behaviors, such as pseudo-listening, listening selectively, or multitasking while listening. Unfortunately, these are not the only detractors from effective listening. Perception traps await the listener as messages are assessed, organized, and interpreted.

Selective perception is the filtering of available stimuli and choosing the bits that match one's attitudes of the moment. An **attitude** is a relatively stable predisposition to act or believe in specific

TABLE 7.1 Internal Listening Barriers

Internal preoccupation:	Using the gap between a speaker's rate of speech (125–250 words per minute) and the ability to comprehend (500 words per minute) to think about other things
Self-involvement:	Focusing on personal needs and ignoring the interests of the other party
Selective attention:	Focusing only on part of the message and ignoring everything else
Listening with an agenda:	Listening for facts to fit preconceived ideas about the conflict
Ambushing:	Listening for points to attack the speaker or his or her ideas
Physiological turmoil:	Attending to pain, hunger, coldness, or other physical conditions
Emotional turmoil:	Feeling strong emotions like anger, euphoria, sadness, or confusion
Multitasking:	Attempting to perform additional tasks or thinking about non-related topics simultaneous to listening
Stereotyping:	Assuming someone will think or behave in particular ways because of the group he or she is perceived to be a part of
Preconceptions:	Letting past interactions or first impressions contaminate how a current message is interpreted

ways. If one's attitude is that another person is untrustworthy, then the behaviors that verify the belief will stick out, and those that do not will recede into the background. For example, if you think a friend is ethical and has good character, you will tend to notice when he loans other friends his truck to help them move to a new apartment and not notice that he sneaks a box of steaks home from the restaurant where he works.

DISCUSSION QUESTION • 7.2

What did you learn about being a good listener as you grew up? Did listening equate to silence? Who taught you about listening? Describe the behaviors of a good listener according to your family.

Where there are gaps in information, people seek closure and fill in the gaps to complete the picture, often with unfounded speculation and attribution errors. For instance, two friends at a party are looking in your direction and laughing, and you wonder what is going on. You might think: "They are just talking about a something funny," or "They are talking about me in an unflattering way." Lacking solid facts about what really happened rarely inhibits people from making up a story and attributing unfavorable motives. Competent conflict managers are aware of the tendency to overjudge and misinterpret others' motives and learn to defer judgment until more information is obtained.

Working on a conflict is difficult when hurt feelings, anger, or other emotions block the ability to listen. While experiencing high emotion, people may reject outcomes that are in their best interest because they are not ready to listen and to problem solve. Competent conflict managers realize that problem solving works best when both parties are ready to listen. The techniques offered later in this chapter help create those opportunities.

Listening and being listened to offers the opportunity to move beyond the hurt feelings into a zone where productive conflict management can occur. Gordon and Chen (2016) explain that "people tend to experience greater relationship quality when they perceive that their partner understands them" (p. 240). In other words, if you want to be understood and listened to, do something so other people think you at least have listened enough to understand them.

DISCUSSION QUESTION • 7.3

Think about two conversations you've had this week. Where would you fall in each conversation on the continuum of listening effectiveness in Table 7.2?

TABLE 7.2 The Continuum of Listening Effectiveness

Pretending to listen	**Ineffective Listening**
Looking for key places to interrupt and to change the topic	↑
Attending to selective content for later rebuttal	
Trying to remember everything exactly as it was said	
Giving full attention and listening for main points	↓
Giving full attention to emotions and content	**Effective Listening**

Listening in Competitive and Cooperative Bargaining

Both competitive and cooperative conflict require skillful listening. Competitors in particular may fall prey to mistaken assumptions about listening. First, competitors may assume that talking is powerful and listening is weak. Second, competitors may assume that listening is the same as agreement. They think, "If someone listens without interrupting, the person must agree with what is being said." Conversely, if the other person does not agree, it must be because he or she did not listen. These assumptions may not only be false, they also may be disadvantageous in competitive bargaining.

Listening is necessary to understand what is standing between you and your goals. After understanding the situation and the facts, one can make strategic decisions about the right response. A final listening error competitors commit is listening only as a tactic to amass information for future counterattacks. Two siblings who are polar opposites politically are in a discussion about presidential politics. When one offers support for her argument by citing a story she saw on a particular news station, her brother sees the opportunity he's been waiting for to attack where she gets her biased information. Listening solely for opportunities to raise disagreement is too focused and may unnecessarily extend the time spent bargaining. To be effective in competitive conflict, listening should lead to uncovering issues, maximizing options, and discovering optimal solutions.

Cooperative conflict managers also prosper through effective listening. They need well-honed listening skills to move efficiently through the early stages of conflict so problem solving can be accomplished. Although listening purely to understand or to show empathy are noble endeavors, cooperative-minded conflict managers who spend all their time on empathy may never get to the problem-solving stage. Competent conflict managers apply empathetic listening techniques strategically toward the goal of managing a problem. Effective listening may seem to take too much effort. In reality, taking the time to listen is efficient because it avoids the time lost in leaping to erroneous conclusions based on false assumptions.

DISCUSSION QUESTION • 7.4

What barriers to listening challenge you the most? Think of examples when specific listening barriers inhibited your ability to listen well.

Types of Listening

Many communication scholars identify six types of listening: discriminative, comprehensive, evaluative, appreciative, empathetic, and dialogic (for example, see Hargie, 2011). **Discriminative listening** is attending primarily for particular signals. When waiting for a text, the faintest beep from a cell phone can be picked out from among other louder noises. The ability to discriminate while listening can be advantageous, such as when listening for the "word of the day" on a radio station to call in to win a prize or when parents pick out their child's call of distress from the raucous noise of dozens of children at play. On the downside, discriminative listening can mask the larger picture if someone listens just for particular words or phrases and doesn't pay attention to the whole context.

Comprehensive listening fosters an understanding of the overall message where the listener attends to the main idea or general theme. When in conflict, listening to grasp the main topic or issue before responding is crucial. Comprehensive listening is effective when the general theme of a message is enough. A shopper trips and falls in the store, but quickly gets up and says to the concerned clerk, "I'm fine." Reading the situation, the clerk determines all is okay and goes back to her work. However, it is less effective when understanding specific details is important or when implicit emotional or relationship messages dominate the exchange. In the previous example, the fallen shopper seems to have a bad cut, but still says, "I'm fine." The clerk, while listening to the words, determines by closer attention to the situation that more attention is warranted and helps the injured shopper to a chair and retrieves a bandage. A variation of comprehensive listening is pure content listening. *Pure content listening* ignores the emotional subtext (the embarrassment of fallen shopper) and focuses on specific message ("I'm fine.") For conflict managers, pure content listening is rarely as helpful as listening to the whole picture, which includes the content, nonverbal cues, and emotional tone.

Evaluative, or **critical listening**, judges the value of a message and gauges the speaker's intentions. The message is critiqued for logic, spin, accuracy, and truthfulness. Evaluative listening is useful in situations where manipulation is anticipated. A salesperson, who has previously asked if you have children, may start touting the benefits of the product you are looking at purchasing for kids. The competent negotiator will correctly recognize the tactic and continue to seek all the information necessary to make a good purchasing decision. When trying to find more information about an item on Craigslist, the seller may say several others are looking at the item to pressure for a quick sale. The strong evaluator will not be swayed by time pressures and will seek all necessary information before making a decision. Citizens should apply evaluative listening to political speech and verify the veracity of campaign information, as there are no rules inhibiting blatantly lying in politics. In general, it is wise to gather more information before making any important decisions rather than relying on any one source. Too much evaluation too soon, however, may bypass a comprehensive understanding of the speaker's intent or create unwarranted defensiveness.

Appreciative listening focuses on the artfulness or aesthetics of a message. For example, relaxing with one's favorite music illustrates appreciative listening. Appreciative listening can foster renewal and reenergize the weary, or it can detract from understanding. One of the authors once was told at a conference that a listener was so struck by her presentational style that he didn't really pay attention to what was said. Appreciative listening removes attention from most of the substance of a message, and therefore it is not a useful skill in interpersonal conflict management.

Empathetic listening gives the other person unconditional space to vent or speak without evaluation or criticism. It is effective when helping someone think through difficulties or when providing validation. Empathetic listening is helpful to conflict managers who are working to moderate emotion or to build rapport. Attending to a friend's story of how his father died when he was young and that his family has continued to have money problems may be a necessary prelude to helping problem solve how to address his spending habits. However, when problems need a resolution, empathetic listening alone is not enough. The conflict manager who only uses empathetic listening is severely limiting the available options for problem solving.

Dialogic, or **relational**, **listening** involves going back and forth between a speaker and a listener role in an effort to understand. In practice, it means joining with the other person to search for an agreeable outcome. Adult sisters both want their parents to travel to their respective cities to visit for the same holiday. Knowing the parents cannot accommodate both at the same time, the sisters instead framed the issue as "How can we ensure that our families get to be with our parents during important family events this year?" Relational listening is closest to the activities involved in mutual gains bargaining, where conflicting individuals actively look for common goals and apply creative thinking to reach a mutually beneficial solution.

Researchers also note that listening can be *supportive* or *unsupportive*. Supportive listeners make comments indicating a focus on the other person and an interest in the conversation, are friendly, make statements about common understanding, and give feedback during the conversation (Bodie, Vickery, & Gearhart, 2013). One sister in the above example states, "I know that your family is really into Thanksgiving. How about mom and dad go there next year instead of our place?" Supportive listeners are attentive and add to a positive conversational flow.

> **DISCUSSION QUESTION • 7.5**
>
> What might happen if someone is expecting one type of listening and gets another type (e.g., expecting empathy and getting evaluation)? Has this happened to you?

Eight Steps for Effective Listening During Conflict

While many skills are helpful for conflict managers, listening may be the most important. To listen effectively and efficiently, apply the eight steps presented in this section.

Consciously Choose the Conflict Management Mindset

Listening starts with self-awareness and the right attitude. One reason for interrupting others is the attitude that "What I have to say is more important than what you have to say." Listening requires discipline and concentration. Preparing to listen means putting aside other tasks and distractions. Listening requires self-control, the strength to not interrupt, and a willingness to let another person express ideas and feelings. Preparation can focus a listener on the goal of understanding *before* evaluating, criticizing, or responding. If engaging in conflict with a reticent person, preparation includes leaving empty space in a conversation to allow the other time to think and respond, rather than rushing to fill what feels to you like awkward pauses.

Wood (2012) labels the mental state of an effective listener as **mindfulness**. She concludes:

> Mindfulness is a choice. It is not a talent that some people have and others don't. No amount of skill will make you a good listener if you don't make a commitment to attend to another person fully and without diversion. Thus, effective listening begins with the choice to be mindful.
>
> (p. 144)

Give the Other Person Your Momentary Full Attention

Full attention is required for two reasons. Being attentive during interpersonal conflict shows that the issue is taken seriously and the other person will not have to struggle to get your attention. You can manage difficulties more effectively if you follow the advice in Table 7.4. When you are perceived as taking other people seriously, they are more likely to show similar respect in return. The second reason full attention is required is that it is more efficient than making mistakes while paying half attention. Getting only part of the story leaves the listener with two options: first, asking for the other to repeat while admitting you were not listening or, second, guessing about the missed content. Both options risk hurting credibility and impeding the conflict management process.

TABLE 7.3 Steps for Effective Listening During Interpersonal Conflict

1. Consciously choose the conflict management mindset.
2. Give the other person your momentary full attention.
3. Determine which type of listening best fits the situation at the moment.
4. Deal with emotions before dealing with substantive issues.
5. Ask questions to get information.
6. Give information the other needs to know.
7. Reframe the problem into an issue where agreement is possible.
8. Check for mutual understanding while problem solving.

TABLE 7.4 Behaviors That Indicate Giving Full Attention

1. Turn the cell phone face down and ignore its pleas for your attention.
2. Put down the remote control and turn off the television.
3. Go to a private space to talk.
4. Turn toward the other person while paying attention.

Full attention also means using all of your senses. Listening uses more senses than the ears and involves more than silent assessment. Nonverbal communication may carry a large part of the meaning in a message and often is more important than the denotative meaning of the words. A parent who states, "Fine. Go out with your friends and don't celebrate your grandfather's birthday with us" may be meaning the opposite—"You should stay here out of respect for your grandfather." Context also can be considered part of listening. A supervisor who considers employees "friends" gives a different message when he speaks while sitting behind a desk than if he is standing in a formal way. Good listeners take a message's possible connotations and its context into account when interpreting what the message means.

The word "momentary" also is important in this step. You do not let the other person hold the floor and speak endlessly. Giving momentary attention before jumping in gives you the opportunity to take advantage of the remainder of the Eight Steps for Effective Listening.

DISCUSSION QUESTION • 7.6

While preparing to listen, what does giving someone momentary full attention mean to you personally? What other activities would cease? What does "giving someone your full attention" look like?

Evaluate Which Type of Listening Best Fits the Situation

Effective listening means discriminating when to focus on the verbal content, when to focus on the relationship implied in a message, and when to attend to the overall emotional tone. For example, if Sara and Ella are having a disagreement about how late into the night visitors can stay in their dormitory room, Ella may agree to Sara's proposed solution, but cross her arms, glare, and sound surly when saying "Yes." The nonverbal message contradicts the verbal message. If Sara is listening mindfully, she will discern that more conversation probably is necessary, perhaps including some empathic listening to more fully understand Ella's perspective.

Not all conflicts start with the disputing parties in the same mental state. Depending on the state the other party is in, the competent conflict manager will respond with empathetic, analytical, or evaluative listening skills. Van Slyke (1999) comments on the outcome of not evaluating which response is necessary:

> The first step we often take toward resolution is to offer additional information intended to demonstrate the logic and reasoning that supports our view of a fair solution. When the parties remain unconvinced, we typically provide further amplification of the position already rejected by those in dissension. When this fails, we persuade, cajole, argue, manipulate, sulk, bully, stamp our feet, arbitrate, or withdraw from the interaction.
>
> (p. ix)

Sometimes one party to an interpersonal conflict calmly and logically presents facts about goal interference and asks the other person to participate in problem solving. For example, a coworker might observe that the work relationship seems to be deteriorating and ask, "Is there something the two of us should discuss?" Other times someone may state a position aggressively and make demands. For example, the coworker might say, "You aren't getting me the information I need on time anymore. I need you to get me the data every day by 1 o'clock." Sometimes the conflict partner talks around the real issue while expressing anger, sadness, or despair. For example, the coworker might talk about how overwhelmed he or she has been lately. The effective conflict manager can use the appropriate type of listening to discover what is really going on. Research examining listening as a goal-directed activity suggests even if people have a preference for one type of listening, they can adapt situationally (Gearhart, Denham, & Bodie, 2014).

DISCUSSION QUESTION • 7.7

What is your greatest challenge as a listener when in conflict with a good friend or significant other?

Deal With Emotions Before Dealing With Substance

When someone criticizes, judges, speaks loudly, or expresses anger, the temptation to respond in kind may be strong. When someone is sad, cries, or expresses emotions the listener finds awkward, the impulse may be to ignore or downplay the emotion. Responding in kind to negative emotions or simply pretending emotions don't exist are inefficient strategies that often make conflict worse. Telling someone, "Don't be so emotional," rarely helps. Devaluing others creates face issues, the conflict becomes more personal, and emotions run higher. Generally, a more productive response is to moderate emotions as they emerge through techniques such as empathic listening.

One of the functions of empathetic listening during conflict is to manage affective events. An **affective event** is any emotional spike. Managing emotions enables the work of conflict management to go forward. When emotions are present, it generally is useful to manage them before confronting substantive issues. Attempting problem solving during an emotionally charged moment is an exercise in frustration. It is difficult for someone awash with emotion to function as a creative problem solver. The emotional mind, as opposed to the rational mind, makes rapid decisions based on associations and perception of facts—and is often wrong (Van Slyke, 1999). Conflict managers have become deeply interested in what neuroscience says about the brain and how emotions and other stimuli lead to automatic reactions rather than higher order thinking (see, for example, Sasscer-Burgos, 2014). A good solution offered to a person in the midst of strong emotions probably will be ignored or misjudged.

Defusing emotions is one skill that should reside in every conflict manager's toolbox. When emotions are high, those in conflict generally benefit from help to get past their personal feelings and move toward resolutions. Empathizing with a highly charged person can lead to a calmer interaction, once the other feels heard and understood.

A general **validation** is any positive statement about the other person. For example, "I can see that this topic is really important to you." Conflict managers often use a general validation to indicate they are listening without judgment. Research shows people who validate others are perceived as supportive listeners (Bodie & Jones, 2012). A validation during conflict might follow the formula: "You are (insert emotion) because (insert cause)." For example, "You are upset because I was late."

Validating at any point during a conflict may be helpful in moving someone from an emotional reaction toward problem solving. Identifying what someone is feeling acknowledges the other's value.

The emotional paraphrase technique is a specialized form of a validation (see Toolbox 7.1). The **emotional paraphrase**, is a method to moderate affective events such as venting or crying. The purpose of the emotional paraphrase technique is to demonstrate that you are listening and show understanding of the feeling that the other person is experiencing. When done properly, the emotional paraphrase will shorten the time spent venting.

TOOLBOX 7.1   The Emotional Paraphrase

Rules:

1.   Give your momentary full attention.
2.   While the other is speaking, you must overlap his/her speech with this technique.
3.   State a two- to six-word emotional paraphrase, then stop speaking.
4.   Use only when the person is exhibiting strong emotions.

The Emotional Paraphrase Equation

A lead in phrase (followed by) *a Feeling word that fits the situation*

You look . . .	Angry/mad/sad/upset
You sound . . .	Concerned/troubled/worried
That must be . . .	Difficult/disturbing/troubling
That sounds . . .	Maddening/upsetting
You seem . . .	Frustrated/ignored/angry

Four qualifications are necessary before you add emotional paraphrases into your conflict management repertoire. First, the defusing of emotion skill is designed for use while emotions are being vented. Waiting until the expression stops before applying the skill makes it too obvious. Second, using the skill when the other is calm and speaking about facts rather than feelings is inappropriate. If someone is not visibly upset, you may use the technique with mild feeling words like "troubled," "frustrated," or "concerned." Third, conflict managers must realize that in conflicts about face or relationship issues, feelings may be the issue. Although moderating emotional display to be able to discuss the issue is important, expecting feelings to evaporate completely after one skill application is unreasonable.

Finally, display of emotion may be a variable of personal and/or cultural style. Culturally expressive individuals display emotion as a part of their process. Nonexpressive individuals incorrectly tend to interpret enthusiastic nonverbal displays as anger, belligerence, or irrationality. Attempting to stop the expression of stylistically or culturally based emotion is not productive. Mirroring the energy level in the emotion of people from expressive cultures is a better choice in some cases. For example, some Italians are more direct and enthusiastic than North Americans. Telling someone with a direct and emotive style to "calm down" generally has the opposite effect. Likewise, being overly calm is open to misinterpretation from an emotive person who might think that you don't care. One strategy is to employ mirroring the volume and tone to demonstrate "listening" from the other person's cultural perspective. Bullying, however, is not the same as cultural expressiveness or an individual with an excitable personal style (see Chapter 11). True bullies should not be allowed the excuse that their excessive misbehavior is just a passionate style of speaking.

Ask Questions to Get Information

Once initial barriers to productive problem solving have been moderated, both individuals benefit if the basic facts and interests that drive the conflict are put on the table. The primary skill for eliciting information is asking questions. Preparing a list of possible questions in advance is helpful. Sometimes the questions one can think of on-the-spot are not artfully phrased and cause defensiveness.

Generally, conflict managers start with broad, open-ended questions. **Open-ended questions** do not have a "right" answer. For example, a coworker being given the cold shoulder by a former friend may say, "I've noticed our relationship has changed a lot, and we're not spending as much time hanging out as we used to do. What do you think about this change?" The answer is not "Yes," "No," or a predetermined fact. Asking broad open-ended questions at the outset allows someone to tell his or her story without feeling interrogated or herded in a particular direction. Starting with close-ended or probing questions may cause defensiveness or miss giving the other person a chance to share important information.

Close-ended questions have a specific concrete answer. "Did you take the money out of my drawer?" is answerable by "Yes" or "No." Close-ended questions can make others feel as if they are being interrogated, but they do have the benefit of getting specific information. For example, "What time did you arrive?" is a close-ended question. Effective conflict managers use close-ended questions sparingly and purposefully.

People who are good independent problem solvers are vulnerable to stepping over the information-gathering stage, relying on close-ended questions, and moving instantly to solutions. Specific questions such as "What do you want me to do?" or "Why don't you just _____?" leap ahead in the process to problem solving before the real issues in the conflict have been determined. Too often, the quick solution has little to do with the real issues. A supervisor may notice a worker is less productive than usual and assume the equipment is inefficient and give the worker a new computer. In reality, the issue could be a conflict with a coworker that is not resolvable by buying a new computer. The supervisor who doesn't take the time to gather information will be disappointed when productivity doesn't go back up after supposedly solving the problem. Leaping ahead in the process often wastes time and resources.

Once the cause of the conflict is determined (values, information, relationship, etc.) through general and open-ended questions, then probing questions are used. **Probing questions** elicit details. "What specifically about how we are working together is a problem?" or "What do you want from me to turn this situation around?" or "So, how do you feel about me taking the kids over winter holiday break and you taking them at Thanksgiving and spring break?" Probing questions might make abstract terms less vague. "When you say we need to spend more time together, what do you have in mind?"

TOOLBOX 7.2 Asking Questions

1. **Open-ended questions** allow an expansive response with no exact right answer.

   "How do you like your work?"
   "How will this decision affect you personally?"
   "What is going on?"

2. **Close-ended questions** have a specific, factual answer.

   "Are you still living in the same place?"
   "Have you ever talked to _____ about this difficulty?"

3. **Probing questions** seek more detail within a topic area.

   "What exactly happened to you that day?"
   "What is it that keeps you from doing your work?"
   "How are you impacted when your roommate is drunk?"

Give Information the Other Person Needs to Know

Asking questions to elicit information is not enough. Information also must be volunteered if it is critical to the issue. Withholding information may allow someone to feel powerful, but it often is an unproductive strategy in the long run. Two general types of information can be given: personal information and factual information.

Personal relationships are developed by symmetry in levels of self-disclosure. A common social rule is that one person's disclosure of feelings or previously unknown facts should be matched with similar information from the other person. If someone relates that he or she feels overwhelmed at work and that nobody will help, sharing a similar story of when you were the new employee may be appropriate. If a wife discloses that she feels angry, it is appropriate for her partner to disclose feelings as well. Of course, sometimes the context or asymmetry in the relationship may make reciprocal disclosure unwise. If a classmate you hardly know discloses in an area where you don't feel comfortable, there is no real obligation to reciprocate. Also, be aware that matching disclosure may come across as one-upmanship (i.e., my life is more interesting than your life). Consider your motives if you respond to a disclosure with a story about yourself. While it may move the relationship forward, it also could inadvertently create a competition.

Putting Facts on the Table . . . Culturally

Not all cultures discuss conflict issues in the same way. North American and many Northern European cultures teach individuals to lay the facts on the table and directly confront the other person. Hammer (2002) relates that individuals from indirect cultures (e.g., some Japanese or Chinese) feel that confrontation and open discussion cause too much social disturbance and loss of face. For individuals with this cultural orientation, problems must be discussed indirectly, metaphorically, or through intermediaries. Open-ended questions at the beginning of an interpersonal conflict episode may create too much social stress for members of indirect cultures. Instead, asking background questions and approaching the problem indirectly is a better strategy. Instead of first asking an open-ended question such as "What is the problem with your workgroup?" one might begin with close-ended questions to set the context. "You've been with the group for how long?" "You work with several teams in the company?" "There have been some difficulties with the work?" Ask probing questions after trust and a relationship has been established. Using this approach, the issues probably will emerge slowly rather than all at once. Asking "What else do I need to know for the good of the group?" will elicit more information. The explanation that follows may be indirect, through a metaphor or a story.

Likewise, if a friend from an indirect culture suddenly starts telling you stories or using a specific metaphor, he or she may be engaging in conflict management behavior. A story about a past friend who was always there to help may be an indirect request for assistance. Listening through the ears of a direct culture will miss these overtures and frustrate both parties.

Understanding intercultural conflict style is complex. We encourage you to research the cultural conflict styles of groups that are prevalent in your lives.

DISCUSSION QUESTION • 7.8

Do you interact regularly with a person from another culture? How is good listening the same or different in each culture? How can you become a better listener when interacting with that person?

Disclosing factual information also is important. In many conflicts, one person will have more detailed knowledge or experience about the topic. For example, a student might be angry about how the instructor is conducting a class and immediately go to the college dean to share that opinion. He will complain about the professor and demand that the dean immediately do something about it. There will come a point early in the conversation when the dean knows that this is a complaint about a faculty member and the student is not following the university policy for these matters. If the dean waits until the student is finished and then says, "I'm not the right person to talk to yet, you have to start by talking to the professor and then your department chair," the student probably will feel humiliated and put-off by the dean. If one is going to share critical information that the other party is not aware of, it is better to do so earlier rather than later.

Frame or Reframe the Issues Onto Common Ground

If you've studied group problem-solving processes, you may remember that the first step always is defining the problem. This step is first so everyone is on the same page when beginning to analyze the problem.

Conflict management also benefits if everyone is one the same page. In conflict management terms, a **frame** is how one or more people formally or informally define an issue. It is common for conflict to emerge because people frame a situation differently. One person may mentally frame getting together Friday afternoon as just something to do and the other may frame it as a date.

People like to frame the topic and scope of a conflict to their personal advantage—it is easier to "win" if the playing field is slanted to one side. **Reframing** moves an issue from a self-interest frame offered by one person into a larger frame that still encompasses the original topic. A reframed statement also moves the focus from positions to more general interests. For example, someone may lead into a conflict discussion with a positional demand: "You have to . . ." The instinctive reaction is defensiveness: "No, I don't" or "No, you have to . . ." A conflict framed in a way to give one party an advantage over the other invites negotiation brinksmanship, and a speedy resolution is unlikely. A way of escaping this dilemma is to reframe the issue into a larger and more general frame where negotiation can occur more fairly.

Joel may threaten his roommate by saying, "You have to pick up my part of the rent this month, or I'll move out tomorrow." The frame is set to pressure compliance. Before the underlying issues can be discovered and the conflict discussed, the frame must be altered. A reframed response ignores the threat or positional statement, takes away the attempt to gain an advantage, and makes the issue larger to seek a common ground where problem solving might occur. The roommate might respond, "So there's some problem with the rent payment? Let's talk about that."

Check Mutual Understanding While Problem Solving

Although it is important in the early stages of a conflict to avoid content paraphrasing while fishing for issues and defusing emotional barriers, content paraphrasing is essential during later stages. **Content paraphrasing** verifies facts and checks for mutual understanding.

Highlighting the content of a message can be beneficial to check the accuracy of information or to pull out important points. For example, a customer comes into the store with a complaint about a computer he purchased. He comments, "The computer gets really hot in the battery area, and I'm afraid it will catch on fire." The shop owner may provide a content paraphrase to make sure the important message has been understood. "So it gets hot in the back left part of the machine?" The customer could agree that the owner understood or offer more explanation if the paraphrase wasn't quite right.

Content paraphrasing is a good skill but one that can be misunderstood, overused, or applied too early. If one partner says to the other, "You've been playing all day while I worked, so you have to fix dinner," a reply phrased as a content paraphrase may come across as sarcastic or demeaning: "I play, you work, so I cook dinner, is that how you see it?" Of course, the interpretation of a message is up to the receiver. Those using content paraphrasing should recognize that it runs the risk of sounding canned or insincere ("So what I hear you saying is . . ."). If used when the other person is emotional, a content paraphrase ignores an important component of the conflict. If used too early, content paraphrasing can fix the topic of conversation in an area that skirts the real issue.

Summarizing is a tool to recognize the primary issues in a conflict. Summaries indicate that concerns have been heard and understood. For example, at the end of a long conversation, a supervisor might say, "You're upset with not getting your reports on time and need a workable system in place for storing data." After a couple has a long talk about money, one might summarize, "You're concerned about all the bills that are piling up and want a plan for managing our budget." Summarizing has an added benefit of helping others move from focusing on the past and into problem solving. For example, a parent has a lengthy list of grievances about her child's teacher to share with the school principal. After some time, she begins to repeat herself. The principal can state, "As I understand, your concerns are about how the teacher communicates with your son, her classroom management, and how often you get progress reports. Does that cover the concerns?" Once there is agreement, the principal can move toward solving the problem with the parent.

Once an agreement is reached, one person should paraphrase what has been agreed to check that the other party has the same understanding. "Just to be clear, we agree that we will use the Thompson report in the future to get our productivity statistics, is that right?" or "So we've agreed that you will come home early, meaning before 11 P.M., right?" If a term in an agreement is vague, someone should use a probing question to clarify, such as: "Just so I understand, what does 'early' mean to you?" Or, put as a question, "We've agreed that you'll be home early on school nights. What do you mean by early?"

If mutual understanding is not checked, both parties may leave thinking the conflict is managed but have quite different pictures in their heads of exactly what the decision meant. An example is the boss who gives an employee vague feedback about not meeting the company image. The employee may vow to do better and will try harder by wearing a tie to work. Unfortunately, the boss wanted the employee to proofread his reports more carefully. The boss will be disappointed and angry that her vision of "company image" has not improved. The employee will feel betrayed and lied to when reprimanded again after having his attempts to improve his image unrecognized by the boss. A simple check of the exact understanding between the parties and careful attention to possible points of misunderstanding can prevent future conflict.

Summary

Listening is a primary way to understand the causes of and possible solutions to interpersonal conflict. Without listening, individuals work from a one-sided and limited knowledge base that is fraught with misassumptions, factual inaccuracies, and self-serving biases.

Listening, unlike hearing, is a learned skill that requires effort to master. The listening process includes attending, organizing, and interpreting data. In each of these steps, a listener can falter. Numerous internal barriers to listening distract from concentrating on messages. Several types of listening are possible, including discriminative, comprehensive, evaluative, appreciative, empathetic, and dialogic. There are benefits to listening for both competitive and cooperative situations. Eight listening steps are the hallmark of effective listeners during interpersonal conflict: (1) choosing a conflict management mindset, (2) giving momentary full attention, (3) selecting the right type of listening, (4) dealing with emotions before dealing with substance, (5) eliciting information through questions, (6) giving information, (7) reframing issues, and (8) checking mutual understanding.

Listening is the quintessential skill of an effective conflict manager. Unfortunately, many people carry poor listening habits into their conflicts. Fortunately, listening abilities can improve with awareness, knowledge, and practice.

Chapter Resources

Exercises

1. Reframe the following positional statements (i.e., remove the positional demand and reframe the general concern).

    A. "The only way we're ever going to finish the project and get a good grade is if we get the teacher to throw Erika out of the group."
    B. "This is the way it's going to be. I'm going fishing so I can finally get some peace and quiet."
    C. "Dr. Reyes, you have to let me retake the test or I'll get a C in your class and won't be able to get into graduate school."

2. Use Toolbox 7.1 skills to defuse the emotion in the following examples.

    A. A client says, "Your staff is so incompetent. They couldn't even get a simple order right even when I held their hand through the whole process!"
    B. A coworker says, "I hate these new policies. How am I supposed to get my work done with all this paperwork I have to process?"
    C. A student in your project group says, "I'm really worried about the project. Everybody else is fooling around, and I'm stuck here trying to find the information before the deadline."
    D. Your best friend has been acting oddly lately. She calls and says, "I hate it when you treat me the way you do. You don't really like me at all. I don't know if I want to hang out with you anymore."
    E. Create your own example.

3. Consider Maureen's listening challenges in the Mastery Case when she returns the call from Danielle. Using the eight steps of listening as a guide, what could Maureen do?

Journal/Essay Topics

1. Are you a good listener? What skills do you possess or need to develop? How does your listening skill level affect those around you?
2. Keep track of your attempts to multitask. How efficient is your multitasking? What are the benefits and deficits to your use of multitasking?

Research Topics

1. Investigate other skills to improve listening. Write a report on at least three recommendations for improving listening that were not included in this chapter.
2. Find peer-reviewed studies that explore listening in a particular context (e.g., workplace, family, or classroom). Report on three different listening studies. What are the similarities and differences in their conclusions?

Mastery Case

Analyze Mastery Case 7A, "The Car Conflict." Which concept from the chapter best explains what is occurring in the case?

The Car Conflict

The National Public Radio show *Car Talk* in July 2005 received a call from Maureen, who described this experience. Maureen's friend, Danielle, owned a truck she had inherited from her father's estate. It was old and had lots of problems, but she was attached to it because it had belonged to her father. Danielle was very generous in loaning the truck to friends when they needed one. Maureen and her partner Jeremy asked to borrow the truck. Danielle said that would be fine, but they would have to jump-start the truck because the battery was low.

Jeremy and Maureen tried to start the truck. Jeremy previously had a car where the battery ran down so he had all the cables and was experienced with the procedure. The truck wouldn't start. Maureen called Danielle and told her about the problem and said that Jeremy could charge the battery overnight in his garage. Danielle said, great, thanks, go ahead. After charging the battery, Jeremy put it back into the truck and nothing happened—not even any clicking or whirring. After consulting with Danielle, they had the truck towed to Danielle's neighborhood mechanic.

The next week, Danielle called and left a message for Maureen demanding $1,400 because she and Jeremy had ruined the battery and the entire electrical system in the truck. Her mechanic said they must have charged the battery backward, and he had to make $1,400 in repairs and put in a new battery.

References

Bodie, G. D., & Jones, S. M. (2012). The nature of supportive listening II: The role of verbal person centeredness and nonverbal immediacy. *Western Journal of Communication, 76*(3), 250–269.

Bodie, G. D., Vickery, A. J., & Gearhart, C. C. (2013). The nature of supportive listening, I: Exploring the relations between supportive listeners and supportive people. *Journal of Listening, 27*, 39–49.

Gearhart, C. C., & Bodie, G. D. (2011). Active-empathic listening as a general social skill: Evidence from bivariate and canonical correlations. *Communication Reports, 24*(2), 86–98.

Gearhart, C. C., Denham, J. P., & Bodie, G. D. (2014). Listening as a goal-directed activity. *Western Journal of Communication, 78*(5), 668–684.

Gordon, A. M., & Chen, S. (2016). Do you get where I'm coming from? Perceived understanding buffers against the negative impact of conflict on relationship satisfaction. *Journal of Personality and Social Psychology, 110*(2), 239–260.

Hammer, M. (2002). *Resolving conflict across the cultural divide: Differences in intercultural conflict styles*. Hammer consulting.

Hargie, O. (2011). *Skilled interpersonal communication: Research, theory and practice* (5th ed.). New York: Routledge.

Lee, J. H. (1991, July 6). Slaying may be linked to pair's use of sign language. *Los Angeles Times*, B3.

Medina, J. (2015, July/August). Mind full. *Leadership*, 34–37.

Sasscer-Burgos, J. (2014). *Our brains on conflict: A neuroscientific explanation: Conflict Resolution Lunchtime Series Presentation, NSA*. www.adr.gov. Accessed 16 September 2016.

Van Slyke, E. J. (1999). *Listening to conflict: Finding constructive solutions to workplace disputes*. New York: American Management Association.

Wood, J. T. (2012). *Interpersonal communication: Everyday encounters* (7th ed.). Boston, MA: Cengage Learning.

Zweibel, E. B., Goldstein, R., Manwaring, J. A., & Marks, M. B. (2008). What sticks: How medical residents and academic health care faculty transfer conflict resolution training from the workshop to the workplace. *Conflict Resolution Quarterly, 25*(3), 321–350.

Chapter 8

Conflict Style and Emotional Intelligence

Vocabulary

Abstract

Accommodation

Avoidance

Collaboration

Competition

Compromise

Concrete

Conflict management style

Conversational style

Distributive engagement style

Emotional intelligence

Escalation

Expectancy violation theory

Five-styles conflict approach

Fractionator

Gregorc style

Gunnysacking

Integrative engagement style

Intercultural Conflict Style Inventory

Maslow's Hierarchy of Needs

Myers-Briggs Type Indicator

Pause gap

Personality style

Postponement

Rapport talk

Report talk

Responsiveness

Root culture

Self-actualization

Self-construal

Social style model

Style

Withdraw-complain cycle

Objectives

After reading this chapter you should be able to:

1. Explain how style differences cause and/or escalate interpersonal conflict
2. Differentiate among personality styles and other types of styles

3. Explain how conflict styles differ across cultures
4. Recognize the advantages of identifying style differences and their impact on conflict
5. Understand how the sixteen characteristics of emotional intelligence impact conflict management.

CASE 8.1

"Yellow"

When I was a teenager—in that stage when my parents could do no right—I was really bothered by something that my father did. When he answered the phone he said, "Yellow." Not "Hello" but "Yellow." It sounded just like he was identifying the color of our neighbor's house: It's yellow. It drove me crazy.

No matter how eloquent my suggestions of alternatives, he would never change—not because he was right and not because he didn't "know better." He didn't change because he liked answering the phone that way. It was his style. He enjoyed it. He thought it was funny. And his style really annoyed me.

It was all right, though, because we were tied together with the bindings of love. Then one day, when I was older, I finally realized *he* wasn't the one who had the problem.

When you have problems with a friend or colleagues at work, would you confront them? Try to smooth things over? Work with them until you find and fix what is wrong? Just let the others have their way? Remove yourself from the situation? Do you feel comfortable politely raising issues, or does even thinking about it create a knot in your stomach? The answers to these questions reveal matters of style. People have preferred ways of communicating and different behavior patterns. In this chapter, we examine how style differences can be at the root of some conflicts.

A working knowledge of communication style is important for two primary reasons. First, people who are aware of their styles can learn to adapt their behaviors strategically to create a greater chance of managing conflict productively. In contrast, people who can only see "differences" and "wrongness" in how others communicate probably will find their lives in constant turmoil.

Second, differences in style can create an expectancy violation. **Expectancy violation theory** suggests that people have preconceived ideas about how others should behave based on perceptions of that individual, the relationship, and the situation. When expectations are violated, we view the other person negatively (Hullett & Tamborini, 2001; Johnson & Lewis, 2010). Style differences can lead to feelings of being obstructed in how communication should occur or how people should behave (goal differences). It is the perception of goal obstruction that leads to conflict.

Style differences can precipitate mistaken assumptions that the other person is intentionally being obstructive. In Case 8.1, the father's verbal style clashed with the daughter's expectations and perceptions of the right way to answer a call. Because they were family, the annoyance wasn't a big problem. Unfortunately, in our everyday work lives, we do not have built-in forgiveness factors to mitigate the effects of those who annoy us or the grace of time to "grow up." Some of Riannon's coworkers in Case 8.2 see her communication style as combative and unnecessarily aggressive. These style annoyances risk becoming conflicts between Riannon and her coworkers. The goal for conflict managers is to acquire skills to deal with those style differences that may cause us angst and interfere with the ability to do our jobs well.

CASE 8.2

Soft Skills

My coworker, Riannon, is an expert in her field, and her opinion is well-respected by those in the office and beyond. She serves on many committees because of her wealth of experience and the information she brings to bear on almost any topic. I appreciate how she is a no-nonsense communicator; if she sees something not adding up, she is direct and rather blunt and doesn't worry about how her opinion comes across. More often than not, she is absolutely right. However, not everyone appreciates how she operates.

On more than one occasion, our supervisor has brought her in to discuss "improving her soft skills" with others because someone has complained. I personally like how I always know where I stand with her and that she will correct my thinking errors. I am not sure if others in the office need to recognize her style as an asset and not be so sensitive or if she should learn to adapt to other people's styles as the boss is suggesting.

What Is Style?

A **style** is a habitual way of communicating: It is what feels natural and right. Styles arise from personality characteristics and become patterned ways of behaving. It is too simple to say that each person has only one style that never changes. As individuals mature, they learn that what feels natural to one person may be offensive to another. Most people find that different styles may be necessary depending on the context. In other words, how one reacts at home, at school, with friends, and on the job may require moving from a preferred style to a style that is effective in each specific situation. For example, someone who is shy who moves into management may need to adopt a more forceful leadership style.

DISCUSSION QUESTION • 8.1

How does your style vary in different contexts? What communication style do you use at home, at work, with your extended family, or with your friends?

For example, Suzanne has a very organized, analytical style. Over the years, she has learned that a direct style offends people in some situations. Many years ago, a student finishing her master's degree brought in a copy of her thesis to show it off. She was proud of her hard work and accomplishment. After looking at the document, this was Suzanne's first comment: "Your margins are wrong." This comment, although sensible within a direct and analytic style, showed a lack of social sensitivity. Teachers who prefer analytical-critical approaches might feel it is efficient to mark only errors on student papers. Through experience, the analytic teacher may discover that, for many students, learning is enhanced when criticism is paired with positive comments.

There are many ways to view style and behavioral patterns. Each viewpoint offers insights into how styles affect behaviors. With knowledge of how styles can clash, conflict managers can make more purposeful choices and not remain trapped in the narrow confines of one style.

Very rarely are conflicts true personality issues. Usually they are issues of style, information needs, or focus.

(Jourdain, 2004, p. 23)

Personality Styles

A **personality style** is a relatively stable pattern of thinking and processing information that, in turn, leads to specific types of behaviors. Personality tests abound and are useful in understanding how one's impulses are similar or different from others. When the conflict manager can recognize personality style differences, behaviors during conflict are less likely to be attributed as intentional interference. Many unnecessary conflicts arise from differences in personality styles. We discuss several personality style typologies to provide insight into how style might confound issues when engaging in conflict.

The Myers-Briggs Type Indicator

The **Myers-Briggs Type Indicator** is a popular test to determine personality styles. Based on Jungian theory, the test categorizes preferred behavior patterns into four paired groups (Table 8.1) (for more information, visit myersbriggs.org).

The *Extrovert/Introvert* (E/I) dimension specifies whether energy and excitement lies with the outer world of social contact or the inner world of ideas. Extroverts tend to be verbally expressive, enjoy interacting in larger groups of people, act first and think through critical details later, and enjoy social contact. In contrast, introverts tend to be private, enjoy quiet reflection alone, think first and act later, and prefer one-to-one interactions.

The *Sensing/Intuiting* (S/N) pairing describes how individuals process information. Sensing individuals relate to external stimuli such as sounds and smells. They mentally focus on the present, have a commonsense approach, remember specific details about the past, prefer known facts, and like clear and concrete data. Intuiters like possibilities and potentials. They focus mentally on the future, are imaginative, remember patterns, work from theories or idealism, and are comfortable with change or with projecting from incomplete data.

The *Thinking/Feeling* (T/F) dichotomy describes how one prefers to make decisions. Thinkers analyze, use objective facts, are task oriented, and make decisions based on criteria. Because of these habits, they can be critical, may observe more than participate, and take a long-term view. In contrast, people with a feeling personality act on emotions or instinct. Thus, they are sensitive to others' needs, seek consensus, are sympathetic, make subjective decisions, understand events through participating in them, make decisions based on values, and may be uncomfortable with conflict or disagreement.

The final pairing, *Judging/Perceiving* (J/P), describes how one views other people and the outside world. Are life decisions structured and organized around a plan or discovered as one goes along? Judgers have plans, are task oriented, like orderly sequences, complete work before deadlines, and are organized. Perceivers make up the plan as they go, like working on many projects at the same time, do best just before a deadline, meander toward objectives, and avoid structures that inhibit flexibility.

Those firmly entrenched on one side of a pair of the Myers-Briggs terms may clash with the other side if they are not prepared to see the value of the opposite trait. If one person is trying to organize work into discrete segments and the other just wants to get started on the project and see

TABLE 8.1 Myers-Briggs Paired Personality Traits

Extrovert (E)	Or	Introvert (I)
Sensing (S)	Or	Intuitive (N)
Thinking (T)	Or	Feeling (F)
Judging (J)	Or	Perceiving (P)

where it goes, a process conflict may emerge about "how to get the job done." Without awareness of style preferences, the differences often are attributed as intentional goal interference or as a personality deficiency.

For more detailed information about specific personality styles, the preferred behavior from each pair in the Myers-Briggs Inventory can be combined (see Table 8.2). For example, one can be an ENFP (extrovert, intuiter, feeler, and perceiver). The Myers-Briggs test is proprietary and can be taken in paper-and-pencil form or online for a fee. Millions of employees in the United States and abroad have taken the test to understand how styles differ in workgroups. Some have gone so far as to put colored dots on each employee's nameplate representing his or her Myers-Briggs combination, so others know what to expect based on personality style.

TABLE 8.2 Sixteen Personality Types

ESTJ: Energy comes from interaction with others. Prefers facts, makes logical decisions, is organized and somewhat impersonal, detail oriented.

INFP: Energy comes from inside. Likes patterns, possibilities, dealing with people, flexibility, is adaptable, and creative. Prefers work with a meaningful purpose.

ESFP: Energy from the outside and spoken words. Prefers facts and takes them at face value. Is present oriented, yet impulsive and friendly. Makes friends easily and likes troubleshooting.

INTJ: Energy comes from the world of ideas. Prefers possibilities about the future, makes decision based on impersonal analysis, is organized, has goals, is skeptical and critical, has a strong intellect, and can deal with details that are relevant.

ESFJ: Energy comes from the outer world of action and ideas. Prefers facts, makes value-based decisions, values friendships, dislikes conflict or criticism, and is very loyal.

INTP: Energy comes from inner thoughts. Prefers dealing with patterns, makes logical decisions, is flexible, quiet, detached, somewhat adaptable, may make a stand on principle, hates routines, and is good with complex problems.

ENFP: Energy comes from the world of action and the spoken word. Prefers patterns, people, value-based decisions, flexibility, new ideas, creativity, uses insight, seeks new ideas, might neglect details or planning, and works toward general goals.

ISTJ: Energy comes from the world of thought. Prefers facts, analytical decisions, organization, logic, quiet, seriousness, preparation, observing, practical, efficiency, and might not express ideas to others.

ESTP: Energy comes from action and the spoken word. Prefers facts, objectivity, logically based decisions, flexibility, action oriented, practical organization, impulsive, troubleshooting work, problem solving, but might neglect follow through.

INFJ: Energy from the inner world of thoughts/emotions. Prefers people-focused possibilities, value-based decisions, organized around people, private sense of purpose, quiet concern for people, likes to help people, has good insights about people that often are not shared.

ENFJ: Energy comes from the outside world and the spoken word. Prefers possibilities for people, value-based decisions, seeks stable relationships, actively promotes personal growth, highly sociable, expressive, finds conflict and criticism difficult, and works best in a team.

ISTP: Energy comes from the inner world of thought. Prefers facts, logically based decisions, flexibility, new information, quiet, somewhat adaptable, thinking through problems and solving them, curious about how things work, impulsive, and sometimes unpredictable.

ENTJ: Energy comes from the outer world of action and words. Prefers possibilities, making thoughtful decisions, logical approach to personal decisions, control, organizing people to complete tasks, being a director, businesslike approaches, and may be intolerant of others who don't seem to be competent.

ISFP: Energy comes from the inner world of thought and emotions. Prefers facts, people, value-based decisions, somewhat adaptable, quiet, friendly, enjoys people in small numbers, is sensitive and caring, helps others, dislikes confrontation, and is a supportive team member.

ENTP: Energy comes from the outer world and spoken words. Prefers patterns and logically based decisions, is adaptable, likes new ideas, works to increase personal competence, an ingenious problem solver, tries new ideas, enjoys a good argument, and likes change.

ISFJ: Energy comes from the inner world of thought and emotion. Prefers facts, people, value-based decisions, organizes life around personal relationships, quiet, observer, conscientious, loyal, wants to be of service to people, perceptive of others' feelings, and dislikes conflict.

DISCUSSION QUESTION • 8.2

What's your Myers-Briggs type orientation? Based on the description in this chapter, guess the item from each pair that best describes your preferred way of behaving. Are there people with whom you are close that would fit in different categories? How might this affect a relationship if not addressed?

Extrovert (E)	_____	Introvert (I)	_____
Sensing (S)	_____	Intuiting (N)	_____
Thinking (T)	_____	Feeling (F)	_____
Judging (J)	_____	Perceiving (P)	_____

The purpose of understanding personality style differences is that people can begin to notice when style is causing problems. After style difference enters conscious awareness, someone can point out that the individuals struggling to work together have different ways of doing things. For example, instead of the extroverts assuming that anyone who wants to go to lunch will just invite himself or herself along, the more social individual will invite their silent, introverted coworkers who may be feeling left out. Sensors can appreciate that intuiters have good ideas but arrive at their conclusions in a different way. Thinkers will better appreciate that feelers will raise issues about how clients will react to a new policy that would never have occurred to the thinker. Companies with employees who have different styles can reduce conflict through style awareness training. Workplaces with homogeneous styles in their employees can identify potential areas of weakness. For example, studies find most students majoring in computer information science had a different style than other business majors (McPherson & Mensch, 2007; Reynolds, Adams, Ferguson, & Leidig, 2016). A one-style workforce might develop habits or blind spots that could harm their effectiveness.

The Gregorc Styles Model

Although the Myers-Briggs Inventory is very popular, other style perspectives are useful to gather more insights into human behavior. The **Gregorc Styles model** places people on a continuum between the perceptual preferences of *abstract* or *concrete* and the ordering preferences of *sequential* or *random*. Abstract individuals are very comfortable living in the world of ideas and concepts, looking at many possibilities, and playing with the what-ifs in decision making. Concretes, in contrast, want ideas backed by facts and experience and prefer to verify rather than to speculate. The Sequential versus Random dimension contrasts how people approach tasks, see time, and organize their world. A Sequential proceeds step by step, has a desire to complete one project before starting another, makes lists, and sees time as fixed. Randoms come at decisions from many different directions, enjoy multitasking, easily move from project to project, handle interruptions well, work from crisis to crisis, and see time as fluid (Gregorc, 1984, 2001; Gregorc Associates, 2017).

In a local business, two partners found themselves constantly at odds. One issue surrounded the morning meetings that the two had agreed to have twice a week on Tuesdays and Thursdays at 8 A.M. Lee was a concrete-sequential and always showed up to the meeting promptly at 7:55 with an agenda for discussion. Stella was an abstract-random. She'd come into the office at 7:30 and stop to chat with her employees. She believed contact early in the day was crucial for efficiency. She often helped employees with situations that could not wait due to customer needs. Stella generally arrived at the meeting with Lee around 8:15 or a little after. Lee saw this behavior as unprepared and lazy.

Conflict habitually arose at the beginning of Lee and Stella's meetings. Lee would be irritated that Stella wasn't prepared. Stella was confused by the formality of the meeting. Stella wanted her employees to know that she was available if needed and that they should interrupt her if they had a problem. Lee considered these meetings to be sacred and believed they should be protected from interruptions.

Lee and Stella became so conflicted that they required third-party intervention. A consultant helped them see each other's behavior as coming from different styles—Stella's abstract/random versus Lee's concrete/sequential tendencies. After exploring the benefits of each style to their business, they worked out an agreement for their meetings. They built in a fifteen-minute buffer to accommodate Stella's possible crisis fixing. During that fifteen minutes Lee would do something else until Stella indicated she was ready. The day before, Lee sent Stella an agenda that Stella could add to. They agreed to tell employees not to interrupt during these meetings. In sum, they became aware of the other's style and worked out a plan that took both styles into account.

DISCUSSION QUESTION • 8.3

What is your style according to the Gregorc model? Do your coworkers/friends have similar or different styles?

Social Style Model

The **social style model,** uses direct observation by a trained viewer to assess a person's behavior. Unlike the Myers-Briggs assessment where individuals rate themselves, the social style model is designed to be more objective. Two basic dimensions create the style: assertiveness and responsiveness.

Assertiveness describes whether a person "asks" or "tells" while interacting with others. Those who are direct and forceful in their communication, speak faster or louder, and have direct eye contact with forceful gestures are called *tell assertive*. Those who are reserved and speak less, slower, or softer while keeping their thoughts to themselves are labeled *ask assertive*.

Responsiveness measures how much emotion is displayed. *Controlled* individuals are more distant, formal, and do not express much emotion. Those who *emote* display feelings openly and are more animated.

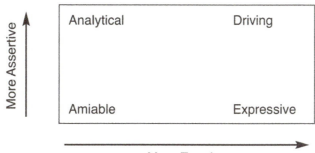

FIGURE 8.1 Social Style Model

Four dimensions are created from the ask-tell and control-emote pairings: High control and high assertive individuals are labeled *driving*—independent, task and results oriented, decisive, fast-paced, and dominating. Low control and high assertive individuals are *analytical*—prudent, task oriented, careful, logical, and low key. Low assertive and low emotive are *amiable*—dependable, relationship oriented, supportive, open, pliable, and conflict averse. High emotive and low assertive are *expressive*—visionary, animated, flamboyant, fast paced, impulsive, and opinionated (Furlong, 2005).

For example, Jamey ordered a hamburger, and the order wasn't exactly what she wanted. If Jamey quickly and forcefully told the waitress who delivered the meal that she doesn't like onions on her burger and ordered her to take them off while simulating gagging to show her disgust, she is tell assertive and emotive. If she waits until the waitress leaves and takes the onions off, she exhibits an ask assertive and controlled style.

Social styles, like personality styles, are useful to identify areas where miscommunication can lead to conflict. Equally competent coworkers with different styles might experience mutual frustration. One seems eager to please but not task oriented (amiable), whereas the other seems cold, heartless, and only interested in getting the job done (driving). The amiable person might withdraw or perceive the driver as a bully. The driver might perceive the amiable colleague as unskilled and slow. Bringing style differences to light could increase mutual respect and productivity.

Conflict Management Styles

A **conflict management style** is a patterned response to conflict situations. Conflict management styles are influenced by personality, culture, and social expectations. Each individual is believed to feel more comfortable with some conflict styles than with others but can, with time and effort, learn to adopt new styles. When they are used strategically rather than habitually, styles create more options for responding to conflict.

The Five Styles of Conflict Management

The most popular conflict management style perspective is a five-style approach adapted from Blake and Mouton's 1964 notion that styles exist at the intersection of one's *concern for personal goal achievement* (assertiveness) and one's *concern for the other party's goal achievement* (cooperativeness) (Hammer, 2005; Holt & DeVore, 2005).

Low concern for self and other leads to **avoidance** of the conflict. Low concern for self and high concern for the other results in **accommodation** of the other's wishes. High concern for self

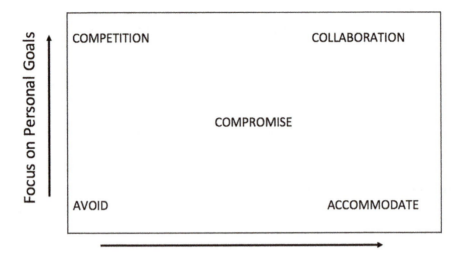

Focus on the Other Person's Goals

FIGURE 8.2 The Five-Style Conflict Management Grid

and low concern for the other person leads to **competition**. High concern for self and other manifests in **collaboration** where the needs of both parties are met. Moderate concern for self and other tends toward **compromise** so each person gives a little to gain a little.

Avoidance

Withdrawing from a situation to avoid it can be advantageous when the conflict is not yet ripe for settlement, the issue isn't very important, there will be little future contact between the individuals, or the situation might be dangerous.

In some families, avoiding hot topics is the only way to spend time together. For the sake of harmony, all family members avoid the areas of potential conflict (e.g., Don't ask CeCe about the tattoo, don't make comments about how Aunt Emily got revenge on her ex, and don't mention Rudee getting fired for sexting!).

DISCUSSION QUESTION • 8.4

Are there topics you do not discuss with your family because it causes conflict?

Disadvantages of avoidance include never engaging issues that need to be confronted. When conflict is suppressed, it typically bursts out in some other form. Several dysfunctional variations of avoidance occur. In the **withdraw-complain cycle**, the avoider withdraws from communicating with the other person in the conflict but complains to friends and family about it. For example, when asked by Cara if anything is wrong, Emma may say everything is fine (withdraw) and then complain to all of her friends about the problem with Cara. Instead of confronting the conflict, she talks about the other person behind her back.

Another dysfunctional practice is called **gunnysacking**. A gunnysack is a bag. When people avoid conflicts as they arise but keep mental score of the grievances, it is as if they are storing each offense in their gunnysack. When too many grievances accumulate, the gunnysack is full to bursting—and that is what happens. All of the issues are let out in one dramatic explosion as the bag bursts open.

Habitual avoidance can lead to a gradual erosion of relationships as avoidance leads to more avoidance. The longer an issue is avoided, the harder it becomes to discuss it. In the long term, unexpressed conflict becomes a weight dragging on the relationship. In frustration, one party may create a crisis—typically through an outburst, verbal aggressiveness, or some extreme measure. The negative encounter leads to less incentive to engage the issue, and both draw even further apart. At some point, it may seem easier to end the relationship than to face the accumulation of conflict.

In contrast, temporary avoidance, or **postponement** of a conflict encounter to a specific time, can be helpful. Because Mason knows that he gets too hot when surprised with a conflict, he learned to postpone discussion on new topics for at least an hour to give him time to adjust. When Abigail blurts out that she made reservations at an expensive restaurant for Friday so they can go out and have a good time, Mason will say, "Let's talk about this in an hour so I'm not distracted," instead of his old pattern, yelling about spending too much money.

DISCUSSION QUESTION • 8.5

When would avoidance be an effective strategy? What possible disadvantages to avoidance do you see?

Inaction chosen strategically to avoid a negative consequence or to not engage a trivial concern, can take three forms: (1) Choose not to confront the other person and withhold comments; (2) If engagement starts, use tactics to prevent more discussion; (3) If more discussion continues, move to have the topic declared taboo (Afifi & Guerrero, 2000; Roloff & Ifert, 2000). Generally, however, avoidance does not get rid of the issue. If the issue is important, it will reemerge. For example, there are a limited number of ways that friends can successfully avoid a topic without it being brought up again (Donovan-Kicken, Guinn, Romo, & Ciceraro, 2011; Donovan-Kicken, McGlynn, & Damron, 2012).

Competition

Competition can be advantageous when there are genuine scarce resources, time is short, it is fun, or achieving a goal is more important than the relationship. If competition is not advanced through tactics that humiliate and destroy people, it can be effective and appropriate. However, one danger of competition is that the loser gains a powerful motivation for retaliation, and destructive power struggles may ensue.

Disadvantages to competition occur when relationships are harmed or the other party feels humiliated. For example, a couple conflicting over which movie to see may result in one person winning. Both will go to the winning person's movie, but the loser can use passive-aggressive tactics to ensure that the "winner" does not have a good time, such as delaying departure so part of the movie is missed or talking during the movie (sometimes called a **lose-lose** result). In some cases, the price of winning may be too high.

DISCUSSION QUESTION • 8.6

Has your use of competition ever backfired and led to a worse outcome? When is competition most appropriate?

Compromise

Compromise can be advantageous because neither party wins or loses everything: Both give a little so nobody loses face. Compromise is quicker than collaboration and a natural fallback position to avoid destructive competition. It also can be used to entice avoiders and accommodators to engage a conflict. A meta-analysis of past studies indicated that in individualistic cultures, females use compromising styles more than males (Holt & DeVore, 2005).

The major disadvantage to compromise is that it sometimes produces a mediocre outcome. Even though compromise is valued as a quick way to settle an issue (let's split the difference), neither party has complete goal attainment. Moving too quickly to compromise doesn't allow for creativity that might mutually benefit everyone. For example, Kasi and Jake broke up after several years together and were preparing to move to new apartments. They had several items that they purchased together. A compromise might be to sell everything and split the money. With more time to explore their needs, however, the couple could determine that because Jake commuted and Kasi was moving near a bus line, the old car should go to Jake. Kasi was more into watching movies, so she should take digital projector and surround-sound system. She also really wanted the leather couch, and he wanted the dining set. Kasi had a refrigerator in her new apartment; Jake didn't, so Jake took the refrigerator. Both parties wanted the computer. Because Jake took the car, which was more expensive, they decided that Kasi should get the computer and Jake would buy a new one. Yes, selling everything and splitting the cash would have worked, but ultimately collaboration got the parties more of what each needed.

Accommodation

Accommodation, like avoidance, is advantageous when the one giving sway has little interest in the outcome, is minimizing a loss, does not want to rock the boat, is atoning for a wrong, or has high or low commitment in the relationship. In cases in which accommodation occurs where there is high commitment, the relationship is so valued that its maintenance may take priority over achieving other goals. In the workplace, the employee may give in because the commitment to, or need for, the job is more important than the issue at hand. Conversely, if the employee has a low commitment, he or she may feel that taking the effort to engage in conflict isn't worth the trouble.

An example of when agreeing with someone else prevented conflict occurred outside a club. While waiting to get in, Stuart made a comment to his date about a very large man urinating against a wall. The obviously drunk man overheard and aggressively came at Stuart saying, "Who do you think you are? Are you trying to be smart?" Stuart replied, "No, I really am stupid." The drunk, confused that he'd won so easily, said, "All right, then," and a fight was avoided. In this case, accommodation showed a high concern for self-preservation.

Disadvantages of accommodation include allowing power to become unbalanced, lack of personal goal achievement, and relationship lethargy. Like avoidance, accommodation can be chosen strategically if the cost of confrontation might be too high. An overbearing and hypercritical roommate may be accommodated because the other roommate determines that the cash coming in is more important than ending the current living situation. The disadvantage occurs when someone changes their view of the cost-benefit in the situation. The accommodating roommate allowed bad habits to become established instead of setting boundaries. When the roommate becomes sick of his overbearing housemate, it will be much harder to negotiate a change in behavior.

DISCUSSION QUESTION • 8.7

Have you ever used accommodation strategically? What damage could occur to someone who always accommodates?

Collaboration

Collaboration sometimes is presented as the best conflict management style. This style encourages the parties to communicate their interests and to work together to find the best alternative, i.e., all parties agree that it is the best solution they can come up with at the time—not necessarily that everyone thinks it is a perfect solution. Advantages include maximizing both parties' goal achievement, engaging in creative problem solving, and gaining commitment to the solution.

However, collaboration is a laborious process. Disadvantages include the length of time it takes, the amount of energy expended, and the potential manipulation of the process by clever competitors. If one or both of the collaborators also are perfectionists, trying to get the outcome to be "perfect" may hinder the process. Conflict managers need to determine if the effort that will be expended to collaborate is in their best interests. Sometimes a quick resolution through competition, accommodation, compromise, or even avoidance may be the optimal strategy. Case 8.3 compares the five styles in action.

DISCUSSION QUESTION • 8.8

What types of situations call for a collaborative style? In what situations would collaboration be ill-advised?

Most style frameworks have limits. For example, the five styles of interpersonal conflict are based on only two characteristics—concern for personal goals and concern for the other's goal achievement. Whenever just two choices (self or other concern) are available, limitations occur. Do individuals who withdraw in potentially violent situations or when they have little investment in the relationship really show a low concern for self? When a person accommodates a loved one to maintain social harmony, doesn't that indicate a high concern for a goal to create a satisfactory home life? Does all competition have to be win/lose in a negative way? If collaboration takes too long, is it really advancing each party's goals? Although the five conflict styles are a convenient way to view conflict, a superficial application of them may overvalue collaboration and undervalue the strategic advantages of avoidance, competition, compromise, or accommodation.

CASE 8.3

The Five Styles in Action

Julia and Layla are assigned as roommates their freshman year. From different backgrounds, they have little in common. Soon their differences begin to surface, and conflict is inevitable. Julia asks if she can borrow a scarf from Layla, who agrees. Soon Julia is borrowing shirts, coats, and whatever else she wants without asking.

If Layla is an avoider, she will suffer silently, think bad thoughts about Julia, and probably complain to friends. If Julia asks what is wrong, Layla will say she has to go study in the library and leave the room.

If Layla is an accommodator, she will say she doesn't mind that Julia borrows things. If Layla has a competitive style, she will confront Julia and demand that all her clothes be washed and never borrowed again.

If Layla uses a compromiser style, she will raise the issue of borrowing clothes with Julia. Then some middle ground will be sought. For example, the clothes can be borrowed if Julia asks every time in advance and washes and irons the clothes when returning them.

If Layla is a collaborator, she will ask Julia to sit down with her to discuss the roommate situation. She will frame the issue in a comprehensive way, asking what it means to be roommates and discussing each of their expectations. At some point, borrowing clothes will be discussed as part of the bigger picture.

Three Conflict Management Styles

The five-styles approach seems intuitive and is helpful in understanding different tactical approaches to conflict, but some researchers support the idea that there really are only three conflict management styles: avoidance, distributive engagement, and integrative engagement. **Avoidance** attempts to minimize the conflict. **Distributive engagement** is direct, competitive, and may include persistent attempts to wrest concessions from the other side. **Integrative engagement** is direct, cooperative, and seeks a mutually satisfactory outcome (Kuhn & Poole, 2000). Accommodation might manifest as a type of avoidance of conflict or as a result when one loses a distributive engagement. Compromise is seen as a tactic in distributive engagement (splitting the difference) or the fallback position when integrative engagement fails.

> ### KEY 8.1
>
> Competent conflict managers are comfortable with many conflict and communication styles.

Conflict Styles Across Cultures

Additional challenges arise for conflict management across cultural boundaries. In fact, the five-style approach to conflict management is built from a European-American perspective. Because European-American culture generally favors openness and direct speech, it is easy for those with its heritage to grasp how to become competent within the five styles. However, Kim and Leung (2000) observe that the application of the five-styles grid across cultures creates a problem. For example, people in some cultures think conflict avoidance is ideal.

> It can help the individual to control emotion, and may at times also allow the passive expressive of discontentment without the dangers of a direct challenge. . . . Avoidance (or withdrawal) strategies can be seen as positive or negative by members of different cultural orientations.
>
> (Kim & Leung, 2000, p. 241; see also Brew & Cairns, 2004)

In the collectivist cultures (discussed in Chapter 5), avoidance is a positive response that shows high concern for the other's face goals. In these cultures, avoidance is a subtle and positive strategy rather than from a European-American viewpoint that sees avoidance as weak.

Different style preferences also exist within geographic areas. For example, the U.S. is not one uniform culture. African-Americans, as well as other ethnic groups in the United States, do not necessarily embrace European-American conflict styles (Holt & DeVore, 2005). Walker (2004) observes that 517 American-Indian tribes use conflict management styles based on a different worldview from European-Americans. The Tsalagi (Cherokee) Talking Circle, Hawaiian Ho'opono-pono, the Haudenosaunee (Iroquois) Great Law of Peace, and the Navajo Justice and Harmony Ceremony, for example, all stem from a focus on involving everyone in a community, using ceremony as a balancing and healing process, bringing authentic emotions and apologies into the process, and building past lessons into the discussion of current conflicts.

Learning how to engage with another culture is a lifelong activity. For example, Melanie, who is a European-American mediator, was asked to facilitate a high-conflict meeting at a hospital on a local Indian reservation. Her Euro-American bias about conflict caused her to rush the stories that individuals were relating in an attempt to move the process along, not realizing that the stories were a culturally competent way of managing conflict. Mid-facilitation, after realizing her approach was not working, she apologized to the group for her cultural bias, discussed what she observed, and engaged in a different style of facilitation that was more culturally appropriate. Cultural lessons should be collected over the course of a lifetime and are considered valuable assets for conflict managers.

Some research tries to establish a common way of examining conflict across cultures, such as Hammer's (2002, 2005) **Intercultural Conflict Style Inventory.** As introduced in Chapter 5, Hammer examines two dimensions: how conflict is expressed and how emotions are expressed (see Table 5.2 in Chapter 5).

Knowledge of intercultural conflict styles is essential in the modern workplace. As Brew and Cairns (2004) state, workplace conflict across cultural groups "are due to differing needs, conflict management styles, assumptions and expectations, and stress related to today's fast-paced business environment" (p. 28). Knowledge of intercultural styles can prevent some conflicts and assist in the management of others.

In addition to personality and conflict management styles, individuals also develop personal communication habits. These communicative habits impact how conflicts develop and how they are managed. The next section discusses three areas: general communication style, escalators versus fractionators, and conversational style.

Communication Styles That Impact Conflict

Folger, Poole, and Stutman (2013) conclude that research indicates several types of communication behaviors serve as styles during conflict: assertiveness, cooperation, disclosiveness, empowerment, activeness, and flexibility. *Assertiveness* occurs when one directly states a goal. *Cooperation* (versus competition) differentiates between consideration of the other's goals or sole focus on one's own goals. How much one tells or reveals goals and strategies is called *disclosiveness*. *Empowerment* assesses whether power is shared or hoarded. The intensity of involvement in managing a conflict when it first arises is a measure of *activeness*. Finally, *flexibility* addresses how open one is to new ideas in managing a conflict. Difficulties arising from general communication style can impact conflict. For example, individuals who are nondisclosive may have trouble talking about personal goals, which is necessary for collaboration.

Escalators and Fractionators

Those who see conflict as a crisis and become very excited have a style of **escalation**. What feels natural to an escalator is making a conflict bigger. At their extreme, escalators add other conflicts to the mix to create a crisis. In contrast, **fractionators** feel it is natural to become calm and go straight to problem solving.

There are obvious areas where escalator and fractionator styles clash. First, they are pulling in opposite directions: One wants drama and the other wants calm. Second, because the behaviors are going in opposite directions, misunderstanding will occur. While the escalator is venting, the fractionator may make comments like this: "If you weren't so emotional, we could work this out." These words probably are perceived as judgmental and that the other doesn't care about the problem. More escalation may result. Fractionators probably see escalators as too excitable and out of control. Ironically, the differences can precipitate a conflict around how to behave during conflict as each person tries to push the other into behaving "correctly." During conflict, fractionators can adapt by withholding the impulse to leap to problem solving and allowing the escalator time to explore the size of the issue emotionally.

In the film *A League of Their Own*, the manager of a 1940s World War II era women's baseball team used an aggressive escalation style. When an error occurred that allowed the other team to score, he responded by yelling and exaggerating the importance of the mistake (escalation)—resulting in some players crying, to which he would exclaim, "There is no crying in baseball!" Toward the end of the film, the manager confronted a player who missed an outfield throw. Visibly shaking with rage, he controlled his natural response and calmly said, "Try to practice the cutoff throw over the winter." The manager had learned to moderate his style.

Conversational Style

With so many options, how can we determine the most effective way to interact with others? **Conversational style** refers to speech and vocal habits—for example, how fast to talk, how long to pause between speakers, and whether to interrupt or overlap while another person is speaking (Beaumont & Wagner, 2004). Individual conversational styles can inflame or subdue a conflict. For example, how long should the pause be between when one person finishes speaking and the other begins? Depending on what was learned while growing up, the **pause gap** could be several beats— before or after the other finishes speaking. Fast talkers may perceive slow talkers to be or uninvolved or even a bit dim. At times, it can be difficult for those with a slower response speed to enter a conversation: Faster people take every pause as an opportunity to capture the conversational lead.

Some linguists (Tannen, 1994, 2007) advance the notion that there are two basic European-American conversational styles: report and rapport. **Report talk** is a style focused on keeping the floor while talking, so the speaker learns many facts, figures, and stories, and gathers techniques for interrupting and capturing the topic from other speakers. For two individuals within this style, a conversation is like the child's game of King of the Hill. Each individual attempts to push the other's topics aside, wrestle for topic control, and gain the conversational high ground. In **rapport talk**, the individuals work together to build a conversation by nodding, making verbal sounds indicating one is listening ("Uh huh"), and telling short stories on the same theme. Then the two switch roles (Tannen, 1994).

Difficulties arise when a report person converses with a rapport person because of style clash. Each will follow the rules for his or her conversational style, and each will encounter unsatisfactory results. The report person will do most of the talking while the rapport person plays the supportive role and patiently waits for a turn. When the floor is not relinquished, the rapport individual perceives the report talker as uncaring, egotistical, and rude. The report person views the rapport talker as uninteresting, uninformed, and less powerful for not joining in the fray. They think if the other person had anything important to say, it should be said without prompting or turn taking. These attributions about the other are a direct reaction to style clash.

Even regional dialect or vocal inflection can cause attribution errors. A coworker may speak quite differently from most of the group and lead to stereotypes that become the basis for an interpersonal conflict. A group of professionals in training were practicing a model in which two individuals worked together while mediating a dispute. After the first half hour, one mediator, with a fast New York City style of speaking, would make a comment, and the other mediator and disputants would ignore him. A few moments later, the other mediator, from Denver, would make the same comment, and the disputants, also from the West, would respond positively. What was happening in this situation? Because of stereotypes of a New Yorker's verbal style as aggressive and uncaring, the others in the room discounted the content of that mediator's remarks. Frustrated at being ignored, it would be easy for the New Yorker to attack the group verbally and precipitate a conflict. At minimum, unconscious attributions about the New Yorker led to some social exclusion.

Conversational styles are important because "research by social psychologists has confirmed that speakers who use similar speech styles rate each other as more likeable, warm, trustworthy and friendly than those who use different speech styles" (Beaumont & Wagner, 2004, p. 340). Similarly, the negative feelings that arise when styles clash can be perceived as goal interference and precipitate conflict. For example, research indicates that adolescents tend to use a *high-involvement conversational style* with frequent interruptions and overlapping speech. Parents tend to exhibit a *low-involvement conversational style* with few overlaps or successful interruptions. This means that parents expect children will not interrupt with excuses while being lectured. According to one study, this difference in style caused frustration on both sides and resulted in higher perceptions of conflict (Beaumont & Wagner, 2004).

Emotional Intelligence

The realization that intellectual intelligence (often expressed as IQ) had little to do with interpersonal competence led to a search for a companion concept to fill in the rest of the picture. **Emotional intelligence (EQ)** encompasses self-awareness, managing emotions, self-motivation, recognizing emotions in others, and handling relationships (Cherniss & Adler, 2000). We should note that current EQ tests emerged from the European-American worldview and are indexed to Western values.

Behind EQ theory is the notion that emotions create energy. Positive energy comes with positive emotions; negative energy comes with negative emotions. Those who test low in EQ have little self-awareness and ability to manage their emotions, are not self-motivating, cannot recognize emotions in others, and don't handle relationships well. People with the opposite characteristics test higher in EQ (Bagshaw, 2000).

Hughes, Patterson, and Terrell (2012) explain that emotions are what we feel, with fear and desire among the most powerful primary emotions. Emotions are processed by the brain automatically "without having to consider them rationally" (p. 13). The brain then orders hormone or chemical reactions that produce physical and mood reactions such as stress, the elation of love, or the excitement of fear. The significance for conflict management is that automatic programs might be overly influencing your behavior. Attention to emotional intelligence helps build the awareness and skills to take back control.

EQ is measured through many copyrighted instruments. After analyzing all the EQ tests, Hughes et al. (2012) found sixteen key competencies that cut across the tests (see Table 8.3).

The competencies are important to conflict management in numerous ways. A better *self-regard*, or positive view of oneself, enables self-confidence and less fear of failure during conflict, allowing new tactics and styles to be developed. EQ researchers find self-regard one of the highest predictors of interpersonally competent behavior.

Self-awareness is the ability to understand what is being felt. Individuals often feel that "something is wrong" or "this is the right thing to do" without consciously knowing why. A higher self-awareness brings the causes of these feelings to the surface. The counterpart to self-awareness is awareness of others' feelings, or *empathy*. Self-awareness helps conflict managers keep their goals in the forefront and not be sidetracked during conflict.

Assertiveness is the ability to express oneself and advocate for goals without being verbally aggressive. Assertiveness is a hallmark of the emotionally intelligent person. Assertive individuals garner the respect of others because they can be depended on to state what is important in ways that don't

TABLE 8.3 Sixteen Key Emotional Intelligence Competencies

- Self-regard
- Self-actualization
- Emotional self-awareness
- Assertiveness
- Independence
- Emotional expression
- Empathy
- Social responsibility
- Interpersonal relationships
- Problem solving
- Impulse control
- Reality testing
- Flexibility
- Stress tolerance
- Optimism
- Happiness

demean others. When individuals in conflict know that someone is assertive, rather than avoidant or aggressive, trust can be developed.

A person who is not overly influenced by a group exhibits *independence*. The opposite of independence might be **codependence**, where a person is so fixated on another individual that he or she can't make decisions without knowing that person's view. Although a degree of independence is required to know one's goals in life, too much independence may be damaging during conflict with significant others. Too much independence can be perceived as selfishness. Competent conflict managers aim to balance independence with *social responsibility*, indicating a concern for the welfare of others.

TOOLBOX 8.1   What's Your Emotional Intelligence?

Reflect back on past interactions with a specific individual. Then answer each of the following while thinking about that relationship. The more "Yes" answers you give, the higher your emotional intelligence.

1. Are you aware of your own feelings?
2. Do you usually sense what others are feeling, even when they don't verbalize them?
3. Does awareness of how others feel lead you to have compassion or empathy for them?
4. When angry, can you still interact with civility and not make the situation worse?
5. Can you focus on the long-term goal without getting distracted or sidetracked?
6. Do you keep trying to reach your goals, even if it is tempting to give up?
7. Can you use your feelings to help make decisions?
8. Can you get the things done that you want when you experience stress, or do your feelings keep you from moving forward?

Source: Excerpted from Bagshaw (2000, pp. 61–62)

Self-actualization involves becoming the best person one can be—to climb to the top of **Maslow's hierarchy of needs**. Self-actualized individuals have attained basic survival resources: have food and shelter (physiological needs), feel safe (security needs), have people to be affectionate with and give affection to (belonging needs), and have self-respect and are respected by others (esteem needs). With the bottom of Maslow's pyramid of needs mastered, they can work on self-actualization, the last step. For Maslow, the highest personal achievement is a balanced inner life and an appreciation of others (as opposed to a need to dominate others). *Expressing emotions* is a way to meet needs.

Many conflicts occur at the lower levels in Maslow's hierarchy—contesting for scarce resources needed to survive, to feel secure, or to gain esteem and affection. By establishing meaningful and mutually satisfying relationships with others, emotional maturity is developed and things like unearned sarcasm are less hurtful when received and less likely to be used by a person with a balanced sense of self-esteem. Much of the bickering and sarcasm that people find so hurtful are attacks on self-esteem. Self-actualization should be balanced with *interpersonal relationships* because it is difficult to know oneself without interacting with others.

Stress tolerance allows an overall higher quality of life without emotional or physical overstimulation and negative health effects. Individuals who can tolerate general stress also can tolerate more uncertainty about the outcome of a conflict while collaborative strategies are developed. Those who can manage stress have more options available during conflict. Controlling stress relates to *impulse control*. Negative impulses drive people to do things that are unproductive and they probably will later regret. Although some impulses may be good, such as grabbing someone who is about to fall, many other impulses are unproductive, such as punching a hole in a wall in anger. Those who think before they act can control the impulse to say hurtful things or to use destructive tactics and will become better conflict managers.

Reality testing means viewing the world as it is rather than how one might wish it to be. It enables a clear view of the real consequences of actions. Hopes and dreams may be comforting, but competent conflict managers can cut through the fog of wishful thinking to see the real world.

Rigidity inhibits the creativity that is necessary for competent conflict management. *Flexibility* in how goals are achieved allows variability in approach, processes used, or the shape of the exact outcome. Flexibility does not mean giving in to the desires of others at the cost of personal goals. Paired with flexibility is *problem solving*. Useful problem-solving skills include being able to define issues, research facts, develop creative ideas, and evaluate which proposal is the best solution

The final two skills of emotional intelligence are *optimism* and *happiness*. Those who believe that problems can be overcome are more likely to work to overcome them. Although it may seem strange to phrase it this way, those who allow themselves to be happy will be more effective conflict managers than those whose self-concept is built on sustaining an image of personal tragedy.

Emotional intelligence provides skill sets and characteristics that make people better conflict managers. People with high emotional intelligence may be more successful in their personal and professional lives than those who have low emotional intelligence.

EQ is an interesting concept for conflict managers, because low EQ may explain the insensitive patterns of interaction that precipitate some conflicts. It also helps explain why some individuals could, with good intentions, believe that everything would work out if the other person would just not be so emotional.

The EQ literature also directly confronts the age-old advice that negotiators suppress emotions and stick mainly to logic. Negotiation scholars are beginning to agree. Katz and Sosa (2015) detail how each of the components of emotional intelligence are strategically advantageous for negotiations. They comment:

> The emotionally intelligent negotiator is acutely aware of the role of emotions in the negotiation process and use the information furnished by emotions to guide her moves and

countermoves. She regards the wholesale suppression of feelings as both unrealistic and unproductive.

(p. 60)

DISCUSSION QUESTION • 8.9

How can each of the sixteen elements of emotional intelligence be of help to you?

Transforming Dysfunctional Communication

This chapter offers many opportunities to speculate about communication style and behavior patterns along a number of style dimensions—personality, conflict management, emotional intelligence, social style, among others. It is important to know how a style interacts with others and whether the style one currently uses works productively or causes more distress; is it functional or dysfunctional?

With awareness, the conflict manager can bring differences in style or emotional intelligence deficits to a conscious level. Sometimes just verbalizing that someone has a different style can transform the negative attributions being made. Saying, "I've noticed that we have different ways of approaching this problem" or "I've noticed that you're better at the detail work and I'm better at the long-range vision" may be helpful. At a board meeting, two individuals were in conflict over whether to hire an executive director. One advocate passionately focused on the vision of making the organization bigger and more successful and was confident that the details could be worked out if the plan was adopted. Another board member argued against the plan because details were lacking, like who would fill out the forms to deduct payroll taxes or what deliverables the executive director would have for each month. When a third board member observed that the two individuals had different styles—one being a visionary and one being detail oriented—and that both styles were necessary for any plan to work, the entire nature of the discussion was transformed from competitive to collaborative. Awareness of styles affords the opportunity to transform dysfunctional conflict into more productive possibilities. Table 8.4 overviews several conclusions about style.

TABLE 8.4 Conclusions About Style and Conflict Management

- Style explains how good people can see the same thing in opposite ways.
- Gut reactions coming from style aren't automatically superior.
- We can't change somebody else's basic style.
- Styles can mesh together if we are aware of our strengths and weaknesses.
- Relationships are stronger if people recognize style differences.
- Strong teams lean into each other's strengths and prop up each other's weaknesses.
- With time and effort, new styles can be learned.

Summary

Styles are patterns of behavior that influence the way individuals communicate. Awareness of differing styles can help us recognize style clashes when they arise and provide options for adapting personal styles to be more effective. Many problems attributed to "personality conflicts" can be understood as differences in style.

Personality styles are a popular way to understand how people approach conflict differently. The Myers-Briggs Type Indicator categorizes people along four distinct pairs: extrovert/introvert, thinking/intuitive, feeling/perceiving, and judging/perceiving. The Gregorc styles model identifies people as abstracts, concretes, randoms, or sequentials. Gregorc style indicates how people see time, deal with details, and organize thoughts. The social style model uses direct observation to assess assertiveness and responsiveness.

The five styles of conflict management typology has been widely used, modified, and adapted since 1964. It includes avoidance, accommodation, competitiveness, compromise, and collaboration. Much of the style research is based in Western culture, and its usefulness breaks down when applied to non-Western cultures. Avoidance and accommodation may be seen as more ideal strategies in collectivist cultures than in individualistic cultures. Communication styles are key in assessing the effectiveness of a conflict manager. The approach to conflict we take includes whether we hide or disclose information, if we empower others or attempt to keep power to ourselves, and our levels of activeness and flexibility. Other communication styles that affect conflict are whether individuals escalate or fractionate conflict. Even conversational styles can affect outcomes. Learning to adapt a communication style to the situation is possible with awareness, desire, and training. The sixteen characteristics of the emotionally intelligent person correlate with conflict management competence. Understanding communication styles and emotional intelligence are key to transforming dysfunctional conflict.

Chapter Resources

Exercises

1. Take and self-score a personality test. Think about how you engage in conflict in one specific relationship that is important to you. Take the test a second time thinking about a different context—perhaps how you engage in conflict at work with your supervisor, at home with a significant other, or with a college roommate. In a group, compare and discuss your scores. Are you surprised by the outcome? Did your score change? Discuss with your group why styles might be different in these two contexts. What are the advantages and disadvantages of your style during interpersonal conflict? (Suggested source: Conerly & Tripathi, 2004)
2. In small groups, observe your classmates to guess their social style. Check to see if your observations match their self-perceptions. How might each social style be an advantage or a disadvantage during interpersonal conflict?
3. Ancient Greeks and Romans categorized four temperaments based on types of fluids in the body: sanguine (cheerful, optimistic, vain, unpredictable), phlegmatic (cool, persevering, needing direction), melancholic (soft-hearted, does things for others, slow to respond), and choleric (stubborn, domineering, opinionated, self-confident). How different or similar are these typologies from modern personality theories?
4. What role does culture or subculture play in your development of a personal style? How do cultural styles affect conflict management between people from different cultures? What are your biggest challenges when in conflict with others?
5. Make a list of tactics that people use to avoid engaging in conflict. When are these tactics productive and when are they unproductive?
6. What's your style?

    Place an X on the continuum to mark your conversational preference at work. What problems might arise when working with someone with an opposite preference?
    Just business _____Social talk OK
    Ask for your help _____Tell you what to do

Single tasker _____Multitasker
Polite talk _____Blunt talk

7.   Select a conflict with a roommate. During conversations about that conflict, identify examples of assertiveness, cooperation, disclosiveness, empowerment, activeness, or flexibility. Explain how those behaviors affected the conflict (for better or for worse).

Essay/Research Topics

1.   Use the social style model while observing a boss, roommate, or friend for one week. Write your observations in a journal. Using your insights as evidence, write an essay that explains the other person's social style. What difficulties might arise for the two of you during conflict because of his or her social style?
2.   Write an essay about your intercultural conflict management style. Using Hammer's four intercultural styles, identify the style of your root cultural group. Do your conflict behaviors match those of your cultural group, or do you fit more comfortably in one of the other categories? What challenges will you face when engaging in conflict with persons from other cultural groups?
3.   Assess your development along the sixteen dimensions of emotional intelligence. In which areas are you the most competent? In which areas could you increase your emotional intelligence?
4.   Examine research on the personality type of your major compared to other majors. Is your major dominated by one personality type?

Mastery Case

Examine Mastery Case 8A, "The Doggie Discontent." What styles are evident in the case?

The Doggie Discontent

Before Tess and Molly became roommates, Tess made sure that Molly would be fine with her lovable little dog Gretel, a five-year-old schnauzer. After about two months, Molly met Tess at the door, obviously upset:

Molly: "We need to talk. I hate living here! I can't stand your dog anymore. She jumps on me and the house smells like a dog. I like some animals, but I hate your dog!"
Tess: (Shocked). "You knew about Gretel when we moved in. She's a schnauzer for God's sake—they love everybody. It's not like she's a pit bull and going to attack you. What did you expect?"
Molly: "I was hoping the apartment wouldn't allow dogs."
Tess: "I wouldn't have moved in with you then. I could never live without Gretel."
Molly: "I think you should get rid of her."
Tess: "That is not going to happen! You knew I had a dog. And I don't have the money to move. You got yourself into this situation, so you figure a way out of it."

Molly left the apartment and slammed the door. Gretel, sensing something was wrong, walked over to comfort Tess.

References

Afifi, W. A., & Guerrero, L. K. (2000). Motivations underlying topic avoidance in close relationships. In S. Petronio (Ed.), *Balancing the secrets of private disclosures* (pp. 165–179). Mahwah, NJ: Erlbaum.

Bagshaw, M. (2000). Emotional intelligence: Training people to be affective so they can be effective. *Industrial and Commercial Training*, *32*(2), 61–65.

Beaumont, S. L., & Wagner, S. L. (2004). Adolescent-parent verbal conflict: The roles of conversational styles and disgust emotions. *Journal of Language and Social Psychology*, *23*(3), 338–368.

Brew, F. P., & Cairns, D. R. (2004). Styles of managing interpersonal workplace conflict in relation to status and face concerns: A study with Anglos and Chinese. *The International Journal of Conflict Management*, *15*(1), 27–56.

Cherniss, C., & Adler, M. (2000). *Promoting emotional intelligence in organizations*. Alexandria, VA: American Society for Training and Development Publications.

Conerly, K., & Tripathi, A. (2004, Summer). What is your conflict style? Understanding and dealing with your conflict style. *Journal for Quality & Participation*, 16–20.

Donovan-Kicken, E., Guinn, T. D., Romo, L. K., & Ciceraro, L. D. (2011). Thanks for asking, but let's talk about something else: Reactions to topic-avoidance messages that feature different interaction goals. *Communication Research*, *40*(3), 308–336.

Donovan-Kicken, E., McGlynn, J., & Damron, J. C. (2012). When friends deflect questions about sensitive information: Questioner's cognitive complexity and explanations for friends' avoidance. *Western Journal of Communication*, *76*(2), 127–147.

Folger, J. P., Poole, M. S., & Stutman, R. K. (2013). *Working through conflict* (7th ed.). Boston: Pearson.

Furlong, G. T. (2005). *The conflict resolution toolbox*. Mississauga, Canada: Wiley.

Gregorc, A. F. (1984). *Gregorc style delineator: Development technical and administration manual*. Maynard, MA: Gabriel Systems, Inc.

Gregorc, A. F. (2001). *Adult's guide to style*. Maynard, CA: Gabriel Systems.

Gregorc Associates Inc. (2017, January 25). Gregorc.com. Accessed 1 February 2017.

Hammer, M. (2002). *Resolving conflict across the cultural divide: Differences in intercultural conflict styles*. Hammer Consulting.

Hammer, M. R. (2005). The intercultural conflict style inventory: A conceptual framework and measure of intercultural conflict resolution approaches. *International Journal of Intercultural Relations*, *29*, 675–695.

Holt, J. L., & DeVore, C. J. (2005). Culture, gender, organizational role, and styles of conflict resolution: A meta-analysis. *International Journal of Intercultural Relations*, *29*, 165–196.

Hughes, M., Patterson, L. B., & Terrell, J. B. (2012). *Emotional intelligence in action* (2nd ed.). San Francisco: Pfeiffer.

Hullett, C. R., & Tamborini, R. (2001). When I'm within my rights: An expectancy-based model of actor evaluative and behavioral responses to compliance-resistance strategies. *Communication Studies*, *52*(1), 1–16.

Johnson, D. I., & Lewis, N. (2010). Perceptions of swearing in the work setting: An expectancy violations theory perspective. *Communication Reports*, *23*, 106–118.

Jourdain, K. (2004). Communication styles and conflict. *The Journal for Quality & Participation*, *27*(2), 23–25.

Katz, N. H., & Sosa, A. (2015). The emotional advantage: The added value of the emotionally intelligent negotiator. *Conflict Resolution Quarterly*, *33*(1), 57–74.

Kim, M-S., & Leung, T. (2000). A multicultural view of conflict management styles: Review and critical synthesis. In M. Roloff (Ed.), *Communication yearbook 23* (pp. 227–269). Thousand Oaks, CA: Sage.

Kuhn, T., & Poole, M. S. (2000). Do conflict management styles affect group decision making? *Human Communication Research*, *26*(4), 558–590.

McPherson, B., & Mensch, S. (2007). Student's personality type and choice of major. *Academy of Information and Management Science Journal*, *10*(2), 1–18.

Reynolds, J. H., Adams, D. R., Ferguson, R. C., & Leidig, P. M. (2016). *The personality of a computing major: It makes a difference.* Proceedings of the EDSIG Conference, Las Vegas.

Roloff, M. E., & Ifert, D. E. (2000). Conflict management through avoidance: Withholding complaints, suppressing arguments, and declaring topics taboo. In S. Petronio (Ed.), *Balancing the secrets of private disclosures* (pp. 151–163). Mahwah, NJ: Erlbaum.

Tannen, D. (1994). *Talking from 9 to 5.* New York: Morrow.

Tannen, D. (2007). *Talking voices: Repetition, Dialogue and imagery in conversational discourse* (2nd ed.). New York: Cambridge University Press.

Walker, P. O. (2004). Decolonizing conflict resolution. *American Indian Quarterly, 28*(3/4), 527–549.

Chapter 9

Negotiation

Vocabulary

Anchor point

Assertive negotiation

Bargaining range

Boulwarism

Coalition

Collaborative negotiation

Commonality

Compliance gaining

Contingency agreement

Directness

Distributive negotiation

Fogging

Gaslighting

Gunnysacking

Hypothetical offer

Integrative negotiation

Interest

Issue

Lose/lose outcome

Metacommunication

Mirroring

Mutual gains

Negotiation

Positions

Postponement

Quid pro quo

Reformed sinner

Reframing

Splitting the difference

Threat

Values

Verbal aggressiveness

Winner's curse

Objectives

After reading the chapter, you should be able to:

1. Differentiate between appropriate and inappropriate tactics in competitive negotiation
2. Differentiate between appropriate and inappropriate tactics in collaborative negotiation
3. Develop a strategy to move competitive negotiators toward more collaborative processes

"They always say time changes things, but you actually have to change them yourself."

Negotiation is a common endeavor, and most people negotiate every day. Merging in traffic, choosing where to eat with a friend, and determining topics for conversation all involve some negotiation. In the broadest sense, a mother's stern glance at her daughter can be a condensed negotiation they engage in every weeknight, with a stern look serving as the winning argument, as it does in Case 9.1.

CASE 9.1

I Don't Have That Much Homework

Mother: "Put down your phone and do your homework."
Daughter: "Can't I have any privacy to text my friends!? You always nag me. I don't have that much homework anyway."
Mother: "Do your homework first and then you can chat with your friends. If you don't have that much, it won't take very long."
Daughter: "Just fifteen more minutes."
Mother: "Two minutes or I'm taking your cell."
Daughter: "Mom, that's so unfair!"
Mother: [Looks sternly at daughter.]
Daughter: "All right, all right, I'm putting it down!"

What Is Negotiation?

As people enter a subway car, one seat is left. The individual who put her bag on the seat may pick it up voluntarily to allow someone to sit, or a nonverbal negotiation may occur. A passenger who has no seat may gesture at the seat as if to say, "Mind if I sit?" Friends negotiate where to go for coffee or when to gather at the local club on Friday night. Couples negotiate where to go on vacation. Students negotiate due dates of assignments with their professors. A common cause of conflict among college roommates is not specifically negotiating expectations and boundaries when they move into an apartment. Who will do the dishes? How often is the house cleaned? What does "clean" mean? Who does what cleaning? Can we have overnight guests? Are there times when the house should be quiet for studying? Upfront negotiation can preserve relationships and make expectations known (McCorkle, 2015).

Negotiation, or bargaining, occurs when one person (or group) engages in conversation with another person (or group) to pursue goals. Fisher, Ury, and Patton (1993) more simply define negotiation as the "ability to persuade someone to do something" (p. 4). There are contrasting approaches to the pursuit of goals: acting persuasively, coercively, entirely egocentrically, or with consideration of the other party. This chapter differentiates between two basic approaches to negotiation—competitive and cooperative—and the tactical choices inherent in each approach.

For negotiation to succeed, several conditions must be met (Table 9.1). First, the individuals need some meaningful connection or common interests. Without an apparent connection, there may be no incentive to negotiate.

TABLE 9.1 The Conditions for Negotiation

- The people involved must have some type of interconnection.
- The outcome must be unpredictable to some degree.
- The difference must be about negotiable issues.
- The people must be willing to communicate.

Second, the outcome of the negotiation is unpredictable. If one party is confident that her or his goals will be met with 100 percent certainty, there will be little or no incentive to negotiate.

Third, the issue must be something that is negotiable. A clash of values at the purely "I'm virtuous and you are not" level really isn't negotiable. **Values** are deeply rooted feelings about right and wrong and generally are not negotiable. For example, people are unlikely to negotiate away their cherished feelings of patriotism toward a country or devout adherence to a religion. However, parties may be willing to negotiate issues such as what behaviors are appropriate when expressing patriotism.

Issues can be classified into the same four categories as goals in conflict: substantive, process, relationship, and image/face (discussed in Chapter 4). In a conflict around a substantive goal of getting a raise, the issue also is substantive. The issue is the part of the conflict being discussed. *Substantive issues* are the points of clash that occur when one person's substantive goals are perceived as interfering with another person's needs. In other words, negotiations around salary, work schedules, or other relatively tangible things are mainly substantive.

Relationship issues arise when individuals negotiate their different goals for the relationship. For example, one may want romantic intimacy and the other wants just to be friends. The negotiation will be about boundaries for behavior in their relationship, or if the relationship will continue at all. Coworkers often have to negotiate relationship issues—are we friends or just working in the same building?

Identity/face issues perhaps are overtly negotiated less often than other issues, but may be more central in many conflicts. Image or face management is a constant part of life. Negotiation sometimes involves a negative tactic of attacking someone's self-concept (face). Some scholars argue that face attacks occur through verbal aggressiveness because the attacker thinks he or she is not skilled enough to achieve goals through persuasion (Aloia & Solomon, 2015; Rogan & La France, 2003). In other words, when people fear that they won't be able to reach their substantive goals, they may shift the conversation to relationship goals or face subversion. It may be easier to call someone "stupid" than to explain one's deeper feelings or look for the facts that support one's assertions. Some point to anger as the predecessor of verbal aggressiveness and suggest anger awareness and suppression are needed skills for these individuals (Aloia & Solomon, 2016). Other scholars suggest verbal aggressiveness is a learned behavior from families and media. Children's television programs contain over 18 acts of verbal aggression an hour, with no negative consequences for the characters portrayed (Glascock, 2013). Many interactive games are based on aggression and violence.

Identifying issues can be problematic due to the dynamic nature of goals and the frequent screening of the real issue with other issues. Is it a relationship issue or a process issue when one partner doesn't consult the other about a major decision? What may begin as a substantive issue (where to live?) can become a conflict over a relationship or about each person's self-identity (face issue), depending on what type of goal interference is perceived. Face issues often are cloaked as a substantive issue (arguing about something trivial like a stapler as a means of scoring points and saving face). As you learn negotiation tactics, keep in mind that identification of the appropriate issue is key to making negotiation efficient and effective.

The final condition for negotiation is a willingness to communicate. If one person is unwilling to engage in negotiation, little progress can be made. Negotiation by its nature involves communication as parties attempt to meet their needs.

DISCUSSION QUESTION • 9.1

Explore the necessity of the four conditions needed for successful negotiation. How important is it for parties to feel interconnected? How does uncertainty affect negotiations? What options exist when one person in a negotiation is unwilling to communicate?

Because the likelihood of a successful negotiation is affected by the presence of the four conditions just described, sometimes an individual will need to help set those conditions in place. For instance, Esther is a supervisor over several employees. In the day-to-day operations, she is not required to negotiate with employees. She has the authority to order employees to do their work in specific ways and can refuse to listen to their requests. When dealing with a high-power person who is uncommunicative or unwilling to negotiate, those in low-power positions must persuade the other person to enter into negotiation. Esther's employees could bring her to the negotiation table in a number of ways. They could convince her that negotiating will serve her interests (an interconnection) or explain if she does not negotiate she won't know what is going on (establish unpredictability). The employees could appeal to a higher authority, the company's owner, to require Esther to negotiate (force communication). Using any of these tactics with a person of higher power, however, does have inherent risks.

Ideally, appealing to someone's interests is the most collaborative way to bring an uncooperative negotiator to the table. Carla wants to change her scheduled shift at the bar where she works. From past experience, she knows that her boss, Ramon, will say "No" if she directly asks for a change in shift. He has the power to say "No" and does not see anything in it for him if he negotiates. Carla analyzes the situation to create a strategy that will engage Ramon's self-interest and persuade him to negotiate. She chooses to say, "Ramon, I know that you have difficulty filling the schedule during the holidays, and I was thinking that if I took some time off now when no one else has anything going on, then next month I could work the two weekend shifts when everyone will want that time off." By focusing on a need that Ramon already recognizes (filling hard spots in the holiday schedule), Carla engages his interest. By not giving too much information at the outset about the specifics of her goal (getting the next two Saturdays off), Carla has a better chance of avoiding Ramon's automatic "No" response.

KEY 9.1

Appealing to the other person's interests can transform an uncooperative negotiator into a cooperative negotiation partner.

Contrasting Approaches to Negotiation

Negotiation strategies and tactics align with the two views of conflict presented in Chapter 3: competition and cooperation. Framing a negotiation as a competition (win/lose) would naturally lead to competitive (power-based) negotiation strategies; conversely a cooperative framework would promote collaborative or mutual gains negotiation techniques (needs-based).

Competitive bargainers place a higher priority on achieving personal goals over meeting the needs of others. Competitors work to control the allocation of perceived scarce resources (**distributive negotiation**). Control is a primary strategy of a competitive negotiator. Commonly, competitive negotiators engage in tactics to manipulate the negotiation process and how issues are framed, and they work to rig the criteria applied to attain an outcome that will achieve their self-interest. If one party is able to maintain control of the process, the other party's bargaining options are reduced significantly. In competition, winning is defined by getting the best outcome for oneself.

The other approach to negotiation, cooperative, also is called **mutual gains**, **collaborative negotiation**, or **integrative negotiation**. Cooperative approaches are designed to keep personal goals clearly in mind while simultaneously considering the interests of the other person. Cooperative negotiators explore mutually beneficial options and seek outcomes allowing maximum goal achievement for both parties. Winning is defined as what is best for all concerned, instead of what is best for only one side.

DISCUSSION QUESTION • 9.2

How does the framing of a negotiation as either competitive or cooperative affect the relationship of the parties? Are you more comfortable negotiating competitively or cooperatively? What influences your preference for one approach over another?

Competitive Negotiation

Competition is driven by a desire to win but can involve a wide array of techniques. Competitors may engage in tactics distinguished by cordial assertiveness, polite dialogue, and appropriate positioning. They also can use manipulation, outrageous demands, dirty tricks, and destructive aggressiveness to gain the upper hand. In an organization where there is one promotion available and the hiring choice will be made from an internal pool of candidates, competitive negotiation can be appropriate and effective if everyone puts forward their best efforts and uses nondestructive tactics. However, the competition can be perilous (to the parties, as well as to the long-term success of the organization) if employees undercut each other, spread rumors, and try to destroy the other applicants in an effort to gain an edge. Although circumstances may call for competition, how one engages in competition is a choice. Recognizing the options available within the realm of competitive negotiation is what distinguishes skilled and ethical competitors from those who leave paths of destruction in their bargaining wake.

Ineffective Competition Versus Effective Competition

At the heart of competition is the power to influence the other to achieve a desired outcome. Some competitors may exhibit one or more unhealthy or destructive approaches in order to win. First, competitors may lose sight of tangible goals and make the outcome of the competition personal. A divorcing couple may be negotiating the division of property, but when one party feels particularly slighted or hurt the goal changes to "making sure he doesn't get a dime!" Competition can become particularly fierce when power, self-esteem, and saving face come into play. Competitors can be convinced of the uncompromising virtue of their proposals and feel offended when others don't immediately comply. Dad tells his son to mow the lawn. The son says he has plans to visit a friend but will do it when he gets back in a couple of hours. Dad sees this response as a threat to his authority and provides an ultimatum to mow the lawn now or he can't go to his friend's house. "Arguers almost always enter a negotiation with the goal of persuading their opponent of the worth of their stance, especially at the beginning of a negotiation. They believe that their position is better and more valid than their opponent's position . . . [or] to determine who will be the more dominant person in a relationship" (Stein & Albro, 2001, p. 114). Sometimes negotiation becomes more about self-identity than about a substantive issue.

A second outcome of negative competition occurs when negotiators fall victim to the winner's curse. The **winner's curse** occurs when someone is victorious in the negotiation but isn't happy with the results. For example, people caught up in the competition of an auction may pay ridiculous prices for mundane objects (Bazerman & Samuelson, 1983). An eBay auction is exciting, but one may lose sight of the goal of getting a good deal and become invested in beating the other bidders. Logically, making a purchase should be simple: Research the value of the item, set a limit, and enter the bargaining arena to get the best price. However, it may not turn out that way. People pay too much for a variety of reasons, including lack of research, poor bargaining skills, fear of losing, emotional involvement with the idea of owning the object, or craving the thrill of victory.

The winner's curse can be understood by looking at what the actual, and often unintended, cost was to the winner. For example, someone may win the issue of who pays for a scratch on the paint of his car, but the cost of winning is that a once-congenial friendship now is marred by resentment. A worker may win the most preferred schedule over other coworkers but lose their respect and help in the future. The winner's curse ultimately is caused by either unfocused goals or a lack of thought about the consequences that winning might incur.

DISCUSSION QUESTION • 9.3

Describe a time when competition over a tangible resource changed to a competition over self-esteem, power, or identity. Can you identify the point where the conflict goal switched?

A third ineffective outcome of competition occurs when an important issue is left unresolved. Competitors may turn a negotiation into a quest for a personal victory rather than solving a problem. They may ignore a good solution offered by the other party ("If it is your idea, it must be bad for me") and judge the success of the negotiation by how much the other person suffers ("If you are really unhappy, the outcome must be good for me"). People involved in this cycle may assume that the best personal outcome is achieved through winning at all costs, but they may not consider that the other's loss translates into more headaches for the winner. Thompson and Nadler (2000) found that losers in a win/lose situation convert the outcome to a lose/lose situation in about 20 percent of negotiations. In **lose/lose outcomes**, the person whose goals are not met may sabotage the system so the "winning" person's goals cannot be achieved. For example, one person may "win" a promotion but find that those she beat to get the job are subverting the win by withholding information, building coalitions, or ruining her reputation in the organization. Thompson and Nadler continue, "Our psychological immune system is so efficient that we do not even realize our judgments are tainted with self-interest" (p. 219). That blind spot may lead competitors to select tactics not in their long-term self-interest.

How you win in long-term relationships matters as much as winning. Engaging in destructive competition may prove to be more damaging than if the competitor did nothing. Destruction to relationships, unintended consequences, and an unhealthy communication climate can make winning an empty victory.

DISCUSSION QUESTION • 9.4

One negotiation philosophy contends, "What is good for you and doesn't harm me is good for both of us." How might managers or parents put this philosophy into practice?

Although the very nature of competition is about setting bargainers in opposition to one another, this dynamic is not inherently negative. Competitive negotiation can be effective and appropriate in a variety of contexts: when resources genuinely are scarce (only one promotion is available), time is limited (we want the kids to clean their rooms before Grandma visits), the topic is deeply valued (we take a stand on drilling for oil in pristine wilderness areas), and/or moderate tactics are chosen (whoever has the highest sales numbers this month gets a gift card for 50 gallons of gasoline).

Competition can be motivating, fun, productive, effective, and result in high morale. Some families and social groups include friendly competitive games as part of valued time together, and many organizations have competitions designed to increase sales or production. To maximize the possibility of productive outcomes, competition should operate in an environment of trust, commitment to fair and equitable treatment, access to information that will affect the competition, and delineated clear criteria for what constitutes a "win."

Competitive Negotiation Tactics

Competitive negotiators have a variety of tactics to choose from as they work toward goal achievement. In this section, we highlight the tactics presented in Table 9.2. Depending on how the tactics are implemented, they exist on a continuum from benign to destructive.

Although not a requirement of competition, verbal aggressiveness is a characteristic often associated with negotiators. **Verbal aggressiveness** is expressed in countless ways—for example, attacking through name-calling, mudslinging, angry tones, loud volume, demeaning personal attacks, criticism, and hostile body posturing. As a tactic, verbal aggressiveness may be successful but is strongly related to destructive conflict, physical violence, and relationship deterioration (Rogan & La France, 2003). Negotiators give more concessions to angry people but dislike them

TABLE 9.2 Competitive Negotiation Tactics

Verbal aggressiveness
Hypothetical offers
Splitting the difference
Force the other to make the first reasonable offer
Manipulate the bargaining range
Offer the same deal they offer you
Do your homework
Use humor to devalue the other's position
Boulwarism
Threats
Promises
Obnoxious persistence
Gaslighting
Coalitions
Frame the issue favorably to your side
Ask for concessions
Enumerate complaints
Manipulate pity, guilt, or other emotions
Lie
Call in debts
Quid pro quo
Ask questions
Tit for tat

more (Van Kleef, De Dreu, Pietroni, & Manstead, 2006). The alternative to aggressive competition is **assertive negotiation**. Assertive competitors advance their interests through persuasion and engage in direct and pointed dialogue to promote their needs without personal attacks.

A competitive negotiator may use **hypothetical offers** to gauge an opponent's willingness to change positions. "What would you think about me taking a week off to go hunting in the fall if I agree to go with you to visit your mother?" "If I were to offer to sell you both the truck and the boat for $10,000, would you be interested?" The strategic nature of hypothetical offers emerges when an offer is not one the negotiator really would make. After discovering the buyer has $10,000 that he would be willing to give for the truck and boat, the offer can be withdrawn—it was just hypothetical—and the seller can try to get a higher price for just the truck. Bringing in another negotiator who must review any offer is a common tactic at this point, as in, "I'll have to talk to my husband about whether he really wants to sell the boat, but I know the truck is worth quite a bit." This tactic has the effect of resetting the bargaining point after gaining new information.

Splitting the difference is a familiar strategy used when a negotiation stalls. When trying to buy a used car, the deal may deadlock with the seller wanting $8,000 and the buyer not wanting to pay more than $7,500. Typically, one party will say, "Let's just split the difference," and a bargain is struck at $7,750. A variation of splitting the difference involves **contingency agreements**. If the real future value of the agreement is unknown, the compromise can be contingent—open to renegotiation if particular events happen (Kray, Thompson, & Lind, 2005). For example, heirs settling an estate can decide to split the profits from the deceased parent's home, but only if it sells for more than $200,000. If it sells for less, the agreement would be renegotiated.

There often is an advantage to *having the other person make an offer first*. With one offer on the table, the second person has an option to respond, ignore the offer, or argue against it (Garcia, 2000). A negotiator might seek to have the other make the first offer simply by saying, "What do you think we should do?" or "What do you think is a fair outcome?" When negotiating a fixed-price item, such as a used car, the one who makes a serious offer first is at a strategic disadvantage because that offer becomes the **anchor point**. An anchor point firmly sets one edge of a bargaining range. The second person can adjust his or her response, knowing that the final price probably will be somewhere in the middle of the first two serious offers. If a seller originally sets an anchor point at $10,000, a buyer can come in with a price of $7,000. The age-old negotiation dance calls for the seller to inch the price downward ($9,500, then $9,250, then $9,000) and the buyer to inch up the offer ($7,500, then $7,750, then $8,000). The bargainers approach the midpoint until impasse is reached or a bargain is made (often by splitting the difference). An important consideration in this type of negotiation is the setting of the anchor point, in this example $10,000. A high anchor point may be used strategically to give the seller room to negotiate and get a higher price.

Negotiators generally have a range of acceptable settlement figures in mind. For instance, the buyer would like to buy a car for $7,500 but is willing to pay as much as $8,500. The seller will take no less than $8,000 but would like to receive as much as a buyer will pay and sets the price at $10,000. When the seller sets the first offer close to what he thinks is a fair value, it leaves room for the buyer to manipulate the **bargaining range**. By decreasing the first offer to $7,000, the buyer creates a midpoint (between $7,000 and $10,000), and the final agreement likely will be around $8,500. If the seller's first offer was $9,000, the midpoint changes to around $8,000.

Any purchase offers an opportunity for competitive bargaining. The familiar dance of competitive bargaining is used to get a better deal from naive bargainers. Buyers use competitive bargaining to get better purchase prices through assertive tactics: laughing at the car salesperson's first offer to downplay it, pitting one dealership against another, doing research to know reasonable pricing, and knowing one's consumer rights. Buyers sometimes can gain a better price in a store simply by asking for one. The magic words, "Is this your best price?" said to a store owner or manager can result in a discount. For example, Melanie was at a shop getting her car fixed. The mechanic quoted a price, including labor. Melanie asked, "Can you knock something off the price because I've brought a lot of friends and family into your shop over the years?" The price came down $75. Individuals with good credit ratings sometimes can obtain lower interest rates on credit card balances or loans simply by calling and asking for them. Those who avoid competition pay the asking price.

TOOLBOX 9.1   Negotiating for a Car

Getting Ready

- The Internet contains information on models, pricing, and so on. Do your homework.
- The sticker price is not a realistic offer. Don't let the sticker price be an anchor.
- Don't give away your trade-in! Negotiate just as hard on the price of the trade-in.
- Work a package deal to your advantage. Make each agreement contingent on the entire deal.
- Get financing in advance. Then negotiate an even better deal with the seller.
- Don't buy a vehicle just because it has a nice sound system or color.
- Always be willing to walk away from a deal. If you fall in love with a car, your negotiation posture is weak.
- Bring a friend along to point out negative features of the car and say things like, "That price is too high." "That's a terrible color."
- Ask for items that you don't need or want to be taken off the price. "I don't care about custom wheels, so take those off or reduce the price."
- When the seller goes to "talk to the manager," call other dealers. Call someone for advice.
- Give a time limit if the dealer takes your keys to show your trade-in to the mechanics. The longer they get you to stay, the more invested you are to the deal. You can give them a time limit or have them set an appointment to see your car.
- Don't share with the dealer your love of the car. Make it seem that you might be willing to settle for it, but you wished there was something better available.
- Don't buy on your first visit; ideally, the seller will call you back with a reduced offer.

Offering the other the deal they offer you is an interesting competitive strategy that could be useful when the other party refuses to move from an unreasonable demand. Jacey and Darla have shared an apartment for two years but are now moving into separate homes. Darla argues that she should get to keep all the furniture and not have to do any cleaning; in exchange Jacey could keep all of the $500 deposit money. This is a good deal for Darla if it would cost more than $250 to replace the furniture, the cleaning is extensive, or getting a deposit refund is in doubt. The deal is not very good for Jacey, however. In response, Jacey could ask Darla if she thinks it is fair for one person to take all the furniture and not have to do any cleaning. If Darla says, yes, then Jacey could say, "OK, I'll take that deal. I'll take all the furniture, you do all the cleaning, and you can keep the deposit."

CASE 9.2

The Dance of Competitive Negotiation

Applicant:	"I really need a starting salary of $75,000."
Interviewer:	"That's a bit out of our range."
Applicant:	"What figure did you have in mind?"
Interviewer:	"We were thinking in the range of the low $50s."
Applicant:	"That really is not enough for my qualification level. I couldn't consider anything less than $70,000."
Interviewer:	"We started our last applicant at $52,000."
Applicant:	"Wasn't that last year? My qualifications plus changes in the market really make this position at least a $68,000 starting rate."
Interviewer:	"Why don't we split the difference and start you at $60,500?"
Applicant:	"That's acceptable to me, if there is an opportunity for a raise every 6 months."

"You aren't paid what you're worth; you're paid what you can negotiate."

—Anonymous

Humor can be used to move the other bargainer off a position. The humor can be minimal, such as laughing with a salesperson at a car's inflated sticker price. Humor also can be aggressive and mean-spirited, such as snickering at someone who stutters or laughing while challenging someone's credibility: "What would a college-kid like you know about business?" Humor can work to move parties to more reasonable offers, or humor can function to undermine someone's credibility and confidence. The ethics of purposefully hurting someone must be considered. However, regardless of how wrong it is, such attacks can be effective.

In negotiation, information is power. The side that has the most knowledge has an edge in competitive bargaining. Doing your homework may involve researching competitive salaries, finding out about someone's financial position from friends, gleaning information from the other while not revealing much about yourself, or knowing the organization's policies better than one's boss.

Boulwarism, named after former GE vice president Lemuel R. Boulware, announces a firm opening offer and the policy of refusing to bargain. Essentially, the Boulware strategy starts the negotiation with a take-it-or-leave-it offer. The other side has no opportunity to develop a negotiation strategy. An add-on to the Boulware strategy is diminishing offers. If the other party attempts to bargain after the take-it-or-leave-it statement is declared, the negotiator takes part of what was offered back off the table. A parent might say: "I expect you home by midnight with no exceptions!" If the daughter tries to negotiate for 12:30 A.M., the mother's timetable would narrow. "Okay, now the time is 11:45." Raiffa, Richardson, and Metcalfe (2002) comment, "The Boulware strategy of making a reasonable opening and holding firm works sometimes, but more often than not it antagonizes the other party" (p. 127). Assuming the daughter continues to try to negotiate the midnight curfew, Mom's winning the battle through Boulwarism may not be worth the increased anger and rancor that the thwarted teen brings to future family dynamics.

Threats and promises are overused in competitive bargaining. A **threat** is a statement that a negative sanction will occur if the other party does not comply. The manager may threaten that if production goals aren't met this week, there will be no bonuses this month. To be credible, a threat must meet three tests: (1) The user must have the power to enforce the threat, (2) the individual must be viewed as willing to carry through with the threat, and (3) the threatened consequence must be seen as undesirable. A *warning* is a threat that the speaker does not have control over: "If you don't buy this car today, you'll regret it for the rest of your life." A *promise* is a statement that a positive reward will occur if the other person complies. "If you meet all your performance targets this year, you'll get a 20 percent salary bonus."

A common strategy of competitors is *obnoxious persistence*. The strategy is to wear someone down by being persistent enough that the negotiator will give in just to get the offensive person to go away. A colleague once lost her airplane ticket. After asking two agents in the terminal for help, she was referred to the main check-in area, where she discovered a long line waiting for assistance. If she stood in line, her plane would leave without her. So she went to the middle of the crowded airport check-in area and loudly repeated over and over: "I've lost my tickets and nobody will help me. I'm going to miss my plane. Why won't anybody help me?" Soon an agent came over and took her aside to get her replacement ticket, and she made her flight.

Gaslighting is a strategy whereby a person, in an effort to gain the upper hand, manipulates the other into questioning their sanity (Sarkis, 2017). The term stems from the 1944 movie *Gaslight*, which portrays a husband manipulating his wife's reality, in particular her lighting, and denying that anything has changed, making her question her own senses. Gaslighting involves blatant lying, even in the face of evidence to the contrary; using your own values against you; bombarding you with attacks, but tossing in positives to keep you off-kilter; building coalitions against you; telling others you can't be trusted or you are crazy; and using your confusion to further manipulate you. Gaslighting is effective at psychologically damaging an opponent and can be immensely effective, even if ethically questionable.

DISCUSSION QUESTION • 9.5

Identify examples when ethical competitive negotiation is appropriate.

Coalitions are formed when people join together to reach a goal that one person does not have enough resources or power to achieve. One student may talk so much that it fills class time with his or her personal questions and comments. When other students try to contribute, they may be unsuccessful in taking attention away from the student who is dominating the discussion. If several students join forces to support each other's comments to keep the stage-hogging student from doing all the talking or to complain to the professor, they are more likely to reach their goal. It is not unusual for several roommates to form a coalition to try to get another roommate to move out. On a larger scale, unions are coalitions created to gain power and engage in collective bargaining.

Competitors seek to *frame the issue favorably to their side*. By controlling how the topic is phrased, a competitive advantage is acquired. If Sergio wants to have a party at the house, he can ask his roommates, "Who should we invite to a party on Friday?" The frame assumes that they will host a party without asking his roommates for permission or agreement.

Competitors may make an offer and then demand concessions or enumerate several complaints in one session. If bargaining with someone with an avoidance or accommodating style, simply *demanding concessions* can be successful. Some competitors simply take resources as entitlements, as if they are socially superior and deserve more than anyone else. For example, an employee may demand a larger office because she's been at the company longer than anyone else. Related to demanding concession is the tactic of *downplaying what the other has to offer*. Even though you may like the color of a used car or covet the rear view camera, competitive-minded car buyers will claim to dislike the color or not care about the camera and demand concessions on that basis saying, "The camera is not a big deal to me so I'm not going to pay extra just because it's there."

Enumerating several complaints may make the negotiator's stance seem stronger than it really is. Related to enumeration is the tactic of gunnysacking, discussed in Chapter 8. **Gunnysacking** occurs when someone avoids direct conflict but secretly keeps a list of grudges. At some point, the grievances become more than the person can bear, and all of the complaints are dumped on the other party in one giant heap. Strategic gunnysacking can be used as a basis to demand concessions.

Manipulation of pity, guilt, or flattery urge others to comply. **Compliance gaining** is the communication of tactics designed to induce the other to do one's will (see Table 9.3). "Won't you make me a

TABLE 9.3 Compliance-Gaining Strategies

1. **Altruism**: Appealing to the other's basic goodness of heart. *"Please send money to help the victims of the tsunami."*
2. **Authority appeal**: Using a power position. *"I'm the mother, that's why."*
3. **Challenge**: Goading others into accepting a dare. *"I bet you can't get your shoes on and be ready to go to school in three minutes."*
4. **Your concern for me**: Seeking compliance by appealing to the other's regard for the person asking the request. *"If you really care about me, you will quit smoking."*
5. **Criticize**: Attacking the other personally. *"You're so cheap. You never take me anywhere."*
6. **Debasement**: Attacking one's own self-worth to encourage compliance out of pity. *"I'm just so stupid when it comes to math. Could you help me with this problem?"*
7. **Debt**: Calling in a favor or something owed. *"Remember when I covered your shift when you got sick? I'm just asking for you to step in for three hours on Saturday for me."*
8. **Demanding**: Commanding the other to act. *"Clean up your mess!"*
9. **Disclaimer**: Dismissing rules or constraints, downplaying the task, or dismissing the cost of compliance. *"It's not that hot outside, so go mow the lawn."*
10. **Duty**: Reminding someone of their responsibilities. *"As a parent you need to watch your children more closely and not let them go in someone else's yard."*
11. **Esteem** (positive or negative): Claiming they will be seen more positively/negatively if they comply. *"If you pay your bills on time, others will see you as a good credit risk; if you don't, you'll be seen as a deadbeat."*
12. **Invoke norm**: Suggesting that they will be out of step with everyone if they don't comply. *"Nobody else has asked for a travel budget; why should you get one?"*
13. **Logic**: Appealing to reason or facts. *"The lease has only our names on it, so we can't let your friend move in."*
14. **Moral appeal**: Claiming the action is the right/ethical thing to do. *"Don't use plastic bags because it is bad for the environment."*
15. **My concern for you**: Asserting one is looking out for their best interests. *"I'm worried that you're not making friends here; why don't you join my softball team?"*
16. **Pre-giving**: Giving a gift or positive action in advance. *"Enclosed in this letter you will find personalized mailing labels for you to use. Please consider sending us a donation."*
17. **Promise**: Offering a later reward. *"If you give me the money for the movie, I'll wash your car when I get home."*
18. **Surveillance**: Informing them they are being or will be watched. *"Don't cheat. I've caught some of the best in my time."*
19. **Disrupt-then-reframe**: Using confusing language followed by an immediate request for compliance. *"The price is 1500 cents. I mean $15 dollars which is a bargain."*
20. **Fear-then-relief**. Set up the possible negative outcome, demonstrate how it was mitigated, followed by a request. *"Your girlfriend came around and asked where you were. Don't worry, I didn't give you away. But can I borrow your car?"*

Source: Adapted from Carpenter & Boster (2009); Dolinski and Szczucka (2013); Kellermann and Cole (1994), among others

grilled cheese sandwich? You make the best grilled cheese sandwiches." Some requests cajole and flatter someone into performing a personal service. Teens commonly complain that parents attempt to gain compliance by making them feel guilty. "Your grandparents drove all this way to see you, and you would rather go out with your friends tonight?" To get one's partner to quit watching TV and clean the house, saying, "Don't mind me. I've worked all day but I can clean up the kitchen, take out the garbage, and finish the laundry by myself," may induce the other to chip in. However, it could be met with an attempt to create pity in return with a reply of "Sounds fair because I spent the whole afternoon cleaning the garage, and moving those boxes was exhausting."

> Liars share with those they deceive the desire not to be deceived . . . their choice to lie is one which they would like to reserve for themselves while insisting that others be honest.
>
> —Bok, 2004

Lies—whether by omission or outright deception—are considered part of the game by some competitive negotiators. Lewicki and Robinson (2004) identified five clusters of lying during negotiation: misrepresentation of a position to an opponent, bluffing, falsification of information, deception, and selective disclosure. In their survey of MBA students, most lying tactics were considered unethical by the respondents. However, deceptive tactics considered acceptable during negotiation included asking around to gain information about the other's strategy, making an opening demand far greater than one expects to receive, hiding the real bottom line, and conveying a false impression that time is not an issue.

DISCUSSION QUESTION • 9.6

Are all lies created morally or ethically equal? Is it ethical to withhold certain information or offer only part of the picture when negotiating? Can any of the types of lies identified by Lewicki and Robinson be considered ethical? If so, under what circumstances?

Competitors may manipulate the perception of concessions to build up future credit. If both participants perceive that a credit exists, one party can *call in the debt* during the next negotiation. The phrase "Okay, but you owe me one" indicates that current goal achievement has been traded for an unknown future favor. If you accept a loan from a friend, the monetary debt may be leveraged to gain all sorts of other favors—lending your car, taking books back to the library, or doing the dishes more often. **Quid pro quo** literally means "something for something." If you help me, I'll help you. The negotiators trade items to reach a decision where both feel they have gained and lost equal value.

Asking questions without giving reciprocal information is another competitive tactic. Competitors may ask questions to discover information that will provide an advantage without sharing information that might help the opponent. A real estate agent may ask many questions to know how to appeal to a prospective buyer's emotions and needs: "How long do you plan to live in the area?" "Do you have pets?" "Do you like to cook or entertain?" "What ages are your children?" "Is this your first home purchase?" Later, the agent can appear to be your friend while using the information or highlighting certain aspects of various homes. If you have a young family, an agent can highlight nearby schools and bike paths. If you like entertaining, homes with large kitchens and decks are shown. An agent may say that homes are going fast, show several overpriced and problematic homes, and then take clients to the house that she wants to sell saying, "This one will probably be gone by this afternoon, so if you are interested in it, you'd better put in an offer today."

A final commonly used tactic is **tit for tat**. Negotiators do what is done to them—incremental move for incremental move, ridicule for ridicule, and so forth. The danger of tit for tat is creating a series of negative and dysfunctional tactics that spiral downward. Two boys were arguing over Legos. When the biggest boy just grabbed the desired piece, the smaller boy took another ten pieces out of the larger boy's pile. Mutual name-calling and snatching of each other's stash ensued. The conflict escalated into mutual destruction of both building projects.

DISCUSSION QUESTION • 9.7

Which competitive negotiation tactics are you most comfortable using? Which are you least comfortable using? Are there any you consider to be wholly unethical?

Cooperative Negotiation

The potential for negative impact of competitive negotiation on relationships and the probability that "losers" will not follow through enthusiastically with their agreements leads some competitors to search for alternatives. Cooperative negotiation, often called **mutual gains bargaining**, starts with the premise that it is possible for both parties to "win" most of what they need if the parties work together. A cooperative approach affords each person the opportunity to disclose real needs and to gain assistance in moving toward goals. Instead of automatically attempting to thwart the other's goal achievement, mutual gains negotiators look for ways for both to prosper. Cooperative strategies, however, are not without drawbacks. Unbridled cooperativeness could result in being taken advantage of by sneaky competitors. The competitor might encourage the naive cooperator to create better outcomes (add value) and then capture the majority of what was on the table (take value) (see Foo, Elfenbein, Tan, & Aik, 2004).

Preparing for Cooperative Negotiation

Because competitive bargaining is so entrenched in European-American culture, it may take some preparation and thoughtfulness to engage in cooperative bargaining. An easy adjustment is adapting physical and psychological space. Space affects how people feel and how they behave. Sitting across from each other at a formal table invites debate, argument, and competition. Creating a more relaxed physical environment may invite a more relaxed negotiation style. Symbolic gestures of engaging in some conversation before jumping into negotiation (called schmoozing in the business world) may thaw a tense situation. A family who bakes some cookies and then sits down to discuss vacation plans with all the electronic devices turned off may have more success than the family who broaches the subject while riding in their car. Bargainers who schmooze and engage in social chitchat sometimes reach superior solutions, in part because they discover social cues that more task-oriented negotiators miss and develop interpersonal linkages that make discovering the other's interests possible. Selecting a time and place that is private and comfortable for both individuals may encourage more mutual gains thinking.

Mutual gains negotiators understand the difference between **interests** (underlying needs) and **positions** (demands that conceal needs). By focusing on interests, all parties might have their needs met. At the grocery store a cashier repeatedly propped open a door to avoid the overpowering smell from a scented product placed by her checkout stand. The clerk at the customer service desk, seeing the door open, repeatedly closed the door because she was cold. The conflict, however, was expressed through positions: "I want the door open" and "I want the door closed." Because the underlying needs were not disclosed (avoiding the smell and being warm), creative or mutually satisfactory solutions never had a chance to emerge.

The need to be right all the time is the greatest barrier to new ideas.

—Cooley, 2005

To negotiate collaboratively, two basic elements must occur: The negotiator must consider the other person's needs and give up the notion that personal ideas automatically are the best. Collaboration must start with a suspension of judgment about what the exact outcome will be. Collaborative negotiators must live with some uncertainty and ambiguity while searching for a mutually satisfactory outcome.

Instead of the "my way" versus "your way" tussle of competitive negotiation, collaborators join together against a mutual problem. A competitor might say, "You drive the car to work most days, so I get it today." A collaborator might frame the negotiation opening differently and say, "I need to go to the bank this afternoon, and you need to get to work. How can we work this out when we only have one car?" The problem to be solved is separated from the individuals in the negotiation, and psychologically, the other person is not forced to defend a position.

KEY 9.2

The initial framing of the negotiation can create either a competitive or a cooperative climate.

After studying the needs of both parties and the emotions or fears that might hinder the negotiation, the negotiator considers how to begin. Sometimes, a comment that both could benefit if they worked together on a solution will help create a cooperative frame and establish an overarching goal. A couple who begins a discussion about finances with an affirmation of their commitment to each other and to making decisions based on what's best for "the team" may find the discussion of money goes more smoothly.

TOOLBOX 9.2   Preparing to Negotiate Cooperatively

1. Research the facts and the situation. Do your homework!
2. Analyze both parties (goals, needs, and fears).
3. Consider strategically how to frame the negotiation.
4. Consider introducing mutual gains bargaining to the other party.
5. Listen and validate the other's needs and fears (as necessary).
6. Ask open-ended questions, particularly those designed to uncover interests.
7. Comment about commonalities.
8. Reframe the issue as something both parties share.
9. Look creatively for mutually beneficial outcomes that meet each party's interests.

Instead of starting the negotiation competitively with a demand, the negotiation might be framed at the beginning with a question. Students who anticipate conflict while negotiating a group project topic might start with the question: "What do we all want to get out of doing this group project?" As each one answers, underlying interests and expectations will emerge. Asking questions and then listening provides information. Several students may only be interested in a good grade. One may want to do something that might lead to an internship placement. Another may just want it not to take up much time or have the project cost any money. With an awareness of everyone's interests, the group is more likely to choose a mutually beneficial topic than if they fought over whose favorite topic would win selection. If someone is distraught at the slightest chance of receiving a mediocre grade on the project, another group member can highlight the interest by saying, "So the grade is the most important thing for you," letting the person know that the concern has been heard and giving voice to that concern for the rest of the group to hear. Groups are more likely to succeed if part of everyone's interests are met.

One published account itemizes how even a trained conflict manager went astray during negotiations when preparation was not sufficient. A professional mediator confronted a neighbor about his barking dogs.

> My first step, prior to the actual conversations with my neighbor, was defining my interests. In retrospect, this stage of the negotiation was woefully inadequate. I had focused solely on my need for a quieter atmosphere, and though I intended to use a friendly tone in our conversation, I chose a strategy of honesty and openness, even bluntness if necessary. . . . In so doing, I failed to consider the prominence of my other main interest, that of having friendly ongoing relations with my neighbors. As a result of choosing a competitive, rather than collaborative, approach to our negotiations, my ability to preserve the relationship was compromised.
>
> (Stringer, 2006, p. 35)

By forgetting his neighbor's fears and interests, he bypassed the critical other half of the conversation and turned what could have been a cooperative discussion into a competitive interaction. The negotiation was engaged by knocking on his neighbor's door and demanding that a new fence be built to stop the barking. Surprising the neighbor with the issue was confrontational, and the opening frame of the negotiation set a competitive tone. By beginning the negotiation with his own preferred solution (position) for the barking dogs, the neighbor was denied a chance to think about the problem and to be drawn into the negotiation or motivated to look for a long-term solution. The dog owner was, unsurprisingly, defensive and angry. The bottom line: Planning matters.

KEY 9.3

Advanced planning improves negotiation.

Cooperative Negotiation Tactics

Several collaborative tactics flow from earlier discussions: searching for interests, preparing a physical and psychological space, and listening. This section focuses on the additional tactics in Table 9.4.

Identifying commonalities is helpful, if not crucial, during mutual gains negotiation. A **commonality** is any trait, attitude, goal, need, or fear shared by the negotiators. Identifying and verbalizing commonalities help individuals see their similarities instead of allowing differences to shape the negotiation. After talking about what each person's goals are for a group project, one member may summarize, "We all need to have something to turn in on the due date, and all of us are concerned about our grade."

Reframing is useful to keep the discussion on productive problem solving. If one person jumps ahead in the process and advances a solution too early, "So let's host a poker tournament and

TABLE 9.4 Cooperative Negotiation Tactics

Preparing a physical and psychological space	Dueling lists
Listening	Magic wand
Identifying commonalities and interests	Asking questions
Reframing	Giving information
Suspending judgment	Putting more than one option on the table at a time
Applying creativity	Something now for something later
Brainstorming	Changing the size of the issue
Challenging the status quo	Focusing on the future
	Patience

give the proceeds to the Red Cross," another group member might reframe: "We want a project we can all agree will get a good grade. Let's talk about what the prof would consider a successful project before we focus on any one idea." Reframing also can focus on issues instead of attacks. For example, if a group member responds to the suggestion of critiquing a movie with "I'm not doing another lame project where we analyze some movie and wind up with a bad grade," another student might reframe away from the attack and toward a central issue: "The project needs to be significant enough to warrant a really high grade."

Mutual gains negotiators must learn to *suspend judgment*. They must accept some uncertainty at the beginning about the exact outcome. They then frame the issue as a mutual problem; that is, they phrase the problem in a way that everyone can join together in finding a mutually beneficial solution. Case 9.3 illustrates some cooperative strategies for a salary negotiation.

CASE 9.3

The Creativity of Cooperative Negotiation

Applicant: "I really need a starting salary of $60,000."

Interviewer: "That's a bit out of our range."

Applicant: "What figure did you have in mind?"

Interviewer: "We were thinking in the range of the low $50s."

Applicant: "That really is not enough for my qualification level. I couldn't consider anything less than $58,000."

Interviewer: "I don't have that much in my budget."

Applicant: "What other incentives do you have to offer?"

Interviewer: "Well, we could start you at $55,000 with a review for your first pay increase after six months."

Applicant: "That sounds promising. How about $55,000, add a onetime signing bonus of $5,000, and pay for my moving expenses?"

Interviewer: "We could offer $2,000 in dedicated training or travel funds but not as a cash signing bonus. We could pay moving expenses up to $2,000. I also could put you in an office that faces the river."

Applicant: "I can see that you have some budget restraints, but this is a workable package for me."

Another key to collaboration is bringing some creativity to the situation. If conflict managers and negotiators think there is only one best solution (obviously the one that "I" thought of), then there is no need for creativity. Once the possibility of other ideas enters the scene, creativity is needed to discover other potential solutions. Brainstorming is a technique to spur creativity and generate ideas that might solve the issue while meeting each party's needs. The cooperative negotiator may need to teach the basic format for brainstorming to the other party (see Toolbox 9.3).

TOOLBOX 9.3 Introducing Brainstorming

Brainstorming is a technique to produce many ideas in a short period of time.

Brainstorming rules:

1. Set a time limit for the brainstorming.
2. Get as many ideas on the table as possible.
3. No criticizing ideas as they are given; that happens later.
4. All ideas are listed on a whiteboard or flipchart.

Starting a brainstorming session might sound like the following.

> "Let's see if we can generate some ideas using brainstorming. What we do is make a list of all the ideas we can think of, even wild and crazy ones. To keep the creative juices flowing, we need to keep from criticizing ideas as they come out; we can do that later. Let's try this for five minutes to see what happens?"

During conflicts, starting from the current situation and assuming that what was done in the past should be done in the future is the easiest route, but is it the best path? Just because one partner always has taken the car in the past doesn't mean that it might not make sense for both individuals to take the subway to work and leave the car at home. Just because a family always has taken a one-week vacation in the summer with the negotiation centering on where to go doesn't mean that other creative options might not be more desirable—if allowed into the conversation. Maybe three long weekend vacations would better meet their needs. Asking questions about assumptions is a powerful negotiation tactic in challenging the status quo.

The dueling lists technique has each individual make a long list of possible solutions. For example, a couple can each create a list of places to go on vacation. Then the two examine the lists to find common ideas that might lead to a mutual solution. If one lists Cancún and the other Mazatlán, they can talk about their common interest in going to a warm place with a beach and lots of parties.

To use the magic wand technique, ask, "What would you really need if you could wave a magic wand and get the outcome that would make you the happiest?" After posing the question, a negotiation would state the magic wand outcome he or she preferred. It sometimes is easier to discuss basic needs and to gain a greater understanding of each other through an idealized viewpoint (Creo, 2005). Questions are asked such as: "What is your idea of a good neighbor?" "What type of communication with coworkers is ideal for you?"

In some respect, mutual gains bargainers rely on two key skills: asking questions and giving information. Questions are asked to elicit information. If one party has key information that the other lacks, the information is shared so a better solution can be crafted. Questions can be asked about assumptions and traditions to see if there are good reasons for them.

Asking a question about tradition can start a conversation about how individuals, groups, or organizations change over time: "Does the way we've always done this task still meet all of our needs today?" Rather than attacking the ways things are, such as "That's a stupid way to do the project," ask, "How does this process help us get the work done?" By keeping the question focused on interests (completing the project) instead of on people ("Your stupid way of doing things"), face goals are less likely to be threatened.

DISCUSSION QUESTION • 9.8

Which collaborative tactics are you the most/least comfortable using? Identify examples when cooperative negotiation is appropriate. What cooperative negotiation tactics would be the most effective in each example?

Meiners and Miller (2004) identify *sharing information* as one of the key characteristics of cooperative negotiation between supervisors and subordinates. They identify three types of information sharing: elaboration, directness, and mutual concessions. The amount of information that is shared is called *elaboration*. The more information is exchanged, the greater the possibility of creative solutions. **Directness** refers to the clearness and openness of the negotiators about their goals and interests. *Mutual concessions*, or a give-and-take exchange, indicates flexibility. Mutual concessions work best when several issues are negotiated at the same time. In the same study, employed undergraduate college students found cooperative negotiation was more likely to occur when the situation was formal than in spontaneous situations—indicating a need to prepare for negotiations in advance if one wishes to use cooperative tactics. Similarly, students using a casual and friendly tone were more successful at integrative negotiation than those using a more impersonal approach.

Another tactic of mutual gains negotiation is to *put more than one option on the table at a time*. Typically, several negotiation steps are involved in buying a car: the new car price, the trade-in value, warranty extension, interest rates, car features, or extras. The savvy purchaser makes each section of the negotiation contingent on the outcome of the other items. Once you state you will buy the new car at an agreed-upon price, the incentive to cooperate in good faith on the other negotiation items is lessened for the seller. By keeping the final purchase decision open, the incentive to think creatively about the next negotiation item is maintained. Because the price of the car was higher than anticipated, the buyer may expect more on the trade-in, a lower interest rate, and/or items added to sweeten the deal—for example, a sound system upgrade or free oil changes for a year. Having several items in play at the same time also allows for the option of trading across items.

Mutual gains negotiators can bring time into the negotiation. *Something now for something later trades* can be advantageous. Instead of fighting competitively to control which movie is seen tonight, a couple can widen the frame of the negotiation and decide what choices will be made over the next three or four times they go out. An employee negotiating for a raise may request more frequent evaluations (quarterly instead of yearly) to increase opportunities for raises when denied a big raise immediately.

If negotiations falter, consider *changing the size of the issue*. If the issue seems too overwhelming, break it down into smaller parts. If negotiation about the house not being clean becomes defensive, focus on smaller parts of the larger issue: Which roommate will do the dishes, who will sweep the floor, and who will do the laundry? If two roommates gang up on a third about not picking up the house, enlarge the issue to overall workload in taking care of the house so everyone's duties are put on the table for consideration and each person's responsibilities become clear.

A trademark tactic of mutual gains negotiation is *focusing on the future*—how to get out of the conflict—more than on the past causes of the situation. Simply stating that one is more interested in how two parties will act toward each other in the future than on past grievances sometimes can change the frame of a negotiation from defensive to more cooperative. Neighbors who have had a tense relationship may both desire more congeniality in the future. The goal to get along helps frame the negotiations in the present and the future rather than in the past. For example, a neighbor might say, "Chances are we're going to be living next door to each other for years. Let's try to figure out a way that we can have a good relationship and move beyond our past differences." When paired with an apology, focus on the future can be a powerful technique, such as: "I know we both probably did things in the past that we wish didn't happen and I'm sorry about my part in that. I would like to have less stress going forward, so do you think we could talk about going forward in a different way?"

A final, important tactical consideration for mutual gains negotiators is *patience*. Working with someone takes longer than making decisions like a dictator. Finding about others' needs and bringing creativity to a situation takes thought and energy. Living with some ambiguity about the final outcome can be stressful. Controlling impatience is necessary for mutual gains bargaining to have time to work.

The Choices Negotiators Make

Negotiators have a philosophical and tactical choice about their behaviors. Where competitive bargainers focus on difference, mutual gains bargainers focus on similarity. Competitive negotiators fight for their share in a world of scarcity, whereas mutual gains bargainers live in a world of potential abundance. The way the negotiation tactics function in competition and cooperation is quite different, as are the consequences to continuing relationships.

DISCUSSION QUESTION • 9.9

As you turn in your first essay in a class, you realize that the second essay is due the next week. You probably won't get the first paper back before the second paper is due and would like to renegotiate the due date. Because the instructor has the power to say "No" to the request, how can you phrase the issue to appeal to the instructor's interests and move toward cooperative negotiation?

Moving From Competition to Cooperation

Collaborative bargaining is not easy. Kolb and Williams (2003) comment, "Bargainers don't naturally trust each other. They worry that in revealing too much they will give the other person an edge. . . . It takes work to change the perceptions that people bring to negotiation and to cultivate a climate of openness and mutual respect. It takes work to keep a dialogue going when the other party's only inclination is to put demands on the table and press for a deal. It takes work to get everyone to own his or her part of the problem" (pp. 236–237). Although collaboration is more labor intensive, the payoffs for improved outcomes makes the effort worthwhile in many cases.

A negotiator may, in good faith, attempt cooperative tactics, only to be rebuffed by a competitive negotiator. Some research suggests that individual disposition and style directly relate to a party's willingness to use nonconfrontational problem-solving strategies and to avoid verbal aggression (Rogan & La France, 2003), but scholars do not believe that style or disposition automatically determine what will occur. People can opt to make other choices, and, with time and effort, they can change their approach.

> The clever thing to do is not to let the negotiation drift toward two mutually exclusive alternatives—your way or my way.
>
> —Management expert Mary Parker Follett

To make a transition from competitive to a more mutual gains approach, a negotiator must have some degree of trust. He or she must believe cooperation can lead to goal achievement. Table 9.5 summarizes specific tactics useful in persuading a competitive individual to try mutual gains negotiation.

Tactics to Move Competitors to Collaboration

Some techniques to move toward mutual gains were discussed in the cooperative section: highlighting commonalities and focusing on interests. Collaborative techniques of recognizing positions and asking questions to uncover the underlying interest are key in creating cooperative interactions. For example, "You've said that you'd like to be the leader on this project. What is it about the leadership position that attracts you?" Some competitors, once they understand that more than one person's goals can be achieved simultaneously, may no longer feel compelled to seek a decisive personal victory.

One method of moving toward collaboration involves *selecting the channel of communication strategically*. Written channels, such as e-mail, texting, and Twitter, are less personal than telephone conversations; phone conversations are less personal than face-to-face interaction. The less personal the channel, the easier it is to compete and use negative tactics. One option when seeking to change the style of negotiation is to move to a more personal channel.

Metacommunication—talking about negotiation processes, styles, and tactics—can be useful. Metacommunication acknowledges that individuals disagree. For example, when a competitor continues to repeat a position over and over with increasing frustration, the other might say, "I know it's tempting to keep repeating the same thing because you think the other person doesn't understand what you are saying. I think I do understand what you are saying but simply don't think we are limited to that option. What I understand your concern to be is _____. Do I have that right?"

TABLE 9.5 Moving from Competition to Cooperative Bargaining

Selecting the right channel of communication
Metacommunicating
Reality checking
Bringing the relationship into the decision
Reformed sinner
Mirroring
Rewriting the past
Apologizing
Fogging
Common fact finding
Postponing
Setting criteria
Adding humor
Asking for help
Engaging in negotiation judo

For some diehard competitors, more direct techniques may be necessary to persuade them to give mutual gains a try. A *reality check* probes the value of winning what the competitor has demanded. For example, "It sounds like the path we are on now would result in both of us not getting what we really want. Is there a way we can work around that and find a solution that better meets both our needs?" "If we give you what you want and you become the leader of the group, are you willing to do all the planning, organizing, and work that is required in the position?" "Do you still want to buy a new plasma TV knowing that it will put our ability to pay for school next semester at risk?" If it is an important relationship, a partner or friend may be more willing to consider other options once the reality of the *impact on the relationship* is brought to the surface. "I know you want your sister to stay with us, but you know she disapproves of my religion and comments on it often, causing a lot of tension between us. Perhaps you can encourage her to stay in a hotel when she visits for the weekend if we pay for part of it?"

Another tactic to move a competitor toward cooperative bargaining is called the **reformed sinner** strategy. In this technique, initially one competes, then switches to cooperation—showing that he or she could compete and win if desired (Folger, Poole, & Stutman, 2013). Sometimes proving that one won't give in is necessary. Ingrid heard through the company grapevine that her counterpart, Fred, in another division was a hard bargainer and ran over people he thought weak, particularly women. When Ingrid and Fred met to work out details on a project, Ingrid chose to start with hard competitive tactics and demanded that Fred's crew meet her schedule. Fred responded with his usual competitive style. Ingrid continued to use competitive tactics and restated her demands. Once an impasse was reached, she used a common goals statement and reality checking to move toward collaboration: "Well, we're both stuck, and at this rate neither one of us will get our projects done. We're both professionals; let's find a compromise where neither of us gets hurt too badly."

Proving a willingness to fight may motivate the other to consider collaboration as a way of getting a better outcome. A colleague used this technique to get a manager to renegotiate a decision by saying, "Look, I don't want to go through the hassle of filing a formal complaint—that wouldn't be good for our continued relationship or the department, but this is important. I'm confident we can work this out between us." By mentioning a possible formal complaint, the manager was aware that the employee knew the system and was willing to bump the issue to the next level. Ultimately the two negotiated a mutually acceptable agreement. If a degree of trust exists, this tactic can lead to more creative negotiation. If it is perceived as a threat, competition may ensue.

Mirroring tactics show that a negotiator understands competition and won't give in if the other insists on hard bargaining. Until the negotiator shows the ability to win competitively, the diehard competitor may persist in the mistaken assumption that the one who prefers mutual gains will eventually just wear down and give in. When Fred and Ingrid met, he spoke loudly and pounded on the table. If she used mirroring, Ingrid would also speak more forcefully and likewise pound on the table to mirror his behavior. After both parties briefly demonstrated their mastery of competitive skills, they were able to move toward more collaborative processes. Both knew that there would not be an easy victory over the other.

If there are hard feelings from the previous encounters, *rewriting the past* may be necessary. One negotiator would express regret about past behaviors and a desire to find a better way (McCorkle & Reese, 2015). Offering an apology for past behavior can be a powerful negotiation technique. If hurt feelings were blocking the negotiation, an apology may lead to significant concessions from the other negotiator or allow a relationship to be rebuilt. If Ingrid unsuccessfully tried competitive tactics with Fred, she might use rewriting and apology tactics to get through the resulting impasse. "Fred, I'm sorry we got off on the wrong foot in our meeting. I've been so focused on my own unit's needs that I've missed some opportunities for us to work together on this. If I had it do over again, I would have spent some time learning more about your department's needs. Can we start over?"

DISCUSSION QUESTION • 9.10

Which tactics to transition to mutual gains would you be most/least likely to use?

Fogging is a technique to take some of the steam out of a competitor's words and create opportunities for change. For example, if the other negotiator uses negative criticism, sort through the comments for items that are true but not relevant. If the criticism is true but not relevant, simply agree with it. Next, reframe the issue to a problem-solving frame. If an angry student accuses a group member of just caring about taking notes on everything, the accused could refuse to take the bait or to become defensive. The criticized student might agree with what is true and ignore the negative implications. "True, I am very thorough in keeping a good record for the group [fogging]. What challenges do we all see in getting the project done? [reframe]"

If the conflict centers around whose facts are correct, instead of deadlocking on an "is so/is not" argument, suggest looking up the facts together. *Common fact finding* clears the air—in a cooperative way—and may help build a better relationship. Jerry and Raoul differ on which topic to pick for a group project. Jerry is convinced that his idea for a poker tournament to raise money for a charity would work; Raoul is sure that state laws prohibit gambling, even for charity. Instead of just disagreeing more and more loudly, Raoul could suggest they use a speakerphone together and call the state attorney general's office to find out if their plan is legal.

Postponement, or time-outs, are effective to let one or both parties cool down when tempers are hot. It might be advisable to say, "I think we will both have a better outcome if we take a few minutes off before we say something we'll both regret later." This strategy is effective only if there is trust that the parties actually will return to the negotiation table. Setting a time to return to the discussion can make this option more attractive to someone who doesn't want to quit for fear of being ignored. Saying, "Let's plan to come back at 1 o'clock, after lunch, so we can think about how we want to proceed" can assure the other that the issue will be discussed further after a time-out. When possible, frame the postponement with mutual gains in mind: "Let's take a 15 minute break and both come back with some ideas that might actually work for both of us."

Focusing on criteria of a good outcome for both people creates a more cooperative frame. If the other person probably will come to the table with a competitive demand, start the discussion by saying, "I know we both have specific ideas that we think will work, but I'd like us to start by thinking about what an outcome might look like that would be good for both of us." Continue to ignore positional statements that might creep into the discussion until mutually agreeable criteria are created. Melanie put an ad in the paper to sell her car for $7,200. The prospective buyer offered $6,500. Rather than focus on the price, which would engage the dance of competitive negotiation, Melanie focused on criteria. When the buyer made the lower offer, Melanie asked, "How did you come up with that amount?" The buyer replied, "It seemed about right." Melanie responded, "Well, we are both looking for a fair deal at the right price. Why don't I show you how I came up with $7,200, and you can decide if what I'm asking is fair." After looking at her comparables and data, the buyer paid the asking price because she felt that the criteria of a fair outcome were met.

For some, *humor* is a technique that might moderate competitiveness. A few people nonverbally stiffen their posture and puff up before making a particularly outrageous demand. Among friends who recognize the pattern and metacommunicate about it in advance, laughing may be the best reaction during the puffing-up stage before the outrageous demand reaches the air. Other demands can be treated humorously instead of seriously to keep the competitive tone from taking command of the situation. When supervisors are negotiating their share of budget increases, one may demand 100 percent of the increase. A colleague could reply with a good-humored laugh and say, "That would be great, wouldn't it! No, really, what are your department's expectations for your share of the increase?" Shared humor builds commonality. Negative humor, however, causes more divisiveness. Humor requires extreme social sensitivity and can be dangerous if not done well. Laughing with people is different than laughing at them.

Humor can be used to break the boundaries of habitual thinking. Many conflict situations occur when people become attached to a personal perspective without consideration of the other person's viewpoint. For example, a story is told of a guest who brings champagne to a party as a special surprise treat. When it comes time to open the champagne, only paper cups are provided. There are very nice champagne glasses in the house, but the host says they would all have to be washed by hand, so why not just use the paper cups? (Sclavi, 2008). The guest who brought champagne is offended that the special treat will be served into tacky paper cups; the hostess is offended that the guest expected for her to perform extra work. The symbolism of the gift becomes lost, and a relationship may be at risk. An astute conflict manager might reflect on whether there is a humorous way to change each person's framing of the situation ("not respectful of the gift" and "interrupting the fun of the party to wash dishes") with something else. For example, another guest who observed the conversation might jovially say, "I bet these glasses are lonely in that cupboard watching the party. They didn't know they would have a surprise chance to come out and shine. A couple of us can get these glasses washed in a few minutes so they can have their moment of glory."

Asking for help may seem like an odd tactic to persuade someone toward mutual gains negotiation. The request is an attempt to engage the other person and build mutual ownership of the problem. If used at the outset, a request for help in solving the problem may be seen as a sign of weakness or bargaining inadequacy. If used after some trust is established, the tactic may meet with more success. In determining departmental budgets, one manager may say to the other, "Help me out with some advice. How much do you allot for travel in your budget?" Asking for help can change the other person's view of their role in the conversation from opponent to adviser.

Finally, *negotiation judo* can build a better climate by ignoring criticism, attacks, and outrageous demands. When occasional criticism or negative comments occur (if not outside the boundaries of acceptance or a bullying pattern), the negotiator does not respond. Instead of becoming defensive, focus is maintained on the issue. Techniques such as emotional paraphrasing or reframing can be used. Thomas Crum's book, *The Magic of Conflict*, explains how conflict management is like the martial art of aikido: If someone is centered and has good self-esteem, other people's attacks do not hurt as much, and in fact, their negative energy can be channeled into more productive paths (Crum, 1987). For example, during a heated discussion Jessie slams her notebook down in frustration. Curtis can use that energy and say, "The frustration in here is high and that is because we are both passionate about doing what's best for our departments. What a boring place this would be if neither of us cared, wouldn't it?" Turning high frustration into positive energy can move parties to more positive interactions.

Summary

This chapter presented three approaches to negotiation: competitive, cooperative, and mixed. The everyday world provides opportunity to engage in ethical negotiation within each of the three approaches. Every person starts from a different place as a negotiator, depending on disposition and experience. Research indicated most people can improve and expand their negotiation techniques and abilities through awareness and training (Soliman, Stimec, & Antheaume, 2014).

People negotiate every day. Negotiation is communication in pursuit of goal achievement. Four conditions are necessary for negotiation to occur: a meaningful connection, outcome unpredictability, issues other than values, and a willingness to communicate.

Negotiation can be categorized as either competitive or cooperative. Competitive negotiation can be destructive if it degenerates to face issues, the winner's curse occurs, or personal victory is sought at all costs. Of the numerous competitive bargaining tactics, some are more constructive than others.

Cooperative negotiators search for a mutually satisfactory outcome for all. Focusing on interests instead of positions is a key skill. Preparing for collaborative negotiation entails several steps and consideration of a different set of tactics. Moving a negotiation partner from competition to cooperation can be difficult, but it is possible through the use of several specialized tactics.

Chapter Resources

Exercises

1. In the following cases, consider the steps in preparing to negotiate competitively versus preparing to negotiate cooperatively.

    ### Case One
    You have been concerned that one of your work team members, "Travis," is not carrying his weight on projects. Travis has been late in getting the data to you that you need and has started avoiding you. You need the data each week by Wednesday noon if you are to be able to submit your report to the director by Friday noon.

    ### Case Two
    You need to have every Friday afternoon off to take your child to music lessons. You have asked your boss to alter your schedule, but he or she just laughed and said "No" before you had a chance to give your reasons.

    ### Case Three
    You can't stand that your colleague in the next office "holds court" every morning for an hour with other coworkers and the administrative assistants. They review everyone's personal life and their favorite cable programs. You are planning to do something about the situation and will talk to your coworker tomorrow.

    ### Case Four
    You have several tests on the same day. You want to ask your instructor to allow you to take the test in this class at a different time.

    ### Case Five
    You overhear your roommate talking with a friend about a party on Friday night. You already have made plans for a party in your apartment on Friday.

2. Discuss the lessons you learned or messages you received about negotiation from your family as you were growing up. Were the lessons and messages you received more competitive or cooperative?
3. As a group, select an episode of a reality television program. Analyze the specific negotiation tactics that are used by the characters. Are most of the tactics more competitive or cooperative? Provide an explanation for your answer.
4. Compare Cases 9.2 and 9.3. What specific tactics are used in each case?
5. Provide five examples of the winner's curse.

Journal/Essay Topics

1. Create and implement a negotiation plan for one of the situations below. Write a one-page report on your plan and its effectiveness.

A. If your credit is good, call your credit card company and ask that your interest rate be lowered on any outstanding balance.

B. If you have been employed at the same place for over a year without a raise and your work record is good, ask your boss for a raise.

C. If purchasing a product over $50 at a small store or market, negotiate the price.

2. Reflect on a specific past negotiation that was markedly successful or unsuccessful. What tactics did you employ?

Research Topics

1. Review the published research that highlights the differences in negotiation by two specific cultures or subcultures. What advice would you give to individuals entering negotiation with either of those cultures?

2. In 2016, Wells Fargo Bank was investigated because a number of employees fraudulently opened false accounts for customers to achieve highly competitive sales goals. Investigate this situation and explain the role that extremely high and competitive sales goals might have played in this situation.

Mastery Case

Analyze the tactics employed in the Mastery Cases 9A Don't Try So Hard, 9B Abbe Has Got to Go, and 9C The Sibylline Books

Don't Try So Hard—You'll Ruin It for Everybody

Cindy, Samuel, and Darius work for a call center selling vacation packages. They have a sales goal of four sales per shift. If the goals are met over the course of a week, a salesperson will get a $100 bonus that week. The highest seller gets an additional $500 at the end of each month.

Cindy and Samuel like sales and work hard to outsell each other, often hitting seven or eight sales per shift. Darius routinely makes his three-hour quota, and has been doing this job for many years, compared to Cindy and Samuel, who started a few months ago. What Darius knows is that if Cindy and Samuel continue to surpass the goal, the goal will increase and make it harder for everyone to get their weekly bonus.

He pulls Cindy and Samuel aside one day and says, "Look you two. I know you're competitive and want the bonus. You two decide who gets the bonus, switch off or draw straws, I don't care. Just quit setting the bar so high because it will ruin it for the rest of us and turn this place into a sweatshop."

Cindy and Samuel make a plan to switch off who wins, agreeing it won't be by too much.

Abbe Has Got to Go

Abbe, Ross, and J.B. were assigned by the teacher to work together on a term project. J.B. is an all-A's-student, Ross typically gets high grades, and Abbe not so much. At the beginning of the project, all three agreed on a topic and that they would split the workload, with J.B. doing the research on one topic and all the final editing of the paper; Ross and Abbe each would do the research and write up the two parts of the paper. They decided to meet after class every other week to talk about how the project was going.

At the first two after-class meetings, Ross and J.B. showed everyone their notes and talked about how the research was going. Abbe just said everything was going great. J.B. followed up after the last meeting and texted Abbe to ask if she could send her list of references for the research so far so he could check for duplication of effort. No reply.

At the next scheduled meeting, Abbe slipped out after class saying she was too busy to meet. Ross and J.B. talked about their progress and shared their mutual concerns that Abbe wasn't doing her work. J.B. e-mailed Abbe and asked for a progress report. No reply.

After class the next day, Ross and J.B. met privately and decided to ask the professor to throw Abbe out of their group.

The Sibylline Books

A mythic story is told about a Sibyl in ancient Cumea who offered to sell nine secret scrolls containing prophecy to a king of Rome. She offered the nine scrolls for a price. He said it was too much. She threw two scrolls into the fire. She said "I now have seven scrolls." He asked how much. She mentioned the same price as before. He said it's too much for seven scrolls. She threw two more scrolls into the fire. She said, "I now have five scrolls of secret prophecies." He asked how much. She said the same price as originally stated for the nine scrolls. He paid the price.

References

Aloia, L. S., & Solomon, D. H. (2015). The physiology of argumentative skill deficiency: Cognitive ability, emotional competence, communication qualities, and responses to conflict. *Communication Monographs, 82*(3), 315–338.

Aloia, L. S., & Solomon, D. H. (2016). Emotions associated with verbal aggression expression and suppression. *Western Journal of Communication, 80*(1), 3–20.

Bazerman, M. H., & Samuelson, W. F. (1983). I won the auction but don't want the prize. *Journal of Conflict Resolution, 27*(4), 618–634.

Bok, S. (2004). Truthfulness, deceit, and trust. In C. Menkel-Meadow & M. Wheeler (Eds.), *What's fair: Ethics for negotiators* (pp. 79–90). San Francisco: John Wiley & Sons.

Carpenter, C. J., & Boster, F. J. (2009). A meta-analysis of the effectiveness of the disrupt-then-reframe compliance gaining technique. *Communication Reports, 22*(2), 55–62.

Cooley, J. W. (Ed.). (2005). *Creative problem solver's handbook for negotiators and mediators* (Vol. 2). Washington, DC: ABA Section of Dispute Resolution.

Creo, R. A. (2005). Creative problem-solving techniques and tactics. In J. W. Cooley (Ed.), *Creative problem solver's handbook for negotiators and mediators* (Vol. 2, pp. 42–54). Washington, DC: ABA Section of Dispute Resolution.

Crum, T. F. (1987). *The magic of conflict*. New York: Touchstone.

Dolinski, D., & Szczucka, K. (2013). Emotional dispute-then-reframe technique of social influence. *Journal of Applied Social Psychology, 43*, 2031–2041.

Fisher, R., Ury, W., & Patton, B. (1993). Negotiation power: Ingredients in an ability to influence the other side. In L. Hall (Ed.), *Negotiation: Strategies for mutual gain* (pp. 3–13). Newbury Park, CA: Sage.

Folger, J. P., Poole, M. S., & Stutman, R. K. (2013). *Working through conflict* (7th ed.). Boston: Pearson.

Foo, M. D., Elfenbein, H. A., Tan, H. H., & Aik, V. C. (2004). Emotional intelligence and negotiation: The tension between creating and claiming value. *The International Journal of Conflict Management, 15*(4), 411–429.

Garcia, A. C. (2000). Negotiating negotiation: The collaborative production of resolution in small claims mediation hearings. *Discourse and Society, 11*(3), 315–343.

Glascock, J. (2013). Prevalence and content of verbal aggression in children's television programming. *Communication Studies, 64*(3), 259–272.

Kellermann, K., & Cole, T. (1994). Classifying compliance gaining messages: Taxonomic disorder and strategic confusion. *Communication Theory, 4*(1), 3–60.

Kolb, D. M., & Williams, J. (2003). *Everyday negotiation: Navigating the agendas in bargaining.* San Francisco: Jossey-Bass.

Kray, L. J., Thompson, L., & Lind, E. A. (2005). It's a bet! A problem-solving approach promotes the construction of contingency agreements. *Personality and Social Psychology Bulletin, 31*(8), 1039–1051.

Lewicki, R. J., & Robinson, R. J. (2004). Ethical and unethical bargaining tactics: An empirical study. In C. Menkel-Meadow & M. Wheeler (Eds.), *What's fair: Ethics for negotiators* (pp. 221–220). San Francisco: Jossey-Bass.

McCorkle, S. (2015). *College roommate kit: How to minimize college roommate conflict.* iTunes. apple.com.

McCorkle, S., & Reese, M. J. (2015). *Mediation theory and practice* (2nd ed.). Los Angeles: Sage.

Meiners, E. B., & Miller, V. D. (2004). The effect of formality and relational tone on supervisor/subordinate negotiation episodes. *Western Journal of Communication, 68*(3), 302–321.

Raiffa, H., Richardson, J., & Metcalfe, D. (2002). *Negotiation analysis: The science and art of collaborative decision making.* Cambridge, MA: Belknap Press.

Rogan, R. G., & La France, B. H. (2003). An examination of the relationship between verbal aggressiveness, conflict management strategies, and conflict interaction goals. *Communication Quarterly, 51*(4), 458–469.

Sarkis, S. (2017, January 22). Gaslighting: Know it and identify it to protect yourself. *Psychology Today.* www.psychologytoday.com/blog/here-there-and-everywhere/201701/gaslighting-know-it-and-identify-it-protect-yourself. Accessed 9 July 2017.

Sclavi, M. (2008). The role of play and humor in creative conflict management. *Negotiation Journal, 24*(2), 157–180.

Soliman, C. G., Stimec, A., & Antheaume, N. (2014). The long-term impact of negotiation training and teaching implications. *Conflict Resolution Quarterly, 32*(2), 129–153.

Stein, N. L., & Albro, E. R. (2001). The origins and nature of arguments: Studies in conflict understanding, emotion, and negotiation. *Discourse Processes, 32*(2–3), 113–133.

Stringer, T. (2006). Barking dog negotiations: A mediator's own story. *ACResolution, 5*(2), 34–37.

Thompson, L., & Nadler, J. (2000). Judgmental biases in conflict resolution and how to overcome them. In M. Deutsch & P. T. Coleman (Eds.), *The handbook of conflict resolution* (pp. 213–235). San Francisco: Jossey-Bass.

Van Kleef, G., De Dreu, C., Pietroni, D., & Manstead, A. (2006). Power and emotion in negotiation: Power moderates the interpersonal effects of anger and happiness on concession making. *European Journal of Social Psychology, 36*(4), 557–581.

Chapter 10

Conflict Assessment

Vocabulary

Comprehensive Conflict Checklist

Conflict assessment

Conflict Road Map

Critical choice points

Flashpoint

Imagined interaction

Interests

Mulling

Positions

Objectives

After reading the chapter, you should be able to:

1. Explain the usefulness of conflict analysis
2. Understand the focus of different conflict analysis tools
3. Apply a conflict analysis tool to a personal conflict

Understanding Conflict From the Inside Out

Conflict involves many factors: the relationship of the parties to each other, the context of the conflict, precipitating events, personal styles, power resources, personal histories, and much more. People find themselves in conflict and wonder, "How did I get here?" "What is really going on?" and "How can we move forward?"

The ability to analyze conflict allows insights that may escape the participants in the heat of an interaction. **Conflict assessment** involves taking a step back to evaluate the many factors that led to this moment. Through analysis, conflict managers can make informed decisions and purposeful moves to foster a goal of productively managing the conflict situation.

In many ways, analysis of interpersonal conflict is all about self- and other-awareness. Self-awareness requires the courage to ask tough questions and to give honest answers. The tandem requirement is an ability to move beyond self-centered attributions about the other person's motives. The level of awareness, maturity, and desire of the parties involved is critical in the successful analysis of a conflict. This is not an easy task. Successful analysis requires both experiencing the conflict and stepping outside of it while it is happening. In particular, one must be able to detect interests and goals. Although often challenging to do, conflict assessment can bring about greater clarification, improved interactions, and relational growth. In short, the effort is worth the work.

CASE 10.1

Dress Code

Kaitlin and William dated for months before recently moving in together. Sometimes William is uncomfortable when other men look at Kaitlin because she likes to wear low-cut blouses and tight jeans. William has asked Kaitlin to "tone down" her wardrobe. She said she understood, but she needed to be herself. One day, William confronted Kaitlin when she dressed for their night out.

William:	"You've got to be kidding. You're not wearing *that*."
Kaitlin:	"What do you mean?"
William:	"You look like a cheap hooker."
Kaitlin:	"A hooker? Are you kidding me?"
William:	"I thought you said you'd tone down your clothes. What were you thinking when you put that on? Do you want everyone to stare at your chest all night?"
Kaitlin:	"I thought I would wear what I wanted, and I don't care what other people think. You used to like this outfit when we first met. I can't believe you are so judgmental and mean!"
William:	"Hey, I'm just telling you what everybody is thinking. You look like a hooker."
Kaitlin:	"So you want me to change and that will shut you up?"
William:	"Hey, I don't really care. I'm just not going out with you looking like that."
Kaitlin:	"You're assuming that *I* still want to go out with *you*."

Analyzing current conflicts can help determine the best strategies to meet the goals of the parties. However, it is useful to scrutinize a past conflict to learn from personal history as a route to escape destructive patterns in the future. Looking for themes and trends in conflicts from the past may prove easier, as time may dilute some of the emotional intensity felt while in the middle of the situation. The benefits of conflict analysis include an opportunity to build a better understanding of a conflict, to learn from past mistakes, and to reflect on productive choices rather than responses from habit.

This chapter discusses some ways to analyze and learn from the past so future conflicts can be managed more productively. It also presents several choices to guide conflict analysis (see Table 10.1). We first present tools that are easier to apply, such as identifying Conflict Causes and Mapping. The next section presents tools for more comprehensive analysis: The Comprehensive Conflict Checklist, the Conflict Road Map, and the Imagined Interaction.

Simpler Conflict Analysis Tools

Locating Goal Interference

As stated in Chapter 1, conflict arises when we perceive goal interference. General areas of goal interference (i.e., causes of conflict) include emotions, values, structure, style, information, and substance.

TABLE 10.1 Conflict Analysis Tools

Tool	Best Use	Adapted From
Locate Goal Interference	Identifying the type of goal interference being experienced by each individual	Mayer's Wheel of Conflict; Moore's Circle of Conflict
Mapping	Identify interests and fears in the conflict	Australian Conflict Resolution Network, crnhq.org
Comprehensive Conflict Check List	Total overview of a conflict	Australian Conflict Resolution Network
Conflict Road Map	Total overview of a conflict; particularly applicable to multi-party conflicts	Wehr
Awareness Wheel	Both parties working through the analysis one person at a time	Miller, Miller, Nunally, & Wackman
Imagined Interaction	Locate flashpoints and plan how to phrase comments during an upcoming conflict episode	Honeycutt & Ford

Emotion-based conflicts arise from hurt feelings, grievances, or other strong emotions. People who perceive attacks feel interference with their self-esteem goals. If any of this type of conflict goes on long enough, an emotional element may be overlaid onto the original conflict. In Case 10.1, Kaitlin and William are experiencing strong emotions. Conflict arising from the emotion area is focused on the feelings each participant has and how they react to hurt or embarrassment. The listening skills discussed in Chapter 7 are useful when immersed in conflict with emotional elements.

DISCUSSION QUESTION • 10.1

In Case 10.1, what might have triggered emotions for William and Kaitlin?

Value-based conflicts are the most difficult to resolve because they require the exploration of underlying beliefs, cultural influences, and deep-seated views of how the world should operate. Those who believe only their values are correct may find the mere existence of other values as a threat. Values may come into play as each person determines what "appropriate" means. Because values are so ingrained in our sense of what is right and what is wrong, values may be non-negotiable in conflict. At times the best we can hope for is to respect the differences and agree to disagree. Just because values are in conflict, it does not mean that people cannot work together amiably.

DISCUSSION QUESTION • 10.2

Identify possible value differences between Kaitlin and William. What do you think the likelihood is that either will modify their values? How else might they manage their value conflict?

Structure-based conflicts are about how ideas, tasks, space and physical settings, or things are organized. People who prefer one way of doing a task may see another's preference for a different method as interference with doing the task the "right way" (i.e., my way). Structure conflicts can be about complicated rules or simple procedures. Rules might include the question of what topics are open for discussion. Every relationship has an implicit rule structure. The structure might be one of equality or of a more powerful and less powerful symmetry.

Style-based conflicts arise from preferred ways of communicating, as discussed in Chapter 8. Because one's style may feel like the best way to communicate, people with different styles may seem to be interfering with the communication process. Discovering if people in conflict communicate in ways that annoy each other can be helpful, as differences often becomes less important once people recognize they are just personal styles.

Information-based conflict is about data or facts. Sometimes these conflicts are about which information is correct. At other times, information conflicts arise when one person withholds information.

Substantive-based conflict is about concrete and tangible things. These things can be counted and distributed, and disagreements occur over how to divide or manage these items. Money, time, use of a car, or any resource can lie at the heart of a substantive conflict.

Where conflict primarily resides matters because the initial actions taken to change a conflict differ for each causal area. The questions in Toolbox 10.1 help identify where a conflict resides. The strategies to transform the conflict vary depending on the type of goal interference experienced. If the conflict is about one person having different sets of data than the other, then conflict transformation starts with a focus on identifying and sharing information. The conflict manager might want to determine if everyone has the same information or negotiate which information will be used as decisions are made. If the conflict falls mainly into the value area, such as whether unmarried couples should live together, then more information probably won't be helpful. Strategies to bring shared values to the surface, to create commonality, or to agree to disagree are paths to conflict transformation.

TOOLBOX 10.1   Conflict Causes Worksheet

Which of the following seem to be driving the conflict?

Emotions

- What emotions are driving the conflict for each party?
- How are emotions being expressed in the conflict?

Values

- Are values different in the conflict?
- What values do both parties share that might be used to create commonalities?

Structure

- What is the setting (i.e., work, home, pub) of the conflict?
- Are there rules (formal or informal) or procedures for conflict in this situation?

- Are there time constraints built into the situation that affect the parties' actions?
- Is the medium used during the conflict affecting how it is expressed (face-to-face, chat room, Twitter)?

Style

- Are communication style differences affecting how the individuals are reacting?
- Are cultural style differences affecting how each person perceives the process?
- Are the parties invested in proving their personal style is the "right" approach?
- Do the individuals have different conflict management styles?

Information

- Do the parties have the same information?
- Is there argument about which information is right?

Substance

- Is the conflict free from emotional content?
- Will resolution of resource issues manage the conflict?

Of course the causal areas discussed above are not mutually exclusive; there may be more than one type of perceived interference in play at the same time. However, analysis at this basic level can lead to insights into which parts of the conflict are more pressing than others at that moment. In Case 10.1, emotions and values predominate for Kaitlin and William and must be addressed first before they can reach a mutually acceptable outcome on the specific issue of what clothes should be worn.

Mapping

A visual representation of conflict can be created through mapping. The Australian Conflict Resolution Network suggests drawing a map for quick analysis of a situation. The method starts with stating the issue of the conflict as proper identification of the issue is important (see the discussion of issues in Chapter 9). For obvious reasons, if the map doesn't start with the right issue, then the rest of the analysis probably will go astray.

After the issue is identified, personal fears are listed about what will happen if the issue is not resolved. Next, the needs to be met in an acceptable outcome are listed. Then, the analysis turns to speculation about the other person's needs and fears. Care should be taken to list these items in good faith, rather than ascribing evil intent to the other person.

Mapping forces attention on the **interests** that underlie **positions**. Someone may *want* an apology (position) but *need* to have some recognition of how she was affected by the other's actions (interest).

A second aspect that the mapping tool highlights is fear. Fear that a goal or interest may not be met could be driving either person's behaviors. Sometimes creative strategies or acknowledgement of each individual's concerns can change the tone of the conflict. According to the mapping model, understanding needs and fears keeps the focus on the basics during conflict and builds empathy toward the other party.

After the incident in Case 10.1, William and Kaitlin didn't go out, and a rift was created between them. William decided to analyze what was going on because he feared the two of them were on the verge of breaking up. Using the mapping worksheet (Toolbox 10.2), William laid out what he thought was going on. He posited that Kaitlin probably feared losing autonomy while he feared the disapproval of his parents, as well as losing her (which manifested in jealousy of other men). Yet this did not provide enough explanation of how their conflict developed. Although mapping was helpful, William needed a more detailed tool to help him think about the conflict.

TOOLBOX 10.2   Mapping Worksheet

Party 1: _____

Needs (Interests): _____
Fears (Barriers to Settlement): _____

The Issue is _____

Party 2: _____

Needs (Interests): _____
Fears (Barriers to Settlement): _____

Source: Adapted from the Australian Conflict Resolution Network

---

Comprehensive Conflict Analysis Tools

When a simple analysis is not revealing, a more complex method of viewing the conflict becomes necessary. By following the steps and answering the questions in a comprehensive tool, the entire dynamic of a conflict is laid bare. Comprehensive tools are useful when it is not obvious at first glance what is driving the conflict or what may be motivating the other person. Several comprehensive tools are discussed in this section: the Comprehensive Conflict Checklist, the Conflict Roadmap, the Awareness Wheel, the Interactive Conflict Map, and the Imagined Interaction.

Comprehensive Conflict Checklist

A companion to mapping, also adapted in part from materials developed by the Australian Conflict Resolution Network, is the foundation of the first tool discussed in this section. The **Comprehensive Conflict Checklist** in Toolbox 10.3 asks a series of questions that reveal an expansive view of the conflict.

TOOLBOX 10.3   Comprehensive Conflict Checklist

Needs

1. Beyond what I want, what is my real need?
2. Beyond what the other wants, what is his or her real need?

Cooperation Potential

3. What do I want as an outcome for both of us?
4. Are our needs mutually exclusive? Can the issue be expanded to find a mutual benefit?

Empathy

5. What is it like to be in the other's shoes?
6. Have I really listened? Do I need to paraphrase or validate to show I'm listening?

Framing

7. How can I state what I need without blaming or attacking the other person?
8. How can I state the problem so we both can be involved in finding the solution?

Power

9. How are each of us using power? Is either party using power inappropriately?
10. Is either party trying to gain more power out of a feeling of powerlessness or of being attacked? How can I allay those fears?
11. Is power too imbalanced? If so, what can I do to manage power?

Emotions

12. What are each of us feeling? What emotions are holding us back?
13. Will telling the other how I feel help the situation?
14. How can I manage my feelings?

Willingness to Resolve

15. Do I really want the conflict to be managed?
16. Does the conflict serve some other function or purpose for our relationship?

Negotiation

17. How can I make this a fair deal for both parties?
18. What do I have that the other wants? What does the other have that I want?

Face

19. Has either of us invested our personality or face into the conflict?
20. How can I help the other save face?

Aftermath

21. What do I want our relationship to be like in the future?
22. What should we do if problems arise in the future?

Source: Adapted, in part, from the Australian Conflict Resolution Network

William from the case earlier in the chapter completed the Comprehensive Conflict Checklist to help him better understand his conflict with Kaitlin. He answered all of the questions, representing Kaitlin's viewpoint as honestly as he could without her input. He gained the insight that each of them only thought of their personal interests and never talked about the situation in ways to permit mutual interests to emerge. He discovered in the *empathy* area that he previously didn't think about her perspective very much and that either of them could have *framed* the conflict better—perhaps like this: How can Kaitlin have independence and individuality in the way she dresses and at the same time William feel less jealous or concerned about other people's reactions? Other areas of the comprehensive analysis revealed more about the dynamic nature of their conflict.

After answering all the questions, William decided which areas were the most critical and offered the most opportunity to manage the conflict more productively. For example, given a different framing, Kaitlin might have been less defensive and able to talk the issue through. Given this knowledge, William felt better prepared to enter a conversation with Kaitlin that would be less hostile and more productive.

DISCUSSION QUESTION • 10.3

How could William approach Kaitlin more productively? What do you think would have to happen to make Kaitlin receptive to working on this issue?

Conflict Road Map

Wehr (1998) recommends answering a series of questions to create a road map of a conflict. Although Wehr's tool was developed for group or international conflicts, we adapted it to analyze interpersonal conflict (Toolbox 10.4). One or both individuals create the road map to seek insights about the conflict. When possible, both parties compare road maps or work together to form a mutual road map—and thereby create a common view of information, goals, and communication processes.

TOOLBOX 10.4   Conflict Road Map

Conflict context

Gather information about the conflict history and context. Conflicts do not exist in a vacuum.

Parties

Place the primary parties who have a stake in the outcome and who are opposing each other in a circle. In an outer circle, place the secondary parties and/or allies who have a stake in the outcome but may not be directly involved in the interaction. Put any mediators or other third parties who try to intervene off to the side.

Causes and consequences

List what seems to be driving the conflict (the goal interference) and the consequences of the conflict (hostility, defensiveness, etc.).

Contrasting beliefs

In two columns, list any contrasting beliefs or values held by the parties.

Goals and interests

In two columns, list what the parties say they want (positions). What interests seem to be beneath the positions?

Dynamics

What is the historical flow of the conflict? Has it escalated? Are the parties polarized? Is each person mirroring the negative tactics of the other?

Functions

Does the conflict have a purpose? What does maintaining the conflict do for each group?

Regulation potential

What is keeping the conflict from getting bigger (self-restraint, rules, laws)? Are there forces that limit the conflict or could help to manage it?

Source: Adapted from Wehr (1998)

After the fight, Kaitlin looked back at the episode in Case 10.1 using the Conflict Road Map. She wrote her recollections in each of the eight areas of the road map. In the *parties* area, she recorded that the conflict was driven, in part, by William's relationship with his parents. Under *contrasting beliefs*, she listed the influence of William's church on his perceptions of appropriate dress. She noted her easygoing attitude from her California beach upbringing, as well as the rebellion she felt in reaction to her own father's conservatism. In the *dynamic* section, she itemized the types of name-calling and mirroring tactics that led them to hurt each other's feelings. After gaining insight from each area of the Conflict Road Map, she retrospectively assessed which areas were most important to the conflict at the time and which behaviors might be altered to manage conflict productively in the future. Using the Conflict Road Map, Kaitlin concluded that because they didn't directly confront their different values and beliefs, the conflict likely would grow and that the tactics each one currently used might create a destructive spiral of negativity.

Awareness Wheel

The conflict analysis tools previously discussed can be accomplished by one person. Another approach is for parties to work through a conflict analysis together.

Miller, Miller, Nunally, and Wackman (1991) created a model of conflict analysis called the Awareness Wheel. While one person can use the tool independently, it is best if both parties participate. The listener and the speaker have specific responsibilities. Two people alternate the speaker and listener roles and answer a specific question in each area (Toolbox 10.5). Using this model, Kaitlin, as the first speaker, starts the process by giving her *observation of data*, presenting a picture of what she has noticed in nonjudgmental terms. The other person takes the listener role. The listener's job is to *attend to the message* fully. The listener may *acknowledge* the speaker verbally or nonverbally but not give an opinion during this stage.

Kaitlin could say to William, "William, I've noticed since we've moved in together that you have commented on my outfits more often than before we moved in together." Next, the speaker presents an *interpretation* of the event. This is an opinion of what the observed behavior means. Kaitlin may say, "I think that you are ashamed of me or really jealous." Presenting how she feels about the situation is the next step. She might say, "I feel confused because I thought you liked how I dressed. I'm feeling hurt when I think I'm being judged." Throughout this process, William's job is to continue listening and indicate his attention through verbal or nonverbal acknowledgments. If he's confused by something, he can ask for more information, being careful not to take the floor from the designated speaker by judging or offering an opinion.

TOOLBOX 10.5   The Awareness Wheel

Sensory Data	What have I seen or heard?
	Kaitlin: William comments on my outfits using derogatory language.
Interpretations	What do I think is going on?
	Kaitlin: "I think you are ashamed of me."
Feelings	How do I feel?
	Kaitlin: "I feel confused because how I dress was what first attracted you."
Wants	What do I want?
	Kaitlin: "I want to express who I am without being criticized."
Actions	What will I do in the future?
	Kaitlin: "I am willing to listen to your concerns if you aren't so negative."

Kaitlin's next step is voicing her wants: for herself, for William, and for the two of them together. She could say, "I want for me to be able to express who I am through my clothing choices without feeling judged. I want for you to be comfortable being seen with me and confident that I am not looking for another guy. I want for us to be able to talk without being mean to each other and to work through this and other problems that might arise." Finally, Kaitlin would indicate what actions she is willing to take. She might say, "I am willing to listen to your concerns about clothes and may be willing to make modifications if I see them as reasonable."

Once Kaitlin completes the wheel and she feels confident that William is aware of her views, they switch roles so the listener role is assumed by Kaitlin and William becomes the speaker. The new speaker works through the five areas of the model while the partner listens.

DISCUSSION QUESTION • 10.4

How might William respond to the five questions in the Awareness Wheel? Discuss the benefits/disadvantages of one party speaking at length while the other listens, as suggested in the Awareness Wheel.

The Imagined Interaction

When approaching an interview, a job candidate:

> buys the right suit, reads the right books, conducts the right company research, and prepares herself for the questions that the potential employer may propose. In preparing herself for those questions, she develops a mental picture of the situation, including likely dialogue. She imagines the questions the interviewer may propose while also developing possible answers she may offer.
>
> (Honeycutt & Ford, 2001, p. 315)

While preparing meticulously for a job interview seems natural, people rarely prepare with the same level of detail for difficult or conflict-laden encounters. Mentally anticipating what will occur during an interaction is called the **imagined interaction**. This activity is different from **mulling**, where one obsessively replays a past negative encounter or frets about what might happen in the future. It is also different from fantasy, which is based on wishful or fanciful thinking.

CASE 10.2A

The Grand Old Opry: Part I

Justin (excited and happy): "Good news, baby! I've got hotel reservations this weekend in Atlantic City and we're going to see a Grand Old Opry Review show."

Hanna (happy at the first part of the news, and then the emotion changes to scorn): "Grand Old Opry Review? I'm not going to any lame country western show while we are in Atlantic City. I want to have some fun!"

Justin (crushed): "I'm trying to set up something nice. You probably want to lie around the pool all day and then drink in some bar all night."

Hanna: "That's right. The pool, the casino, some great music, and dancing. There's not going to be any lame country western thing. It's like I should have that big Dolly Parton hair and wear a funky little cowgirl hat. No way."

Justin (getting mad): "Fine. We'll just stay here and I'll watch the games all weekend with my friends."

Hanna: "Now don't get all sulky and mad." Justin leaves, slamming the door.

The imagined interaction can be an important tool for developing new scripts to use in the future. It also can be adapted as a tool for analyzing past conflicts. Case 10.2A Part I illustrates a past conflict episode written like a small short story or play, with dialogue and context.

If Hanna applied the imagined interaction tool, she would analyze the conversation retrospectively to determine her goal, Justin's probable goal, any goal interference that occurred during the conversation, and the **flashpoint** where the conflict emerged. After understanding the conflict through the initial analysis, Hanna then rewrites the dialogue to what she wished would have happened (Case 10.2B Part II).

By rewriting the dialogue, Hanna forms a new mental script that is available when similar conflicts begin in the future. Instead of just reliving the past in her mind, which keeps the conflict alive, she changes the scenario. She can identify the flashpoint in a conflict where her comments provoked defensiveness and with this awareness watch for it showing up in the future. With a new script and new tactics in mind, she has more choices. Imagined interactions are mental rehearsals in preparation for the next conflict encounter.

CASE 10.2B

The Grand Old Opry: Part II

Justin (excited and happy): "Good news, baby! I've got hotel reservations this weekend in Atlantic City, and we're going to see a Grand Old Opry Review show."

Hanna (happy about the surprise weekend away but cautious about the show plans): "Atlantic City! That's fabulous! What a great idea to get out of town together this weekend."

Justin (happy and proud of himself): "Yeah, I've been planning this special weekend for a couple weeks. It's been hard not telling you, but I wanted it to be a surprise."

Hanna (still praising Justin): "That's so nice. What about this Old Opry thing? You know I'm not crazy about that twangy country music."

Justin (cautiously; he knows this might set Hanna off): "I know. I know. You like dance music in bars. But this is so special. The hotel is amazing with an inside atrium. The show has the stars from that talent contest program that you're addicted to. You love that show, so I was thinking we could go and see something that I like for a change, and it shouldn't be *too* painful for you. It's only a couple of hours, and we can do something else afterward if you want."

Hanna (thoughtfully): "You're right that I can't stand that country western stuff, but it'd be fun to see some of those contestants. As long as I don't have to wear one of those cowgirl hats. And casinos are open all night, right?"

A final way that Hanna could use this analysis tool is to share what she wished she had said to Justin by reading him her imagined script. This action has the benefit of showing Justin that she is willing to consider his views and his efforts. The process of introducing the imagined interaction into the conversation allows the parties to reenter negotiations on a positive note.

> **KEY 10.1**
>
> Use analysis to discover what is keeping the conflict alive.

Transformation Is the Key to Changing Conflict

Conflict assessment can assist in understanding past conflicts, locate how to transform a current situation, or provide a guide for future interactions. Without knowledge, choices seem limited and negative patterns are more likely to be repeated. Without understanding how individuals fall into conflict, it is difficult to work one's way out of conflict or prevent destructive interactions. With knowledge, choice multiplies.

To alter the shape of a conflict, some aspect of it must be *transformed*. Some part of the conflict has to be changed. Because the strategy of persuading the other person to change his or her behavior rarely works, the possibility of change is in the hands of the student of conflict management. Now that you know more about conflict, you are the one who can make a move to keep relationships from becoming crippled by dysfunction.

Assessment will determine the critical pattern or behavior that turns an exchange dysfunctional or keeps a conflict alive. An unexamined conflict is like a ball of string where everything is tangled together. People must find the end of a thread to pull and release the tangle. Pulling the string without planning can make the knots more difficult to untie. Conflict assessment identifies the specific thread of a conflict that might unravel the complex mass.

After assessing the conflict, one can create a plan for transformation. Change in any one aspect of a conflict may affect the entire dynamic. Some aspects that might be transformed include changing perception of the other person's motives, expectations, goals, information shared, communication styles, structural barriers, how decisions are made, moving relationally closer or further away, boundaries, power management, cultural differences, face concerns, and/or common values.

Summary

Conflict analysis is a beneficial method to develop self-awareness and options for future conflict management. Locating goal interference is a tool to see where a conflict primarily resides (communication, emotion, value, structure, style, or substantive). The Australian Simple Mapping tool presents a straightforward analysis of the needs and fears driving an issue. The Comprehensive Conflict Checklist and the Conflict Road Map are detailed tools to analyze a conflict systematically. The Awareness Wheel provides speaker and listener roles and responsibilities to help parties navigate through a discussion of a conflict. The Imagined Interaction is helpful to locate the behaviors that turn a conflict toward the unproductive side and allows individuals to rehearse conversational strategies that might transform a conflict.

The key to conflict management is transformation of some element of the conflict. Analysis uncovers the critical place to focus transformative action.

Chapter Resources

Exercises

1. *Creating Your Own Analysis Tool*

Sometimes the tools created by others aren't exactly right for a specific conflict. For example, some conflicts seem to erupt simply because two people have different styles and one can't stand how the other person behaves. If a style difference is the basis of a conflict, the tools described in this chapter are less useful. Instead, use the style chapter to create your own method of analysis.

Create a tool to analyze communication style based on the concept of escalators and fractionators. Put your name and the other's name in two columns on a sheet of paper, and then list the behaviors and style characteristics each person exhibits. Draw a line at the bottom of the characteristic section. Then list how each person perceives the other's style. Hanna might analyze her interactions and discover that she has an escalatory style that relies on exaggeration and sarcasm, whereas Justin has a more fractionator style—but will become defensive and blow up when he feels rejected. Knowing that these style differences exist, Hanna can choose to ask questions instead of escalating the conflict through sarcasm. By understanding **critical choice points** in the conflict, a different path can be selected.

Using the above concept of escalators and fractionators or a tool you create using a different concept from Chapter 8, analyze a conflict you experienced that was driven by differences in communication style.

Journal/Essay Topic

1. Describe a conflict from your personal history. Apply one of the tools in this chapter to analyze the past conflict. After analyzing the conflict, identify what was sustaining the conflict and critical choice points where you could have used a different tactic or made a different choice to transform the outcome.

Research/Analysis Topics

1. Record an episode of any situation comedy. Choose one of the tools in this chapter to analyze the conflict in the episode. (Hint: If you take out the humor, what would the episode be about?)

Mastery Case

Which concepts from the chapter best help explain Mastery Case 10A, Roadblocks at the Bank?

Roadblocks at the Bank

After discovering that her bank was charging a fee of $25 per year on each of her Roth IRA accounts (which was more than she was earning in interest), Dana wanted to move her account to a bank that didn't charge fees. The new bank filed the paperwork three times to make the transfer, and the old bank either ignored the requests or found some minor error each time. They didn't notify anyone of the errors, so months would go by before Dana discovered the money hadn't been transferred.

She called the toll-free number on her account and was told that she had to visit the local branch. After arriving at the local branch, she was told that they couldn't do anything, and she should call the national toll-free number. Dana explained that she had called the number and was told to come to the branch. The information clerk called the number and heard the instructions and then consulted with branch managers in her office. The clerk returned to say that they couldn't do anything, and the new bank should just send in a request. Dana said, "They have sent three requests already. Are you saying you don't have the authority to do anything or that you are choosing not to do anything?" The clerk replied, "We can't do anything." Dana repeated her question and the clerk repeated her answer, becoming red in the face. Dana explained that she wanted to know if the lack of action was a policy or an internal decision. The clerk left and returned with the branch manager. Dana repeated her question. The branch manager explained that they couldn't get into the retirement accounts with their computers and had no control over them. Dana expressed frustration that the national number sent her to the local branch when they don't have the authority to do anything, and she left.

References

Australian Conflict Resolution Network. (2017). *Resolve the conflict guide*. Crhnq.org. Accessed 7 February 2017.

Honeycutt, J. M., & Ford, S. G. (2001). Mental imagery and intrapersonal communication: A review of research on imagined interactions (IIs) and current developments. In W. B. Gudykunst (Ed.), *Communication yearbook 25* (pp. 315–345). Thousand Oaks, CA: Sage.

Miller, S., Miller, P., Nunally, E., & Wackman, D. (1991). *Talking and listening together*. Littleton, CO: Interpersonal Communication Programs.

Wehr, P. (1998). *Conflict mapping*. Colorado.edu/conflict/peace/treatment/cmap.htm. Accessed 24 June 2008.

Section III

Conflict in Specialized Circumstances

Dealing with difficult behaviors saps our energy and can make life miserable. People who are normally rational, under stressful situations, can become difficult. There also are individuals who seem to relish wielding their power who become bullies. Bullying in the workplace is a common experience that only has recently emerged into our consciousness. Regardless of the causes or motivations of people who exhibit difficult behaviors, conflict managers need practical response strategies because the standard rules of engagement may not apply in these special circumstances. Chapter 11 answers the questions: What makes a difficult person difficult? What behaviors may make people escalate conflict? How prevalent is bullying? What can be done about bullying? Chapter 12 examines what happens when individuals no longer can manage their conflicts and others are called in to assist, with special attention to mediation. Chapter 13 looks beyond the obvious to determine the effects of strong emotion on conflict, as well as the role of anger, apology, forgiveness, and reconciliation.

Chapter 11

Bullies and Difficult People

Vocabulary

Bullying

Bystanders

Cyberbullies

Griefers

Happy slapping

Mobbing

Outing/Trickery

Psychological terror

Unearned criticism

Objectives

After reading the chapter, you should be able to:

1. Understand the error of attributing motives to difficult behaviors
2. Explain the critical lessons about difficult encounters
3. Explain how bullying differs from incivility
4. Discuss the prevalence of bullying in schools and workplaces
5. Contrast the three theories about what causes bullying

CASE 11.1

New Boss/New Rules

Tamara works as the Tutoring Coordinator in the Math Department at a medium-sized college. She has a master's degree in education and a bachelor's degree in mathematics. As professional staff, she works directly with students, helping them with the coursework, and manages the tutoring staff of 15. Under the previous Department Chair, Tamara was treated as a member of the faculty, invited to all meetings, and her opinion was regularly solicited and followed. When the old Chair retired, they brought in Dr. Reginald in her place.

Dr. Reginald has very particular ideas about who should have a voice in the college, and it wouldn't be professional staff like Tamara. She realized she got off to a rocky start when she introduced herself to him by putting out her hand and saying, "Hi, I'm Tamara." Dr. Reginald didn't return the handshake and said pointedly, "I'm *Doctor* Reginald" and fixed her with a look that made it seem she had broken a rule of decorum. Initially Tamara took opportunities to share her opinions and advice by email, thinking she was helping to orient Dr. Reginald into his new job, but was told by Dr. Reginald's assistant that it annoyed him.

Over the first semester he was chair, Dr. Reginald disinvited Tamara to the faculty meetings and sent a memo to all professional staff that he would meet with them as a group once a month to brief them on upcoming work. He made a point to mention he wanted any communication to go through his assistant, and not directly to him. Tamara knew this was directed at her.

Things started changing for Tamara at work. She was told by close colleagues that Dr. Reginald was talking to other staff about how difficult Tamara was to work with, and questioning her credentials and the quality of her work. She noticed that some faculty who were friendly with her before he came were now distant. She also noted that other professional staff could joke with Dr. Reginald, but he only spoke to her in clipped tones. But she loved her job, the students loved her, and she didn't let this friction get to her.

In March she had her first evaluation with Dr. Reginald. Whereas she had always had glowing evaluations, Dr. Reginald found her to be below average in most areas and put her on an improvement plan—a first step to getting fired. Tamara was surprised and upset, and realized she had no idea how to make this situation better.

If life were easy, all conflicts would be about simple issues, people would treat each other with courtesy, and everyone would have compatible communication styles. Sadly, we occasionally meet and work with people who seem difficult to get along with. This chapter examines the causes, dynamics, and strategies for difficult encounters. The chapter also examines bullying, as it is now recognized as a prevalent problem on college campuses, workplaces, and social encounters. Although we recognize the danger of labeling someone "difficult," we are starting from the viewpoint of the recipient of problematic behavior. It is the perception of difficulty that produces feelings of goal interference and hence conflict. We also recognize that the term "bullying" can be overused. In the section on bullying, we will differentiate between the behaviors of bullies and difficult people.

These are the first questions often asked after a difficult encounter: "What did I do to deserve that treatment?" or "Why can't I make the other person treat me better?" The truth is that those who suffer the brunt of annoying or difficult behaviors may or may not have provoked the episode. Sometimes the people we find difficult to work with have personal problems or extreme skill deficiencies. But, as we discussed in Chapter 3, personal behaviors, such as a superior tone or evaluative comments, sometimes *do* provoke defensiveness. Sometimes the styles of the two people grate across each other's sensibilities. In Chapter 8, we noted that polar opposite styles might give rise to a perception of goal interference based entirely on personal preference. Whatever the cause, the effective conflict manager is responsible for trying to diffuse difficult situations and work toward more productive outcomes.

An Overview of Difficult Encounters

> **DISCUSSION QUESTION • 11.1**
>
> Describe the behaviors of a difficult person you've encountered. Are their behaviors similar or dissimilar to how you generally act toward others? How did the difficulties get resolved, if at all?

Just as there are many contexts and variables of interpersonal conflict, there are many complexities of difficult encounters (Duck, Kirkpatrick, & Foley, 2006). What makes these encounters "difficult" is that the conversation does not unfold as expected and customary communication strategies don't work. The anticipated give-and-take of conversation in an office may not occur because one employee does all the talking or aggressively steps in to tell everyone else what to do. A financial aid counselor's comment that a student's parking tickets must be cleared before a check could be awarded may be met with extreme anger and personal attacks. Attempts to get a group member to do her share of the work on a class project may be met with belligerent defensiveness and a retort that the leader always picks on her. Asking a sincere question to clarify a policy may be met with personal attacks about how the questioner is a presumptuous troublemaker.

Once we can recognize difficult behaviors, the next step is to think about why customers, family members, coworkers, friends, or acquaintances might behave in these strange ways. Table 11.1 lists some possible motives of people during difficult encounters.

When experiencing a difficult situation, it is tempting to attribute negative motives or a defective personality to the other person. For example, if a coworker speaks loudly when giving instructions, one might attribute that he needs to control the situation because he thinks he is superior. We tend to combine our past experiences, some speculation, and a few facts to create a story: He is trying to push me around. We then act in response to the "story" we created, based on a guess about why that person is behaving as he is.

A discussion with a group of librarians elicited an encounter that evidently repeats almost daily in the library. The patron arrives with an overdue fine grasped in his fist. The patron approaches the desk in a huff and angrily states, "You people don't keep very good records here. I am sure I returned this book, and it is probably on the shelf right now." The librarian feels attacked, thinks the patron is an ogre, and wants to respond with something like "Too bad! Pay the fine or get out." If the difficult encounter is managed poorly, the librarian will suffer more verbal abuse, the library misses its end goal of serving the public and getting the book back, and the patron will still have

TABLE 11.1 Possible Motives of Difficult People

A desire to control the situation
A need to exert power
A cover for embarrassment
Fear of loss of self-esteem or loss of "face"
Fear of economic loss
Need to be recognized
Low self-esteem
Cultural habits
Need to feel superior

an unpaid bill—leaving all parties unsatisfied. Is the patron really an ogre, or could the difficult behavior be masking something else?

One of the critical questions in learning to deal with difficult people is to ask, "How can we tell which motive matches which behavior?" The simple answer is: We can't. Unless you have telepathy, you cannot know what motivates a person's behaviors at any given moment in time. What one person interprets as snobbish or superiority may be motivated by something else entirely: insecurity, cultural upbringing, or even poor hearing. Because we can't read people's minds, we must rely on communication skills, experience, patience, and lessons learned from research to guide our responses.

KEY 11.1

It is virtually impossible to know the exact motives behind someone else's communication.

Critical Insights About Difficult Encounters

The First Critical Insight: Distrust First Impressions

The first lesson in dealing with difficult encounters is to distrust first impulses—often to attack or defend—and to withhold judgment until more information is obtained. As in the case of the patron with the library fine, the difficult behavior is masking a real need—perhaps avoiding paying a bill for a mistake or to be able to use the library even if he has no money to pay the fine. Unfortunately, some people have not learned how to state their needs gracefully or how to ask for help. They fear being taken advantage of by "the system" or in starting off in a weak negotiating posture. Instead of making a rational argument, they become belligerent, exaggerate their claims, and even conceal the real problem behind a show of anger, whining, or misdirection.

One of the underlying factors exacerbating difficult encounters is poor communication skills. Some people lack the skills to be assertive without being aggressive. Others use extreme tactics because they are afraid of appearing weak. Many individuals simply continue to use the tactics they know or that have worked for them in the past. Mirroring these behaviors with equal aggressiveness can cause a difficult situation to spiral out of control. Learning to withhold gut reactions and to take a moment before responding helps set the stage for a more satisfactory resolution.

The Second Critical Insight: You Can Be the Change Agent

The second insight is that if the relationship is important to you, you must be the one to look for the real interest in the situation. Typically, the person who is acting in a difficult manner will not change unless provided good reasons to do so. By developing skills to discover the interest underlying the difficult behavior, the situation sometimes can be made less difficult, relationships can be strengthened, and negative patterns can be transformed.

DISCUSSION QUESTION • 11.2

What do you think Tamara's goal is in the relationship with Dr. Reginald in Case 11.1? Do you think it is possible for her to achieve it?

The Third Critical Insight: Build Self-Awareness

The third insight is the value of self-awareness, which is important during difficult encounters on two levels. First, becoming aware of personal reactions when entering a difficult encounter creates a position of strength. Understanding the types of comments that you find the most distressing can insulate you against them. These are the types of behaviors that, for you, might provoke an unproductive response. For example, if being called a particular name really pushes your buttons, having a plan for how you'll respond when and if it happens puts you in control.

Second, self-awareness requires an honest look at where you might be being difficult. Sarcasm, biting retorts, or superior tones of voice are unproductive habits for a conflict manager. Table 11.2 lists some behaviors that many people find offensive. Where you might think you're being "funny" and trying to lighten the mood, others might find you difficult or caustic. Many of the items in Table 11.2 provoke other people because they feel attacked. Self-awareness helps determine if one's behaviors are inviting others to become difficult.

The Fourth Critical Insight: Look for Hidden Interests

The fourth insight is to discover hidden needs. In every difficult situation, the other person wants something. They could want a specific favor, have a need to feel important, or harbor any one of thousands of motivations. The effective conflict manager is adept at using questioning and listening tools to discover what the other needs. Using the listening skills in Chapter 7 and searching for the interests behind the difficult behavior refocus energy into productive communication.

Difficult people expect your attention. For some individuals, simply listening to them is the essential step to transform the situation. In the business setting, clients may be afraid of the faceless bureaucracy when they reach for the telephone, so they attack the voice on the other end of the line. Acknowledging feelings or the challenging situations people are facing, without agreeing with them, opens doors to find the underlying problem. In a very real sense, businesses run on relationships. Thirty seconds of strategic listening can save considerable time later when customers become calmer and clearer about what they need and want. As a problem solver and conflict manager, you can use this insight to encourage others through their "difficult" stage quickly so you can respond to the real need. The skills for moving difficult people past their aggressiveness or anger are feeling paraphrases and validations (see Chapter 7). Likewise, many difficult encounters with family or friends are better met with validation, feeling paraphrases, or questions than with a mirroring of the negative behavior.

Skills When Facing Difficult Encounters

Bookstores are filled with advice for dealing with difficult people in a variety of contexts. For example, Hakim and Solomon (2016) provide helpful strategies when dealing with bosses who are narcissists. Characteristics of narcissistic bosses include being ego-driven and having expectations

TABLE 11.2 Behaviors That Make Matters Worse

A superior tone of voice (implying "I am better than you")
Giving deceitful or wrong information
Appearing not to care about other people or their possessions
Putting personal needs in front of everything else ("me first—every time")
Threats
Comparing someone to a negative example ("You're just like your father!")
Personal attacks
Persistent negativity

of loyalty, although not demonstrating it themselves. They are unpredictable; they love you one minute and detest you the next. Hakim and Solomon suggest surviving a narcissistic boss involves setting goals for being respected, attempting to reduce angry outbursts, and working to build trust. Specifically, they suggest that clarifying expectations and highlighting priorities can mitigate the damaging effects of a narcissistic boss. The authors also provide insights to deal with difficult coworkers and others, from prima donnas to bootlickers.

While every difficult encounter must be analyzed before choosing a specific response, the following techniques may be useful in dealing with various types of difficult behavior.

Four-Step Feedback

TOOLBOX 11.1   The Four-Step Feedback Technique

Step 1:   Focus on One Specific, Recent Event

"Today, I noticed that you left your books all over the living room and kitchen table."

Step 2:   State a Consequence

"As a result, I was embarrassed when my parents arrived. They had no place to sit, and I had to clean the kitchen table off before we could eat."

Step 3:   State the Desired Reformed Behavior

"When you say you are going to clean up the house, I really need to know I can depend on you."

Step 4:   Ask for Agreement or Input

"Can you do that?" or "What do you think we can do to avoid this in the future?"

People who continuously interrupt, argue, or give endless excuses when you are trying to give feedback provide a special type of difficult encounter. In these cases, memorize what you want to say in advance using a specific formula for giving feedback (see Toolbox 11.1). The *Four Step Feedback Technique* helps the speaker stay on track and avoid being distracted by interruptions or excuses. If a messy roommate has excuses, politely listen and then go back to the top of your message and restate all the steps. Step 4 is important to test agreement and the other's willingness to comply. If the answer is a surly, "Yeah, sure," you may wish to test the depth of the commitment. "It sounds like you're not really interested. Is there something else that's going on that I need to know about? Maybe you have some other ideas on how we can work this out?"

Dealing With Interruptions

Several different techniques are useful in responding to people who constantly interrupt. Four suggestions are provided. First, an assertive statement of understanding without agreement may help, such as "I understand your perspective. You think _____. Now I'd like you to understand my perspective. Please listen for a moment." A second technique is to refuse to follow their lead to another topic. For example, after being interrupted, simply go back to your original topic and flow of thought: "Now, as I was saying . . ." A third, more assertive technique is to interrupt the interruption: "Excuse me, I am not finished." A fourth technique, useful with people who change the subject to avoid conflict, is to agree with their subject change but postpone the new topic. For example, "I'd be glad to discuss that after we finish this topic" or "We seem to be off track. Let me recap where we started . . ." Be aware that all of these techniques can be blueprints for being difficult, so be sure to check your motivations as you use these tools.

Responding to Unearned Criticism

Dealing with unearned criticism is another type of difficult encounter. **Unearned criticism** occurs when you are accused unjustly of generic faults such as being a barrier to success, inefficient, a troublemaker, always late, or not helpful. Three techniques can be used to reply to unearned criticism. First, ask for specific examples when you behaved in the way criticized. If the boss says you are "inefficient" and you sincerely don't know what is being referenced, say, "Can you give me a specific example of when I was inefficient? I want to be sure I know what you mean by that." The second technique is to agree at some level. If you are unfairly accused of not holding up your end of the work on a group project, reply in principle that "Yes, I agree that reports should be timely" or "Yes, the group's performance concerns me too." Agreeing in principle allows some validation of the speaker and may open the channel for joint problem solving. A final technique is to beat the other to the punch with a solution to a general criticism. For example, "I couldn't agree more that the group needs to increase its performance, and I have some ideas on what we might do."

CASE 11.2

The Delayed Evaluation

Denny and his boss Christine both started this year at the Get Well Quick Physical Therapy Group. Denny, a physical therapist, moved to this city and brought an outstanding record of service as a therapist for over fifteen years. Even with his experience, he was on a six-month probationary period because of the company's policy for all new employees. Christine had been a therapist for eleven years before moving into management, and she was three years away from retirement age. Denny and Christine seemed to get along fine, often trading good-natured banter. After a few weeks, Denny noticed that Christine made critical comments about other therapists behind their backs and mocked patients. He'd heard that she didn't leave her last job on good terms with many of the therapists.

Christine was a go-getter, worked very hard, and had an expectation that the therapists would work as hard as she did. She was irritated when she looked around at 4:30 P.M. and saw most of her staff was gone. Single and without family obligations, she stayed until 7 P.M. or later most nights, taking extra patients that helped keep the overall numbers for her group very high. Christine was scheduled to provide Denny with an initial evaluation by October, but she was too busy to do it. Denny assumed that all was fine because Christine and he were on such good terms and he'd been helping with the company's new computer software.

Finally, in March, Christine scheduled Denny's evaluation. Denny had no more than sat down when Christine pulled out a list of complaints—mostly about his lack of commitment, his cluttered work area, a couple of incidents where patients talked to her about their concerns with the therapy (over which Denny had no control because it was prescribed by the doctor), and a barrage of personal criticisms about his lackadaisical attitude. Denny was too shocked to react and was still reeling when he left her office. This evaluation could derail his job and reputation in town.

DISCUSSION QUESTION • 11.3

How could Denny respond to Christine's negative evaluation in Case 11.2? How can he turn this around so he can be proactive and regain some power in the situation? What mistakes must he avoid?

Bullying

Bullying is an extremely difficult behavior that occurs in a variety of settings, such as schools, work, faith communities, family, and friendship circles. Few people can say they have never experienced bullying, as a victim, perpetrator, or observer. Bullying involves the oppression of an individual through a series of negative behaviors that range from purposeful humiliation to sabotage, destruction, isolation, manipulation, coercion, control, and sometimes even violence.

In the United States, bullying garnered little attention until it was related to high-profile workplace violence and school murders. Although no single factor could explain the tragedy, a shooting rampage by two Columbine High School students in Littleton, Colorado, led to intense scrutiny of the link between school violence and bullying (Chapell et al., 2004; Fried & Fried, 2003). It seems every year, another workplace or school shooting illustrated how violence can become the response when someone who is psychologically at risk meets social isolation, bullying, or adversity. Sadly, examples of societal violence are plentiful. Given the prevalence of bullying in U.S. society, we may be fortunate that so few targets seek retribution.

Defining Bullying

Bullying research began in Europe, where it sometimes is called **mobbing** or **psychological terror** (Sheehan, Barker, & Rayner, 1999; Stein, 2001; Zapf & Wolfgang, 1999). **Bullying** is distinguished from other antisocial behaviors by five key characteristics: (1) The harassment is frequent, (2) it involves a pattern over time, (3) it does harm, (4) it begins with or results in a power disparity between the bully and the target, and (5) recipients perceive themselves to be the specific target of the bully (Tracy, Lutgen-Sandvik, & Alberts, 2005; Lutgen-Sandvik, Tracy, & Alberts, 2007,). Zapf and Gross (2001) provide a definition specific to workplace bullying:

> Bullying occurs, if somebody is harassed, offended, socially excluded, or has to carry out humiliating tasks and if the person concerned is in an inferior position. To call something bullying, it must occur repeatedly (e.g., at least once a week) and for a long time (e.g., at least 6 months). It is not bullying if it is a single event. It is also not bullying if two equally strong parties are in conflict.
>
> (p. 498)

> **Happy slapping**, a disturbing trend first reported in England, is an illegal assault. The happy slapper walks up to a stranger and slaps him or her in the face while a friend takes a camera shot of the victim's expression. A disturbing number of examples are available on YouTube. In the United States and elsewhere, happy slapping has been linked as a precursor to more serious violence, such as cases of unprovoked physical beatings and random murders ("Stark Warnings," 2008).

Bullying is so large a problem that it has gained the attention of legislators. European Union Parliament passed a resolution against workplace bullying, and many European countries have specific anti-bullying legislation (Seward & Fahy, 2003). The British were so frustrated by the behaviors of neighbors, coworkers, and bosses who, in the words of then former Prime Minister Tony Blair "make life absolute hell," that they passed an Anti-Social Behavior law that can ban incalcitrant bullies from swearing or making sarcastic remarks (Lawless, 2004; Anti-Social Behaviour Act, 2014). Britain's Anti-Social Behaviour, Crime and Policing Act was strengthened and updated in 2014. Bullying goes beyond incivility to a concerted effort at making a specific person's life miserable.

All of us are difficult on occasion. Bullies are difficult on purpose.
—Bullying expert Sam Horn, 2002

In the U.S., laws were enacted to protect groups subject to persistent social harassment and bullying (Fredericksen & McCorkle, 2013). Sexual harassment and discrimination based on sex, race, and religion is illegal, and, if enforced, provides some protection from those manifestations of bullying. Public schools in most states have been required to establish anti-bullying policies. However, in many jurisdictions, there remains no universal clear legal protection against social bullying.

Bully behaviors fall into five basic types: (1) Attacks on self-expression and the way communication happens (interruptions, yelling, criticism, threats), (2) attacks on social relations (isolation, invisible treatment), (3) attacks on reputation (rumors, ridicule, accused of being mentally ill, name-calling), (4) attacks on career (no special tasks are given, given meaningless work, tasks given below one's ability to affect self-esteem or above ability to question competence, supervisors sabotage the work area), and (5) direct attacks on health (physically strenuous work, threats of physical violence, physical violence, physical or sexual abuse) (Blase & Blase, 2003). Any single instance of these behaviors might be reprehensible, but it does not technically constitute bullying. Bullying is the persistent repetition of abuse over time. Table 11.3 details common bully behaviors.

According to research by the Workplace Bullying and Trauma Institute (2013), the most popular bully tactics include falsely accusing someone of errors (71 percent); staring, glaring, nonverbal intimidation (68 percent); discounting the person's thoughts in meetings (64 percent); and silent treatment or icing out the victim from coworkers (64 percent).

School Bullying

Information on school bullying has become robust since the year 2000. An eight-year international study by the World Health Organization (WHO) found school bullying decreased somewhat in many countries, but still was too prevalent, with one-third of all children reporting bullying—around 14 percent during the previous six months. WHO declared bullying a health hazard that must be addressed by policy-makers (Cosma & Hancock, 2010). Children stay home from school

TABLE 11.3 Bully Behaviors

Nonverbal Bullying	Verbal Bullying
Aggressive eye contact	Convincing lies
Staring	Angry outbursts
Dirty looks	Yelling
Snubbing	Putdowns
Ignoring/the silent treatment	Malicious rumors
Rude gestures	Public humiliation
Invasion of physical space	Threats
Finger pointing	Name-calling
Slamming/throwing objects	Unfounded criticism/blaming
Sarcasm	Unreasonable job demands
Rolling eyes	Stealing credit
Exclusion/social isolation	

because they are afraid of what will happen on the way to school, in the locker room, or on the playground. Bullying creates an environment of fear, where it is difficult to concentrate on learning.

Some studies report that most primary school bullying occurs during recess and that student peer mediation programs significantly reduced physical aggression in schools (Cunningham et al., 1998; Heydenberk, Heydenberk, & Tzenova, 2006). Another form of bullying occurs in texting, chatrooms, and social media. **Cyberbullies** send hurtful text messages, post derogatory comments, secretly take unflattering pictures and splash them on social media, or send the target's e-mail address to porn sites.

National news followed the case of 13-year-old Megan Meier, who after a falling out with a girlfriend, allegedly was victimized by her ex-friend's mother in a bizarre cyberbullying attack (Welch, 2008). Stories said the friend's mother, posing as a boy interested in the victim, flirted and established an online relationship with Megan. Once Megan's trust had been won, the messages changed. The "boy" then broke up with Megan in a series of humiliating e-mails, the final message from "him" saying, "The world would be a better place without you." The case only came to light after the distraught girl committed suicide. The mother/bogus boyfriend has been indicted in the case ("Missouri Mom Indicted," 2008). Children are reluctant to disclose the torment of cyberbullying to adults because of the fear that a parent will take away their technology access (Snider & Borel, 2004).

CASE 11.3

Being the Bully

Everyone has something that they wish they could take back—something that was so bad you want to be able to rewind that moment and record over it. Back in junior high school, my friends and I would always make fun of a certain kid just because he was different. He wasn't the "typical cool" person and didn't fit into any of the cliques. He would try to play sports, but we would give him a hard time because he always came in last place. We made fun of him just because he had red hair. If he hadn't had red hair, we would have found something else to taunt him about.

I know that this was in junior high and we were very immature at the time, but I still feel bad for giving him such grief. I don't know where he is today because he went to a different high school. I hope that he realizes how young we were and that I feel bad about the way we treated him. I think we acted that way because we could. We thought that it was fun to make fun of someone else to make us feel better about ourselves. Junior high is tough enough, so I can't imagine what it must have been like for him to have us on him day after day. It must take a lot of courage to show up for school every day and take the verbal and mental beatings he took.

Variations of cyber abuse that may or may not fit the technical definitions of bullying include griefers, outing/trickery, and online ostracism. **Griefers** deliberately offend or disrupt others in sites such as Second Life or interactive gaming. **Outing/trickery** occurs when embarrassing information about someone is revealed—sometimes by tricking the victim into thinking the other person is a friend to get to the hidden information. *Online ostracism* might include blocking a specific individual from a website, list, or blog.

Public school bullying has consequences for those who experience it. Those bullied in high school have greater difficulties adjusting and succeeding in their first semester of college (Goodboy, Martin, & Goldman, 2016). Apprehension that new college or work settings will be a continuation of past victimization is a strong demotivator to success.

Workplace Bullying

While it is difficult to pin down an exact number, surveys consistently show about a quarter of the U.S. workforce has experienced bullying (Namie, Christensen, & Phillips, 2014). In the United States, eyes are slowly opening to the human and business costs of bullies (Tracy, Lutgen-Sandvik, & Alberts, 2006). It's estimated the U.S. loses $180 million of productivity time per year because of inefficiencies and other effects of workplace bullying.

Bullying affects the bully, the victim, and the organization. In the workplace, the effect of bullying on the organization includes both opportunity lost and direct costs. Bullying takes time and leads to supervisor intervention, which also takes time. Productive employees who are bullied take more sick leave and are more likely to quit, causing more hiring and training costs due to a hiring-bullying-resignation cycle (the bully remains and the productive employees leave). Bystanders of bullying may fear retaliation or being selected as the next victim. Managers and supervisors already spend at least 20 percent of their time managing routine conflicts among employees; bullying only makes their jobs more difficult. Add in the costs of turnover and litigation, and the price of letting bullying continue becomes alarmingly high.

TABLE 11.4 The 2014 Workplace Bullying Institute Survey Findings

Men (69 percent) are more likely to be bullies than women (31 percent)
Women are targets in over 60 percent of cases
Bosses (56 percent) bully more than coworkers (33 percent) or bottom-up (11 percent)
Bullies are everywhere: government, small business, family business, and nonprofits
Most (60 percent) observers of bullying did nothing or helped the bully.

Source: Namie, Christensen, & Phillips (2014)

TOOLBOX 11.2   De-escalating Potential Violence

According to the Occupational Safety and Health Administration nearly 2 million American workers report being victims of violence at their workplace (Workplace Violence, 2017). While getting to safety is a primary goal, knowing strategies to de-escalate a violent person should be part of everyone's skillset.

When Someone Threatens Violence, *Do* . . .

- Project calmness: move and speak slowly, quietly, and confidently.
- Be an empathetic listener; encourage the person to talk and listen patiently.
- Focus your attention on the other person to demonstrate you are interested.
- Set a relaxed yet attentive posture at a right angle rather than directly in front of the person.
- Acknowledge the person's feelings. Indicate that you can see he or she is upset.
- Establish boundaries if unreasonable behavior persists. Calmly describe the consequences of any violent behavior.
- Use delaying tactics, which will give the person time to calm down. For example, offer a drink of water (in a disposable cup).
- Be reassuring and point out choices. Break big problems into smaller, more manageable problems.
- Accept criticism in a positive way. When a complaint might be true, use statements like "You're probably right" or "It was my fault." If the criticism seems unwarranted, ask clarifying questions.
- Ask for recommendations. Repeat back what you feel he or she is requesting.
- Arrange yourself so your route to the exit is not blocked.

Source: This list was adapted in part from a violence crisis response training at the University of Nebraska, Lincoln, and the Department of Labor, OSHA website.

Causes of Bullying

Coloroso (2003) commented:

> Bullies come in all different sizes and shapes: some are big, some are small; some bright and some not so bright; some attractive and some not so attractive; some popular and some absolutely disliked by almost everybody. You can't always identify bullies by what they *look* like, but you can pick them out by what they *act* like.
>
> (p. 11)

Victims of bullies, whether children or adults, are selected for a reason. The reason, however, may have little to do with the target's physical, social, or mental characteristics. Fried and Fried (2003) tell the story of one child who was selected as a target merely because she was the first to get on the bus and the last to leave. Workplace victims may be selected because they are different, popular, competent, or perceived to threaten the bully's "place" in the organization (Workplace Bullying and Trauma Institute, 2003). The research on causes of bullying center on three elements: the target, the bully, and culture.

While in no way justifying bully behaviors, one view holds that the target somehow invites bad behavior from others. This view would propose that a timid individual is an easy target for the bully. Contradictions abound in the research about what a typical target of bullying looks like, with research showing virtually anyone is the workplace is open to targeting (Fox & Cowan, 2015).

TOOLBOX 11.3   What Not to Do When Faced With Violence

The Bureau of Labor Statistics Census of Fatal Occupational Injuries (CFOI) report that of the 4,679 workplace fatalities in 2014, over 400 persons died of workplace homicides. (Census of Fatal Occupational Injuries Summary, 2015). Employees should be aware that workplace violence is a possibility and know what not to do when faced with a violent person.

When Someone Threatens Violence, *Don't* . . .

- Use styles of communication that generate hostility such as apathy, the brushoff, coldness, condescension. Don't go strictly by the rules or give the runaround.
- Reject all demands from the start.
- Pose in challenging stances, such as standing directly opposite someone, hands on hips, or cross your arms. Avoid any physical contact, finger-pointing, or lengthy fixed eye contact.
- Make sudden movements, which can be seen as threatening. Do moderate the tone, volume, and rate of your speech.
- Challenge, threaten, dare the individual, or make him/her feel foolish.
- Criticize or act impatiently toward the agitated individual.
- Attempt to bargain with a threatening individual.
- Try to make the situation seem less serious than it is.
- Make false statements or promises you cannot keep.
- Try to impart a lot of technical or complicated information when emotions are high.
- Take sides or agree with distortions.
- Invade the individual's personal space. Make sure there is a space of 3 to 6 feet between you and the person.

Source: This list was adapted in part from a violence crisis response training at the University of Nebraska, Lincoln, and the Department of Labor, OSHA website. See the OSHA website and your college's safety office for current recommendations

A second view proposes that bullying is a personality fault of the bully. Bullies feel superior, entitled, and intolerant. They may disrespect others, like to dominate situations, enjoy hurting people when there are no consequences, view weaker people as prey, blame others to explain personal shortcomings, and/or have a craving for attention (see Coloroso, 2003; Randall, 1997). Smugness, self-centeredness, narcissism, power mongering, prejudice, or elitism may drive bullies (Fried & Fried, 2003). Some experts view bullying primarily as a manifestation of power—either the bully covets power or has power and behaves badly because he or she can (Simpson & Cohen, 2004).

A third explanation is that culture causes bullying by permitting it (Freiberg, 1998; Porhola, Karhunen, & Rainivaara, 2006; Simpson & Cohen, 2004). For example, a culture of bullying could be created if popular students are allowed by teachers to make fun of less popular students. Gender or race-based bullying acts may be allowed as a way of reinforcing social elitism. Supervisors who bully their employees model bad behavior for other workers, which may, in turn, induce more bullying.

The Bullying Process

Bullying typically builds gradually. There are four phases of workplace bullying: (1) An incident occurs that triggers the bully's attention; (2) over time, the bully wears down the target and separates him or her from other employees; (3) management notices the target's loss of productivity; and (4) someone gets reprimanded or fired, usually the target.

A key feature of the bullying process is that it is incremental. Small successes lead to more extreme bullying. For example, Davis mentions to his coworker, Miranda, that the two of them might improve their work output by adopting his suggestions. The comment, although well-intended, is threatening to Miranda. She begins a rumor campaign to alienate other workers from Davis. Davis is confused and hurt, but mostly he ignores Miranda's behavior. Seeing no repercussions yet, Miranda makes fun of Davis and, if he complains, tells everyone he "doesn't have a sense of humor." Davis finally complains and is labeled as a troublemaker. Gradually, coworkers begin to avoid Davis. Davis' work suffers. Miranda sabotages his work area, lies about his ability, and encourages others not to help or share information with him. Management begins to notice a drop in productivity within the unit. When management asks what is going on, everyone points to Davis. He receives a reprimand. Research predicts a high likelihood that Davis either will leave voluntarily or eventually be fired.

Table 11.5 lists some responses bullies use to mask their aggression. The subtle masking of bully behaviors is important when put into an organizational context. A study found that before

TABLE 11.5 The Bully's Favorite Responses and Excuses

"I was just kidding."
"Why are you so sensitive?"
"You need to lighten up."
"You need to learn to take a joke."
"What's the matter? A little joke going to make you cry?"
"I'm just hot tempered."
"That's just the way I am—get used to it."
"If I didn't act like this nothing would get done."

Source: See MacIntosh (2006)

Human Resource professionals would call a behavior bullying, they needed to judge that it was intentional on the part of the perpetrator and the behaviors could be verified by other workers (Cowan, 2012). As stated earlier, these are factors that are often concealed during the late stages of the bullying process and might explain why Human Resources officials sometimes seem to cast a blind eye on workplace bullying.

Bystanders

> Evil prospers when good people do nothing.
>
> —Adaptation of philosopher Edmund Burke

Bullies do not work in isolation. Many of the behaviors of bullies involve **bystanders** who witness or participate in the process. Bystanders can be supervisors, friends, or those who are supposed to prevent bullying, such as human resource departments or teachers. Table 11.6 lists the types of bystanders.

Strategies for Victims

Most experts agree it is best to stop bullying in its larval stage (Glendinning, 2001; Horn, 2002). As previously noted, most bullying is incremental, starting with an equal power situation that gradually is eroded, particularly if the victim lacks assertiveness and conflict management skills. Even though many individuals prefer to avoid all conflict, accommodation and avoidance will be ineffective with bullies: Once bullying begins, it rarely will simply go away. People who successfully cope with bullying actively engage the behavior and respond with emotional intelligence. They find ways to maintain a strong sense of self and feelings of competence.

Conflict managers must separate early and late stages of bullying. In the early stages, bystanders, supervisors, or targets may be able to change the situation using conflict management skills. In the late stages, the life cycle of bullying reduces the target's power and his or her ability to manage the situation without help. Intervention from a powerful source such as a teacher or manager is required in the late stages of bullying.

DISCUSSION QUESTION • 11.4

What messages did you receive growing up about how to deal with bullies?

TABLE 11.6 Bully Bystanders

Angry witness:	May be annoyed at the target for creating the situation
Fearful witness:	Thinks about intervening but are afraid the bully will turn on her or him
Voyeur:	Gets some pleasure from watching
Accomplice:	Laughs at the bully's putdowns and becomes an active audience
Helpful witness:	Challenges the bully
Inactive witness:	Tries to avoid the situation

Source: Fried and Fried (2003)

Setting boundaries with a bully may stop the gradual worsening of bully behaviors. For example, when a bully demeans or is sarcastic, wait until the person is calm and tell him or her how the comment affected you. One might also respond in a good-natured way, saying, "I don't appreciate that kind of humor." If that does not help, instead of avoiding or becoming defensive, the target could say, "Excuse me? What did you say?" to highlight the inappropriate comment or begin to record all the bully's behaviors. Say to the bully, "Let me write that down. You said . . ." One formula for setting boundaries is the following statement: "If you continue to_____, I will need to _____." For example, "If you continue to withhold the information I need to do my reports in a timely fashion, I will need to take this list of documented occurrences and witnesses to the next level." If the offending behavior does not stop, the target must be willing to act. Unrealized threats are clear signs of weakness. Because power is part of the bullying dynamic, targets can benefit from analyzing their sources of power and developing new options (see Chapter 6, Table 6.2).

> Workplace bullying is "a constant drumbeat, a relentless picking away at what they do, what they say, how they look, how they sound, and how they work."
> —Communication scholars Tracy et al., 2005

MacIntosh (2006) found three levels of dealing with bullies: formal, informal, and general. Each of the three levels uses different strategies to reclaim power from a bully. *Formal strategies* involve using work or community resources, such as an employee assistance program (EAP), union, or legal assistance. *Informal strategies* include educating oneself about the company's rules, policies, and grievance procedures; keeping a written record of all incidents in a safe place away from work; saving messages, memos, or e-mails; requesting that discussions or reprimands take place in open public spaces; following up verbal agreements with e-mail confirmation; asking for copies of any reprimands in writing; recording conversations (if legal); carefully increasing other workers' awareness of the bully's behavior; taking another employee or witness to meetings; and directly letting the bully know how his or her behavior impacts others. *General strategies* require working hard to maintain mental and physical health during the stressful situation and finding a support network at work or away from work. Lutgen-Sandvik (2007) recommends three tactics: (1) formal or informal complaints, (2) precise written documentation of bullying, and (3) using experts or providing research about bullying to management.

The best response to bullying includes institutional support, unbreakable self-confidence, and communication competence. Have a clear and small goal in mind such as stopping teasing. Use only assertive behavior rather than becoming aggressive or accommodating. Be positive and persistent. These strategies serve to gain power back from the bully and put a stop to the unpleasant behavior. Knowledge of the behaviors of bullies can stop bullying before it poisons the workplace. Early intervention, boundary establishment, application of conflict management skills, and/or the intervention of appropriate third parties may halt most bullying. The strategies and tactics in the first part of this chapter on dealing with difficult people also may be helpful during the initial stages of bullying.

KEY 11.2

Stop the bullying in its larval stage.

TOOLBOX 11.4 Should I Take On the Bully?

Assess Your Work Context

- Is my human resources department effective or ineffective in responding to bullies?
- What evidence of the bullying do I have if I go to my supervisor or human resources?
- Do I have any support (network, union, family, friends, boss)?

Assess Your Communication Skills

- Do I have a strategy for how to respond?
- Do I know my boundaries, and can I express them?

Assess Your Options

- Am I tied to this job emotionally, professionally, and financially? Can I leave if I have or want to?
- Can I succeed in a complaint, grievance, or lawsuit?
- Can I put in for a transfer?

Assess the Possible Costs

- What will it cost me to challenge the bully?
- Can my family absorb the cost (either the financial cost or the emotional costs) if I leave my job?
- What will it cost me to take the abuse? How much am I willing to risk?
- Can I put up with this without it killing my spirit?

Assess Your Goals

- Do I want to change the organization and how it treats employees?
- Can I change my boundaries, my limits, and/or my reaction?

It is important to realize that taking on the bully is not without risk. If a bully wants to retaliate, the reality is the bully will do so (White, 2014). Given that the majority of workplace bullying involves a superior to subordinate, a likely outcome is that the subordinate will lose in a head-to-head confrontation with the bully (Smith, 2013). Furthermore, the ability to effectively counteract a bully boss is dishearteningly low. Swaity (2016) offers important strategies if you find yourself bullied. First, don't blame yourself. Bullyonline.org reports that targets are often chosen for their strengths and not their weakness. Sometimes being good makes you a target. Swaity suggests avoiding being consumed by the bullying and realizing that things might not get better. The power of documentation is yours, and starting early is best. She recommends making sure there is a paper trail for all meetings, with a follow up of what was discussed. Staying strong and staying connected to others is also important for maintaining your self-esteem. Being the target of bullying is exhausting, and taking care of yourself is paramount.

Summary

Like conflict itself, dealing with difficult people seems inevitable. Difficult encounters occur in many contexts, and determining the motives of difficult people is problematic. Four critical insights guide responses to difficult people. First, control the impulse to label motives and reactions based on attributions. Second, change the situation to require the recipient of the unwelcome behavior to take positive action. Third, engage in two types of self-awareness: awareness of comments from others that cause an emotional reaction and comments to others that cause defensiveness. Fourth, develop listening and questioning skills necessary to discover the interests behind the difficult behavior. Specific difficult encounters include giving critical feedback, responding to interruptions, and unearned criticism.

Bullying is a growing concern in society, particularly in schools and the workplace. Bullying is the harassment of someone over time that results in or comes from unequal power. Few people have not experienced or observed bullying in educational and/or work settings. Three explanations for bullying are that it is provoked by the target, it is a personality flaw in the perpetrator, and it is encouraged by culture. In the early stages of bullying, targets can respond using the conflict management skills discussed in this book. In the later stages of bullying after the victim has lost power and become stigmatized, the intervention of powerful superiors may be required.

Chapter Resources

Exercises

1. Visit one of the national anti-bullying websites. Find a tactic for responding to bullies that is different from the ones in this chapter and bring it to class. Be prepared to present your tactic to the class and discuss whether you personally could use the tactic.

2. Discuss the following case and decide as a group how to respond.

   You have been with a company for a long time. You know your job well and the jobs of those around you. You are transferred to another site where you are now working for a newly instituted manager, Carmen, who has little experience in the company. You get along well with others and with Carmen. You shared your insights about the company and top management with Carmen. Fast-forward one year. You are in line for a promotion, and Carmen has started telling others that you are unhappy with the company. In addition, you seem to be in trouble with Carmen all the time now—called on the carpet for minor, even meaningless, infractions. You suspect that she is trying to keep you down because you may surpass her. You overheard her talking to another staff member about you. What do you do?

3. Discuss the following case and decide as a group how to respond.

   You've worked for XYZ Company for three years; you have a colleague, Xavier, who just doesn't seem to like you. You need to have data from this person by the third week of the month so that you can compile a report to send "upstairs" by the fourth week. Consistently you receive this data late, and only then after several requests. On two occasions, you have not delivered your report upstairs by the deadline and were spoken to about it by upper management. You have tried talking to Xavier, but he says, "If you worked harder, you could get it done." Xavier is a good friend of your immediate supervisor, and your supervisor backs him. Xavier gossips about you at the office, and you are noticing that coworkers are less friendly than usual. You think that you do quality work and Xavier is instigating this anti-you campaign to get you to quit or be fired.

4. Watch a political panel discussion over any controversial topic on a news channel. Identify techniques moderators and guests use to deal with interruptions and attempts to control the conversation. Which techniques worked and which did not? Report back to your class.
5. Examine Tamara and Dr. Reginald's (Case 11.1) behaviors and consider what the possible motives might be for each of them (from Table 11.1).
6. A boss yells at an employee. What are the risks and benefits for each of these employee responses to the situation?

    A. Say, "Wait. Before you continue, I don't think everyone heard you yelling. Bob, Ann, Mark, come here. Jean has something to say to me."
    B. Apologize for something you didn't do and quietly stew about the unfairness of the situation.
    C. Wait until the manager is out of earshot and say to the group, "Someone had too much caffeine today."
    D. Acknowledge the error and get back to work.
    E. Say to the manager, "I won't be yelled at. If you have something to say, act professionally, and then I'll listen to you. It's okay; I'll wait."
    F. Attempt to diffuse with humor, "Dang. I lost that $5. I bet someone that I wouldn't get yelled at before noon!"
    G. Do an impersonation of the manager as soon as she leaves for those who missed the show.
    H. Ask the manager to explain the unfair criticisms in private and when calmer.

Journal/Essay Topics

1. Describe your experience or observation of bullying in the workplace.
2. Described bullying you have observed in a college classroom or in the workplace. Who was involved? What type of bystanders were involved? What behaviors might have changed the bullying patterns?

Research Topics

1. Find up-to-date statistics on school and workplace bullying. Write a summary that illustrates trends in the prevalence of bullying.
2. Conduct research and/or interviews to determine if your college/university has anti-bullying policies. If so, analyze the policies and state if you think they are sufficient. If there is no policy, explore the pros and cons of formal anti-bullying policies.

Mastery Case

Examine Mastery Case 11A, "Micah's Internship." Which concepts from the chapter help explain the behavior patterns in the case of both the bully and the target? What strategies might help Micah?

Micah's Internship

Micah signs on to a marketing firm for his senior internship that, he hopes, will result in a job offer. Micah's field supervisor, Ben, has been with the firm for a long time and has a reputation as a difficult person. Micah is energetic and popular with the younger workers at the firm. At first, Ben seems to want friendship and is very helpful in training Micah on his job duties.

Micah confides in Ben that he is having a conflict with his fiancé and second thoughts about marriage. Soon, Micah notices that others stop talking when he enters a room and aren't available to go to lunch as they were in the past. A coworker finally admits that Ben has been telling everyone that Micah's work is no good because he spends all his time in bars and "having fun" with lots of different women. Micah is shocked. He confronts Ben with the rumor; Ben denies saying anything to others and calls Micah paranoid.

In the next group meeting, Ben spends forty-five minutes tearing apart Micah's last report, yelling at him for being incompetent, and predicts that he will never get a job in advertising. Micah tries to do better, even though he is now unsure about what is expected. Ben gives him last-minute assignments that are beyond his training and publicly humiliates him when he does a poor job. Ben contacts his university supervisor and reports that Micah has a sexual addiction problem and isn't mature enough to be employed anywhere. He recommends a "D" for Micah's final grade.

References

The Anti-Social Behaviour, Crime and Policing Act 2014. Legislation.gov.uk.

Blase, J., & Blase, J. (2003). *Breaking the silence: Overcoming the problem of principal mistreatment of teachers*. Thousand Oaks, CA: Corwin Press.

Census of Fatal Occupational Injuries Summary, 2015. *Bureau of labor statistics*. Bls.gov/news. release/cfoi.nr0.htm. Accessed 6 February 2017.

Chapell, M., Casey, D., De la Cruz, C., Ferrell, J., Forman, J., Lipkin, R., Newsham, M., Sterling, M., & Whittaker, S. (2004). Bullying in college by students and teachers. *Adolescence, 39*(153), 53–64.

Coloroso, B. (2003). *The bully, the bullied, and the bystander*. New York: HarperCollins.

Cosma, A., & Hancock, J. (2010). *Bullying victimization Trends: 2002–2010*. World Health Organization. Hbsc.org. Accessed 16 September 2016.

Cowan, R. L. (2012). It's complicated: Defining workplace bullying from the human resource professional's perspective. *Management Communication Quarterly, 26*(3), 377–403.

Cunningham, C. E., Cunningham, L. J., Martorelli, V., Tran, A., Young, J., & Zacharias, R. (1998). The effects of primary division, student-mediated conflict resolution programs on playground aggression. *Journal of Child Psychology and Psychiatry, 39*(5), 653–662.

Duck, S., Kirkpatrick, D. C., & Foley, M. K. (2006). Difficulty in relating: Some conceptual problems with "problematic relationships" and difficulties with "difficult people." In D. C. Kirkpatrick, S. Duck, & M. K. Foley (Eds.), *Relating difficulty: The processes of constructing and managing difficult interactions* (pp. 1–14). Mahwah, NJ: Erlbaum.

Fox, S., & Cowan, R. L. (2015). Revision of the workplace bullying checklist: The importance of human resource management's role in defining and addressing workplace bullying. *Human Resource Management Journal, 25*(1), 116–130.

Fredericksen, E. D., & McCorkle, S. (2013). Explaining organizational responses to workplace aggression. *Public Personnel Management, 42*(2), 223–238.

Freiberg, P. (1998). Bullying in the workplace is a violence warning sign. *APA Monitor, 29*(7).

Fried, S., & Fried, P. (2003). *Bullies, targets and witnesses: Helping children break the pain chain*. New York: M. Evans and Co.

Glendinning, P. M. (2001). Workplace bullying: Curing the cancer of the American workplace. *Public Personal Management, 30*(3), 269–287.

Goodboy, A. K., Martin, M. M., & Goldman, Z. W. (2016). Students' experiences of bullying in high school and their adjustment and motivation during the first semester of college. *Western Journal of Communication, 80*(1), 60–78.

Hakim, A. C., & Solomon, M. (2016). *Working with difficult people* (2nd ed.). New York: TarcherPerigee.

Heydenberk, R. A., Heydenberk, W. R., & Tzenova, V. (2006). Conflict resolution and bully prevention: Skills for school success. *Conflict Resolution Quarterly*, 24(1), 55–69.

Horn, S. (2002). *Take the bully by the horns*. New York: St. Martin's Press.

Lawless, J. (2004, September 1). Britain cracks down on behavior ranging from shouting to sarcasm. *Idaho Statesman*, A5.

Lutgen-Sandvik, P. (2007). How employees fight back against workplace bullying. *Communication Currents*. Communicationcurrents.com. Accessed 1 December 2008.

Lutgen-Sandvik, P., Tracy, S. J., & Alberts, J. K. (2007). Burned by bullying in the American workplace: Prevalence, perception, degree and impact. *Journal of Management Studies*, 44(6), 837–862.

MacIntosh, G. (2006). Tackling work place bullying. *Issues in Mental Health Nursing*, 27(6), 665–679.

Missouri mom indicted in MySpace cyber-bullying, suicide case. (2008, May 15). *Information Week*.

Namie, G., Christensen, D., & Phillips, D. (2014). *The 2014 WBI U.S. workplace bullying survey*. Workplacebullying.org. Accessed 16 September 2016.

Porhola, M., Karhunen, S., & Rainivaara, S. (2006). Bullying at school and in the workplace: A challenge for communication research. In C. Beck (Ed.), *Communication yearbook 30* (pp. 213–257). Mahwah, NJ: Routledge.

Randall, P. (1997). *Adult bullying: Perpetrators and victims*. London: Routledge.

Seward, K., & Fahy, S. (2003). Tackling workplace bullies. *Occupational Health*, 55(5), 16–19.

Sheehan, M., Barker, M., & Rayner, C. (1999). Applying strategies for dealing with workplace bullying. *International Journal of Manpower*, 20(1/2), 50–56.

Simpson, R., & Cohen, C. (2004). Dangerous work: The gendered nature of bullying in the context of higher education. *Gender, Work, and Organization*, 11(2), 163–186.

Smith, J. Forbes: How to deal with a bullying boss. (2013, September 26). *Workplace bullying institute*. Workplacebullying.org/forbes-5/. Accessed 2 February 2017.

Snider, M., & Borel, K. (2004). Stalked by a cyberbully. *Maclean's*, 117(21–22), 76–77.

Stark warnings over "happy slapping." (2008, March 18). *BBC News*.

Stein, D. (2001). Introduction. In R. Geffner, M. Loring, & C. Young (Eds.), *Bullying behavior: Current issues, research, and interventions* (pp. 1–5). New York: The Haworth Maltreatment & Trauma Press.

Swaity, S. (2016, September 21). What not to do when being bullied at work. *Tough Nickel*. toughnickel.com/business/When-You-Are-Bullied-At-Work. Accessed 2 February 2017.

Tracy, S., Lutgen-Sandvik, P., & Alberts, J. K. (2005). *Escalated incivility: Analyzing workplace bullying as a communicative phenomenon*. International Communication Association Annual Meeting, New York.

Tracy, S. J., Lutgen-Sandvik, P., & Alberts, J. K. (2006). Nightmares, demons, and slaves: Exploring the painful metaphors of workplace bullying. *Management Communication Quarterly*, 20(2), 148–185.

Welch, W. M. (2008, May 16). Mom indicted in 'cyberbullying' case. *USA Today*.

White, M. C. (2014). Bullying at work: How to make it stop. *Time*. Time.com/17168/bullying-at-work-how-to-make-it-stop/. Accessed 5 February 2017.

Workplace Bullying and Trauma Institute. (2003). Bullyinginstitute.org.

Workplace violence. *United States department of labor, occupational safety and health administration*. Osha.gov/SLTC/workplaceviolence/. Accessed 6 February 2017.

Zapf, D., & Gross, C. (2001). Conflict escalation and coping with workplace bullying: A replication and extension. *European Journal of Work and Organizational Psychology*, 10(4), 497–522.

Zapf, D., & Wolfgang, J. (1999). Organisational, work group related and personal causes of mobbing/bullying at work. *International Journal of Manpower*, 20(1/2), 70–85.

Chapter 12

Mediation and Other Conflict Interventions

Vocabulary

Adjudication	Impartiality
Alternative dispute resolution (ADR)	Interests
Arbitration	Intrusiveness
Balanced Model of Mediation	Issues
Bargaining range	Mediation
Binding arbitration	Negative settlement range
Brainstorming	Neutrality
Close-ended/Open-ended question	Positions
Closure	Positive settlement range
Commonalities	Problem-solving mediation
Confidentiality	Reality testing
Conflict coaching	Reframing
Content paraphrase	Rights-based
Directiveness	Settlement range
Evaluative mediation	Validation
Feeling paraphrase	

Objectives

After reading the chapter, you should be able to:

1. Differentiate among types of third-party conflict resolution processes
2. Explain the phases in the Balanced Mediation Model
3. Differentiate between evaluative and facilitative mediation
4. Recognize key communication strategies of effective mediators

There are many ways to respond to conflict: We can avoid it, escalate it, work on it directly with the other person, or attempt to change ourselves and hope we transform the conflict. Because of its complex nature, people sometimes find they are unable to manage conflict effectively without assistance. Thus far, we have focused on the main theme of this book: personal conflict management. However, competent conflict managers know that sometimes a conflict goes beyond the point where personal management is effective and the help of others is beneficial. This chapter explores some of the ways that third parties can assist with conflict management, with a special focus on the process of mediation.

CASE 12.1

We're Still Parents

Jack and I (Lola) were married for eight years, and we now have two girls, ages seven and three. We were too young, too broke, and too selfish to make it work at the time. Of course, I thought it was all Jack's fault—if he had been more understanding, kinder, or patient it might have worked. I'm sure he thought, "Lola made this mess." He used to say I was the one who changed. When we finally decided to divorce, we were so angry at each other. We had failed our marriage and our children. We couldn't talk about anything together without it turning into a huge yelling match.

The court required us to go to mediation to work out child custody arrangements, and I dreaded being in the same room with Jack. But the mediator helped us break down our problems into manageable bits, and I felt that I was heard. When Jack was talking to the mediator, he even said he felt bad about the marriage's failure. The mediator taught us that while we're divorced, we're still parents and that won't change for our entire lives. We needed to decide what kind of role models we wanted to be for our girls. The mediator made us focus on the issues rather than fall into our old patterns of bickering and blaming. The mediator made it safe to listen to each other and work on the problem together. I have hope we'll be good parents, even though we're divorced.

Approaches to Solving Conflict

The philosophical approach to conflict an individual takes dramatically affects the type of third-party intervention process chosen. Generally, third-party resolution strategies involve one of three approaches: a focus on power, a focus on rights, or a focus on interests (Table 12.1).

Power-Based Intervention

Resolving conflict through **power** is competitive. In competition, whoever has the most ability to influence—whether through physical might or the use of resources like money, knowledge, communication skill, or connections—is favored to win.

> Power concedes nothing without a demand. It never has and it never will.
> —Nineteenth-century abolitionist, Frederick Douglass

In Western society, where competition is the standard negotiation approach, the English language is riddled with references to the quest for and necessity of power: "Might makes right," "She's power

TABLE 12.1 Three Perspectives on Resolving Disputes

Type of Approach	Benefits	Disadvantages
Power-based	Winner declared Often expedient Violence avoided by credible threats Power resources easy to identify	Negative peace Lack of satisfaction by one party Low power may lead to violence Low positive expression of concerns
Rights-based	Clear rules for engagement Specific requirements for evidence The law is the same for everyone People can be represented by attorneys Process is more open to public scrutiny Precedents are set	Emotional issues disallowed Some interests disallowed Decisions are made by judges or juries Laws may prohibit creative solutions Personal data is made public Usually very time consuming
Interest-based	People speak for themselves Open to exploring emotions of parties Solutions can be unique to the parties Flexible solutions Quicker than litigation	Some are weak negotiators Can become mired in emotions Private justice instead of public No precedent set Lack of consistency in practice

Source: Adapted in part from McCorkle and Reese (2015)

hungry," "Knowledge is power." "Money is power." Don't forget to wear a "power suit" when interviewing for that "high-powered position." Power frequently is seen as a negative yet necessary evil. However, while we are warned that power corrupts and absolute power corrupts absolutely, we're also told that power can be good if used wisely and with "great power comes great responsibility." We are encouraged to empower ourselves and others and to balance power to create more even playing fields. Despite these popular adages, power in and of itself is not bad or good. It is a resource to cultivate and exists in all relationships. Power in cooperative conflict resolution is about having enough influence to gain compliance or, at minimum, sufficient power to assert oneself into the decision-making process.

Those with less influence may see resolution by power as inherently unfair. In a power-driven universe, the big corporation has more resources to prevail over the employee, the bully rules the home or workplace, and big government overwhelms the individual citizen. In Case 12.1, "We're Still Parents," the physically stronger parent who assumes a power focus may be able to intimidate the other parent, or the one with the most money can seek advantage by hiring the better attorney. If we do not possess enough power individually to win, our goal in a competitive system is to find someone to fight on our side—somebody bigger (stronger, smarter, richer, better connected) than the opponent.

Although we cannot deny the critical role that power plays in conflict resolution, civil society has tried to move beyond awarding victory to the side with the most power. One alternative system stems from the science of rights.

Rights-Based Intervention

Western society has a well-defined, yet evolving process for resolving conflicts through the promotion and protection of individual rights. The court system uses a **rights-based** view of resolving conflicts. The goal in **adjudication**, or **litigation**, is to balance the process so every person can have a case decided by legal precedent, not brute force. The employee who is fired because he is considered too old can have recourse through legal rights stemming from federal age discrimination laws to triumph over a big corporation. The courts can intervene if one parent wants to deny the other parent access to their children. Of course, there are flaws within the legal system because more money can buy better representation, lobbyists could influence what laws are enacted, or elites can erode the enforcement of the few rules and laws that do exist. Still, the cornerstone philosophy is that legal rights should prevail regardless of influence.

The rights-based system developed through historical precedents and complicated legal interpretations of complex written declarations of rights (such as the U.S. Constitution). Knowledge of the rights-based system requires extensive training. Individuals seeking justice may find it prudent to have trained experts advocating on their behalf (attorneys) in making arguments and appeals to decision makers—typically judges or juries.

In the rights-based system, the locus of control over the decision generally lies outside of those experiencing the conflict. The outcome is determined by a judge who will rule in favor of either the defendant or the plaintiff. Although decisions can be appealed, once the case enters the system, the outcome no longer is in the sole purview of those directly involved in the conflict. In other words, someone else makes the decision and not the disputants.

Interest-Based Intervention

Both power- and rights-based processes tend to be driven by an individual's desire to win—to have one's way at the expense of others' needs or to protect individual rights against unwanted intrusions. A focus on interests takes a different approach. As discussed earlier, **interests** are the underlying needs that drive a conflict. An *interest-based approach* focuses on meeting one individual's needs and at the same time meeting the other's needs—as much as possible. An interest-based approach can consider issues of fairness or other criteria that are important to each party but that may not be resolved in a rights-based system.

In Case 12.1, the rights-based system is well-prepared to determine how much child support should be paid or how Lola and Jack's property would be divided. But what about how Jack feels when Lola remarries and wants the kids to call her new husband "Dad"? The court system is not designed to explore feelings of hurt, abandonment, distrust, or fear. Unless there is a legal issue, a rights-based system is generally mute.

Mediation, discussed later in this chapter, offers a third-party intervention from an interest-based perspective.

DISCUSSION QUESTION • 12.1

Compare the probable impact on the relationship between Jack and Lola from Case 12.1 had their case settled in a court vs. them making their decisions in mediation. How does an interest-based approach help parties focus on the emotional and relationship needs they may have?

Conflict Coaching

The interest-based practice of an expert helping one person (or sometimes both) in a conflict through private coaching emerged in the United States in 1996 as one of the services offered at Temple University's conflict management center and grew into a bedrock service of many conflict centers (Jones & Brinkert, 2008). **Conflict coaching** "is the process in which a coach and disputant communicate one-on-one for the purpose of understanding the conflict, developing communication strategies, and enhancing interaction skills" (Brinkert, 2006, p. 518).

Brinkert (2006) proposed a five-stage model for conflict coaching that leads an individual through a first telling of the story/conflict, the building of multiple perspectives about the conflict, creating a view of a successful outcome, developing skills to transform the story, and systematically reviewing the entire conflict analysis. Through these five stages, a professional conflict manager can assist individuals with the perspective, strategies, and skills to transform their conflict.

Third-Party Resolution Processes

Many interest-based processes fall within the term **alternative dispute resolution (ADR)**. ADR delineates those conflict management practices that are alternatives to formal adjudication. Although some conflicts must be handled in litigation, many do not. The overburdened court system has been active in seeking strategies to reduce its workload by diverting some cases to mediation, arbitration, or other court-mandated programs.

Arbitration is one form of ADR where a neutral third party or panel (typically a judge or experts in a particular field) is empowered to make a decision for the conflicting parties. When people decide in advance to accept the decision of the arbitrator as final, it is called **binding arbitration**. If you have a smart phone or use the services of a bank, you probably agreed to arbitration when you open your service accounts. You agreed to put your facts in a dispute to the third party designated in the contract and to be bound by that arbitrator's decision. Arbitration is a standard means of resolving many retail/consumer disputes because it is a quicker and less expensive alternative to adjudication. This practice is increasingly controversial as it is open to misuse by large corporations who wish to avoid lawsuits, and a bias in favor of the corporation may develop.

Another increasingly common ADR method is mediation. **Mediation** is "the process whereby a mutually acceptable third party, who is neutral and impartial, facilitates an interest-based communicative process, enabling disputing parties to explore concerns and to create outcomes" (McCorkle & Reese, 2015, p. 14). Mediation has been used to handle a multitude of issues outside of the courtroom.

In European-American models, the mediator typically has no prior relationship with either disputant and does not favor one person more than the other (**neutrality**). The mediator also has no stake in the outcome of the dispute (**impartiality**). Where a child custody decision may be handled through the courts in terms of the rights of each parent and the children, during mediation a third party helps the parents negotiate their view of what options are in the best interest of their children. The mediator controls the process to help the parents arrive at a solution that can be tailored to the needs of the individuals involved.

The mediator brings specialized skills to help the parties find personalized solutions, see each other's needs, and understand each other's perspectives. For example, Lola and Jack (Case 12.1) went to mediation prior to submitting a parenting plan to a judge. As decision makers, they knew their work schedules and family situations, and determined, with the help of a mediator, that it was best for their girls to be with Lola on major holidays and with Jack during school breaks and birthdays. A judge, who may not have the time to find out about each parent's life, might have made a dramatically different decision.

In sum, the differences in the interventions of adjudication, arbitration, and mediation generally are based in highlighting either rights or interests. However, the biggest difference between mediation and the other types of intervention is where control of the decision is located. In a courtroom, and usually in arbitration, the decision is the responsibility of the judge or arbitrator. The parties present their cases (or have their attorneys present their cases), and the judge/arbitrator renders a decision. In mediation, the decision lies with the parties. A mediator serves, in part, as a facilitator, but the outcome is the responsibility of the people involved in the conflict.

Mediation is an accessible and affordable process used in a variety of contexts. Many universities have mediation programs designed to resolve conflicts between faculty, students, roommates, and university employees. Community mediation centers provide alternative dispute resolution services to neighbors, homeowner associations, and organizations. Mediators in private practice handle virtually any kind of dispute, including environmental issues, child custody cases, school district and parent conflict, civil complaints, contract disagreements, and real estate disputes. Mediators even helped resolve issues at the Burning Man annual festival (Hedeen & Kelly, 2009). The growth of mediation makes it likely that you will be involved in mediation at some point in your work or personal life. The next section examines the mediation process and reveals some of the techniques that mediators use.

> ### KEY 12.1
>
> When you've exhausted your personal options or reached an impasse, seek third-party solutions.

Mediation

Why Mediate?

The reasons people come to mediation are as varied as the issues to be resolved. Sometimes parties find that they just can't seem to work out issues themselves because of the emotional nature of the subject. Sometimes personalities or styles get in the way of solving a problem without rancor. Juvenile justice programs may require victim-offender mediation before seeing a judge. Mediation may be tasked by a judge to see if parties can work out their concerns before taking up the court's time. Some small claims courts have diversion programs where parties must meet with a mediator prior to seeing the judge. Mediation may be pursued as an option for disputes that don't qualify as a legal issue but need to be addressed. Some businesses require mediation for employee disputes. Many communities offer dispute resolution services for cases such as barking dogs, property line issues, parking, or landlord-tenant problems. Your campus may have a student mediation program. The thread that runs among all types of mediation is the philosophy that the locus of control over decisions belongs to the parties.

Benefits and Disadvantages of Mediation

The benefits of mediation lie primarily in the self-determination given to the disputing parties, flexibility, speed, moderate cost, and confidentiality. Although the legal system works well for a resolution based on the rights of the individuals, other issues may be at stake for the disputants. Mediation is ideal in cases when the parties have a continuing relationship that needs to be repaired.

Another benefit to mediation is its response time compared to the court system. Cases may have to wait months or even years to be resolved through the courts. Mediation usually can be scheduled and completed relatively quickly. Although some individuals seeking mediation also have the additional costs of legal counsel, generally the expense of mediation is a fraction of the cost of litigation. Business and government use of mediation and other ADR methods is believed to accrue substantial cost savings.

A final benefit to mediation is **confidentiality**, i.e., mediators will not talk about the details of a case unless compelled to do so by a court of law. When the process is private, no public record is created, unless filed with the court, as occurs automatically with adjudication. When looking at the reasons a piece of property went to a sheriff's auction, Suzanne went to the county courthouse and read the court documents on the case. In the process, she learned all about a local celebrity's financial troubles and unflattering comments made by the opposing attorney in the case (who called the defendant a spoiled rich banker's son). What is said during mediation is not open to the general public, and mediators pledge to keep the details confidential.

Mediation, however, is not without disadvantages. Privacy and the ability of parties to negotiate on their own behalf are two possible downsides to mediation. Although privacy may have advantages for the individuals involved, it may be detrimental to the public interest. The private nature of mediation may allow for abuse or neglect of individual rights. For example, an undertrained mediator may not recognize a willingness to agree quickly as a possible symptom of spousal abuse or a pattern of abuse by a workplace bully. Additionally, a decision rendered in mediation would not establish a legal precedence. Imagine the delay in social justice that might have been incurred if civil rights pioneer Rosa Parks had mediated with the Montgomery Bus Company instead of going to court. Her public defiance of the rules that literally relegated her to the back of the bus opened the door for legal action to overturn unjust and discriminatory practices and spurred a wave of civil rights actions. Mediation, however, may have resulted in only Parks being allowed to sit at the front of the bus in Montgomery, and one of the sparks that ignited the modern civil rights movement quietly would have been extinguished.

DISCUSSION QUESTION • 12.2

What factors can we use to determine when mediation is appropriate and when mediation would be inappropriate?

Another concern about mediation lies in its dependence on the abilities of the parties. Disputants who are skilled negotiators may have an unfair advantage over those who are less adept. Disputants must be able to express their needs—with encouragement, reframing, and synthesizing by the mediator. In a court of law, the unskilled negotiator would have an advocate presenting the case. In mediation, individuals are responsible for making their interests known. Although part of a mediator's job is to ensure that needs are discussed and that people are making informed choices, there is a risk for individuals who are not savvy about what information is necessary, are reticent, or who don't know what rights are involved. Furthermore, just like any other industry, there are good mediators and those who are not so good. However, unlike in a public court system, mediators who are less skilled may go undetected because of the private nature of their work.

DISCUSSION QUESTION • 12.3

What advice would you give someone who wanted to hire a mediator? How could you determine a good mediator from one who wasn't?

Mediator Responsibilities

The mediator serves many roles during the mediation process. Table 12.2 summarizes some of what a mediator does. Mediators must have a clear understanding of conflict management techniques, listening skills, factors that affect communication, and the dynamics of interpersonal conflict. They must be able to chart the mediation process, make strategic decisions that will move the process forward, and ensure the parties are well served. Mediators must be strong at synthesizing complex information and tracking multiple stories and details while validating both parties and

TABLE 12.2 Mediator Responsibilities

Facilitator/process controller:	The mediator moves the process forward and ensures participation by both parties.
Coach and trainer:	The mediator models how to communicate effectively and appropriately. The mediator may meet privately with disputants to coach them on how to raise their concerns in a joint session.
Impartial and neutral:	The mediator has no stake in the decisions nor bias toward or against either party.
Legitimizer:	The mediator helps parties bring issues important to them to the table and validates their concerns.
Face manager:	The mediator redirects negative comments to reduce embarrassment and helps parties find ways to move past grievances and positions.
Power manager:	When the parties have inequitable power or abilities, the mediator ensures that the less powerful has a chance to engage the process.
Resource expander:	The mediator ensures that all parties have access to necessary information so they make informed choices.
Agent of reality:	The mediator helps parties assess the workability of decisions and aids in the recognition of unrealistic goals or problematic plans.

Source: Adapted in part from McCorkle and Reese (2015) and Moore (2014).

appearing not to favor one individual over the other. The multitude of roles and tasks may seem daunting. Beginning mediators typically receive at least 40 hours of in-depth training, and some states require much more to be certified. During their training, mediators develop the ability to fulfill their roles as facilitators, coaches, power balancers, agents of reality, and the rest of their responsibilities.

Mediator Approaches

Just as there are options for the type of interventions available, there are different philosophical approaches to conducting mediation. Generally, mediators differ along two dimensions: how much they intervene in the process and the desired outcome of the session.

Intervention Styles

Purely *facilitative mediators* strictly hold to the rule that mediators do not intervene in the outcome. They create a process to aid the disputants in making their own decisions and never make suggestions. *Evaluative mediators* use their expertise as attorneys (or other professionals) to provide the parties opinions about their case. For example, if a disputant asks, "What do you think the judge will do if this goes to court," a purely facilitative mediator would say: "That's not for me to say. What do you think the judge will decide when all she has to look at are legal facts?" An evaluative mediator might say, "The judge will only look at the factual evidence, and the evidence you have isn't very compelling."

Outcome Styles

Conciliatory mediators are primarily concerned about the relationship of the parties. Bush and Folger (1994) were early advocates of the conciliation approach in their book *The Promise of Mediation*. The goal of conciliation mediation is to transform parties from adversaries into individuals who see the value of the other and their relationship. Once transformed, the parties have the basis to create long-lasting and meaningful solutions. The conciliatory mediator thinks a focus on solutions is too limiting.

The goal of **problem-solving mediation** is to help the parties work through issues and find a resolution to their problems. The problem-solving approach to mediation generally follows prescribed phases designed to move parties toward agreement. Mediation, from this approach, focuses primarily on substantive issues (e.g., money, distribution of resources, or procedures).

The Balanced Model of Mediation

The **Balanced Model of Mediation** (McCorkle & Reese, 2015) is a facilitative approach that contains elements of conciliation and of problem solving. Rather than determining in advance how conciliatory or problem focused the mediation will be, the balanced model mediator gathers cues from the disputants and then delivers what the disputants need. The Balanced Model contains phases that deal with the parties' emotional or relationship issues, when necessary, and then walks the parties through a problem-solving process. If the parties have no strong emotions blocking their ability to problem-solve, the mediator minimizes that phase. Because the mediator is crosstrained with problem-solving and conciliatory skills, he or she can better meet the needs of the parties. Table 12.3 presents the six phases of the Balanced Model: opening statement, storytelling, agenda building, problem solving, testing and writing the agreement, and closure. Generally speaking, the phases are in chronological order, but the skilled mediator may adapt the phases as appropriate to guide the parties toward satisfactory resolution.

DISCUSSION QUESTION • 12.4

In the Balanced Mediation Model, the mediator is required to be a neutral and impartial third party. How could mediation be impacted if the mediator is not neutral or impartial? Are there times or cultures when it is better to have a mediator who is known to the parties rather than a stranger?

The Opening Statement

Most mediation sessions start with the mediator giving an overview of the mediation process and laying out expectations. The opening phase includes a statement about the mediator's commitment to **confidentiality**, which is a pledge that the mediator will not divulge the details of the negotiation unless required by law. In the opening statement, the mediator also discusses what will occur during the session and sets ground rules for behavior. The importance of the opening statement is

TABLE 12.3 Phases in the Balanced Model of Mediation

Opening Statement
Storytelling
Agenda Building
Problem Solving
Testing and Writing the Agreement
Closure

Source: McCorkle and Reese (2015)

to set the stage, both structurally and psychologically, for the mediation to unfold. For some mediators, this is a formal process involving signed agreements to mediate. For others, this is simply the introduction to the process and is quickly dispatched.

Storytelling

At the heart of mediation lies the opportunity for each party to feel heard and understood. The mediator starts this phase by probing what brought the parties to the table. Each person is offered sufficient time to express his or her concerns, perceptions, and view of the situation. The mediator is responsible for listening actively to the story, validating the storyteller's emotions (if necessary), and making sure that each party has an opportunity to learn new facts and viewpoints.

The mediator employs a variety of communication skills to encourage storytelling. Early in the mediation, validations or the feeling paraphrase may be used. **Feeling paraphrases** identify probable emotions underlying a speaker's statement. One person may wave his arms in the air in frustration and say, "I just don't understand her. She wants me to be more involved, but then she won't talk to me when I come over." The mediator could attempt to identify the emotion of the speaker, even though the speaker didn't verbally label his emotions. The mediator could state, "You're confused by this." A feeling paraphrase serves to validate the speaker (and must contain a feeling word, such as "confused"). If the feeling paraphrase was an accurate identification of the disputant's feeling, the speaker might respond, "Yes, it is very confusing and I just want to get this figured out." If the mediator does not select an appropriate feeling paraphrase, the speaker might say, "No, I'm not really confused. I am irritated that she doesn't seem to know what she wants." Either response from the speaker is productive because the emotional issue has been brought to the surface and clarified.

Once the disputants begin to talk about the more substantive issues, content paraphrasing may come into play. **Content paraphrasing** is a tool that the mediator uses to capture and rephrase a comment for the purpose of clarification, emphasis, or to be remembered during the negotiation phase. For example, an individual might say, "The only time we talk to each other, we seem to yell, and that can't be good for the girls to see from their parents." The mediator could provide a content paraphrase by focusing on the heart of the message: "The girls see you arguing and that's not an example you want to set for them." Other techniques child custody mediators might use are in Table 12.4.

Effective mediators are curious and desire to get a picture of the situation. Mediators ask questions to clarify and uncover details so all parties have access to the same information. **Close-ended**

TABLE 12.4 Strategies of the Successful Child Custody Mediator

1. Help parents recognize they'll continue to be parents for life.
2. Help parents see value in the other parent's role in the child's life.
3. Set the criteria that any agreement has to be in the best interest of the child. Help parents recognize hurting each other hurts the child.
4. Encourage cooperative parenting strategies.
5. Help parents see the world through the child's eyes and frame needs through what the child needs.
6. Expand resources to help parents cope with the challenges of parenting independent of one another.
7. Recognize power differences and screen for presence of abuse.
8. Consider what life will look like in 3, 5, 10, and 20 years into the future (consider not yet present significant others, connections to extended family members, etc.)
9. Encourage cooperative problem solving for the future conflicts that will inevitably arise.

Source: Saposnek (1998)

questions (those that can be answered with a yes, no, or limited response) are used sparingly in mediation, particularly during the early phases. More helpful and common are **open-ended questions** that invite fuller responses. Open-ended questions are one of the mediator's best tools. Common open-ended questions include "How did that affect you?" or "What was the situation like before this happened?" or "What do you do on an average day in your job?" Open-ended questions help the parties tell their stories and provide the mediator with information to keep the process moving forward. Statements that encourage detailed responses serve the same purpose as open-ended questions. "Give me some examples of how holidays were handled in the past." "Help me get a better picture of the situation and describe what happened last time you met." The goal of these approaches is to flesh out the story to get at necessary details.

Reframing is a skill that takes a message and reconstructs it in a way that benefits the media-tion. If a landlord makes an offensive statement about a tenant such as, "He is just scum. You should have seen the way he trashed the apartment," the mediator works to reframe that statement to keep the important issue the speaker identified while discarding the insult. A reframing of the landlord's statement could be, "You are concerned about the condition of the property." A probing question probably would follow: "Please describe what you found when you entered the apartment after he vacated" (moving the speaker back to the issue). Reframing sometimes is used with *strategic interrup-tion*. Rather than letting one person continue with a rant about the other person, the mediator might interrupt, reframe, and then redirect the conversation in to a more productive tone. An example of a strategic interruption could be talking over the ranter and saying, "You've got a lot to say on this, and I need to make sure I get the full picture. Describe the damage to the drywall for me."

A major goal of the storytelling phase is to help people separate positions from interests. The individuals usually come to mediation knowing the solutions they want to see implemented or the **positions** they hold. Common positions are "I demand an apology," "I want a raise," "I want full custody of the kids," or "I expect to receive that payment immediately." The mediator's job is to look behind those positional statements and identify the **interests** that the parties need to have addressed. For example, behind "I demand an apology" may be an interest of needing acknowledg-ment of hurt feelings. Behind "I want a raise" may be an interest of wanting recognition. Expec-tation may be driven by interests of fairness or desires for compensation. Once identified, needs sometimes can be met in other ways than one side's initial opening position.

Part of a mediator's job is bringing multiple skills to the table. While listening, validating, and reframing, the mediator simultaneously is making a list of the implicit issues. **Issues** are the dis-puted items or processes that will become the focus of negotiation. The parties arrive with a general idea of the main issue they want to discuss, for example: division of property, settling Mom's estate, child custody, or roommate responsibilities. The mediator ensures that all the necessary issues are put on the table for negotiation and interests are uncovered.

DISCUSSION QUESTION • 12.5

What is the likely outcome of a mediation where the mediator let positional statements stand and didn't identify underlying interests?

In a court of law, if an issue is not a legal issue, the system is not designed to deal with it. Com-munication and trust are common bones of contention in mediations where there is a continued relationship between individuals. Family conflict offers a rich source for communication and trust concerns. For example, how are kids to talk with parents? How can teens demonstrate that they are trustworthy and therefore responsible enough for later curfews? Will one divorcing parent turn a child against the other? Is it appropriate for the ex-husband to still be friends with his ex-wife's family, and what will that look like if she remarries? Issues such as these can be explored in mediation. Once identified, issues become the road map for the mediator to help the disputants negotiate.

The final job for the mediator during this storytelling phase is to discover and highlight commonalities. **Commonalities** are traits, experiences, or feelings that the parties share, but often don't express aloud. Two people in an office both may want a respectful and productive work environment. Divorcing parents both want their children to be safe and secure. Roommates who disagree about what portion of a cable bill is each person's responsibility may still want to preserve the friendship. Neighbors with different views of what makes for a nice yard may both want to live harmoniously next to one another. Bringing implicit commonalities to the surface allows people to see the problem as the issue to be solved, not the other person as the enemy.

Agenda Building

The issues identified in the previous phase become the agenda to be negotiated. Mediators are savvy about phrasing agendas to be as neutral as possible. For example, Margot would feel at a disadvantage if an agenda item were phrased this way: "One item on the agenda is to make sure that Margot pays her fair share of the utilities." Instead, the mediator would say, "One item is to discuss each party's share of responsibility for the utilities." As the mediator hears issues, they are placed on a list that is revealed at the beginning of the agenda phase.

For experienced mediators, the session may flow easily from storytelling to negotiation without a formal agenda. In all cases, however, the mediator is responsible to ensure that issues that were important to the parties are put on the negotiation table.

Problem Solving

Mediation models vary in how involved the mediator will be during the negotiation and problem-solving phase. In most mediation models, the parties are responsible for decision making. Mediators who offer suggestions for specific solutions are **intrusive**. Disputants may think these suggestions are the "best" solution because an authority figure made them. When the parties do not come up with the ideas, they often are less committed to following through with their agreements. Subsequently, many mediation approaches discourage or outright forbid mediators from offering solutions. The Balanced Mediation model is non-intrusive.

Directiveness relates to the amount of control a mediator exerts over the mediation process.

> A high-directive mediator might lead the disputants through several problem-solving exercises to help them assess their options and to generate possible solutions. . . . A low-directive mediator will lean back and let the disputants talk their way through the negotiation—acting only when the disputants become too emotional or are deadlocked.
>
> (McCorkle & Reese, 2015, p. 157)

How directive a mediator is depends on how cooperative the disputants are and how comfortable the mediator is relinquishing some control over the process.

Mediators bring many skills to the table to help parties negotiate. We only discuss two skills in this chapter: brainstorming and determining the bargaining range. **Brainstorming** is a popular technique to get parties to think more creatively. As mentioned previously, people typically enter negotiations with a solution already in mind. Brainstorming prompts parties to put their solution on the table, but it also encourages them to consider it only as one option among many possible solutions. A mediator might open a brainstorming session by saying, "Let's make a list of as many possible solutions that you two can come up with for this issue. We won't bother with whether the solutions will work right now or evaluate them because the goal is to come up with as many options as possible in the next two minutes. Feel free to be as creative as you can be." The mediator then serves as recorder—if necessary, reminding individuals not to evaluate solutions (yet). If parties are reticent about brainstorming in front of the other party, a mediator may encourage them to write silently and indicate when at least five options are on the list. This independent creativity may aid in effective joint brainstorming later.

In conflicts about money, mediators help determine if there is a positive or negative **bargaining range**. For example, Aidan repaired Jesse's car and billed him $650 for it. The mediator has a private conversation with Aidan and asks a series of questions about what his needs are. Because Aidan is tired of waiting for his money and knows that Jesse doesn't have much cash, he is willing to settle the debt for $570. In a private session with Jesse, the mediator discovers that Jesse has offered to settle the debt for $520 for the car but can go as high as $590 if payments are allowed. The settlement range would look like this:

Aidan	$570 ———————————— $650
Jesse	$520 ———————————— $590	

The **positive settlement range** is between $570 and $590: the overlap in the amounts they are willing to pay and to receive. However, if Aidan wasn't willing to go below $600 for the debt, there would be a **negative settlement range**—no overlap in their offers. After privately determining if there is a positive or negative settlement range, the mediator might bring the disputants back together and say, "Both of you are in the range where a settlement seems possible" or "At this point, you are a bit far apart in your initial ideas about a settlement, and I would like you to think about what you most value in the outcome of this dispute as you go forward in the negotiation." In a negative settlement range, the parties must negotiate ways to put other value on the table if they are going to settle. For instance, Aidan may agree to take $500 in cash if he gets it that day, and take two tickets to a Minnesota Vikings football game for the balance of the debt.

Testing and Writing the Agreement

Once the parties have determined a course of action, the mediator has the responsibility to make sure the agreement is strong. Strong agreements are specific, workable, represent parties fairly, and fit the reality of the individuals involved.

Disputants may come up with agreements that state their goodwill but are too vague. Two employees who have been fighting in the workplace may agree to "respect" each other. After securing that agreement, the mediator's job is to delve into what "respect" means by making it *specific* in behavioral terms. When parties agree to notify each other if a dog is barking too loudly, the mediator helps the parties make the agreement more specific: How will the contact occur? What might the notification sound like?

Likewise, strong agreements are *workable*. To test the workability of an agreement, mediators **reality test** it to see if it meets the needs expressed earlier in the session and if the parties can actually do what they've agreed to do. If someone of low income agrees to make $400 payments on a debt, the mediator should probe to see if that is realistic and what challenges may exist to keeping that agreement.

Reality testing may require the mediator to look back to the interests that each party expressed. If Carmella agrees to give up her dog as part of an agreement with her neighbor, the mediator might compare this decision with an interest that Carmella stated earlier. The mediator could say, "Carmella, earlier you said that you got the dog so you would feel safe living in your apartment alone. Now you are agreeing to give up the dog. Could you talk to me a bit about how your need for safety will be met?" The mediator is not trying to talk Carmella out of her decision to give up the dog; he is reality testing the agreement to make sure it will hold up once the parties leave the mediation table. The best agreements are the ones that meet both parties' needs. In this case, Carmella may inform the mediator that she's decided to take the money she'll save not buying dog food and invest in a burglar alarm system. Her brother wants the dog anyway.

Closure

Depending on the type of mediation and the needs of the parties, solidifying the agreement can be formal or informal. Some mediations end with handshakes; others require a written agreement signed by both parties for closure to occur. Some mediations may end without the parties coming to a resolution at all. In all circumstances, bringing **closure**, or a sense of finality, is an important responsibility of the mediator.

When the mediation is done, mediators should acknowledge the hard work and commitment the parties brought to the session. Congratulations on agreements are appropriate. When mediations do not end in a settlement, the mediator's responsibility is to help the parties realize that, even though they are not walking away with an agreement, they now have a better understanding of their issues and greater awareness of how the other party sees the situation. Mediators may engage disputants in identifying next steps or other resources available in their community.

The bottom line of any mediation is that the parties feel they have been heard and understood, at least by the mediator, if not by the other party. If this has been accomplished, then the mediation can be deemed successful whether it ends in agreement or not.

Summary

Individuals assume one of three approaches when seeking third-party intervention: power, rights, or interests. Power-based approaches focus on gaining an edge that allows one party to influence the other. Adjudication through the courts uses a rights-based focus. An interest-based approach focuses on meeting both parties' underlying needs and permits discussion of issues of fairness. Mediation is a prime example of an interest-based intervention.

The term alternative dispute resolution encompasses many third-party processes, including arbitration and mediation. In arbitration, the third party renders a decision that the parties have agreed beforehand to be binding or nonbinding. Mediators are neutral and impartial third parties who help the disputants reach a decision rather than determine the outcome for them. Mediation occurs in child custody, business, personnel, and many other contexts.

The benefits of mediation are flexibility, speed, and confidentiality. Disadvantages of mediation include its privacy and possible communication weaknesses of the parties. Mediators fulfill many roles to help the disputants reach a decision, including power balancing, facilitating, coaching, and acting as an agent of reality.

Mediators philosophically implement conciliation, problem solving, or a model that uses both conciliation and problem solving. Conciliation mediators try to transform the inner states of the conflicting parties. Problem-solving mediators focus on helping the parties make decisions. The Balanced Model of Mediation contains elements of conciliation and problem solving that are emphasized according to the needs of each individual case. The six phases in the Balanced Model of Mediation are opening statement, storytelling, agenda building, problem solving, testing and writing the agreement, and closure. Generally, mediators pledge to be confidential and not disclose the details of the case unless required by law.

Mediators employ skills such as feeling paraphrases, content paraphrases, closed- and open-ended questions, reframing, brainstorming, and determining bargaining ranges. Mediators separate positions from interests and focus the negotiation phase on meeting the underlying needs of each individual. The mediator uncovers the issues that become the topics of negotiation and highlights commonalities between the disputants.

Mediators who make specific outcome suggestions are intrusive, which many models prohibit. Those who keep firm control over the process are directive. Regardless of which mediation style is used, the bottom line is that disputants should feel they have been heard and understood. Successful mediations are not gauged solely by the agreement reached. If parties have greater understanding, clarity on key issues, and an awareness of the other's perspective, the mediation was successful.

Chapter Resources

Exercises

1. Examine one of the cases earlier in the book. For each person in the case, explain the story from his or her perspective. Make a list of any positions each person may have. What do you think are each person's underlying interests? What commonalities do they share? If the parties are deadlocked in that case, which process would be the best next step: mediation, arbitration, or adjudication?
2. Does your college or university offer mediation services to students? If so, interview a campus mediator to discover how he or she was trained and what kinds of cases come to mediation. What philosophical assumptions do the mediators make about the process?
3. Provide an example of a conflict either you have experienced or is currently in the news involving at least two parties. Identify the issue(s) in contention and provide at least one commonality the parties share.

Journal/Essay Topics

1. Choose a conflict in your local community. What were the positions and interests of the parties? How might third-party intervention change the outcome of the conflict?
2. Many states require child custody cases to go to mediation before coming to the courts. What do you think the reasoning is behind this practice? Can you foresee any problems that this practice might bring?

Research Topics

1. Research one of the following contexts of mediation and write a position paper describing what type of cases are handled and how mediators approach their task differently in that context than in other mediation contexts: domestic violence, juvenile victim/offender, divorce and family, or small claims court.
2. What ethics are mediators required to uphold? Review journal articles or codes of mediator conduct. Are items like confidentiality, neutrality, and impartiality treated the same in all codes of conduct?
3. Examine the practice by large corporations of requiring clients to agree to binding arbitration if disputes arise. Are there examples of misuse of this practice? What are the risks to consumers who agree to binding arbitration?
4. Explore the qualifications to become a mediator in your state. Is there a statewide mediation organization in your area? Explore their standards of practice. What are their rules for neutrality? Confidentiality? Training? Conflict of interests? Membership?
5. Investigate and distinguish among all of the court-annexed ADR processes used by your state.

Mastery Case

Analyze Mastery Case 12A, Anti-Social Networking. What type of dispute resolution processes is suitable for this case?

Anti-Social Networking

Tanya and I are best friends. So, of course, when she asked for the password for my blog, I gave it to her. Weeks later, I started getting funny looks from some of the other kids at school. I started getting a lot of weird pornographic e-mail. One of my so-called friends finally told me that somebody had hacked into my blog about a week before, posted these awful pictures of me, and started writing all this sexual stuff like I was some kind of super slut. Well, I know who must have done it. Just because I started dating Tanya's old boyfriend is no reason for her to do something like that. I know just what to do to get back at her.

References

Brinkert, R. (2006). Conflict coaching: Advancing the conflict resolution field by developing an individual disputant process. *Conflict Resolution Quarterly, 23*(4), 517–528.

Bush, R. A., & Folger, J. P. (1994). *The promise of mediation: Responding to conflict through empowerment and recognition.* San Francisco: Jossey-Bass.

Hedeen, T., & Kelly, R. (2009). Challenging conventions in challenging conditions: Thirty-minute mediations at burning man. *Conflict Resolution Quarterly, 27*(1), 107–119.

Jones, T. S., & Brinkert, R. (2008). *Conflict coaching: Conflict management strategies and skills for the individual.* Los Angeles: Sage.

McCorkle, S., & Reese, M. J. (2015). *Mediation theory and practice* (2nd ed.). Thousand Oaks, CA: Sage.

Moore, C. W. (2014). *The mediation process* (4th ed.). San Francisco, CA: Jossey-Bass.

Saposnek, D. T. (1998). *Mediating child custody disputes: A strategic approach* (Rev ed.). San Francisco: Jossey-Bass.

Chapter 13

Managing the Aftermath
Anger, Apology, Forgiveness, and Reconciliation

Vocabulary

Compensational forgiveness

Cool posing

Expectational forgiveness

Fake apologies

Genuine forgiveness

Grievance story

Group forgiveness

Hollow forgiveness

Impulse control

Interpersonal forgiveness

Interpersonal reconciliation

Lawful expectational forgiveness

Positive intentions

Restitutional forgiveness

Restorative justice

Revengeful forgiveness

Semi-apologies

Silent forgiveness

Sincere apologies

Social harmony forgiveness

State anger

State forgiveness

Trait anger

Trait forgiveness

Unforgiveness

Objectives

After reading the chapter, you should be able to:

1. Differentiate among state and trait conditions
2. Differentiate between forgiveness and reconciliation
3. Explain what forgiveness is and is not

Moments of anger, hurt, disappointment, and/or tragedy shade every person's life. The events that cause hurt can be dramatic—such as abuse, violence, and betrayal—or subtle, such as not getting an expected promotion or an unreturned text message. The darker side of family relationships include betrayal, jealousy, envy, gossip, codependence, obsession, abuse, and abandonment (Olson, Baiocchi-Wagner, Kratzer, & Symonds, 2012; Spitzberg & Cupach, 1998).

CASE 13.1

Winning the Lottery

JJ and Trini met about six months ago and just became engaged. They plan to be married June 14. Trini is a longtime lottery player and faithfully buys her tickets each week. JJ makes fun of her, saying she is wasting her money. Trini started buying the tickets when JJ wasn't around to avoid his ribbing.

JJ teased her about it—until today. Trini's numbers hit a $100,000 jackpot! She was so excited when she told him that she didn't even hear when he said, "Wow. We can really get a great start in our marriage now." When Trini told her parents the good news, they were happy for her. When she told them she was going to surprise JJ with a trip to Austria for their honeymoon, they replied, "Hey, slow down. You need that money to finish your last year in college so you don't have to work. That's what JJ would want, too."

She told JJ that her parents were being funny about the money and wanting her to spend it all on school. JJ got angry: "I thought we were going to decide together about the money." Trini didn't say anything, but she thought, "This from the guy who always said the lottery was a stupid waste of money? It is my money."

JJ's parents were pressuring him to be sure the money was used for a down payment on a house—and to pick up their share of the wedding expenses. His uncle was starting a new business and wanted them to invest, saying it could really pay off down the road.

Trini's friends started saying to blow off JJ and have a last bit of fun before she got married. They were lobbying for that bright red BMW convertible that Trini always yearns over and maybe taking a trip to Vegas.

Trini went to pick up the lottery check by herself. She opted for the lump sum payment, and after the taxes were taken out, the check was for $72,500. She went to a different bank and opened a new account in just her name. She then made two stops: She traded in her old car for a $20,000 used convertible, thinking she would compromise rather than get the new BMW that she really wanted. That left about $50,000. Her second stop was to a travel agent where she booked and prepaid ($13,000) for a two-week honeymoon in Austria and Hungary.

When Trini arrived at JJ's house in her convertible, he threw a fit. Trini just said, "Hey, even though we're not married, I saved some money that we will decide about together." They both fumed for a while but quickly made up and started to joke about the "lucky" car. He seemed pleasantly surprised at the reception after taking their vows when she handed over tickets for a two-week honeymoon.

Trini's parents were happy that they didn't have to help pay for a honeymoon, but in the years that followed, they often told Trini that she wasted her biggest opportunity to finish college early. JJ's family took every opportunity to admonish Trini for her "wastefulness" and "selfishness." It actually became a family ritual to mull over the old lottery situation right before the couple arrived at family gatherings. Whenever JJ doesn't like something Trini does, he still brings up the lottery money.

Interpersonal conflict may carry pain or disillusionment as part of its baggage. Even after a conflict is managed, the bad feelings may continue. In Case 13.1, the conflict over what to do with the lottery money was settled by Trini's unilateral actions. The hurt JJ and his family felt, however, was nurtured and sustained for years. For Trini the situation is over and forgotten, but because JJ and his family did not find satisfaction and harbored hurt feelings, they may never find resolution. As long as JJ holds a grudge and his family mulls over the past grievance, the ugly side effects of the conflict may live on and grow stronger.

The role of anger, the value of apologies, the nature of forgiveness, and the possibilities of reconciliation are important components of effective conflict management. Previously, forgiveness and reconciliation were considered in the realm of religious studies or counseling/psychiatry. Psychiatrists and physicians investigated these issues to help patients who experienced mental and physical debilitation. Although few research studies from a pure conflict management perspective test the value of reducing anger, giving or accepting apologies, achieving forgiveness, or achieving reconciliation, we can learn much from research done in the medical and counseling community and apply those findings to interpersonal conflict management.

Anger

Proponents of emotional intelligence (Chapter 8) identify primary emotions as including fear and desire. Masking primary emotions are a number of secondary emotions, including anger. Angry behavior often is driven by fear of things like embarrassment, loss of control, losing face, losing a relationship, or losing power. Both primary and secondary emotions play significant roles in conflict.

The idea of defensive-provoking communication and face were introduced earlier in the book (Chapters 3 and 4). For some, anger is a consequence of defensiveness and fear of losing face. Researchers studying how emotions affect negotiation ability discovered that words used to label a person negatively or to tell someone what to do were the most frequent catalysts of anger and frustration (Schroth, Bain-Chekal, & Caldwell, 2005). Examples of negative labeling included judgmental phrases like, "You are a bunch of liars," or "It was your fault," and words like unfair, silly, and stupid. Telling someone what to do was illustrated through phrases such as "You need to give me a better deal" or the words can't, must, no way, have to, never, or ought to. One negotiation scholar claims the casual use of the word "no" causes such negative reactions and anger that people should just stop using it (Ury, 2007). For conflict managers, insight into words and behaviors that provoke anger is important because anger affects the quality of communication encounters—usually for the worse.

> If you kick a stone in anger, you will hurt your own foot.
>
> —Korean proverb

Anger and Strong Emotions

Strong emotions can be expressed or hidden through coping mechanisms such as **cool posing**. Pretending apathy by acting "cool" in the view of one's peers is a way of managing anger—particularly among groups processing historic institutionalized oppression such as young African American males (Glenn & Johnson, 2012; Stevenson, 2002).

Impulse control, being able to forestall impulsive negative behavior, is one hallmark of the emotionally intelligent person (Hughes, Patterson, & Terrel, 2012). However, controlling the anger response is harder for some individuals than others.

DISCUSSION QUESTION • 13.1

Have you ever sent an e-mail or text when you were really angry? Were there negative consequences to your message? What advice would you give to others who are about to send an e-mail or text while consumed with anger?

Researchers separate trait and state anger. **State anger** is momentary and caused by occasional events. Conversely, **trait anger** is a relatively stable personality characteristic distinguished by a predisposition to react to events with angry outbursts. For example, a man was observed stomping and cursing as he walked alone through the student union. He would be exhibiting state anger if his behavior was unusual for him and brought on by the convergence of a flat tire, being late to class, and losing his wallet—all in one afternoon. On the other hand, if he displayed aggression and cursing for almost any minor adversity that happened, from losing a preferred parking spot to having to sit in another chair than his first choice, he would be exhibiting signs of trait anger.

Research on date and spousal abuse provide insights into how anger is linked to violence. The National Coalition Against Domestic Violence (2017) claims 20 people per minute are abused by an intimate partner in the U.S. Anger is a complicated emotion. For example, men's trait anger itself did not predict violence against women (see Chapter 15 for more discussion on violence in intimate relationships). Rather, those with trait anger combined with misogynistic attitudes (e.g., believing women to be stupid, greedy, irritating, irrational, selfish, spiteful, and vindictive beings who should be put in their place) seemed to produce most of the violence toward women (Parrott & Zeichner, 2003).

Jealousy and Anger

Both romantic jealousy and friendship jealousy are common sources of conflict. Romantic jealousy can be defined as "the cognitions, emotions, and behaviors that follow a loss or threat to self-esteem and/or existence or quality of a romantic relationship" from a real or imaginary third party (Bevan & Samter, 2004, p. 14). Jealousy can arise from fear that a romantic partner will engage in sexual intimacy with someone else, but it also stems from numerous other causes, such as loss of trust, seeing a friend sharing time with new people, or fear of losing a friendship.

Most interestingly, jealousy emerges in friendships with greater frequency than in romantic situations. Bevan and Samter found some people experience jealousy over the romantic partner of a friend, seeing a friend enjoy other friends and doing activities with others, or a friend withholding personal information that was shared with others. They even found it possible to be jealous of a computer when a friend or partner spends time surfing the net or playing online poker.

The downside of jealousy is that it frequently leads people to act in ways that do not endear them to the object of their desire—and may in fact drive the other person away. Anger, threats, physical abuse, and murder of "loved ones" unfortunately can, and do, occur (Leary, Koch, & Hechenbleikner, 2001).

Research into anger among at-risk youth showed promise for the success of anger management programs. Prompted by a growing number of school shootings in the United States, Herrmann and McWhirter (2003) tested the Student Created Aggression Replacement Education program (SCARE) and found at-risk youth who completed the anger reduction program felt more confident in their ability to respond productively toward those exhibiting anger toward them, as well as personally exhibiting less trait and state anger. Booster training, however, was necessary to sustain the reduction of anger over time.

> Nothing external can make us suffer . . . we suffer only when we want things to be different from what they are.
>
> —Epictetus, first century philosopher

Other training programs aim to redirect irrational or defective thinking that result in anger. Levinson (2006) identified several irrational beliefs that lead to anger (Table 13.1). The training goal is to replace each irrational belief with a rational one. For example, even though we would like everyone to love and approve of us, the reality is they won't. Instead of dwelling on rejection and becoming angry or depressed, the training goal is to focus on how one can be happy, even after being rejected. Feeling happy is better than letting others' lack of approval lead to misery. Ultimately, happiness is a choice. Rational responses include expecting some things to be difficult, for life to be uncertain, that we will make mistakes, and that revenge will not make hurt disappear. Internalizing rational thought translates to positive and productive behaviors in conflict.

KEY 13.1

Happiness is a choice.

The Recipient of Anger or Strong Emotions

Being on the receiving end of anger is not fun. At minimum, the situation is unpleasant; at its worst, anger may be a precursor to violence. Successful strategies used to manage the anger of others have been identified and used effectively in a variety of contexts. Table 13.2 summarizes

TABLE 13.1 Irrational Beliefs Linked to Anger

Belief	Response
Things should be quick and easy.	Most things are not quick and easy. Delay reacting to let logical thought come to the surface.
People should love/approve of me.	Rejection is inevitable. Self-acceptance is much more important than the acceptance of others.
Other people *make* me angry.	We choose to become angry. There are other choices.
I must have certainty in life.	Certainty is not the norm; uncertainty is more common.
I must do well in everything I try.	Trying is more important than being the best at everything. Most people are not really good at everything. The expectation is too high.
I must seek revenge for past harms.	Revenge will not change the past. The hurt feelings or embarrassment will still exist and probably increase through a cycle of mutual retaliation.

Source: Levinson (2006)

TABLE 13.2 The OFTEN Strategy

Observe	Make an objective and descriptive observation of what occurred to you (or in some cases, to the other person).
Feel	Use an "I" statement about how the behavior makes you feel.
Think	Speculate on what has been going on with the other person.
Expectations	Discuss what each person expects about the situation.
Negotiation	Brainstorm how to meet those expectations.

Source: Welch (2001)

the OFTEN strategy (Welch, 2001). This model requires conflict managers to respond to anger by (1) observing and describing what occurred, (2) identifying the feeling being experienced, (3) thinking about how the other person is experiencing their world, (4) exploring expectations we may have for the situation, and (5) negotiating the best ways to meet expectations. The following example illustrates the OFTEN strategy.

Lucas had a conversation during which one of his coworkers became very angry and yelled at him. Lucas didn't appreciate being yelled at and wanted to make sure the yelling didn't become a pattern. (1) Lucas inwardly reviewed what occurred—"I was just finishing the inventory job when Owen came up and started yelling at me about the orders we had to fill next week." (2) Lucas identified how he felt: "I felt attacked for no reason and a little afraid." (3) He then speculated on what might be going on: "Maybe something happened to Owen somewhere else and I just happened to be a handy scapegoat or maybe I did something wrong." (4) With that preparation, Lucas had a conversation with Owen. Lucas said, "Owen, this morning I was working then you came up and raised your voice to me regarding some new orders. I was concerned about that and felt attacked for no reason. Maybe there is something going on that I don't know about or should know about." (5) Moving into negotiation, Lucas added, "If there is a problem, I'd like to talk about how we can have these conversations in the future without us having to yell at each other." It should be noted that if someone is in an angry frame of mind, calling them on their behavior may escalate matters. We recommend letting dust settle before engaging in the OFTEN approach.

Apologies

Engaging in angry and hurtful behaviors can be the impetus for a need to apologize or to receive an apology. Taking responsibility for one's actions is an appropriate ethical behavior. Additionally, an apology perceived as sincere also carries tactical advantages. This section discusses both the personal and strategically beneficial aspects of a well-developed and effectively executed apology.

Fake, Semi, and Sincere Apologies

Should Trini, from Case 13.1, apologize to JJ for spending the majority of the lottery money on herself and not including JJ in the decision making? Maybe. If she arrives at the point where she sincerely is remorseful, an apology is appropriate.

There is a difference between a fake and a sincere apology. A **fake apology** is expedient. While going through the motions of expressing regret, inside the fake apologizer feels no remorse and still thinks the offensive behavior was fine. Fake apologies can be outright lies. They may also take the form of **semi-apologies**, which are phrased to disallow personal responsibility, such as, "I'm sorry you feel that way."

In contrast to fake apologies, **sincere apologies** arise from a genuine feeling of regret about past behaviors. If Trini doesn't feel bad about her actions, a fake apology may make things worse. If the situation continues to affect their relationship, Trini may reexamine her feelings to see if there is some part of the situation she feels responsible for that warrants expressing her regret. Perhaps she feels bad that she was not honest and upfront with JJ and went by herself to the lottery office. She could apologize for the parts of the situations that she does regret. The sincere apology covering areas where she feels remorse could demonstrate to JJ that she recognizes how her actions affected him. Research indicates only sincere apologies are related to later forgiveness among U.S. college students (Bachman & Guerrero, 2006) and to less anger among romantic couples (Hubbard, Hendrickson, Fehrenbach, & Sur, 2013).

The giving and accepting of an apology is a social dance that can smooth a conflict. However, sometimes apologies are not accepted. Because those who apologize generally think their apology will be accepted, an expectancy violation occurs when an apology is rejected. These rejections not only keep the conflict alive, they may paradoxically give the one who caused the hurt reason to take offense (Chiles & Roloff, 2014).

Culturally Appropriate Apologies

It is important to distinguish between culturally appropriate indirect apologies and fake apologies. In cultures where direct conflict communication is not polite, a formulaic apology may be the most appropriate and culturally sensitive strategy (see the culture discussion in Chapter 5). A European American who says, "I'm sorry that happened" may be avoiding responsibility by using vague terms in a culture that prefers directness. Someone from a high-context culture who says, "Sometimes regrettable things happen," may be making a sincere apology because the speaker and listener share a context where indirectness is preferred over directness.

The aftermath of the accidental sinking of a Japanese ship illustrates how American and Japanese cultures approach the act of apologies on an international level. Japan was offended at what was perceived to be an insincere apology by the captain of the U.S. Navy submarine that surfaced on February 9, 2001, near Hawaii and accidently collided with the *Ehime Maru*, a Japanese ship with a group of high school students aboard. Nine Japanese nationals died, including several students. The U.S. Navy released a statement of "sincere regret" over the incident while an investigation was launched to determine who was at fault. U.S. Navy Captain Waddle was silent, as was expected from U.S. norms because the investigation was still ongoing. But tensions with Japan grew as days passed without an apology that was acceptable to them. The U.S. president offered an official apology and sent diplomats to Japan to deliver it personally to the families of the victims. Although respectfully received, Japan was still deeply offended by the Americans. Nineteen days after the accident, Captain Waddle offered a written letter with his "sincere regret" for the incident. The apology was rejected and considered insufficient in scope for the loss by Japan (Drumheller & Benoit, 2004; Lingley, 2006).

The families of the victims expected Capt. Waddle to demonstrate his regret and remorse in a public act of contrition where he would accept responsibility for the accident and acknowledge the grief of the victim's families. A Japanese apology is marked by one's submission, humility, and action. If necessary, an apologizer subjugates oneself through unconditionally surrendering to the mercy of the victim. The act of apologizing is most important. Even formulaic responses are acceptable if matched by appropriate submission. Japan expected Capt. Waddle to bow in submission and acknowledge the pain he caused.

In contrast, the Japanese apologies in 1972 for a group of Japanese terrorists killing several people in an Israeli airport were swift, ongoing, and shared by the Japanese people. Apologies came from Japanese youth groups, citizens from across Japan, as well as heads of state. The outpouring of regret and remorse was seemingly unending from the Japanese people. Japan's expression of accountability was never matched by the American counterparts for the 2001 accident at sea. The connection of guilt that Americans associate with the act of apologizing offers a striking contrast to the Japanese effusive and humble messages of regret. The act of apologizing holds different cultural meanings for different groups.

Barriers to Apology

The many reasons why people won't apologize include barriers such as anger, defensiveness, feelings of virtuous superiority, not wanting to admit a wrong, seeing the offense as the end of a series of events rather than as a single event, fear of punishment, feeling morally wrong, or shame (Exline & Baumeister, 2000). Researchers determined that compounding why some may not feel an apology is warranted is the fact that "perpetrators tend to perceive their transgressions as less harmful and serious than victims do" (Exline & Baumeister, 2000, p. 140). Those who hurt others may justify their actions by saying it wasn't that big a deal or the other person shouldn't be so sensitive.

CASE 13.2

The Missing Food

Warren was visiting Randolph and asked him if he had any food in the house. Randolph said, "There is some leftover pizza. Take what you want." Warren opened the fridge and saw the pizza. He also saw a chocolate cake that looked really good. He cut a piece out of the cake and ate it while the pizza was in the microwave. He took the pizza back into the TV room and watched the end of the game, then left.

That night, Warren called and was furious. "How could you eat that cake! That was special, and I went to a lot of trouble to buy it because my parents were coming to dinner. You knew my parents were coming over!" Randolph replied, "You said I could have what I wanted, don't be such a baby."

In Case 13.2, Warren was cavalier about the miscommunication that led to him ruining his friend's dinner for his parents. Warren's options represent a range of possible responses. He could (1) refuse to apologize and deny responsibility, (2) apologize without admitting responsibility ("I'm sorry your dinner didn't turn out well"), (3) apologize without admitting responsibility and offer to help make the situation better ("I'm sorry your dinner was ruined. I'll buy flowers for your parents"), (4) apologize, admit responsibility, and negotiate a reasonable compensation for the mistake ("I'm sorry I cut and ate that cake. It was an honest mistake, and I thought you told me I could. What can I do to make the situation better?"), (5) apologize and take full responsibility for the loss ("I'm so sorry for my thoughtlessness. I will apologize to your parents"), or (6) apologize, express regret, and promise not to do the behavior again ("I'm so sorry I ate the cake. I feel horrible about it. In the future, I'm going to bring food when I come over so I'm not mooching off you all the time"). Expressing regret is useful when the harm was not intentional or was the result of an accident.

Another barrier to an apology might be that even though an individual may want to apologize, she or he fears legal action. Sometimes people are prohibited from apologizing by a third party, such as an employer or a spouse, or in Captain Waddle's case, the U.S. Navy.

DISCUSSION QUESTION • 13.2

Have you been the recipient of a fake or semi-apology? If so, how did it make you feel? Imagine that you are the recipient of Warren's semi-apology, "I'm sorry you didn't have the cake for your parents' dinner." How might this semi-apology affect the relationship of the two friends in the future?

Part of the problem with some malpractice lawsuits is that the patient who was harmed wants an apology from the physician. An apology and sincere promise to guarantee that the issue won't happen again might settle the issue. But because an apology could be taken as an admission of guilt (in a legal sense), the apology is not forthcoming.

Restorative Justice

Apologies are a standard part of the **restorative justice** model, a view that promotes justice is better served by restoring balance to an individual or a community than by mere punishment of the wrongdoer. For example, one specialized form of mediation helps people deal with the strong emotions they feel after being the victim of a crime (Umbreit, Vos, Coates, & Brown, 2003). When victims see their offender tried in court, they may achieve retribution but are not allowed to face the offender or have a role in selecting restitution. Victims may be trapped in fear or anger and wonder why the offender picked them. In carefully screened cases, victim-offender mediation allows victims to question the offender in person and to work out a restitution plan for the offense. Victims may or may not personally forgive the offender, but they sometimes are able to let go of the fear and anger after being able to express it directly to the offender. Offenders may or may not apologize.

Swanson (2004) noted that victims of crimes want several things when they file charges against offenders: (1) They want to know why the crime happened to them. (2) They want the offender to hear their story and how the crime impacted them. (3) They need empowerment. (4) They want restitution or vindication. Apologies fit into the fourth category as a part of the restitution process.

The Strategic Side of Apology

There are strategic and personal advantages to a sincere apology. Refusing responsibility for one's actions can lead to negative attributions from others and concerns that there might be more severe moral failings. In addition, justifying one's actions may convey a tone of superiority that elicits defensiveness from others. Over time, moral failings, negative attributions, or defensive-provoking behaviors can erode personal credibility, the quality of relationships, and the ability to succeed in personal and business contexts. Finally, not apologizing may require more effort in the long term than apologizing. Strategically, not apologizing may have more costs than benefits. Sincere apologies are an opening through which business or personal relationships can be repaired or sustained.

Forgiveness[1]

Defining Forgiveness

Early in the twentieth century, individuals of faith virtually were the only group to study forgiveness. Social scientists began to examine forgiveness in the 1930s, but its exploration did not flourish until the 1980s. The 1980s and 1990s saw forgiveness research explode onto the scene, with around two hundred empirical studies published (Harris et al., 2006). Researchers investigated questions such as these: Is the capacity to forgive related to moral development? Are there mental or physical advantages to forgiving versus not forgiving? Is the ability to forgive related to specific personality types? (McCullough, Pargament, & Thorensen, 2000).

Interpersonal forgiveness occurs when one person forgives another. Murphy (2003) explains that interpersonal forgiveness involves situations where one person *gives forgiveness* to "an unfaithful spouse, a betraying friend, a malicious colleague, a government agent by whom one has been tortured, or . . . a criminal by whom one has been victimized" (p. 5). In contrast, **group forgiveness** applies to larger frames, such as national, ethnic, or faith groups, where a *group asks forgiveness from another group*. For example, the U.S. government apologized and offered reparations to Japanese Americans subjected to the World War II internment camps.

> The first person that forgiveness changes is the person doing the forgiving.
>
> —Enright, 2001, p. 9

Part of the development of forgiveness research involves consideration of how the term should be defined. Harris et al. (2006) assert that:

> Although no "gold standard" definition of interpersonal forgiveness exists, there is general agreement among theorists and researchers about what forgiveness is not: It is not pardoning (legal term), excusing (implies good reason for offense), condoning (implies justification), denying (implies unwillingness to acknowledge), forgetting (implies failed memory, something outside conscious awareness), or reconciliation.
>
> (p. 716)

For example, it is possible to forgive an abusive spouse but never consider reconciliation because the abuser has not changed.

Defining what forgiveness is seems more difficult than deciding what it is not. Luskin (2002) describes the feeling of forgiveness:

> Forgiveness is the feeling of peace that emerges as you take your hurt less personally, take responsibility for how you feel, and become a hero instead of a victim in the story you tell. . . . Forgiveness does not change the past, but it changes the present. Forgiveness means that even though you are wounded you choose to hurt and suffer less.
>
> (pp. 68–69)

To some degree, forgiveness requires giving up any dreams of having had a different past. Mortensen (2006) differentiates between types of real and fake forgiveness. **Hollow forgiveness** accepts an outward apology ("He said he was sorry and brought me a present") without inner contrition ("But even though I said I accepted the apology, I still harbor deep hurt feelings and animosity toward him"). **Silent forgiveness** genuinely forgives but shows no outward sign of the forgiveness. The longer process of **genuine forgiveness** reduces personal animosity and may increases benevolence toward the transgressor.

> There is Power in Forgiveness. "Open your eyes to what anger and resentment are doing to you. Take your power back from those who have hurt you. . . . Hatred, anger, and resentment eat away at the heart and soul of the person who carries them. . . . [Ultimately] those who love you don't get you—they get the bitter shell of who you once were.
>
> —McGraw, 1999, pp. 200–202

Two general kinds of forgiveness emerge in the literature. **Trait forgiveness** describes a personality that tends to forgive rather than one that tends to hold a grudge. **State forgiveness** involves the act of forgiving a particular offense. Both types of forgiveness are found to have measurable cardiovascular benefits (Lawler et al., 2003).

DISCUSSION QUESTION • 13.3

What is your reaction to the phrase, "Forgive and forget." What do you think is meant by the term "forget" in this phrase?

Enright and Fitzgibbons (2000) discuss five forgiveness conditions (see Table 13.3). If a committed partner is unfaithful, the offended partner might only forgive after specific conditions are met, depending on the type of forgiveness being applied. **Revengeful forgiveness** might occur only after the other partner does something hurtful (such as also having an affair). In **restitutional forgiveness** or **compensational forgiveness**, the offender might be forgiven after a sincere apology and compensation (a new car) is awarded. Within **expectational forgiveness**, parents or friends pressure the victim to rise above the situation. If the partner belongs to a group or religion that advocates forgiveness, **lawful expectational forgiveness** may come into play. A victim may forgive because his faith tradition says it is the right thing to do. Finally, the victim might take a universal, **social harmony forgiveness** position that love and peace are better than anger or hate, and forgive because it is the morally right thing to do.

Examples of programs working toward forgiveness (as well as toward reconciliation) are found in areas that suffered dramatic political violence. The religious, ethnic, and racial violence in places like Bosnia, North Ireland, Rwanda, and South Africa gave rise to efforts to help individuals move beyond their personal tragedies (de Vries & de Paor, 2005; Gibson, 2006). Even though these programs work toward political reconciliation, personal forgiveness is the cornerstone on which the social structure is rebuilt. Pope John Paul II asked forgiveness for historic failures of the Catholic church ninety-four times during his reign (Accattoli, 1998), including the church's indifference to the persecution of Jews during World War II, the historic oppression of women, the Inquisition, and alienation from Muslims since the Crusades. Pope Francis said the church should seek forgiveness from homosexuals for the way they have been treated. The belief that healing and forgiveness are inextricably linked is a compelling motivation in these examples of public contrition.

DISCUSSION QUESTION • 13.4

Wachovia Corporation, once one of the largest U.S. banks, issued a public apology for its part in the exploitation of African Americans in the 1800s. What is the value of such apologies? Can reconciliation occur *without* apology and forgiveness?

TABLE 13.3 Types of Forgiveness

Revengeful	Forgive after you get even.
Restitutional	Forgive after being restored or compensated.
Expectational	Forgive because people think you should.
Lawful expectational	Forgive because you are required to.
Social harmony	Forgive because it is the morally right thing to do; peace is better than conflict.

Forgiving Versus Unforgiving

Interpersonal rejection may be at the heart of many grievances that promote anger, sadness, guilt, embarrassment, lost self-esteem, or isolation. A former partner's last words before departing might be: "I never loved you." A parent may have given more love and attention to one sibling, abandoned her or his children, or left all the family's assets to a favorite child. Someone you wanted to be your best friend may not have wanted to reciprocate the friendship. Each of these situations probably would sow feelings of rejection and resentment. Some of these actions might be difficult to forgive.

Researchers have investigated those who hang on to old grievances. **Unforgiveness** has been defined as mulling over an offense after the fact, "including resentment, bitterness, hostility, hatred, anger, and fear" (Harris et al., 2006, p. 716). Wade and Worthington (2003) posit that actions such as taking revenge, denying the hurt, reframing the event, taking legal action, or justifying the offense may reduce active unforgiveness. Unforgiveness at its worst allows "vindictiveness to take over their very selves—turning them into self-righteous fanatics so involved, even joyous, in their outrage that they will be satisfied only with the utter cruel annihilation of the wrongdoer" (Murphy, 2003, p. 33). Interestingly, those who are more religious do not forgive more than non-religious individuals (Wade & Worthington, 2003).

The benefits to relationships through the act of forgiving are well-documented. Fincham, Beach, and Davila (2004) argue that forgiveness in marriage not only stops negative conflict management behaviors, but it sets the stage for reconciliation, which seems necessary for long-term survival of the relationship. They observed that positive conflict management strategies are unlikely to emerge from the smoldering embers of an unforgiven hurt. In fact, the existence of unforgiven events may be used as a justification by one partner for future retaliation or mistreatment. Those who take offenses more personally have been shown to hang on to hurt feelings, ruminate more about the hurt, and seek revenge (Miller & Roloff, 2014). The ability to forgive seems to be a key conflict management skill.

Benefits of Forgiving

Healing takes longer than inflicting the wound. Without forgiveness, moving on with life can seem impossible. The old grudge weighs on one's thoughts and taints all relationships—it saps energy and gives the person who caused the hurt a continuing source of power. Cloke and Goldsmith (2000) comment, "Forgiveness also is a kind of boundary. It means giving up all hope of having a better past. It means releasing oneself from the conflict and letting the other person go. It means surrendering one's false expectations for how the other person ought to have behaved, releasing the other person to his or her own fate, and taking responsibility for clarifying the boundaries in one's own life" (p. 172).

Those who do not forgive suffer additional harms, particularly to their mental and physical health. In a review of over five years of forgiveness research, Lawler et al. (2003; see also Maltby & Day, 2004) summarized the near universal conclusion that forgiveness is positively related to health. Those who forgive have less anxiety and depression. State forgiveness is related to fewer symptoms of poor physical health, less reliance on medication, better sleep quality, and less fatigue. The researchers concluded that not forgiving literally causes tension and stress on the body that are relieved when forgiveness occurs. Benefits of forgiveness are relational (stops relationship deterioration and allows relationship continuance) and personal (physical and mental health improves, guilt is reduced, and self-esteem increases).

Barriers to forgiveness include not wanting to cancel the debt that sustains the anger, not wanting to give something up without seeming to get anything back, fearing repetition of the act, fearing appearing weak, believing justice will not be served, losing the benefits of victim status, losing potential money in reparations, losing the justification for one's own bad behaviors, or losing sympathy from others (Exline & Baumeister, 2000). Table 13.4 presents several myths about

TABLE 13.4 Myths About Forgiveness

Forgiving is forgetting.
Forgiving tolerates what was done.
Forgiving is excusing the other person from the wrong behavior.
Forgiving means what was done was not really wrong, bad, or evil.
Forgiving shuts off seeking justice or compensation.
Forgiving invites the other person to victimize again.
Forgiveness can be conditional on the other person changing.
Forgiveness means you once again trust the person who wronged you.

forgiveness. Goens (2002) demonstrates the benefits to organizations and argues that business leaders should forgive to maintain personal integrity, ground relationships in reality, allow people's full talents and abilities to emerge, and permit transformation within organizations.

Hanging on to the hurt so tightly that it taints all aspects of your life gives the person who hurt you more power. A past grievance should not become your best friend. Holding on to a hurt can poison all other relationships and sap potential happiness. Forgiveness provides an opportunity to put the past into the past: not to forget, but to move on.

Actions Leading to Forgiveness

The steps to arrive at a place where forgiveness can occur are many and varied. Forgiveness research has no universal advice because everyone seems to take a personal journey toward forgiveness. Forgiveness has no timetable, and some journeys are longer than others. There is no right time to forgive—no magic amount of time before forgiveness occurs.

A few research findings have emerged that provide a path toward forgiveness. For example, merely expressively writing about the offense does not seem to reduce the negative health effects of unforgiveness (Landry, Rachal, Rachal, & Rosenthal, 2005). British researchers Matlby and Day (2004) determined that individuals who use neurotic defenses, such as fake forgiveness (saying one forgives but not meaning it) or reaction formation (demonstrating active hostility toward the other), are less likely to forgive. They conclude that some active mental transformative process is required to reap the benefits of forgiveness.

One study on the efficiency of forgiveness training programs found that training did speed up forgiveness, but a majority of participants experienced no recovery during the training programs (Harris et al., 2006). Clearly, forgiveness is not easy.

Enright (2001) proposed several guideposts to forgiveness. Not everyone passes the guideposts at the same pace; some may not need every step; sometimes a step has to be revisited several times. One of Enright's guideposts for forgiving is of particular interest and closes the link in the theme of this chapter: anger, apology, forgiveness, and reconciliation. Enright's first guidepost requires the uncovering of anger. A first step is understanding that anger and shame underlie the motive for unforgiveness and that anger is not healthy. Similarly, anger is the first step in Luskin's (2002) four general stages to forgiving: identifying self-justified anger, awareness that bad feelings aren't helping, remembering how much better one felt after forgiving in the past, and becoming resistant to offense and being able to "let things go."

Although most of the forgiveness processes discussed thus far are internal and unilateral processes, other formats for forgiveness are possible. Negotiated forgiveness in restorative justice requires the presence of a perpetrator who is prepared to make three offers: a confession, ownership of the offending behavior, and repentance (Andrews, 2000). Victims of crimes often want to be made whole (garner restitution) and to feel some vindication. They also sometimes feel a need to forgive themselves and forgive the perpetrator. Swanson (2004) tells the story of a victim-offender mediation session between an embezzler and a business owner. The three principles of restorative justice were applied so the embezzler could see how the crime was a violation of a specific person and their relationship, that the violation created obligations, and that the embezzler had an obligation to put right to the wrong. During sessions in which the embezzler heard the owner express how deeply hurt she had been by the crime, the perpetrator sincerely apologized. Being heard and receiving a sincere apology allowed the owner to forgive; she experienced "emotional healing and closure" (p. 17). International truth and reconciliation processes also are premised on negotiated forgiveness.

Luskin (2002) claims continued grievances are nurtured by unenforceable rules that people try to enforce. Table 13.5 lists some unenforceable rules that can make life miserable. For example, faithfulness is a choice that partners make that one person in the relationship cannot enforce. If a partner chooses to be unfaithful, the "rule" can take on a life of its own and preempt any chance of forgiveness. In Luskin's view, a change in perspective must precede forgiveness when unenforceable rules are the basis for holding on to an unforgiven grudge.

Earlier in the book, we discussed how humans are storytellers who make inferences and attributions. Cloke and Goldsmith (2000) argue that people who have suffered because of the behaviors of others can tell stories to "mend the fabric of their perceived reality" (p. 5). Unfortunately, some stories mainly keep anger and hurt alive. Conversely, healthy stories show recovery from loss or how one overcame adversity. How personal stories are framed is what makes a difference in the healing process.

Luskin (2002) suggests reframing a grievance story to acknowledge positive intentions. A **grievance story** focuses on the bad things that happened and stars the other person as the villain. After divorce, an individual may create a story on how his life was ruined because of his wife's betrayal. As long as the betrayal story is the energy focus, he is caught in the past. A **positive intention** is a goal. When the relationship started, the positive goal was to share intimacy and have a loving family. Luskin says, "Your positive intention of having a loving family . . . has taken a hit. For the sake of this exercise, picture your loss as a tire blowout on the road of intimacy. . . . Many will stay stuck on the side of the road complaining about how unfair this is" (pp. 144–145). Instead of deciding never to trust your car again, get back on the road. As long as the past grievance is enshrined, the positive intention of having intimacy and a loving family is less likely to happen. Remembering and focusing on the positive intention, over time, makes moving forward possible and encourages the healing process to take hold.

Rediscovering the positive intention begins by changing the story one tells from being the victim to being the hero. Dr. Luskin's work with Northern Ireland families who experienced the murder of a loved one discovered that even the darkest circumstances can uncover a positive intention. Love does not expire, it can be shared with other family members, used to help others in similar situations, build memorials, or create change.

While victims may seek the benefits of forgiving, perpetrators may have a difficult time in accepting the forgiveness of others. People stuck without self-forgiveness are full of guilt.

TABLE 13.5 Unenforceable Rules

My partner has to be faithful.
People must not lie to me.
Life should be fair.
People have to treat me with kindness.
My life has to be easy.
My past should have been better.
My parents should have loved me more.
Bad things shouldn't happen to me.

Source: Adapted from Luskin (2002)

Self-forgiveness is all about taking power over one's thoughts and actions. An individual can make amends to those whom he or she has harmed, can apologize, or can reward oneself for changing bad habits to better ones. Luskin's (2002) three basic steps can be used for self-forgiveness: Take something less personally (you are not the only person to ever make a mistake), take responsibility for your feelings (don't blame the actions of your past self for your current self's behaviors), and tell a positive intention story (don't talk about how bad you were in the past; focus on what your positive goals are for the future and what you have learned). Being stuck in shame doesn't help us to grow or mature. Working toward self-forgiveness allows us to move ahead toward a better life.

> Forgiveness is not a quick fix. It is hard, sometimes painful, work. Serious emotional wounds require serious medicine.
>
> —Enright, 2001, p. 74

Reconciliation

Defining Reconciliation

Reconciliation occurs when individuals rebuild a relationship. Unlike forgiveness, which can be accomplished without the other party, reconciliation requires communication among the disaffected individuals. A simple definition of reconciliation is to bring back together that which was forced apart. **Interpersonal reconciliation** is the rebuilding of a broken or tarnished relationship. The literature on interpersonal reconciliation seems inextricably tied with social justice.

When Reconciliation Is Right

The choice to move toward reconnection is personal. It is not, however, always a choice that is made freely. In the business context, a level of reconciliation may be required. Sometimes, we do not have the leisure of choosing not to associate with a specific person without uprooting employment, family, or other important parts of one's life. In these cases, a public partial reconciliation may be chosen to sustain employment or family harmony. For the good of the larger community, a partial reconciliation may be orchestrated.

Skilled mediators can assist individuals in negotiating the boundaries of contacts in professional or family contexts where full reconciliation has not occurred. For example, coworkers who were best friends may have an irreconcilable falling out. If their friendship dissolution affects their productivity, a level of reconciliation may be necessary so they can continue as coworkers, even though other aspects of their relationships have been severed.

In other circumstances, reconciliation may be chosen. Estranged family members may choose to transcend a past rift and rebuild a relationship. Sons and fathers may reconcile after years of silence. Best friends who stop talking after hurting each other's feelings may begin to communicate again. With or without forgiveness, those who reconcile find a way to reshape their relationships.

When offenses occur, forgiveness and reconciliation may or may not go together. Freedman (1998) described the four options after an offense occurs (Table 13.6). In Case 13.2, Randolph may forgive Warren and reconnect their friendship (forgive and reconcile). In the second forgiveness

TABLE 13.6 Reconciliation Options

Forgive and reconcile
Forgive and not reconcile
Not forgive and interact
Not forgive and not interact

condition, Randolph might privately forgive but not reconnect with Warren (forgive and not reconcile). He might continue to interact without forgiveness and hold a grudge against Warren (not forgive and interact). Finally, Randolph could hold a grudge and not interact (not forgive and not interact). The choice that is made about forgiveness and further contact will alter the path of both men's futures.

Ideally, reconciliation occurs after the offending party has reformed the attitudes or behaviors that caused the original injury. Reconciliation without genuine reform and regret by the offending party is an invitation to re-victimization.

Summary

Disappointment and hurt are a part of the life process. Anger is a secondary emotion that masks some primary emotion, such as fear. Anger itself can be masked through strategies such as cool posing or moderated through training programs to reduce the emotion. Trait anger is a relatively stable personality feature, whereas state anger is precipitated by a specific event. Strategies such as OFTEN can assist those who are recipients of anger.

Apologies can be fake, semi-apologies, or indicate sincere regret about a behavior. People avoid apologies for reasons such as guilt, fear of punishment, shame, viewing events differently, or seeing only the other's behavior and not one's own. Sometimes fear of legal consequences forestalls an apology. Sometimes not apologizing takes more effort and leads to worse personal consequences than apologizing.

Interpersonal forgiveness is giving up the hurt and anger toward another. Forgiveness does not condone the behavior or require reconciliation of the relationship. To reap the mental and physical health benefits of forgiveness, it must be real, not hollow or fake. Trait forgiveness describes a personality that tends to forgive, and state forgiveness is linked to specific offenses. Sometimes people put mental conditions around forgiving, such as revengeful forgiveness, compensational forgiveness, lawful expectational forgiveness, expectational forgiveness, or social harmony forgiveness. Research shows that unforgiveness, the active state of mulling over past grievances, produces negative health and psychological effects.

Forgiveness is a process rather than a single action. It may take more time for some individuals than for others. Keys to forgiveness include giving up one's anger and changing from a victim's grievance story to a positive intention. Interpersonal reconciliation is rebuilding a relationship with a person and requires direct communication.

Chapter Resources

Exercises

1. Identify an example, real or fictitious, to illustrate the five types of forgiveness from Table 13.3.
2. Are there historic or current issues in your community or state that a forgiveness or reconciliation process could help?

Journal/Essay Topics

1. "Anger is the wind that blows out the candle of the mind." How has anger affected your life or the life of someone you know?
2. How has forgiveness helped you move beyond a hurtful event?

Research Topics

1. Investigate and write a report on one nation or ethnic group's reconciliation efforts.
2. Read and report on a book about reconciliation such as Desmond Tutu's *No Future Without Forgiveness* or Nancy Friday's *My Mother, Myself*.
3. Compare and contrast two reconciliation models and provide your opinions on the usefulness of each model.
4. What have nations apologized for? How do formal apologies for past behaviors of a country affect relationships?

Mastery Case

Examine Mastery Case 13A, "Memory Boxes." Which concepts from the chapter can be applied to the case?

Memory Boxes

After my father's death when I was eight years old, we moved in for a short time with his mother, my paternal grandmother. Mom and Grandma's relationship always seemed a little strained, but I know that Mom was grateful for her willingness to take us in for that rough time.

Mom was a collector of memories and saw her role as the family historian. She kept newspapers dated the day each of her three kids were born. She had every newspaper that included any mention of family members—birth announcements, wedding announcements, obituaries, graduations, and anything newsworthy. She acquired this tradition from her mother, who passed on her own collection to my mom.

When Mom found a place for us to live, she was in the process of moving when she realized that the memory box of newspapers and clippings was missing. She asked Grandma about it. Grandma replied, "That box of old newspapers? I threw them out. That kind of thing will just collect bugs." To make matters worse, it was clear to Mom that Grandma had gone through all of the packed boxes and got rid of "junk" that she felt was unnecessary—and helped herself to mementos of Dad's.

Mom was livid and heartsick at the same time. We left Grandma's house that day in silence. Mom refused to talk to Grandma from that day forward. Whenever anyone brings up any memory, Mom relives her anger and hurt anew about what Grandma did. Years have passed and we kids are grown, but we still have little contact with Grandma because of the newspaper incident so many years ago.

Note

1 The view of forgiveness emerging in Western research is influenced by Christian theology. Other theologies may lead to other views of forgiveness (e.g., Gassin, 2001).

References

Accattoli, L. (1998). *When a pope asks forgiveness: The mea culpa's of John Paul II* (J. Aumann, Trans.). Boston: Pauline Books & Media.

Andrews, M. (2000). Forgiveness in context. *Journal of Moral Education, 29*(1), 75–86.

Bachman, G. F., & Guerrero, L. K. (2006). Forgiveness, apology, and communicative responses to hurtful events. *Communication Reports, 19*(1), 45–56.

Bevan, J. L., & Samter, W. (2004). Toward a broader conceptualization of jealousy in close relationships: Two exploratory studies. *Communication Studies, 55*(1), 14–28.

Chiles, B. W., & Roloff, M. E. (2014). Apologies, expectations, and violations: An analysis of confirmed and disconfirmed expectations for response to apologies. *Communication Reports, 27*(2), 65–77.

Cloke, K., & Goldsmith, J. (2000). *Resolving personal and organizational conflict: Stories of transformation and forgiveness.* San Francisco: Jossey-Bass.

Drumheller, K., & Benoit, W. (2004). USS Greeneville collides with Japan's Ehime Maru: Cultural issues in image repair discourse. *Public Relations Review, 30*(2), 177–185.

Enright, R. D. (2001). *Forgiveness is a choice.* Washington, DC: American Psychological Association.

Enright, R. D., & Fitzgibbons, R. P. (2000). *Helping clients forgive.* Washington, DC: American Psychological Association.

Exline, J. J., & Baumeister, R. F. (2000). Expressing forgiveness and repentance. In M. E. McCullough, K. I. Pargament, & C. E. Thorensen (Eds.), *Forgiveness theory, research, and practice* (pp. 133–155). New York: Guilford Press.

Fincham, F. D., Beach, S. R. H., & Davila, J. (2004). Forgiveness and conflict resolution in marriage. *Journal of Family Psychology, 18*(1), 72–81.

Freedman, S. (1998). Forgiveness and reconciliation: The importance of understanding how they differ. *Counseling and Values, 42*(3), 200–216.

Gassin, E. A. (2001). Interpersonal forgiveness from an Eastern Orthodox perspective. *Journal of Psychology and Theology, 29*(3), 187–200.

Gibson, J. L. (2006). The contributions of truth to reconciliation: Lessons from South Africa. *Journal of Conflict Resolution, 50*(3), 409–432.

Glenn, C. L., & Johnson, D. L. (2012). "What they see as acceptable:" A co-cultural theoretical analysis of black male students at a predominantly white institution. *The Howard Journal of Communication, 23,* 351–368.

Goens, G. A. (2002). The courage to risk forgiveness. *School Administrator, 59*(2), 32–35.

Harris, A., Luskin, F., Norman, S. B., Standard, S., Bruning, J., Evans, S., & Thoresen, C. C. (2006). Effects of a group forgiveness intervention on forgiveness, perceived stress, and trait-anger. *Journal of Clinical Psychology, 62*(6), 715–733.

Herrmann, D. S., & McWhirter, J. J. (2003). Anger & aggression management in young adolescents: An experimental validation of the SCARE program. *Education and Treatment of Children, 26*(3), 273–302.

Hubbard, A. S., Hendrickson, B., Fehrenback, K. S., & Sur, J. (2013). Effects of timing and sincerity of an apology on satisfaction and changes in negative feelings during conflicts. *Western Journal of Communication, 77*(3), 305–322.

Hughes, M., Patterson, L. B., & Terrell, J. B. (2012). *Emotional intelligence in action* (2nd ed.). San Francisco: Pfeiffer.

Landry, D. F., Rachal, K. C., Rachal, W. S., & Rosenthal, G. T. (2005). Expressive disclosure following an interpersonal conflict: Can merely writing about an interpersonal offense motivate forgiveness? *Counseling and Clinical Psychology Journal, 2*(1), 2–14.

Lawler, K. A., Younger, J. W., Piferi, R. L., Billington, E., Jobe, R., Edmondson, K., & Jones, W. H. (2003). A change of heart: Cardiovascular correlates of forgiveness in response to interpersonal conflict. *Journal of Behavioral Medicine, 26*(5), 373–393.

Leary, M. R., Koch, E. J., & Hechenbleikner, N. R. (2001). Emotional responses to interpersonal rejection. In M. R. Leary (Ed.), *Interpersonal rejection* (pp. 145–166). New York: Oxford University Press.

Levinson, M. H. (2006). Anger management and violence prevention: A holistic solution. *ETC*, *63*(2), 187–199.

Lingley, D. (2006). Apologies across cultures: An analysis of intercultural communication problems raised in the Ehime Maru incident. *Asian EFL Journal*, *8*(1). Asian-efljournal.com. Accessed 7 January 2017.

Luskin, F. (2002). *Forgive for good*. New York: Harper-San Francisco.

Maltby, J., & Day, L. (2004). Forgiveness and defense style. *Journal of Genetic Psychology*, *165*(1), 99–109.

McCullough, M. E., Pargament, K. I., & Thoreson, C. E. (2000). The psychology of forgiveness. In M. E. McCullough, K. I. Pargament, & C. E. Thoresen (Eds.), *Forgiveness theory, research, and practice* (pp. 1–16). New York: Guilford Press.

McGraw, P. C. (1999). *Life strategies: Doing what works, doing what matters*. New York: Hyperion.

Miller, C. W., & Roloff, M. E. (2014). When hurt continues: Taking conflict personally leads to rumination, residual hurt and negative motivations toward someone who hurt us. *Communication Quarterly*, *62*(2), 193–213.

Mortensen, C. D. (2006). *Human conflict: Disagreement, misunderstanding and problematic talk*. Lanham, MD: Rowman & Littlefield.

Murphy, J. G. (2003). *Getting even: Forgiveness and its limits*. London: Oxford University Press.

National Coalition Against Domestic Violence (2017). *National statistics*. Ncadv.org. Accessed 17 February 2017.

Olson, L. N., Baiocchi-Wagner, E. A., Kratzer, J. M. W., & Symonds, S. E. (2012). *The dark side of family communication*. Cambridge: Polity Press.

Parrott, D. J., & Zeichner, A. (2003). Effects of trait anger and negative attitudes towards women on physical assault in dating relationships. *Journal of Family Violence*, *18*(5), 301–307.

Schroth, H. A., Bain-Chekal, J., & Caldwell, D. F. (2005). Sticks and stones may break my bones and words can hurt me: Words and phrases that trigger emotions in negotiations and their effects. *International Journal of Conflict Management*, *16*(2), 102–127.

Spitzberg, B. H., & Cupach, W. R. (Eds.). (1998). *The dark side of close relationships*. Mahwah, NJ: Erlbaum.

Stevenson, H. C. (2002). Wrestling with destiny: The cultural socialization of anger and healing in African American males. *Journal of Psychology and Christianity*, *21*(4), 357–364.

Swanson, C. (2004, Summer). Friendship and forgiveness in the face of embezzlement. *ACResolution*, 15–17.

Umbreit, M. S., Vos, B., Coates, R. B., & Brown, K. A. (2003). *Facing violence: The path of restorative justice and dialogue*. Monsey, NY: Criminal Justice Press.

Ury, W. (2007). *The power of a positive No: How to say No and still get to Yes*. New York: Bantam.

Vries, J. de, & de Paor, J. (2005). Healing and reconciliation in the L.I.V.E. program in Ireland. *Peace & Change*, *30*(3), 329–358.

Wade, N. G., & Worthington, E. L. (2003). Overcoming interpersonal offenses: Is forgiveness the only way to deal with unforgiveness? *Journal of Counseling & Development*, *81*(3), 343–353.

Welch, M. (2001). The O.F.T.E.N. strategy for conflict management. *Journal of Educational and Psychological Consultation*, *12*(3), 257–262.

Section IV

Conflict in Context

Section IV examines how conflict unfolds in several specific contexts. Each context challenges our conflict management abilities in unique ways. A conflict strategy or tactic may be effective in one context and inappropriate or ineffective in the next. Section IV offers useful information as we navigate the ubiquitous contexts of family, intimate relationships, work, and social media.

Managing conflict in the family setting is something that everyone experiences—first as a child, then, for many, as a parent. Chapter 14 provides a base of information about family structures and family communication, then delves into family conflict. Suggestions for conflict management in the family conclude the chapter. Another common context for conflict occurs as adults learn to share their space and time with a partner. Chapter 15 provides a focus on positive and negative patterns of conflict in romantic relationships.

In Chapter 16 we examine the world of employment. Given that many people spend more time interacting with coworkers than with friends and family, workplace conflict deserves special attention. How conflict is managed in the workplace makes an enormous difference in people's quality of life, both personally and professionally.

Finally, the ubiquitous nature of technology necessitates a focus on social media. Use of the internet both causes conflict and is a medium through which conflict is addressed. Chapter 17 provides theories and strategies for managing our lives online.

Chapter 14

Families and Conflict

Vocabulary

Biased punctuation of conflict

Closeness

Consensual family

Extended family

Family boundaries

Family communication

Family meeting

Family of choice

Family of origin

Family secrets

Family stories

Gay/lesbian family

High-involvement/High-considerateness conversational styles

Illusion of transparency

Laissez-faire family

Nuclear family

Pluralistic family

Protective family

Satisfaction

Social learning theory

Taboo topics

Unmet ideals hypothesis

Objectives

After reading this chapter, you should be able to:

1. Differentiate among family types and their strengths and weaknesses
2. Discuss the factors that impact family satisfaction
3. Explain several tools families can use for conflict management

> The family. We were a strange little band of characters trudging through life sharing diseases and toothpaste, coveting one another's desserts, hiding shampoo, borrowing money, locking each other out of our rooms, inflicting pain and kissing to heal it in the same instant, loving, laughing, defending, and trying to figure out the common thread that bound us all together.
>
> —Erma Bombeck, Family—the Ties That Bind . . . and Gag!

The Family As a Communication System

Families can be characterized in numerous ways. There are **nuclear families** (husband, wife, and their children), **extended families** (traditional or nontraditional families with multiple generations), **gay/lesbian families** (same-sex couples and their children), and **families of origin** (the family into which one was born). Families can live under the same roof or live in different geographic areas. Some people even create families out of friendships, called **families of choice.**

Communication scholars paint with a broad brush when defining the family. Early researchers of family communication, such as Turner and West (1998), define a family as:

> a self-defined group of intimates who create and maintain themselves through their own interactions and their interactions with others; a family may include both voluntary and involuntary relationships; it creates both literal and symbolic internal and external boundaries, and it evolves through time: It has a history, a present, and a future.
>
> (pp. 7–8)

The "family" is a social construct and a legal entity, i.e., sometimes a family is what a set of individuals perceive a family to be and sometimes a family is defined by law. The legal definition of "family" changes who is eligible for social services or can be listed on an employee's health care coverage, who can immigrate to the U.S., and who is listed on a tax form (see Degtyareva, 2011; Dunning, 2015; Sugarman, 2008). Even though a rising number of people in the U.S. consider gay couples to constitute a family, heteronormativity prevails as a majority opinion (Oswald, Blume, & Marks, 2005; Powell, Bolzendahl, Geist, & Steelman, 2010). A Supreme Court decision, *Obergefell v. Hodges*, 576 U.S. (2015), had the U.S. join many nations around the world who legally recognize gay marriage.

DISCUSSION QUESTION • 14.1

In your definition, what constitutes a family? Do you belong to several families?

According to the 2010 U.S. Census, 68 percent of households comprise a family of one or more parents with one or more children, compared to 81 percent in 1970. Thirty-one percent of households had one person living alone. Five percent (over 5.4 million) were unmarried, same or opposite sex households. An interesting note to the census report explains that up to 28 percent of the households reporting as opposite-sex partners might be same-sex partners due to marking errors. The highest percentage of husband/wife households were in Utah, the lowest in New York and Louisiana. Over five million Americans live in multi-generational families (Households, 2012).

Family boundaries determine who is included and who is excluded. Sometimes the act of exclusion is a divorce or legal disinheritance, and sometimes the boundary is communicative—for example, when children who break custom or tradition are told they are no longer welcome in the family home or when persons who have no blood ties are informally labeled as "one of the family."

A family, however defined, is a unique system where individuals develop a common view of the reality that governs their behaviors that is (more or less) shared among family members (Arnold, 2008; Galvin, Dickson, & Marrow, 2006). As a system, family members interact in ways that both create and sustain them as a unit. What one family member does affects everyone else in the system. The degree to which family members agree about their shared identity and rules of operation, the number of conversations they have about their shared identity, and the ways in which family identity is sustained all have a deep impact on how well the family functions and the amount of dysfunctional conflict that occurs (Koerner & Fitzpatrick, 2004). A key insight from research is that family communication patterns change over time. Each time a child is born or someone new enters the family by marriage, the family system must readjust its relationships. As children progress through stages of development, relationships change again.

This chapter examines the nature of family communication and how communication within the family affects and reflects its overall health.

In 2006, 51 percent of those surveyed considered pets to constitute a family. Thirty percent considered pets to constitute a family but a gay couple not to constitute a family.

(Powell et al., 2010)

Role of Communication in Families

Communication is the tool that humans use to make sense of the world, convey information, and sustain traditions. Communication is how meaning is created and shared. **Family communication** is a process through which the family system—as individuals and collectively—attributes meaning to the events in their lives, creates and sustains their interpretation of cultural rules, defines and changes relationships among each other, and carries on with everyday life. In simpler terms, communication is how a family creates its reality.

Family communication starts with what a child learns in the **family of origin**. When a young adult leaves home, packed among the other baggage is a template of what it means to be a family. Some aspects of the family of origin's traditions, rules, culture, and communication expectations pass down through the generations; other traditions and habits may be transformed to suit the needs of new family configurations. For example, a marriage between a Jew and a Catholic may struggle with what to do during Hanukah and Christmas or in which religion the children should be raised. Merging systems is a common area for conflict to occur.

Types of Families

A well-developed line of research categorizes families according to their high or low degree of conformity and use of conversation (Fitzpatrick, Marshall, Leutwiler, & Krcmar, 1996; Koerner & Fitzpatrick, 2004, 2006). As Table 14.1 illustrates, **consensual families** (high/high) encourage discussion but expect conformity. For example, family members can discuss politics, and everyone is expected to participate, but when they go to vote individually, they should follow the family's party affiliation. **Pluralistic families** (low/high) encourage discussion and allow children to develop their own opinions. A pluralistic family may discuss many different kinds of religions and encourage individual exploration. **Protective families** (high/low) emphasize conformity without discussion to create an illusion of harmony. This family looks the part and acts the part of a tight-knit group, although they have no idea what anyone else is thinking because they do not talk about their beliefs. **Laissez-faire families** (low/low) neither encourage conversation nor pressure children to conform. Early research indicates many boys in low-conformity families may do well using self-restraint during elementary school, but they require more parental control and communication as self-restraint crumbles during middle and high school, whereas girls from laissez-faire families are vulnerable to social withdrawal at all ages (Fitzpatrick et al., 1996).

Researchers use family typologies in assessing many aspects of family communication. One study found U.S. families more consensual and Japanese families more laissez-faire, perhaps due to Japanese cultural values of self-control, silence, and concern for face (Shearman & Dumlao, 2008).

In early research, it became evident that family types have different opinions about how much conformity is appropriate and whether conformity is contextual (Ritchie & Fitzpatrick, 1990). For

TABLE 14.1 Family Types

	Pluralistic	Consensual
High / Conversation	• Open, unrestrained discussions • Emphasis on the individual rather than the family unit • Openly address conflict and develop positive strategies of conflict management	• Pressure to agree and preserve the family • Open communication and idea exploration • Avoid unimportant conflict (family conflict is negative) but engage if necessary—usually aggressively
	Laissez-faire	*Protective*
Low	• Value individuality and make connections outside the family • Little overall family communication • Conflicts are rare	• Emphasize obedience and conformity • Communication used to enforce family rules • Members are expected not to have conflicts, so few skills are developed to manage conflict

Low ←——————————————→ **High**
Conformity

example, should the family obey the norm of not discussing sexual behaviors in front of young children? At what age is it appropriate for a child to question a parent's instructions instead of simply obeying? Are a child's attempts to negotiate about restrictions a violation of family rules or an expected part of child development leading to maturity and eventual autonomy? One study of family communication found general support for the predictions of how family types communicate. It concluded that during conflict:

> Children and parents of pluralistic families were particularly apt to enact patterns of direct, nonconfrontational communication. By comparison, high conformity families were more likely to be mutually confrontational (especially protective families) or engage in demand-withdraw (especially consensual families).
>
> (Sillars et al., 2014, p. 14)

KEY 14.1

Family patterns of communication are constantly evolving. What worked today may be ineffective tomorrow. It requires constant effort to keep family communication functional.

CASE 14.1

Let's Have Flowers!

My mother and dad eloped on a weekend trip to Nevada during a visit to my mom's aunt. It was Memorial Day, and all the shops closed down for the entire weekend in the tiny town. After finding out about the impending nuptials, there was a little party. Mom's aunt and her best friend had a bit to drink, and they decided it was not going to be a proper wedding without flowers.

The next morning when Mom and Dad showed up at the chapel, they found it full of fresh flowers! The room was beautifully decorated. They didn't notice until after the ceremony that the garbage cans were full of "In Memoriam" signs. Although this event happened years ago, someone inevitably ends up telling this story when the family gets together, usually followed by a comment of what irreverent, slightly shady, and wacky stock we come from!

Stories Sustain Family's Identity

Family stories sustain the vision of the family as a group and often are related to family rituals. Like the family experience in Case 14.1, the recounting of a funny episode during a family vacation or holiday gathering may start with the words "Do you remember when . . ." Family stories can be positive or negative—uplifting the family as they recount how they survived an awkward situation or demeaning an individual who is the unwilling butt of family jokes. Stories can function much like a parable to teach lessons about how one should behave (or not behave). Table 14.2 summarizes how family stories function.

Through stories, the collective meaning and social reality of a family are constructed. Family stories help children understand the changes in rules and roles as they mature. Most families tell stories that can be categorized into common types (Fiese et al., 2002). First, stories may tell *how the family came to be*. These stories relate how parents met or chronicle a birth story. A McCorkle family story relates how Fred McCorkle and Edith Neal went on their first date and he spilled a bowl of chili on Edith's lap. The moral is not to be deterred when things go wrong. A teenage daughter is told often about how she had almost died as a baby from meningitis as a reminder to make every day count because we never know what tomorrow brings. In the 2011 film, *We Bought a Zoo*, Matt Damon's character is picking up the pieces of his shattered family after his wife passes. Stories are shared with the children of how their mother's spirit is still part of their new family adventure as zoo owners and as a new person is redefining the family unit.

DISCUSSION QUESTION • 14.2

What stories were told in your family? Which story type best matches your family stories? Are there other types of stories that aren't part of the list in Table 14.2?

TABLE 14.2 Functions of Family Stories

---

1. Family stories help keep the past alive.
2. Family stories provide family and individual identity.
3. Family stories teach moral lessons.
4. Family stories develop individual and family esteem.
5. Family stories teach members how to change.
6. Family stories provide stability.
7. Family stories pass lore from generation to generation.

TABLE 14.3 Family Story Types

The family creation
Parents are people too
Passages to adulthood
The family stands together
The family's core identity

A second family story reveals that *parents are real people*. Family members or friends may tell stories of what parents were like when they were children or give examples of their human frailty. A father might relay a tale of when he made a rash purchase and ended up in debt for a car that was a lemon. The hope is that the daughter will make a better decision than he did in his youth.

The third family story type highlights the *transition from childhood to adulthood*. These stories relate events that mark a passage to adulthood or a characteristic that earns additional privileges in the family. Parents may talk about their first jobs and how that changed their responsibilities in the family as a way of indirectly telling children to do their parents' bidding until they pass the traditional threshold of getting a job. Being given a set of keys to a car may mark a transition to more independence.

The extent to which *a family will stand behind its members* is the subject of the fourth theme. Stories may relate what the family did or didn't do in stressful times to help each other. Janelle's mom was the eldest girl of six kids. Her father (Janelle's grandfather) died when she was only five, requiring her mom (Janelle's grandmother) to work outside the home to keep the family afloat. A common message in Janelle's youth was "everybody pitches in" to keep the family together. Everyone should sacrifice for the benefit of the family. If that meant the ten-year-old had to cook, do laundry, and raise her siblings, it was just what you had to do.

Stories that establish a *family's core identity* are the final type. Families share stories that clarify what it means to be a member of this particular family. Family stories may emphasize "We aren't quitters" or "Everybody does a stint in the military." Another example comes from Melanie's Grandpa Reese. While running cattle with his sons, he fell from a spooked horse and broke his collarbone. Although the pain was excruciating, he got back on the horse and finished the remaining three days of the long cattle drive because the cattle had to be moved. He said, "Cows don't care about collarbones." The message implicit in this story was that you *have* to take care of your responsibilities. There isn't a "quittin' time" on a farm—you work until the work is done and then rest later.

In addition to classifying family stories, research indicates that the type of story told to typify a family is associated with satisfaction within the family. How happy are you with your circumstance (**satisfaction**) is a common measurement in family research. Stories that illustrate care, togetherness, adaptability, and humor positively correlate with satisfaction; stories containing disregard, hostility, chaos, divergent values, and personality attributes negatively correlate with family satisfaction (Vangelisti, Crumley, & Baker, 1999). Of course, not every member of a family may experience the story in the same way—particularly if a story features that individual in an unflattering way (Thorson, Rittenour, Kellas, & Trees, 2013).

Rules Structure Family Behavior

Rules determine what is appropriate and guide family members' decisions on how to act. Because children soak up family rules as soon as they become aware of the world, family rules may not be obvious. We may not recognize a family rule or custom until it is broken by a newcomer. For example, Tom married Stella. When Tom's sister, mother, and grandmother visited the new wife, they brought along a ham and corn on the cob to share a traditional family meal. To be helpful, the new wife sliced the cold ham for sandwiches and cut the corn off the cob to make it easier to eat. The round of shocked expressions underscored that the family rituals for this type of food had been broken. A ham was a special extravagance that should be baked and lovingly basted while corn was shucked and served on the cob—all work that could be shared over conversation. Stella learned the role food preparation played in building family community and the lesson of asking questions before acting around Tom's family.

Family rules can help or hinder the communication process and be functional or dysfunctional. Sometimes rules involve **family secrets**. Implicitly or explicitly, some families know that if the illusion of family harmony is to be maintained, they can't talk about **taboo topics** such as an interracial marriage, sex, sexual orientation, money, or psychological conditions. Other taboo subjects can be joked about or discussed only if some family members are kept out of the loop. Family members may know that their son/brother is gay, but the entire family conceals that information from the grandparents. Both functional and dysfunctional families have rules not to talk about some topics outside of the family. In other cases, some family members may be privy to secrets that are hidden from other family members (e.g., "Don't tell Mom I'm living with my boyfriend.").

Imber-Black (1993) extends the concept of family taboos to delineate four types of family secrets. *Sweet secrets* have time limits and usually are related to good surprises, such as a party or a gift. For example, the entire McDonald clan banded together for months to hide preparations for Jim and Aretha's fiftieth anniversary surprise party. *Essential secrets* establish boundaries and identity among family members, such as disclosures among partners/parents that are withheld from children. As a teenager, Suzanne went with her parents to the bank while they were completing paperwork for a real estate deal. The agent asked a series of routine questions, including if either parent had been married before. Much to her surprise, her father answered that he was married and divorced once before. Later the same year, she visited her aunt's house in California and dated the boy next door. Her aunt told her she couldn't date him anymore because even though he didn't know it, the boy next door was the aunt's son (i.e., Suzanne's cousin). It was not unusual in those days for the parentage of a baby born outside of marriage to be concealed. Singer Bobby Darin grew up in the 1930s with an older sister, who in reality was his mother, a secret only revealed to him as an adult. All of these secrets were known to the elder generation but concealed from the younger generation.

Toxic secrets have a destructive effect on the family or its members. Some secrets conceal substance abuse or guard the family's economic and social standing. Toxic secrets conceal information at someone's expense. If a family member loses a job or flunks out of school but keeps leaving at the same time every day, it creates a lie that easily becomes a toxic situation. A murder case in Salt Lake City resulted from a husband's years of lying about his job and career prospects. He told his wife and family he had gotten into medical school. When his web of deceit started to unravel, it made more sense to him to murder his wife and claim that a stranger abducted her than to face up to his web of lies.

Dangerous secrets put individuals in physical harm, such as physical or sexual abuse and threats of murder or suicide. A family may know that an elder uncle molested children, but no one turned him in. Everyone instead makes sure that he is not alone with any of their kids.

Vangelisti and Caughlin's (1997) research indicates almost all families have at least one family secret—information intentionally withheld from outsiders. Most of these secrets involve taboo topics such as marital problems, substance abuse, finances, sexual preference, mental health, extramarital affairs, and physical, sexual, or psychological abuse, although some involve positive features such as family wealth. The next chapter will take a deeper look at how privacy functions in intimate relationships.

Communication Affects Satisfaction Levels

As mentioned earlier in this chapter, one measure of how close family members feel toward each other and the overall success of their communication is a variable grounded in **social learning theory** (discussed in Chapter 4) called **satisfaction.**

Caughlin (2003) presents two theories arising from satisfaction research. The **distressful ideals hypothesis** claims the match between one's ideal for relationship communication and one's experiences in communicating with the other person would determine satisfaction or dissatisfaction. The **unmet ideals hypothesis** suggests satisfaction results from the match or discrepancy between one's relationship ideals and one's relationship experiences. Caughlin's research found the unmet ideals hypothesis was implicitly mentioned by family members when describing their communication, e.g., "We don't talk about things like a family should." It is interesting that dissatisfaction could result because one's ideal communication is not held by other family members or because everyone holds the same standard but is not meeting the standard for some reason.

DISCUSSION QUESTION • 14.3

What makes a family happy? Compare your experience with what researchers have determined characterizes satisfactory families and relationships.

Contentment with romantic partners is one line of satisfaction research. Another line examines factors that affect the satisfaction of the rest of the family. Research indicates that fathers and sons may have more distant relationships now than during past historical periods. Fathers report being more affectionate toward their adult sons than what is perceived by that son (Floyd & Morman, 2005). Apprehension and dissatisfaction may lead to avoidance or other negative communicative behaviors.

The degree of openness about adversity may affect a family member's satisfaction levels. For example, children's satisfaction in their relationships with parents can be affected adversely by how news of an impending divorce is communicated. Even though parents may have protective intentions while hiding an upcoming divorce, children over the age of seven are keen at discerning relationship messages and deception. When the "secret" is revealed by parents who did not prepare children for a separation, long-term dissatisfaction with both parents may occur, and the child's self-esteem may be lowered (Thomas, Booth-Butterfield, & Booth-Butterfield, 1995). The relationship with the noncustodial parent suffers the most permanent damage in these cases.

A concept related to satisfaction is the **closeness** that family members feel for one another. Table 14.4 summarizes a study of adult children's perceptions of ten critical moments that changed

TABLE 14.4 Closeness Change Moments

---

1. An increase in physical distance (a child moves out)
2. A time of crisis
3. A change in one's habitual communication patterns
4. The rebellious teenager years
5. Parents' acceptance of a new partner or spouse
6. Birth of a child
7. Spending more/less time on activities with parents
8. Sibling jealousy
9. Alcohol or drug abuse
10. Parental acceptance of dating or cohabitation

Source: Golish (2000)

relationships with their parents—for better or for worse. Research strongly supports that families who conceal more secrets are less satisfied than families who conceal fewer secrets (Vangelisti & Caughlin, 1997). Not surprisingly, research shows that when parents treat children differently, or the children think one sibling is getting preferential treatment, there is more hostile and competitive conflict in the family and less closeness among those children when they become adults (Phillips & Schrodt, 2015).

Conflict and the Family

Believing that conflict is inherently bad is a common fallacy. However, to say conflict is normal does not mean that families should experience conflict all the time. Rather, the inevitable nature of conflict means that healthy families will have goal differences that create conflict situations from time to time.

As many people from highly emotional families can attest, disagreement and loud volume does not have to result in negative outcomes. According to Peterson, Peterson, and Skevington (1986), a conflict approached calmly or managed through "heated" discussions makes no difference in overall satisfaction in the family—if the emotion is a family style, cultural, and/or moderated by positive affection. In fact, the same study suggested teenagers in healthy families gained cognitive development advantages from heated arguments.

Just like other interpersonal conflict, most family conflicts can be distilled to two basic issues: power (who has control) or self-esteem (who feels good about themselves). Sillars, Canary, and Tafoya's (2004) review of family conflict research found young siblings may conflict as frequently as six times an hour, much to a parent's dismay. Anyone who has been around young siblings can attest to the research finding indicating that the more contact that occurs among young siblings, the more conflict occurs. Routine squabbling is not necessarily negative. However, an interesting research finding is that regardless of the type of conflict, high-conflict families rear children with lower self-disclosure skills, who are more likely to experience loneliness as adults. (Burke, Woszidlo, & Segrin, 2012).

Conflict Topics and Causes Change As Families Change

Another way to sort the types of conflicts families experience follows stages of family development summarized by Lulofs and Cahn (2000). Each stage of family development carries with it topics that require negotiation and are potential sites of conflict. In stage one, *selecting a mate*, conflicts can arise regarding if and when to marry or formalize a bond. Stage two, *beginning marriage/partnership*, requires numerous changes for each individual, negotiation of how to live together, what parts of old systems to merge, and what to create anew, as well as what it means to be a committed couple. Conflicts in the first two stages are the focus of the next chapter.

Stage three, *childbearing and preschool years*, require parents to rearrange their lives, social contacts, and renegotiate relationships with in-laws. As children age, they naturally conflict with parents and siblings for control, time, attention, and self-esteem. *School-age* children's needs dominate stage four. Parents again must renegotiate their lives to reflect the often-competing transportation, economic, and interpersonal demands of children. As parents become involved in their children's activities and school, they meet and work with other adults who are coaches, teachers, or parents of the child's friends. Stage five, *adolescence*, brings more changes as children test their independence against parental needs for control. At stage six, *launching*, children leave the home. Parents must renegotiate their lives to adapt to a home without children. Families in the last two stages of *middle* and *older years* begin to deal with the issues of caring for aging parents, relationships with grandchildren, multigenerational families, children who return to the family home as adults, and/or health issues.

This model, of course, is only appropriate to the roughly 50 percent of marriages that don't end in divorce. Divorced families have additional influences that bring conflict opportunities.

Patterns of Family Conflict

Conflicts happen in families. Whether those conflicts result in strengthening the relational bonds or in eroding a loving environment will depend on how family members handle conflict.

A potential contributing factor for a positive outcome is style. Chapter 8 discussed the role of general style in the creation and escalation of interpersonal conflict. It should be no surprise that style differences also exist within families. One way to measure conversational style is differentiating between high-involvement and high-considerateness. **High-involvement conversational style** is characterized by a fast rate of speech, lots of simultaneous speech, and short pauses. **High-considerateness conversational style** exhibits slower speech rate, longer pauses within and between turns, and few overlaps while speaking. Research indicates teenagers tend to use a high-involvement style in conversing with parents, particularly with mothers, whereas parents more often exhibit a high-considerateness style (Beaumont & Wagner, 2004). The style difference offers ample opportunity for misunderstandings and conflict. For example, a teen may be quick to interrupt and argue, which may trigger negative responses from a mother with a high-considerateness conversational style. Parents, exhibiting high considerateness, see high involvement as a mark of disrespect, often shutting down the teen who can't seem to talk without arguing. However, being shut down only frustrates the high-involvement teen who wants nothing more strongly than to be considered as an equal. No wonder parents and teen's conversations can go so quickly awry.

The family typologies discussed earlier in this chapter are significant when understanding how families manage conflict (see Table 14.1). In a study of families containing at least one teenage child, **pluralistic** families avoided conflicts less and had few examples of negative venting. **Consensual** families reported numerous conflicts and negative venting during conflicts. The social support among consensual family members, however, seemed to negate negative effects. **Laissez-faire** families tended to avoid conflict and viewed their conflicts as unimportant. **Protective** families reported conflict avoidance and negative venting. The underlying assumption of Koerner and Fitzpatrick's theory (2004, 2006) is that these family types create schemas that guide family communication.

CASE 14.2

The Broken Truck

Trevor is 30 years old and lives in the same town as his dad, William. When Trevor's car died, William let him borrow his old truck that was nearly worthless; in fact, he had been planning to sell it for scrap metal but hadn't gotten around to it. Trevor has a history of financial trouble, and recently quit his job (again) because he got mad at his boss. When Trevor has money, he likes to be the guy who buys presents for people and picks up the tab for dinner. When he's broke, which is often, he has no problem letting others pay the tab figuring it all works out in end.

Trevor got a $25 dollar parking ticket in William's truck and didn't pay it. William received a bill in the mail for the $25 fine with a late fee of $20 included. This is not the first time that Trevor has cost William money. Trevor defaulted on his student loans several years ago that William co-signed on, and William ended up paying. Trevor had damaged an apartment in his early 20s that William stepped in and paid to have repaired. There are numerous times that Trevor has "borrowed" money that William never saw again. Trevor always promises he will pay it back—and he intends to—but nothing materializes. But this parking ticket and late fee really made William angry. He wondered when the boy would grow up and take responsibility for his life and quit using people.

When Trevor next visited his dad, William made dinner and presented Trevor with the ticket. Trevor apologized and said he'd pay it, but he didn't have money right then because he is between jobs. William agreed to pay it to avoid additional charges, but insisted Trevor pay him for it as soon as he could. Trevor agreed.

Fast forward two weeks and Trevor has not paid for the ticket. Trevor texts his dad saying the truck has died and could he borrow some cash to replace the water pump. William texts back, "I'll help with the truck when I see the $45 dollars you owe me for the parking ticket." Trevor responds, "I said I'd pay you and you know I just started a new job. Why are you being such a jerk?" William stops texting back and makes plans to have the truck towed to the scrap yard.

DISCUSSION QUESTION • 14.4

Trevor and William in Case 14.2 are having two different conflicts. Explain the conflict from William's view and again from Trevor's perspective. How would each punctuate the beginning of the conflict and what assumptions are each making about their transparency of their emotional cues?

Judgmental Biases and Conflict

How individuals define the beginning of a conflict is called the **biased punctuation of conflict** (Thompson & Lucas, 2014). According to this explanation, punctuation bias occurs when:

> Actor A perceives the history of conflict with another actor, B, as a sequence of B-A, B-A, B-A, in which the initial hostile or aggressive move was always made by B, obliging A to engage in defensive and legitimate retaliatory action. Actor B punctuates the same history of interaction as A-B, A-B, A-B, however, reversing the roles of aggressor and defender.
>
> (p. 262)

A conversation between Paul and Becky illustrates how biased punctuation occurs. Paul promises to pick up groceries but forgets. He arrives home just in time for the new episode of his favorite program, and Becky talks to him about groceries during the program. Both are subsequently angry. Paul states, "I wouldn't have gotten mad and said what I said if you hadn't been so rude and talked while I was watching my favorite show." Becky counters, "I wouldn't have interrupted your precious show if you had done the shopping like you said you were going to do." Both Paul and Becky are punctuating (starting) the conflict at the place that benefits them, attempting to demonstrate the justification of their reactions.

In addition to punctuation bias, parties may find themselves suffering from the **illusion of transparency**. According to this theory, people with a shared history (especially family members) may assume that their motives and internal states have been expressed. However, individuals often overestimate their effectiveness at transmitting emotional cues, yet expect that the other should have known what they were thinking or feeling (Gilovich, Savitsky, & Medvec, 1998; Thompson & Lucas, 2014). As Becky in the previous example talks to Paul, she assumes he is aware of how important the shopping task had been, since he should know how stressed she is about making sure this dinner she's preparing for her grandparents goes well. Paul, oblivious to Becky's stress about the grandparents' visit, only watches one show a week and thinks Becky should know how much he looks forward to this 60 minutes of escape. Both assume the other should be aware of their respective emotional states and are confused when the other doesn't pick up on "obvious" cues.

Privacy Management

How rules operate in the family is best explained using Petronio's **communication privacy management theory**. Petronio (2000, 2002) posits that individuals manage the disclosure of private information by creating rules or boundaries about what they will tell and what they will withhold. Very few people tell everybody everything all the time—they choose what is private and what is public information and with whom to share information. Privacy management occurs in many settings—work, friendships, intimate relationships, and families.

Privacy rules attempt to control what is revealed within the family what will be revealed about the family to outsiders. Petronio (2002) advances suppositions to explain how and why people do or do not disclose private information (Table 14.5).

CASE 14.3

Privacy Among Sisters

Gabriela and Patricia are sisters who are in frequent phone contact with their cousin Martin, who lives in another state near his parents. Two weeks ago, Martin mentioned to Gabriela that he was having some surgery soon and asked her not to tell "the family" because his parents would freak out. A week ago, Gabriela told Patricia about that conversation and passed on Martin's desire not to let the family know. Today, when Patricia talked to her mother (Martin's mother's sister), she forgot that the information was secret and asked if her mother had heard how Martin's surgery turned out. Her mother said, "What surgery?" Patricia felt her heart sink, knowing that as soon as she got off the call with her mother, the phone lines would be buzzing throughout the whole family.

TABLE 14.5 Five Privacy Rules

1. People believe they own information about themselves and can control who knows what.
2. People control private information through the creation of personal rule boundaries.
3. When others are given access to private information, they become co-owners of that information.
4. People create rule systems to try to control disclosure.
5. Privacy management involves dialectics.

Rule 1: People believe they own and have a right to control their private information.

Some interpersonal communication theories posit that self-disclosure is the most important activity in building cohesive bonds in relationships. Through sharing personal information, bonds are built. Petronio, however, notes that self-disclosure may or may not create greater intimacy. For example, disclosing something that a family member finds repugnant may create division. Also, deciding not to reveal information is just as important as disclosure. There are multiple reasons why someone would or would not disclose information—to build intimacy, exert power, prevent a wrong, display ethics, or cause a reaction from others.

Petronio emphasizes that people feel they "own" information about themselves and should be able to exert control over how that information is distributed. What people feel is private can vary widely. Each individual consciously or unconsciously will create rules to help manage personal information. For example, an individual might think, "I won't tell strangers about my sexual orientation, but I will tell my best friends because they will keep that information private."

In one application, communication privacy management theory was used to explain children's distancing from parents as the child tried to establish independence. Researchers tested how adolescents used "fortification" of their rooms to create privacy or adopted evasive tactics to keep parents from discovering what they really were doing. Children also set boundaries through topic avoidance and deception (Mazur & Hubbard, 2004). A parent asked her high school sophomore daughter how school was that day, to which the daughter responded with, "Fine." Mom knew her daughter was called into the principal's office for skipping class, but she hoped her child would feel safe enough to share that information. But, the daughter was attempting to maintain a boundary between her school life and her home life. She was unlikely to volunteer information that bridged those two worlds.

Another application of privacy management theory compared privacy tendencies to Koerner and Fitzpatrick's family types (Bridge & Schrodt, 2013). Protective families (high in conformity and low in conversation) had the strongest tendencies to hold strict privacy rules. Children in laissez-faire families (low in conversation and low in conformity) developed the most permeable privacy boundaries, perhaps because they received little instruction from parents about what should be held private.

DISCUSSION QUESTION • 14.5

When friends or coworkers know details about you that you consider "private," how do you feel? Does sharing of private information help you feel closer or is it somehow threatening? If you are in a position of knowing a not commonly known detail about a sibling or friend, how responsible do you feel for managing that information (deciding who, if anyone, to tell)? If you receive a "D" on an essay in this course and the instructor waved the paper around so others could see the grade, would you feel that was a violation of your privacy?

Rule 2: People control private information through the creation of personal rule boundaries.

As soon as a child develops an identity, the potential for secrets exists. An internal boundary rule is created when a child thinks, "I really don't want someone else to know that I regularly sneak my carrots away from the table and flush them down the toilet." The child is trying to set boundaries around what information is public and what is private. In later life, siblings may or may not impose rules about the disclosure of information. If a sister sees her older brother smoking marijuana, a violation of a parental rule, the declaration "Don't tell mom" is the brother's attempt to control what the sister discloses by establishing a boundary rule—"We don't have to tell our parents everything."

Petronio (2002) elaborates on five factors that affect how personal rules are developed and change over one's lifetime: culture, gender, motivation, context, and cost-benefit ratio. As discussed in Chapter 5, people around the world have different cultural thresholds when it comes to the disclosure of private information or the amount of embarrassment that would result if private information about oneself or a family member became public.

Gender roles also seem to affect how privacy rules are developed. Petronio discusses how gender identity impacts the creation of the rules adopted by some boys and girls (women and men). Men who adopt traditional gender roles may feel it is weak to discuss feelings, and women who adopt traditional roles could feel a need to disclose feelings.

What an individual needs at a specific time affects the motivation to conceal or reveal information. For example, someone looking for new friends might experimentally make personal disclosures, expecting reciprocal disclosures from the potential friend. Someone who is motivated by a need to feel in control may not reveal any personal information.

For most people, context matters when deciding what and when to disclose. A work context implies a rule of less disclosure than a family context. A traumatic event can create a special context invoking a change of normal rules. For example, a suicide in a family may stop any discussion of a sensitive nature until the initial shock wears off. Someone working on personal development might seek out venues that require disclosure, such as Alcoholics Anonymous or Weight Watchers. Part of the success of therapy groups is that people are more likely to talk about subjects such as abuse, alcoholism, or sexual difficulties among others with the same life experiences.

Finally, Petronio identifies a cost-benefit analysis as a factor to affect disclosure. While it may not be done consciously, most people weigh the potential risks of sharing or concealing information with their possible benefits. Will sharing private information about oneself or about someone else probably result in positive effects for the one disclosing (such as we become closer) or negative effects (such as personal rejection)? Breshears and DiVerniero (2015) studied children of gay, lesbian, bisexual, or transgendered parents and how they managed their parent's relational information. They found the child's decision to tell others about their parents was based on the cost-benefit ratio of how open or friendly someone was versus the risk of recrimination.

Rule 3: When others are told or given access to a person's private information, they become co-owners of that information.

When information becomes known to more than one person, everyone "in the know" has partial "ownership" of that information. This is particularly true in families where each individual has daily opportunities to observe, overhear, or be told information about family members. The difficulty with co-ownership is that even though each person feels they have a right to control what is known about them, others may disclose that information anyway.

A study of children (now adults) whose parents came out as gay or lesbian to them during childhood found some felt the information about the parents' sexual orientation was owned just by the parent, and some felt the information was owned by the whole family. In either case, the children said they felt some responsibility for managing the information even though there were no overt discussions on who to tell and who not to tell (Breshears & DiVerniero, 2015).

Families with a strong internal privacy orientation (i.e., rules about who gets to know what within the family) had more satisfaction than families with a stronger external privacy orientation (rules about what outsiders get to know about the family). It was speculated that because families can have many separate dyadic relationships (among siblings, between parents and children, between parents, and so forth), families who worked at maintaining internal privacy boundaries had more certainty in their communication than other families (Carmon, Miller, & Brasher, 2013).

Another study noted that many interracial couples also use co-ownership of the information disclosed about their relationship. For example, one woman asked friends not to tell her parents about her new dating partner so they didn't learn of it indirectly. In other cases, the family tried to control which people in their social and familiar network would be informed about the interracial couple (Brummett & Steuber, 2015).

DISCUSSION QUESTION • 14.6

In the age of global social media, sexting, and frequent posting of private details by "former" friends, privacy rules may seem fuzzy. Once information is digitized in any form (e-mail, text, streaming video, photo), what expectations should you have about the privacy of personal information?

Rule 4: People create rules to try to control disclosure.

Rules are created internally by individuals to guide their personal decisions and collectively among those who co-own information. Once an individual learns a bit of private information, the mutual holders of that information should negotiate how private the information is. It is preferable to negotiate who gets to know before the private information is disclosed.

DISCUSSION QUESTION • 14.7

What is your response when someone begins a conversation with: "You have to promise not to tell anyone this"?

One study of sibling privacy management showed changes in both explicit and implicit rules as children aged. Explicit rules were statements like "Don't tell anyone," and an implicit rule might be "We both know that unless I say 'It's OK to tell mom' that things stay private" (Brockhage & Phillips, 2016).

It is not uncommon for students to approach a professor with information about another student and to preface their disclosure of the information with: "I don't want you to tell anyone else, but I thought you should know that . . ." The student is trying to negotiate non-disclosure without actually disclosing the information. Most university professor and officers will stop the conversation by saying something like: "I can't guarantee that I won't tell others because it really depends on what you are about to say." For example, if the "private" information is an illegal act under the university or state's codes (such as a hate crime, threat, or sexual harassment), there is a legal duty for the person who knows the information to disclose it to proper university authorities. In any setting, there are numerous personal and social ethics that might make promising not to tell before knowing the details a really bad idea.

In June of 2016, a U.S. citizen killed 49 people in an Orlando, Florida, nightclub. His wife disclosed that she had tried to talk him out of using violence. For whatever reasons (gender, culture,

TABLE 14.6 Types of Boundary Violations

Intentional Rule Violations/Betrayals. Information is maliciously disclosed. For example, a sibling posts embarrassing photos of her brother on Facebook.

Mistakes. Someone forgets or is socially inept in managing information. For example, a child mentions that the family is on food stamps to a neighbor.

Fuzzy Boundaries. It is unclear what can and cannot be shared. Family members never actually discuss what can and cannot be shared with outsiders. For example, is it acceptable to let others know Aunt Ella is in prison or are we supposed to just tell everyone she moved?

Different Boundary Rules. Individuals have conflicting boundaries. For example, trouble will inevitably result if a newly married couple come from families where the one family had the rule "Always tell your mother everything," and the other had the rule, "Parents shouldn't know the private details of their adult children's lives."

Public Boundary Borders. Boundaries change when an individual enters the public domain. For example, politicians and celebrities must deal with situations where others do not feel bound to keep secret information about someone who has become newsworthy. Privacy border use also occurs when one individual discusses a private topic in a public place, such as an elevator, restaurant, or classroom.

family privacy), the shooter was able to control what others disclosed about his tendencies, and she did not warn authorities of her husband's dangerous state of mind.

A significant cause of conflict emerges when individuals do not concur about the privacy rules. Simply put, when there is a lack of agreement about what can be disclosed or when the privacy rules are broken, it isn't good for the relationship. The one whose information has been "leaked" feels betrayed. Petronio posits several common ways that boundaries are violated and relationship turbulence is created (Table 14.6).

Rule 5: Privacy management involves dialectics.

A dialectic involves inherent contradictions. For example, the idea of intimacy contains both the promise of joy and the risk of disappointment. Privacy management theory focuses on the dialectic between needs for information to be public and the need for information to be private.

It is common for people not to tell critical information to a doctor because they don't want that fact to be put in their file (sexual preference, symptoms of a sexually transmitted disease, loss of bladder control, or any other embarrassing experience). Petronio notes that every choice about the management of private information involves a dialectic—in this case, the weight of momentary embarrassment and a permanent note in one's medical file versus having an important medical condition properly diagnosed and treated.

> **DISCUSSION QUESTION • 14.8**
>
> What dialectics about privacy have you experienced in your close relationships?

The Dark Side of Family Conflict

The family is the place where children receive their basic programming—what to value, how to communicate, and their place in the world. Sometimes families operate in ways that nourish an individual's self-esteem, build emotional intelligence, and confer appreciation for those who are different from the family group—and sometimes families teach something else. The basic socialization received from the family is the voice in your head that tells you how to feel, what is right or wrong, ways to communicate and interact that feel "normal," and a myriad of other messages.

In the preface to one of the first books on family dysfunction (Spitzberg & Cupach, 1998), the authors note it is the paradoxes of communication that give rise to problematic family communication patterns—the dark side of family communication. In other words, family communication can be positive or do great harm. In the prologue to *The Dark Side of Family Communication* (2012), the authors elaborate:

> the family system is a key site where lives are formed, developed, and changed across time. For many, their lives are nurtured and sustained by their families, providing them with a source of security, comfort, and support. Unfortunately, however, many others may find that their family system is a site of much pain, suffering, stress, maltreatment, and perhaps even abuse.
>
> (Olson, Baiocchi-Wagner, Wilson-Kratzer, & Symonds, 2012)

Dysfunction can embrace the entire family or stem from one person who negatively affects others. For example, unmanaged child physical and social aggression and a mother's use of negative conflict management styles affects family members and probably is predictive of future problems for the child (Underwood, Beron, Gentsch, Galperin, & Risser, 2008).

Dysfunctional families may differ from their more functional counterparts both in *what* they talk about and *how* they communicate with each other. Family communication researchers try to discover patterns in how successful and unsuccessful families interact and talk to one another on a daily basis.

Some psychological factors seem to correlate with poor family interaction patterns. For example, neuroticism, narcissism, depression, substance abuse, and Machiavellianism tend to correlate with self-involved individuals who care little about how their communication affects other family members (Olson et al., 2012).

Canary and Canary (2013) highlight numerous specific ways that dysfunctional family communication is harmful:

- When parents use negative communication and conflict tactics, the spillover results in children who become more withdrawn and exhibit their own negative communication behaviors.
- Children tend to perceive their parents' conflicts as their fault.
- When parental behavior threatens emotional security, children more easily become maladjusted.

Negative messages have significant effects on adults and children. Stafford and Dainton (1994) identified two important aspects of rejection in the family. First, a child may experience a debilitating erosion of self-esteem when parental messages consistently are disconfirming. *Disconfirming messages* either ignore the child's attempts at attention or directly label the child as worthless and bad. Telling a child "You are so stupid" runs counter to helping that child develop a positive sense of self. Second, some of the compliance-gaining strategies used by parents may be damaging, such as coercion or withdrawal of love. Some research, however, indicates that higher self-esteem moderates disconfirming messages. In romantic relationships, hurtful evaluative messages were more face threatening than similar comments about personality or appearance, with high self-esteem individuals showing less concern about disconfirmation (Zhang & Stafford, 2008).

While the motivation for specific negative family communication behaviors may vary, Yoshimura and Boon (2014) claim a desire for revenge spurs many personal conflicts. Those using revenge tactics thought the action would cause the other person to change, remedy an injustice, make the other suffer, or lessen the pain of a perceived hurt. After taking revenge, some individuals feel guilt and others felt a positive result occurred (in the other person or in themselves). In families, the effects of revenge may be magnified. With greater exposure, there are more opportunities for one person to feel attacked, slighted, or treated unfairly. Abuse, neglect, and violence occur in many families and sow the seeds of desire for revenge. Those who find affection and advanced communication skills absent within the family and who despair in finding safety and justice may consider violence as an option on the dark side of family life.

Even so-called normal families have their occasional troubles. It is a myth that at some point in history, families were happier and more successful than current families. Stafford and Dainton (1994) comment on the myth of the golden age of family relations, typified by classic television shows like *The Waltons*, *Little House on the Prairie*, or *Father Knows Best*. They state:

> During this fictitious utopian era, divorce was unheard of, children respected their elders and knew right from wrong, multiple generations dwelled blissfully in the same home, and family members spent their abundant leisure time together engaged in wholesome activities such as eating stone-ground bread that had been baked in their own ovens from plates they made themselves at their joint pottery class.
>
> (p. 261)

It is commonly held in the communication discipline that relationships require communication skills and work to keep them healthy. Sadly, many families may talk primarily about who should take out the garbage (a task) and not about issues or feelings that are critical to family satisfaction. Thus little time is invested in productive conflict management and relationship maintenance. Research indicates that most people believe maintaining relationships is work; they just don't do the work (Stafford & Dainton, 1994). We may wind up practicing more careful communication with coworkers and strangers than with spouses and children.

Conflict Management Skills for Families

What Makes a Family Strong?

The term *family strength* describes a family unit that is able to bond together and solve its problems in productive ways. The International Family Strengths Model developed by DeFrain and others claims six qualities make families strong:

1. Appreciation and affection—strong families care about each other
2. Commitment—strong families put energy into each other's well-being
3. Positive communication—strong families talk and listen to each other, as well as work to solve problems and conflicts
4. Enjoy time together—strong families are happy when together
5. Spiritual well-being—strong families use ethics and values to help self and others
6. Effective management of stress and crisis—strong families survive and are able to reframe a crisis into something tolerable

(DeFrain & Asay, 2007)

Among the many challenges to family life today, communication scholars and others try to locate the positive aspects that make a family functional amongst social turmoil. A theme in the research literature states that what makes a family strong is resilience created through a variety of communication skills that assist in coping (Schrodt, 2009).

One of the most powerful ways to manage conflict in a family is to learn healthy and productive communication skills. Families can expand their conflict management skills in a variety of ways. Couples can attend communication and relationship building classes. Parents can use facilitators or counselors to work out expectations and communication behaviors before stepfamilies join together. Adults can teach new skills to their families, including the adults reading this book. Children learn conflict management skills at school and can share those ideas with their parents. For change to occur, the environment must be considered safe to experiment and make mistakes. Just knowing a skill isn't enough. Diligence, desire, and practice are the means to create new habits. Any change in habits takes a concerned commitment (see Reeder, 2014).

As with general interpersonal conflict, listening is one of the most critical skills for family conflict management. Coakley and Wolvin (1997) emphasize that parents must learn different listening skills to use with a child as he or she ages. The act of listening itself is confirming, helping the individual feel as if his or her views are valued. Parents may be deterred from effective listening for a variety of reasons, some of which are featured in Table 14.7.

KEY 14.2

Most people believe that maintaining relationships is work; they just don't do the work.

Creating purposeful time for positive interactions is important for building healthy communication in families. The family meeting or family home night is a widely used practice that enables families to work on issues before they become overwhelming or devolve into negative criticism. Simply put, a **family meeting** is a regularly scheduled time set aside for family communication and problem solving. Families may hold a particular night of the week for "family talk" or have a rule that any family member can call a meeting. Usually, families use a set agenda that includes time for "gripes" or issues, as well as mention of personal achievements and success. After the ritual sharing, the family sets an agenda of which issues to discuss and how the family can address the concern.

Selecting the right time and place for a couple or a family to discuss issues is critical. Because many families may often have no set time when they are all together, working on family issues or conflicts rarely occurs naturally. When everyone knows that two hours are reserved to deal with a family issue, there is less impulse to drift to other activities. Typically, a family meets in a place in the home that is comfortable for everyone and away from distractions. For example, no media should intrude into the conversation and no "outsiders" should be present. Some couples who are trying to break a pattern of raising their voices with each other or cutting off a conversation early can schedule a meeting to discuss issues at a restaurant, using the social setting as a reason to maintain

TABLE 14.7 Myths About Listening in the Family

- Listening undermines parental authority.
- Listening to a child means agreeing with what the child is expressing.
- Listening obligates parents to change their views.
- Listening just leads to hearing hurtful criticism.

low tones. Other families may have informal mechanisms to achieve the benefits of the family meeting, including ensuring at least three nights a week of having dinner together, or regarding one weekend a month as sacred family together time.

When families are not able to work out their conflicts, *family mediation* is an option. Mediators facilitate family interaction in a safe setting and through a controlled agenda that encourages family members to work out their own agreements (Burrell & Fitzpatrick, 1990; Plenert, 2017).

For parents who learn mediation skills, additional benefits may accrue. A study of family conflicts after parents learned mediation skills found the management of their children's conflict had more constructive results, less yelling, more listening, and better involvement from the children who often were able to solve their issues (as opposed to a parent "ruling" on who was right in the conflict) (Smith & Ross, 2007).

A study of conflict among Anglo-American, African-American, Latino, and Asian-American married couples found that negative interactions played a dominant role in creating marriage dissatisfaction. They concluded:

> Based on an entire body of research, we believe that successful treatment for couples will often include provision of a safe place for issues to be addressed in treatment as well as efforts to help couples develop reliable methods for talking safely and openly at home.
> (Stanley, Markman, & Whitton, 2002, pp. 670–671)

Specifically, couples need to learn how to refrain from hurtful comments, negative attributions of the partner's motivations, and how to stay in conversation about difficulties rather than withdrawing (a pattern of behavior in 42 percent of males and 26 percent of females).

Developing any of the skills discussed in this section can help families deal with conflict. Even so, how people feel about each other and the skills being applied may be more important than the skill itself. After examining ten years of research and training programs on parental conflict, Reynolds and her colleagues concluded: "Couples who related to each other with warmth, affection and [humor] (positive emotionality) even during disagreements, somehow protected themselves from the potentially damaging impact of their poor problem solving and communication skills" (Reynolds, Houlston, Coleman, & Harold, 2014, p. 8).

CASE 14.4

My Family Meeting

When my teenagers were fighting excessively—which might actually vary according to how much I could take on a particular day—I would call a family meeting. The three of us sat down at the kitchen table, and I set a few ground rules: Everybody gets an equal chance to talk without interruption, and no negative comments while the other is talking. Each teenager then had a chance to vent about what was going on. Then we would brainstorm. I'd tell them that we wouldn't criticize or make faces when we were brainstorming ideas. We brainstormed how each could accommodate the other and not infringe on each other's privileges as family members. By the end of the family meeting, my teenagers would be laughing, talking together instead of fighting—coming up with the silliest ideas. In among all of the silly ideas, there always seemed to be a way through the difficulty that started their bickering.

Summary

Families come in all types and sizes, from nuclear, to extended, to families of choice. Some families function well, others are at risk of losing their effectiveness when trouble occurs, and some are dysfunctional.

Family communication encompasses how the individuals attribute meaning to events in the life of the family and how rules and norms are created and sustained. Assumptions about family life and patterns of interaction were learned in the family of origin. The quality of family communication is related to family satisfaction.

Research has identified four types of families according to their high or low degree of conformity and how the family converses: Consensual families encourage discussion, but expect conformity; pluralistic families encourage discussion and allow some personal variability; protective families emphasize conformity without discussion; and laissez-faire families don't encourage anything in particular. Pluralistic families seem to provide the most beneficial social learning environment for children. Even so, the amount and type of conformity that is expected evolves over a family's lifespan as children change and age.

Family stories are a type of communication that sustains an image of the group, as well as conveying norms and life lessons. Family rituals, in contrast, are repeated behaviors that a family enacts.

In addition to stories, rituals, and traditions, families have norms and rules for interaction. Norms develop early in a couple's association and may set the standards for behaviors for a family's lifetime. Norms are customary behaviors, so they are somewhat more flexible than family rules, which strictly govern how one should behave. Some family rules include secrets, which can be sweet, essential, toxic, or dangerous.

Research in family satisfaction finds that dissatisfied marriages are more negative and critical than more satisfied marriages. Related to satisfaction in families is their feeling of closeness and whether critical events lead to more closeness or more distance.

Two styles of family conversation, high involvement and high considerateness, may affect how family conflicts are perceived and managed. Pluralistic families provided the most effective foundation for productive conflict management. Additionally, there are significant differences in family communication and compliance behaviors across cultural groups that give rise to conflict in multicultural families. The biases inherent in how parties punctuate their conflict as well as the tendency to assume they've been transparent in the ways they've expressed their emotions can lead to escalated conflict and dissatisfaction with outcomes.

Privacy management is a source of conflict in the family. Petronio's theory of privacy management contains five rules: people believe they own information about themselves; people create rules to control their private information; those given access to private information become co-owners; people create rules to try to control disclosure; and privacy management involves dialectics.

In addition to the usual range of interpersonal conflict management skills, families may moderate conflict through changing their individual communication behaviors, establishing family meeting times, or mediation.

Chapter Resources

Exercises

1. In groups, select a film or television episode to view. Determine what kind of family communication is occurring and if family members have secrets that are concealed. If secrets are concealed, what are the consequences? Suggested sources: *Transparency, Modern Family, Home for the Holidays, The Family Stone, Little Miss Sunshine, The Royal Tenenbaums, Rachel Getting Married, Rumor Has It, Mrs. Doubtfire, Captain Fantastic, Running with Scissors, The Queen, Winter Passing,* or *The Full Monty.*

2. Compare at least two films portraying stepfamilies (e.g., *Raising Helen, Stepmom, Yours, Mine and Ours, The Santa Clause, Man of the House*, or *Tumbleweeds*). What types of conflicts are portrayed in stepfamilies?

3. Compare the change moments in your personal history to those in Table 14.4. Did your family communication get better, worse, or stay the same after a change moment?

4. How do the following challenges to family success, discussed by DeFrain and Asay (2007), affect family communication? Are some types of families better able to handle these stresses?

- High stress, materialism, and competition
- Lack of time for self and family
- Childcare outside the family
- High divorce and remarriage rates
- Violence, victimization, and fear
- Sex as a national obsession
- High alcohol, tobacco, and drug use (and related diseases)
- Changing gender roles and related stress
- Urban overcrowding
- Overspending and financial problems
- Ethical and cultural tensions
- War and terrorism

Journal/Essay Topics

1. How would you classify your family of origin? How is the style of your family of origin affecting you as an adult?

2. If you have children, or if you plan to have children someday, would you want your children to experience the same family communication style that you learned? What lessons in family conflict would/will children learn from you?

3. Does your family use any version of a family meeting? If not, do you think the establishment of a regular family meeting would enhance communication among your family members?

Research Topics

1. Investigate family structures and norms in a culture other than European-American. What does research say about these families?

2. Investigate best practices for family meetings. Which practices would be the most effective in your family?

Mastery Cases

Examine Mastery Case 14A, Too Many Moms, or Case 14B, The Family Feud. What concepts from this chapter shed light on the case?

Too Many Moms

When Debbie was eight, her parents divorced. Her dad, Frank, remarried quickly, and Debbie's mother, Elaine, expressed disdain for the new wife. It was clear to Debbie that her mother feared losing her children's affection and allegiance. Elaine would become jealous whenever Debbie mentioned her stepmother's birthday or if she gave her stepmother a gift on Mother's Day.

When Debbie grew up and married, her husband's mother expected Debbie to call her "Mom" like her other daughter-in-law did. Debbie couldn't bring herself to call her mother-in-law "Mom" and called her by her first name, Eva. Even though her own mother passed away, to call anyone else "Mom" seemed awkward or like a betrayal of her mother's memory. Eva was hurt and always winced when called by her first name instead of by "Mom," and she took the refusal to comply with her wishes very personally.

The Family Feud

Todd and Karen are brother and sister. They were very close in the past but drifted apart during their parents' prolonged illnesses. Karen provided home care for her parents for the last ten years, which dramatically affected her life. Todd refused to help. He was in his second marriage and said he had his own life and career and didn't have time, so she would just have to handle it. Karen took care of their parents until they died.

After their mother's death, probate started. In probate, all of the parents' estate must be vetted through the courts, taxes paid, and the remaining assets distributed to the children according to the will. The will named Karen and Todd as co-executors—meaning they must work together to settle the estate. After the funeral, Karen started working on what needed to be done. Two months passed. There was a lot of tedious, time-consuming sorting to be done, and Karen wanted Todd to help. Todd agreed to meet at the family house.

It's Sunday at 2 P.M. when Todd arrives. Karen is surrounded by boxes and sorting through the items in the estate. Todd helps her carry items from the house to the garage.

Karen: "As you can see, there is a lot to do here—80 years of accumulated personal property that has to be sorted, inventoried, appraised, and distributed. I need you to help out more."

Todd: "I'm too busy with my work and my own family to get bogged down in this. I have more important responsibilities than dealing with this junk."

Karen: "You agreed to be co-executor! That means more than picking up your check from the attorney. It's only right that you help with this stuff. I'll keep working, but you have to come by every weekend and help sort this out."

Todd: "You don't realize how hard I work. I have a life. I don't have time. You don't have Mom and Dad to take care of anymore, so you have lots of time on your hands. You can do it."

Karen: "I've worked really hard the last ten years caring for our parents. Where were you? I am tired and could use your help. I'm anxious to get this taken care of so I can have a life. I've been in this house for ten years taking care of our parents, and I'm ready for a change of scenery."

Todd: "I worked hard here when I was a kid. That should count for something! I shouldn't have to do much now that I have a business of my own."

Karen: "We didn't work that hard as kids, come on. Mom and Dad worked hard."

Todd: "I worked hard, whether you remember it or not."

Karen: "That was a long time ago. We need to figure out what we're going to do now."

Todd: "If I was in charge, I'd get a big dumpster and just get rid of everything! It's all crap anyway."

Karen: "You can't be serious. There's a lot of valuable stuff here—not to mention all the family pictures. How do we know what's here until we look?"

Todd: "Go ahead! Look away. I don't have time to look at all this junk when we're just going to throw most of it out. If you want me to help, I'll have to do it my way. I'll get some dumpsters in here and be done with it."

Karen: "Go for it! At least you'll be doing something. It's all in your hands. Call me when it's time for me to pick up my check on the estate settlement."

Karen leaves and slams the door. Two days later, Todd contacts Karen and says he's ready to work out a schedule to sort through the stuff. Karen says she's glad they will be working on it together.

References

Arnold, L. B. (2008). *Family communication theory and research*. Boston: Pearson.

Beaumont, S. L., & Wagner, S. L. (2004). Adolescent-parent verbal conflict: The roles of conversational styles and disgust emotions. *Journal of Language and Social Psychology, 23*(3), 338–368.

Breshears, D., & DiVerniero, R. (2015). Communication privacy management among adult children with lesbian and gay parents. *Western Journal of Communication, 79*(5), 573–590.

Bridge, M. C., & Schrodt, P. (2013). Privacy orientations as a function of family communication patterns. *Communication Reports, 26*(1), 1–12.

Brockhage, K., & Phillips, K. E. (2016). (Re)negotiating our relationship: How contradictions emerge in sibling privacy boundaries. *Southern Communication Journal, 81*(2), 79–91.

Brummett, E. A., & Steuber, K. R. (2015). To reveal or conceal? Privacy management processes among interracial romantic partners. *Western Journal of Communication, 79*(1), 22–44.

Burke, T. J., Woszidlo, A., & Segrin, C. (2012). Social skills, family conflict, and loneliness in families. *Communication Reports, 25*(2), 75–87.

Burrell, N. A., & Fitzpatrick, M. A. (1990). The psychological reality of marital conflict. In D. D. Cahn (Ed.), *Intimates in conflict: A communication perspective* (pp. 167–186). Hillsdale, NJ: Erlbaum.

Canary, D. J., & Lakey, S. (2013). *Strategic conflict*. New York: Routledge.

Canary, H., & Canary, D. (2013). *Family conflict*. Malden, MA: Polity Press.

Carmon, A. F., Miller, A. N., & Brasher, K. J. (2013). Privacy orientations: A look at family satisfaction, job satisfaction, and work-life balance. *Communication Reports, 26*(2), 101–112.

Caughlin, J. P. (2003). Family communication standards: What counts as excellent family communication and how are such standards associated with family satisfaction? *Human Communication Research, 29*(1), 5–40.

Coakley, C. G., & Wolvin, A. D. (1997). Listening in the parent-teen relationship. *International Journal of Listening, 11*(1), 88–126.

DeFrain, J., & Asay, S. M. (2007). Family strengths and challenges in the USA. *Marriage & Family Review, 41*(3–4), 281–307.

Degtyareva, V. (2011). Defining family in immigration law: Nontraditional families in citizenship by descent. *The Yale Law Journal, 120*(4), 862–908.

Dunning, M. (2015). Employers rethink benefits after gay marriage ruling. *Business Insurance, 49*(14), 3.

Fiese, B. H., Tomcho, T. J., Douglas, M., Josephs, K., Poltrock, S., & Baker, T. (2002). A review of 50 years of research on naturally occurring family routines and rituals: Cause for celebration? *Journal of Family Psychology, 16*(4), 381–390.

Fitzpatrick, M. A., Marshall, L. J., Leutwiler, T. J., & Krcmar, M. (1996). The effect of family communication environments on children's social behavior during middle childhood. *Communication Research, 23*(4), 379–406.

Floyd, K., & Morman, M. T. (2005). Fathers' and sons' reports of fathers' affectionate communication: Implications of a naïve theory of affection. *Journal of Social and Personal Relationships, 22*(1), 99–109.

Galvin, K. M., Dickson, F. C., & Marrow, S. R. (2006). System theory: Patterns and (w)holes in family communication. In D. O. Braithwaite & L. A. Baxter (Eds.), *Engaging theories in family communication* (pp. 309–324). Thousand Oaks, CA: Sage.

Gilovich, T. D., Savitsky, K. K., & Medvec, V. H. (1998). The illusion of transparency: Biased assessments of others' abilities to read our emotional states. *Journal of Personality and Social Psychology, 75*, 332–346.

Golish, T. D. (2000). Changes in closeness between adult children and their parents: A turning point analysis. *Communication Reports, 13*(2), 79–98.

Households and Families: 2010. (2012). *2010 census briefs*. Census.gov. Accessed 31 May 2016.

Imber-Black, E. (1993). *Secrets in families and family therapy*. New York: Norton.

Koerner, A. F., & Fitzpatrick, M. A. (2004). Communication in intact families. In A. L. Vangelisti (Ed.), *Handbook of family communication* (pp. 177–195). Mahwah, NJ: Erlbaum.

Koerner, A. F., & Fitzpatrick, M. A. (2006). Family communication patterns theory: A social cognitive approach. In D. O. Braithwaite & L. A. Baxter (Eds.), *Engaging theories in family communication* (pp. 50–65). Thousand Oaks, CA: Sage.

Lulofs, R. S., & Cahn, D. D. (2000). *Conflict: From theory to action* (2nd ed.). Boston: Allyn & Bacon.

Mazur, M. A., & Hubbard, A. S. (2004). "Is there something I should know?" Topic avoidant responses in parent-adolescent communication. *Communication Reports, 17*(1), 27–37.

Obergefell v. Hodges. (2015). *Legal information institute*. Law.cornell.edu. Accessed 13 June 2016.

Olson, L. N., Baiocchi-Wagner, E. A., Wilson-Kratzer, J. M. W., & Symonds, S. E. (2012). *The dark side of family communication*. Cambridge: Polity Press.

Oswald, R. F., Blume, L. B., & Marks, S. R. (2005). Decentering heteronormativity: A model for family studies. In V. L. Bengtson, A. C. Acock, K. R. Allen, P. Dilworth-Anderson, & D. M. Klein (Eds.), *Sourcebook of family theory and research* (pp. 143–165). Thousand Oaks, CA: Sage.

Peterson, C., Peterson, J., & Skevington, S. (1986). Heated argument and adolescent development. *Journal of Social and Personal Relationships, 3*(2), 229–240.

Petronio, S. (2000). The boundaries of privacy: Praxis of everyday life. In S. Petronio (Ed.), *Balancing the secrets of private disclosures* (pp. 37–49). Mahwah, NJ: Erlbaum.

Petronio, S. (2002). *Boundaries of privacy: Dialectics of disclosure*. Albany, NY: State University Press.

Phillips, K. E., & Schrodt, P. (2015). Sibling antagonism and shared family identity as mediators of differential parental treatment and relational outcomes in the sibling relationship. *Western Journal of Communication, 79*(5), 634–654.

Plenert, W. (2017). *A transformative parenting mediation model*. Mediate.com. www.mediate.com/articles/PlenertW1.cfm. Accessed 6 March 2017.

Powell, B., Bolzendahl, C., Geist, C., & Steelman, L. C. (2010). *Counted out: Same-sex relations and Americans' definitions of family*. New York: Russell Sage Foundation.

Reeder, H. (2014). *Commit to win: How to harness the four elements of commitment to reach your goals*. New York: Hudson Street Press.

Reynolds, J., Houlston, C., Coleman, L., & Harold, G. (2014). *Parental conflict: Outcomes and interventions for children and families*. Bristol, UK: Polity Press.

Ritchie, L. D., & Fitzpatrick, M. A. (1990). Family communication patterns: Measuring intrapersonal perceptions of interpersonal relationships. *Communication Research, 17*(4), 523–544.

Schrodt, P. (2009). Family strength and satisfaction as functions of family communication environments. *Communication Quarterly, 57*(2), 171–186.

Shearman, S. M., & R. Dumlao. (2008). A cross-cultural comparison of family communication patterns and conflict between young adults and parents. *Journal of Family Communication*, 8(3), 186–211.

Sillars, A. L., Canary, D. J., & Tafoya, M. (2004). Communication, conflict, and the quality of family relationships. In A. L. Vangelisti (Ed.), *Handbook of family communication* (pp. 413–446). Mahwah, NJ: Erlbaum.

Sillars, A., Holman, A. J., Richards, A., Jacobs, K. A., Koerner, A., & Reynolds-Dyk, A. (2014). Conversation and conformity orientations as predictors of observed conflict tactics in parent-adolescent discussions. *Journal of Family Communication*, 14, 16–31.

Smith, J., & Ross, H. (2007). Training parents to mediate sibling disputes affects children's negotiation and conflict understanding. *Child Development*, 78(3), 790–805.

Spitzberg, B. H. (2010). Intimate violence. In W. Cupach, D. J. Canary, & B. H. Spitzberg (Eds.), *Competence in interpersonal conflict* (2nd ed., pp. 211–252). Long Grove, IL: Waveland.

Spitzberg, B. H., & Cupach, W. R. (Eds.). (1998). *The dark side of close relationships*. Mahwah, NJ: Erlbaum.

Spitzberg, B. H., & Cupach, W. R. (Eds.). (2007). *The dark side of close relationships*. Mahwah (2nd ed.). NJ: Erlbaum.

Stafford, L., & Dainton, M. (1994). The dark side of "normal" family interaction. In W. R. Cupach & B.H. Spitzberg (Eds.), *The dark side of interpersonal communication* (pp. 259–280). Hillsdale, NJ: Erlbaum.

Stanley, S. M., Markman, H. J., & Whitton, S. W. (2002). Communication, conflict, and commitment: Insights on the foundations of relationship success from a national survey. *Family Process*, 41(4), 659–675.

Stanley, S. M., Markman, H. J., & Whitton, W. S. (2002). Communication, conflict, and commitment: Insights on the foundations of relationship success from a national survey. *Family Process*, 41(4), 659–675.

Sugarman, S. D. (2008). What is a "family"? Conflicting messages from our public programs. *Family Law Quarterly*, 42(2), 231–261.

Thomas, C. E., Booth-Butterfield, M., & Booth-Butterfield, S. (1995). Perceptions of deception, divorce disclosures, and communication satisfaction with parents. *Western Journal of Communication*, 59(3), 228–245.

Thompson, L. L., & Lucas, B. J. (2014). Judgmental biases in conflict resolution and how to overcome them. In P. T. Colman, M. Deutsch, & E. C. Marcus (Eds.), *The handbook of conflict resolution* (pp. 255–282). San Francisco: Jossey-Bass.

Thorson, A. R., Rittenour, C. E., Kellas, J. K., & Trees, A. R. (2013). Quality interactions and family storytelling. *Communication Reports*, 26(2), 88–110.

Turner, L. H., & West, R. (1998). *Perspectives on family communication*. Mountain View, CA: Mayfield.

Underwood, M. K., Beron, K, J., Gentsch, J. K., Galperin, M. B., & Risser, S. C. (2008). Family correlates of children's social and physical aggression with peers: Negative interparental conflict strategies and parenting styles. *International Journal of behavioral Development*, 32(6), 549–562.

Vangelisti, A. L., & Caughlin, J. P. (1997). Revealing family secrets: The influence of topic, function, and relationship. *Journal of Social and Personal Relationships*, 14(5), 679–705.

Vangelisti, A. L., Crumley, L. P., & Baker, J. L. (1999). Family portraits: Stories as standards for family relationships. *Journal of Social and Personal Relationships*, 16(3), 335–368.

Yoshimura, S. M., & Boon, S. D. (2014). Exploring revenge as a feature of family life. *Journal of Family Theory & Review*, 6, 222–240.

Zhang, S., & Stafford, L. (2008). Perceived face threat of honest but hurtful evaluative messages in romantic relationships. *Western Journal of Communication*, 72(1), 19–39.

Chapter 15

Conflict in Intimate Relationships

Vocabulary

Assurances

Cascade Model

Communication infidelity

Contempt

Criticism

Demand-withdrawal pattern

Defensiveness

Emotional disengagement

Essentialist approach

Four Horsemen of the Apocalypse

Independents

Infidelity

Intimate violence

Openness

Positivity

Power differences approach

Relational framing

Relationship maintenance

Repair work

Separates

Sharing tasks

Social networks

Sound Relationship House

Spousal Discrepancy Theory

Stonewalling

Traditionals

Objectives

After reading this chapter, you should be able to:

1. Explain how conflict can be both positive and negative in relationships
2. Recognize common conflict topics and what the possible underlying causes may be
3. Explain how patterns of negative conflict can lead to relational dissolution
4. Understand the skills necessary for maintaining healthy relationships in light of conflict events

Intimate Relationships and Conflict

The message that healthy relationships require constant attention is pervasive in pop culture for good reason—it is true. As partners navigate building a life together, differences have to be negotiated, challenges to values and beliefs settled, and everyday conflicts managed (Gordon & Chen, 2016; Walsh, 2012). While conflict can create understanding, it also has the potential to damage the relationship beyond repair (Gere & Schimmack, 2013; Laursen & Hafen, 2010).

The challenges of maintaining an intimate relationship can be understood by charting the rate of marriages that end in divorce. Peaking in the 1980s, around 50 percent of U.S. marriages ended within the first 15 years. The rate of divorce has decreased over recent decades with first marriages ending in divorce about 43–46 percent of the time. Forty-two percent of whites divorce within the first 15 years (with blacks at a higher rate of 55 percent and Hispanics at a lower rate). Explanations for the difference in divorce rates include increased stressors for some groups in socioeconomic/employment status, immigration difficulties, or cultural differences such as beliefs about marriage or the average age of marriage. Across cultures, each successive marriage increases the risk for divorce, with nearly 60 percent of remarriages not succeeding (Amato, 2010).

Until recently, research on relational conflict has focused on young, heterosexual couples. Researchers asked questions such as: "What causes divorces?" or "What is the secret of those relationships that endure for decades or until death they do part?" (Walsh, 2012). In more modern times, research looked beyond the limited type of relationships formerly studied, and has come to reflect the society at large—including same sex relationships, adolescent relationships, older couples, second (and more) marriages, among other relational types (Grych, 2016; Ogolsky & Gray, 2016; Prager et al., 2015; Reczek, 2016; Ruggles, 2016; Toubia, 2014; Volpe, Morales-Aleman, & Teitelman, 2014).

Conflict Topics Among Intimates

For couples, the act of parenting provides abundant conflict opportunities. Money matters are reported to be a top conflict topic for all couples, even those who are financially secure. Newly committed couples have more conflicts about chores than established couples who have worked out those negotiations earlier in the relationship (Stanley, Markman, & Whitton, 2002).

In many of these conflicts, the flashpoint may or may not comprise the underlying cause of the conflict. For example, a conflict expressed over the topic of money really could be about other things such as control, security, or how love is expressed. Conflicts about a partner's time with friends could be based in fear of abandonment or desire to be more connected. While the research has yet to reach the same level of analysis for same-sex couples as has been the case for heterosexual couples, conflict topics seem relatively consistent and are affected by environmental factors such

TABLE 15.1 Marriage Statistics for U.S. Population

- Sixty-six percent of the U.S. male population is or has been married, 50 percent of those have been married only once.
- Seventy-two percent of the U.S. female population is or has been married, 54 percent of those have been married only once.
- Twenty-seven percent of whites, 47 percent of blacks, and 40 percent of Hispanics have never married.
- Foreign born U.S. residents are more likely than U.S. born to be married only once.

Source: Lewis and Kreider (2015) US Community Survey

as whether couples are parents, their level of financial stability, the level of commitment in their relationships, and the length of time the couples have been together (Mohr, Selterman, & Fassinger, 2013). For women, sexual satisfaction as it predicts relationship satisfaction is similar whether the women are in a same-sex or heterosexual relationship (Holmberg, Blair, & Phillips, 2010).

Toubia (2014) examined the interplay between gender role conflict and role division for gay men in committed relationships. Their review of pertinent research showed gay men do not have the same conflicts as heterosexual men about role division, egalitarianism, and gender roles. Heterosexual couples are more influenced by traditional sex-roles and norms in their relationships. Gay men must negotiate more of these roles and norms given the absence of a female partner. From Toubia's work, we can conclude that conflict about topics surrounding sex-roles, like who cooks, who cleans, and who handles the children's doctor's appointment, might be more prevalent in same-sex relationships, as issues are negotiated without the assumption of sex-role stereotypes.

Noting contradictory research about whether financial disagreements are predictors of divorce, researchers studied the impact of financial disagreements on married couples (Andersen, 2005; Britt & Huston, 2012; Dew, Britt, & Huston, 2012; Stanley et al., 2002). Studies determined that the topic of money predicted divorce more than other disagreements. Researchers analyzed over 4,500 responses to the National Survey of Families and Households to discover how financial well-being, financial disagreements, and perceptions of financial inequity correlated with divorce rates. Husbands and wives' reports of financial conflicts were most predictive of divorce, with wives reporting sex as the only other predictive topic. Interestingly, economic pressures like level of debt, the couples' financial status, and the value of their assets were not predictive in this study.

When money troubles are predictive of conflict, this stressor on relationships can be moderated with quality communication. The findings of Dew et al. (2012) support that the communication strategies used by couples can mitigate potential relationship problems inherent in disagreements over finances. The higher the marital satisfaction the couples reported, the less impact financial disagreements had on their relationships. However, the effect of financial disagreements on relationships, particularly in the early stages of the relationship, does negatively affect marital satisfaction (Britt & Huston, 2012).

A common cause of partner/marital conflict is **infidelity**, the breaking of a partner's trust through unfaithfulness, which can be expressed physically or emotionally. **Communication infidelity** might include behaviors such as telling a partner you love her or him without meaning it, expressing love or providing considerable attention to a cyber-friend in a chat room while hiding the relationship from the at-home partner, joking about leaving a partner for someone you are attracted to, sharing flirtatious episodes with a coworker, or telling others intimate details about one's partner. One study discovered that women, more so than men, consider communication infidelity worse than physical infidelity (Podshadley & Docan, 2005–2006). Deception regarding love is a significant source of conflict among intimates. Lying and rumor telling also are significant sources of conflict for teens (Scott, 2008). Table 15.2 identifies common relationship conflict topics and possible root causes. Note: Sometimes the topic is the underlying factor and sometimes it is concealing another type of conflict. Underlying causes are presented only as examples.

DISCUSSION QUESTION • 15.1

What topics are the most common causes of conflict in your current or past intimate relationships?

Gere and Schimmack (2013) examined how conflict over long-term goals (e.g., "Should we move so I can go to graduate school in another state?" vs. "Should we stay so you can advance your career?") affected the quality of couples' relationships and individual well-being. Their study

TABLE 15.2 Relationship Conflict Topics and Possible Underlying Root Causes

Conflict Topic	Possible Underlying Cause
Money	Control of resources, loss of independence, future stability, decision-making processes, priority identification, perceived value in the relationship
Children	Values, beliefs, fear, presenting a united front, parenting skill levels, resource control, tradition
Relatives/Friends	Relational boundaries, level of independency, privacy, security, control, belongingness, emotional involvement, fear of abandonment or loss of intimacy
Religion	Values, beliefs, future consequences, independency, resource control, traditions, comfort with alternative ideas
Task division	Gender and role expectations, fairness, physical ability, beliefs, values, power, control
Politics/Social Issues	Values, beliefs, presenting a united front, independence, traditions, comfort with alternative ideas, control
Relationship commitment	Expressions of love, stability, security, level of emotional involvement, independence, fear of abandonment, beliefs about what defines being a couple
Frequency/satisfaction with sex	Expectations, values, feelings of attractiveness and desirability, expression of affection, control, independence

followed 105 couples, dating for at least two months, but not living together. They found that the more goal conflict, the lower their positive well-being and relational quality. While limited in scope, the study shows how the relationship dialectic between a need to fulfill long-term goals and the expectation of short-term support affects feeling about ourselves and our partners.

CASE 15.1

Two Stories About Family Conflict

Robyn's story: My mom and dad never fought, as far as we three kids knew anyway. Their roles were pretty stereotypical, where dad made most of the money for the family and mom took care of most of the child-rearing and house duties. I was the last kid living at home in my senior year of high school when mom and dad informed me that after 24 years of marriage, they were calling it quits. I did not see that coming and neither did my siblings. There was no anger. It made no sense to us whatsoever.

Charlie's story: My parents fought all of the time I was growing up. Everything seemed to be a battle. How to pack the car for a trip, whether carrots should be in a meatloaf, what time Thanksgiving dinner should be, who should be president—everything seemed like a hill worth fighting over. The common pattern would be that there was a loud exchange, a final angry word, one of them stomped off, and then a short time later a kiss on the cheek and they would laugh at themselves. It's weird, but they both claim they're still in love and happy after 30 years. They call their arguments "spirited," but they always stressed me out.

Conflict in Relationships: Good or Bad?

The answer to the question of whether conflict in relationships is good or bad is it can be both. While it is useful to know what couples conflict about to be prepared when these topics arise, the topic of a conflict seems to be less important than how people act during conflict. Laursen and Hafen's (2010) review of close relationship conflict research summarized costs and benefits that may arise for couples (see Tables 15.3 and 15.4). The researchers assert that "Conflict is bad (except when it's not)," noting the paradoxical findings in the field about what affects conflict outcomes.

In an effort to understand how and when conflict could be beneficial and healthy in a relationship, yet detrimental and damaging in other situations, different theories have emerged. Some have supported that conflicts about ideas that use positive argument skills are more likely to be healthy than those conflicts characterized by hostility or attempts to coerce (Howe & McWilliam, 2006).

The Cascade Model and the "Four Horsemen"

Gottman's early research (1994) led him to create the Cascade Model to explain how interaction types and frequency have more impact on intimate relationship than the topics in conflict. The **Cascade Model**, supported in subsequent research, posits that the ratio of good to bad interactions is predictive of relational outcomes. In other words, conflict is a valuable part of healthy relationships, but the way in which conflict is handled determines if it is beneficial or not.

Driver et al. (2012) examined seven longitudinal studies, with 843 racially diverse, married couples, looking at what leads to relationships characterized as "happily married," "unhappily married," or "divorced." In the study, both partners needed to report independently their satisfaction with the relationship for a relationship to be categorized as "happily married," otherwise the relationship was coded as distressed or "unhappy." The researchers found that distressed couples express the negative conflict behaviors Gottman coined "The **Four Horseman of the Apocalypse**." The Four Horseman are criticism, contempt, defensiveness, and stonewalling (Table 15.5).

TABLE 15.3 Potential Costs of Relationship Conflict

Decreased trust
Decreased relational satisfaction
Debilitating physical stress
Psychological distress
Increased likelihood of violence and hostility
Impact on decision-making effectiveness
Impact on the support system leading to isolation
Dissolution of relationship

TABLE 15.4 Potential Benefits of Relationship Conflict

Relationship development
Cognitive and analytical improvement
Clarity and understanding
Increased perspective taking and emotional sensitivity
Personal growth
Psychological well-being
Positive social adjustment

TABLE 15.5 Four Horseman of the Relationship Apocalypse

Criticism	Critique involving a personal attack	"The garage is a pigsty! You are so inconsiderate."
Contempt	Condescension, disgust, and disrespect	"You couldn't have been more stupid if you had tried."
Defensiveness	Protecting oneself from attack by deflecting blame	"I would have been on time if you had bothered to put gas in the car."
Stonewalling	Blocking attempts at meaningful dialogue	"Okay, whatever." "I'll be working late all this week."

Criticism is the act of negatively critiquing, usually in a demeaning way or calling into question the spouse's character. For example, Margie says to Tobias, "I can't believe you forgot to call the bank this morning to transfer that money. You are so irresponsible!" Different than a complaint ("The money didn't get transferred and we're going to bounce checks."), criticism attacks the other person (calling Tobias "irresponsible"). A complaint would communicate irritation about the behavior or situation but not question Tobias' character. Criticism is linked to a chilling of communication among couples and subsequent relationship dissolution (Olson, Baiocchi-Wagner, Kratzer, & Symonds, 2012).

Contempt, Goffman's second Horseman, is supremely corrosive to relationships and goes beyond criticism to convey disgust and disrespect. Margie, continuing her criticism of Tobias, states, "You evidently don't care about our credit or that we might want to buy a house someday. You're just like your brother—totally useless when it comes to money." Contempt can be conveyed verbally through sarcasm, insults, and biting humor, or it can come through nonverbal communication like shaking the head, eye rolling, and sneering. Belittling the other is a common type of contempt, such as: "Did you think that this problem would just go away? Are you that naive to think the bank wouldn't notice the lack of funds? Or, are you just stupid?" Contempt makes productive conflict behaviors harder to implement and often escalates the conflict.

The third Horseman is **defensiveness**. Even if Margie merely observes she didn't see the transfer on their account balance (a non-critical observation), Tobias may respond defensively with, "We wouldn't be in this situation if you didn't spend all of our money going out with your friends." Instead of owning his part of the conflict and taking responsibility for not calling the bank, Tobias deflects the attack by trying to pin the blame on Margie. The conflict devolves into blaming and trying to protect oneself from being at fault. No problem solving can occur in this destructive cycle.

Gottman's final Horseman is stonewalling. Relationships marked with a high ratio of conflicts involving criticism, contempt, and defensiveness, may make one partner weary and wanting to avoid any additional conflict. **Stonewalling** can happen nonverbally. The next conflict between Margie and Tobias finds his response as non-committal, not providing any feedback, avoiding eye contact, and looking for the nearest exit point from the conversation. By essentially ignoring Margie, Tobias is hoping to protect himself from a negative spiral, as he knows what will happen having lived this pattern over and over. This stonewalling activity frustrates Margie because she wants to address the conflict at hand.

Any of the Four Horsemen can lead to the demand-withdraw pattern identified by many scholars (Christensen & Heavey, 1990; Christensen, Eldridge, Catta-Preta, Lim, & Santagata, 2006). The **demand-withdrawal pattern** occurs when one partner tries to engage and the other withdraws. For example, a female partner tries to start a conversation about the couple's relationship and her male partner suddenly decides he needs to take out the garbage. The pattern leads to frustration and escalation. Margie really wants to address her concerns with Tobias, but whenever she brings up the topic, he seems to brush her off or not engage with her. She increases her efforts to bring him to the conversation, and his efforts to not communicate are equally fierce. She laments, "You never talk to me about things." He responds with, "We never get anywhere and just end up in a fight, so why bother?"

Emotional Disengagement

In addition to the Four Horseman, Driver et al. (2012) identified emotional disengagement as a predictor of divorce. **Emotional disengagement** is exhibited when couples do not show positive affect for their relationship or each other. Couples may appear to be happy insofar as there is no outward expression of dissatisfaction, but also show "little interest, affection, humor, and concern characteristic of happy couples" (p. 60). Partners may have underlying conflict issues, but do not let them rise to the surface, in an effort to maintain the illusion of harmony. They may appear to be working together in parenting, for example, but are living in separate worlds—merely coexisting in the same physical space. While avoiding conflict, the couple also avoids intimacy and do not grow together, ultimately "editing out parts of their personality and become hidden from their partners" (p. 60).

While the Four Horseman and emotional disengagement are predictors of relational dissolution, researchers indicate that timing matters. Couples exhibiting behaviors described by the Four Horsemen divorce earlier, generally within seven years (Gottman & Levenson, 2000). Emotionally disengaged couples stay with the relationship longer, divorcing after 7–14 years. People who know disengaged couples are often left wondering "What happened?" because things didn't seem bad between them. On the other hand, couples who engage in constant criticism, contempt, defensiveness, and stonewalling may have onlookers saying, "We saw that coming."

Gender and Personality Factors in Relationships

Popular culture instructs us to believe men and women come from different planets where the communication and conflict norms are opposite from one another (Gray, 1992) due to biology (called the **essentialist approach**). Another view, however, is that the differences are due to desires to change (called the **power differences approach**). In this view, while differences do exist between the sexes, men and women act more alike than not, and share about 75% of behaviors (Cupach & Canary, 1997; O'Neil, 2008). Research favors the power differences approach (Holley, Sturm, & Levenson, 2010), explaining that while men do withdraw more than women, those behaviors flip when the male seeks a change and the woman wants the status quo.

What we can take away from the research on biological sex is that patterns are more complex than simply gender-based, but conflict patterns do exist, such as men tend to withdraw more, women tend to pursue conflict more (Christensen et al., 2006), and men exhibit competitive styles earlier and more often than women (Berryman-Fink & Brunner, 1987).

Regardless of gender, personality factors such as impulsivity, submissiveness, neuroticism, and insecurity have been linked to increased marital dissatisfaction (Caughlin, Huston, & Houts, 2000). The connection between partner personality and marital distress was studied by Kilmann and Vendemia (2013), building upon work done by Kurdek (1993) on Spousal Discrepancy Theory.

Spousal Discrepancy Theory suggests that if partners have wide personality differences, they are more at risk for relationship distress than those who are closer in personality. Kilmann and Vendemia (2013) studied couples in marital therapy and found that couples in relationships of a shorter time had more discrepancy than those who had been together longer. They reported that husbands in shorter-term marriages had more "impulsivity, exploitive and insensitive characteristics; and rated themselves as more controlling and competitive, and less cooperative, less dependent, and less responsible" (p. 207) than the women in the study rated themselves. Relationships of longer duration, on the other hand, included behaviors that were less impulsive and contained fewer perceptions of partner exploitation or insensitivity. Self-centeredness as a personality trait reported by the couples were the lowest variable in long-term relationships. Their findings also supported that the greater the discrepancies, the greater the couples' marital distress.

Spousal Discrepancy Theory does not suggest that couples must be alike to be successful. However, personality characteristics that demand a response (e.g., a controlling personality demands accommodation from one's partner) is predictive of greater marital distress. Vater and Schröder-Abé (2015) conclude that the personality characteristics of extraversion, openness, agreeableness, and conscientiousness are correlated with the ability to regulate negative emotions, which in turn predicts positive communication. Specifically, they found extraversion resulted in individuals expressing themselves more. Openness and agreeableness were traits correlating with higher perspective taking (seeing the other's point of view and being able to articulate it). Conscientiousness resulted in higher levels of self-control, lower aggression, and taking a problem orientation to the conflict.

Understanding Relationship Conflict: Lifespan, Types, and Patterns

In a comprehensive summary of marital conflict research, Donahue and Cai (2014) discovered three trends. First, researchers focused on the lifespan of intimates in conflict, from young to older couples. For example, young couples have relationship stressors that come with establishing a life together, including financial challenges and young families. They have to learn to live together and establish themselves as independent from other relationships. These couples often use confrontation, as well as humor, in resolving conflicts. Midlife couples exhibit stability and have worked out many of the bugs in their relationship, making them less confrontational and more analytical. Older couples "avoid intense analyses of relational issues and are more passive in their conflict interactions" (p. 33). Donahue and Cai explain that as couples age, their conflict events become more problem-centered and less relationship focused.

A second research trend offered by Donahue and Cai concerns marital types or behavioral patterns. Researchers (notably Fitzpatrick, 1988) categorize marriages into types such as traditionals, separates, and independents (Table 15.6). **Traditionals** accept gender roles as stereotypically assigned. **Separates**, while in a marital relationship, see themselves as separate entities and are individually goal driven. **Independents** see the relationship as mutually beneficial and develop joint goals together.

A third area of marital conflict research examines the communication patterns couples develop and how those patterns contribute to marital satisfaction. Gottman's Four Horsemen of the Relationship Apocalypse typifies this research area. The topics of conflict, personality factors, whether couples are traditionals or independents are important, but not as predictive of relational success as the patterns of interaction couples routinely engage in. How couples manage their conflicts, and more importantly the repair-work they engage in afterwards, are the most salient factors (Gottman & Levenson, 2000). A couple that uses positive humor at strategic points can break the tension during conflict. A mutual acknowledgement of the silliness of an argument works to repair any

TABLE 15.6 Types of Committed Relationships

Traditionals	Roles often defined by gender, many conflicts avoided by adherence to roles
Separates	Each person identifies and works toward independent goals, conflict likely to arise when goals interfere
Independents	Partners identify mutual goals that benefit the relationship, negotiation a common element of relationship

damage that may have occurred and effectively wipes the slate clean for the couple. In the conflict described earlier between Tobias and Margie, Tobias could break the tension cycle by stating, "You know, Margie, we could just live off the grid and avoid banks altogether by escaping into the wilderness." If Margie plays along, this break could relieve the immediate tension and allow the couple to refocus with less anger when they come back to problem solving in reality.

Another aspect of research into dysfunctional communication patterns identifies misunderstanding as a primary cause of conflict (Gordon & Chen, 2016; Gordon, Tuskeviciute, & Chen, 2013). Gordon and Chen conclude that "perceiving a romantic partner as able to 'get' one's thoughts, feelings, and point of view can be thought of a key component of perceived partner responsiveness" (p. 240)—in other words, feeling understood was important in productive conflict management. They found that when partners remembered a conflict, their reports of relationship satisfaction were reduced only if they did not feel understood at the time the conflict occurred. In other words, feeling understood counteracts the negative effects of conflict. A takeaway from this research is learning to communicate understanding is a key component to improving relationships.

> **KEY 15.1**
>
> Demonstrating genuine understanding of your partner's concerns can mitigate the negative effects of disagreement.

Relationship Maintenance

Relationship maintenance is defined as the mindset and outward actions necessary to keep relationships healthy, stable, and trending in the desired direction (Stafford & Canary, 1991). Relationship maintenance can be strategic (e.g., buying flowers on an anniversary or scheduling date nights) or routine everyday actions (e.g., doing dishes, saying "I love you," making coffee, or kissing goodnight).

Ogolsky and Bowers (2013) conducted research to see if the relationship maintenance behaviors previously identified for heterosexual couples held true for same-sex couples. The five relationship maintenance factors examined were: positivity, openness, assurances, social networks, and sharing tasks.

Positivity describes the demeanor of the parties—how happy they seem when together. Do couples smile at each other, laugh together, and communicate gratitude for the relationship? **Openness** concerns how much the couple shares information about themselves and discusses their relationships. These couples take the time to ask about their partner's day at work and share opinions. **Assurances** are behaviors that communicate one's commitment or faithfulness. A couple who, at age 30, project themselves decades into the future to discuss where they want to retire are making assurances. **Social networks** are those relationships outside of the couple that serve as support and relationship growth. Friends, family, and coworkers may help couples or individual partners reflect on their relationships and guide decisions. Socially, are the partners seen by others as a couple? Finally, **sharing tasks** addresses the assignment each person is expected to perform. Whether the tasks are assigned by gender expectations or are negotiated, how the partners feel about the fairness of the tasks is critical. Engagement in these relationship maintenance activities increases feelings of commitment and satisfaction.

Additionally, the researchers looked at how expressions of daily conflict affects maintenance efforts and if negative emotions from conflicts interfere with relationship maintenance behaviors. Ogolsky and Bowers (2013) found that conflict did bring about higher levels of negative emotion,

TABLE 15.7 Relationship Maintenance Activities

Positivity	Demonstrating and communicating the positive value put on the relationship
Openness	Willingness to self-disclose
Assurances	Communicating commitment to the relationship
Social networks	People outside of the couple who serve to strengthen and validate the relationship
Sharing tasks	The division of labor of activities and obligations

and that negative emotions were associated with lower relationship maintenance activities. If Tobias and Margie are still feeling upset the next day after their discussion about transferring money, it stands to reason that they will be less enthused about expressing positivity toward each other or providing assurances of their commitment. However, Ogolsky and Bowers did find that partners with constructive communication skills lessened the effect of negative emotions, which in turn increased relationship maintenance activities (Table 15.7). In other words, learning how to communicate about conflict and work through issues productively is paramount for helping maintain healthy relationships.

What may be most helpful to couples wanting to maintain their relationships are research findings that negative emotions are less impactful the more the partners use constructive communication. In other words, productive communication works to mitigate the negative emotions partners' experience and increases the effectiveness of relational maintenance efforts. Considering the inevitable ups and downs of normal relationships, learning how to cope and communicate better is a necessity for relationship durability.

Even when good communication skills are applied, conflict can challenge relationship bonds and cause a need for relationship repair-work. **Repair-work** is balancing negative and positive interactions and means individuals have enough commitment to a relationship to put some effort into it. According to Gottman, a ratio of 5:1 is ideal—meaning five positive interactions to overcome one negative. Positive efforts might include friendly humor, compliments, smiling, positive touch, and statements of positive regard. These positive efforts are powerful predictors of relationship success (Gottman & Levenson, 2000). Prager et al. (2015) examined the lingering effect of negative emotions following conflict. Individuals who are more secure individually and in their relationships didn't experience negative emotions for as long or to the same degree as those who had higher anxiety in their relationships. While intimate behavior seemed to lessen the impact of conflict in creating negative emotion, so did self-disclosure (not related to the conflict). Repair-work following conflict, including intimacy and increased self-disclosure, works to decrease the negative emotions that naturally accompany conflict.

One tool for improved outcomes for couples is relational framing. **Relational framing** occurs when a conflictual topic begins with a statement of relational commitment. Margie could start her conversation with Tobias with, "Tobias, I need to talk to you about our finances, but before we start, I want to say how much I love you and how I am committed to making things work between us. This is just a money issue—this isn't a concern about us." By placing the potential conflict topic apart from the relationship, Margie is helping to lessen the impact the forthcoming disagreement may have on their relationship.

When Conflict Turns Violent

To this point we have discussed conflict patterns and research concerning couples in non-abusive or non-violent relationships. The U.S. Center for Disease Control's (CDC) National Intimate Partner and Sexual Violence Survey reveals disheartening degrees of **intimate violence**, which involves physical or emotional abuse of one partner (Breiding et al., 2014). According to the Center for Disease Control, "Intimate partner violence, sexual violence, and stalking are important and widespread public health problems in the United States. On average, 20 people per minute are victims of physical violence by an intimate partner in the United States. Over the course of a year, that equals more than 10 million women and men. Those numbers only tell part of the story—nearly 2 million women are raped in a year and over 7 million women and men are victims of stalking in a year" (Breiding, et al., 2014). With the prevalence of violence across all relationship types, this topic is deserving of more attention than we can give in this chapter. We strongly encourage those who may be experiencing violence in their personal relationships to seek professional guidance and social support immediately.

Winstok (2012) notes contradictory theories for what primarily causes violence in relational conflict. Some theorize that gender differences, driven by biology and socialization of boys and girls, are the significant factor. Violent behavior of men against women is significantly higher than female against male violence. Others, while acknowledging that male violence against women is statistically higher, hold that both genders engage in violence and other factors beyond biology require consideration.

Researchers are attempting to uncover patterns that might predict when intimate relationships may become violent. Relationships that start off with one partner, of either sex, engaging in mild coercion and surveillance of the other while dating are shown to escalate those behaviors as relationships progress (Williams & Frieze, 2005). Alcohol use increased the potential and severity of male-to-female violence or female-to-male abuse (McKinney, Caetano, Rodriguez, & Okoro, 2010). Female alcohol use may increase the severity and prevalence of violence against them.

Bradley and Gottman (2012) cited higher occurrences of violence among couples with lower incomes or those with children and explored the impact of relational skills training on decreasing situational violence. The researchers evaluated the success of The Creating Healthy Relationships Program (CHRP) based upon the Sound Relationship House Theory (Gottman, 1994). The training program involves working with both partners together to build communication skills.

In Gottman's **Sound Relationship House**, there are seven "floors," which provide the framework for the skills training in CHRP. The house's foundation would be to "build love maps." This floor represents teaching friendship-building strategies for getting to know and continuing to learn about each other. Building up from there is the "share fondness and admiration" floor, where partners focus on what the other is doing right, as compared to the complaint pattern discussed earlier in this chapter. The third floor is to "turn towards," with efforts aimed at building connections among partners and working to meet the others' emotional needs. The fourth floor is "positive perspectives," where couples work to see the other as a partner and friend in the relationship and not an adversary. "Managing conflict," the fifth floor, is where couples focus on preventing escalation and practicing problem-solving. The sixth floor, "making life dreams and aspirations come true," focuses on the continued work of making relationships successful, not just the reduction of conflict. Finally, the attic is where couples learn to "create shared meaning," by focusing on building their life together, setting goals together, sharing experiences, and creating priorities that reflect who they are to each other.

The CHRP program did produce results supporting the benefit of training in reducing incidents of violence in relationships. This finding, however, speaks to situational violence (violence arising from situational factors where one may not have developed the skills to cope or manage that situation). However, relationships marked by systemic violence fall outside the scope of their findings and are much more complex in terms of underlying causes and possible strategies for reducing violence.

Additional research (Hays, Michel, Bayne, Colburn, & Myers, 2015) explored the benefits of skill training for couples in efforts to decrease relational violence among college students. The HEART program has a foundation in feminist therapy, which includes promoting independence, assertiveness, and self-worth in efforts to empower women. The HEART program involves group interactions designed to "educate men and women together as members of the college community to collectively work to decrease relationship violence on campus" (p. 53). While not specifically working with couples involved in violent or potentially violent relationships, these group sessions sought to increase the participants' knowledge and self-awareness about violence in relationships. College students in this study reported a greater understanding of themselves and a commitment to self-improvement. Many reported that the HEART program was a wake-up call about their relationship patterns and the impact of violence in the greater society. Perhaps, as the authors note, this training may "help prevent relationship violence before it begins" (p. 61).

Summary

The common wisdom on relationships is that they take work. With nearly one-half of first marriages ending in divorce, this chapter examines what causes conflict and how we can improve the likelihood of relationship success. While most research in this area has focused on young European-American heterosexual couples, more and more research is examining relational conflict experienced in other cultures as well same-sex unions.

What couples argue about is less related to their socioeconomic status, sexual orientation, or culture, and more affected by environmental factors such as if the couple has children and how long they have been together. In answering the question whether conflicts are beneficial or detrimental to relationship, the answer is: Yes—conflicts can either benefit or be a detriment to the relationship. How conflict is expressed and managed is more important than the existence of the conflict or the topic. Certain behaviors expressed in relationship conflict are predictive of divorce, specifically the Four Horseman of criticism, contempt, defensiveness, and stonewalling.

A common negative pattern of relational conflict is the demand-withdrawal pattern where one partner wants to pursue the conflict and the other tries to escape interaction. The presence of emotional disengagement is another factor predictive of relational dissolution. Personality factors may affect relationship conflict, particularly when there is a wide difference in personality traits, as explained by Spousal Discrepancy Theory.

Three primary trends of relationship research include lifespan patterns of young, intermediate and older couples; types of marriages, such as Fitzpatrick's categories of traditionals, separates and independents; and communication patterns. Relationship maintenance speaks to the efforts both strategic and routine that partners engage in to support and maintain relationship health, such as positivity, openness, assurances, social networks, and sharing tasks.

Finally, a discussion was presented on when conflict turns violent. There are contradictory explanations on whether gender differences explain a propensity to violence or if environmental factors such as skill and social acceptance are to blame. Regardless, as violence in conflict exists, the more important consideration is to ensure that help is sought for those involved. An exploration of potential causes and the value of relational skill training was discussed for improving relationships involving situational violence.

Chapter Resources

Exercises

1. As a group, identify topics of past relational conflict you have either experienced or witnessed. Determine if there were underlying causes beyond the issue of the conflict itself.
2. Make a list of stereotypical gender roles and how those are supported or countered in popular culture.
3. Review a film or television program where the primary premise is relational conflict (e.g., *War of the Roses*, *Love is Strange*, *Who's Afraid of Virginia Woolf*, *Divorce*, *Eternal Sunshine of the Spotless Mind*, *Blue*

Valentine, or *Take this Waltz*). Identify examples of the Four Horseman. What suggestions would you make for characters to implement repair-work at strategic times?

4. As a group, brainstorm some example for relational framing that could be used prior to entering into a difficult topic.

5. In a group, create a list of topic areas couples should discuss prior to entering into a long-term commitment.

Journal/Essay Topics

1. What lessons from your family did you learn about relationships and relational conflict? Have these lessons benefitted or disadvantaged you in your adult life?

2. What repair-work skills have you used and to what effect? What skills would you like to develop? How might you gain those skills?

3. Create a list of topics that couples should discuss prior to entering into a long-term commitment. What topics are "non-negotiable" for you and why?

Research Topics

1. Compare current research on gender differences in conflict for the past five years, and compare your findings to how men and women are conceptualized in popular self-help books. What assumptions are made that are either backed up by the research or discredited by the research?

2. Identify resources available either through your college or community to couples seeking to improve their communication and relationship skills. Who can access those resources? What resources should be available but are not?

3. Assess the availability and effectiveness of crisis intervention resources for addressing intimacy violence in your community.

4. For a relationship that is ending, other than the court system, what options are available to help couples, particularly those with children, separate in healthy ways?

Mastery Case

Which elements from the chapter shed light on Mastery Case 15A?

Pre-marriage Class

Rachael and Trent decided to attend pre-marriage classes. Trent was somewhat reluctant because he thought that soul mates didn't need to go to all that effort. Besides, he assumed things would be like they were in his parents' very traditional marriage where his mom did the "girl" things like cook and clean and his dad did the "man" things like barbeque steaks on the weekend and mowing the grass.

One of the first things in the class was a survey about who would do what tasks once they formed a permanent household. Rachel assumed that if they were both working, they would spend Saturdays doing the big cleaning and yardwork together and would alternate days on cooking and cleaning during the week. Trent had never contemplated anything other than watching sports with his buddies on Saturdays.

References

Amato, P. R. (2010). Research on divorce: Continuing trends and new developments. *Journal of Marriage and Family, 72*(3), 650–666.

Andersen, J. D. (2005). Financial problems and divorce: Do demographic characteristics strengthen the relationship? *Journal of Divorce & Remarriage, 43*(1/2), 149–161.

Berryman-Fink, C., & Brunner, C. C. (1987). The effects of sex of source and target on interpersonal conflict management styles. *The Southern Speech Communication Journal, 53*(1), 38–48.

Bradley, R. P. C., & Gottman, J. M. (2012). Reducing situational violence in low-income couples by fostering healthy relationships. *Journal of Marital Family Therapy, 38*(s1), 187–198.

Breiding, M. J., Smith, S. G., Basile, K. C., Walters, M. L., Chen, J., & Merrick, M. T. (2014). Prevalence and characteristics of sexual violence, stalking, and intimate partner violence victimization—National Intimate Partner and Sexual Violence Survey. Cdc.gov. *Surveillance Summaries, 63*(SS08), 1–18.

Britt, S. L., & Huston, S. J. (2012). The role of money arguments in marriage. *Journal of Family and Economic Issues, 33*(4), 464–476.

Caughlin, J. P., Huston, T. L., & Houts, R. M. (2000). How does personality matter in marriage? An examination of trait anxiety, interpersonal negativity, and marital satisfaction. *Journal of Personality and Social Psychology, 78*(2), 326–336.

Christensen, A., Eldridge, K., Catta-Preta, A. B., Lim V. R., & Santagata, R. (2006). Cross-cultural consistency of the demand/withdraw interaction pattern in couples. *Journal of Marriage and Family, 68*(4), 1029–1044.

Christensen, A., & Heavey, C. L. (1990). Gender and social structure in the demand/withdrawal pattern of marital conflict. *Journal of Personality and Social Psychology, 59*(1), 73–81.

Cupach, W. R., & Canary, D. J. (1997). *Competence in interpersonal conflict*. New York: McGraw-Hill.

Dew, J., Britt, S., & Huston, S. (2012). Examining the relationship between financial issues and divorce. *Family Relations, 61*(4), 615–628.

Donahue, W. A., & Cai, D. A. (2014). Interpersonal conflict: An overview. In N. A. Burrell, M. Allen, B. A. Gayle, & R. W. Preiss (Eds.), *Managing interpersonal conflicts: Advances through meta-analysis* (pp. 22–41). New York: Routledge.

Driver, J., Tabares, A., Shapiro, A. F., & Gottman, J. M. (2012). Couple interaction in happy and unhappy marriages: Gottman laboratory studies. In F. Walsh (Ed.), *Normal family processes: Growing diversity and complexity, 4th ed.* (pp. 57–77). New York: Guilford Press.

Fitzpatrick, M. A. (1988). *Between husbands and wives: Communication in marriage*. Newbury Park, CA: Sage.

Gere, J., & Schimmack, U. (2013). When romantic partners' goals conflict: Effects on relationship quality and subjective well-being. *Journal of Happiness Studies, 14*(1), 37–49.

Gordon, A. M., & Chen, S. (2016). Do you get where I'm coming from? Perceived understanding buffers against the negative impact of conflict on relationship satisfaction. *Journal of Personality and Social Psychology, 110*(2), 239–260.

Gordon, A. M., Tuskeviciute, R., & Chen, S. (2013). A multimethod investigation of depressive symptoms, perceived understanding, and relationship quality. *Personal Relationships, 20*(4), 635–654.

Gottman, J. M. (1994). *What predicts divorce? The relationship between marital processes and marital outcomes*. Hillsdale, NJ: Erlbaum.

Gottman, J. M., & Levenson, R. W. (2000). The timing of divorce: Predicting when a couple will divorce over a 14-year period. *Journal of Marriage and the Family, 62*(3), 737–745.

Gray, J. (1992). *Men are from Mars, Women are from Venus: A practical guide for improving communication and getting what you want in your relationships*. New York: HarperCollins.

Grych, J. H. (2016). Increasing precision in the study of interparental conflict and child adjustment. In A. Booth, A. C. Crouter, M. L. Clements, & T. Boone-Holladay (Eds.), *Couples in conflict* (pp. 173–182). New York: Routledge.

Hays, D. G., Michel, R. E., Bayne, H. B., Colburn, A. A., & Myers, J. S. (2015). Counseling with HEART: A relationship violence prevention program for college students. *Journal of College Counseling*, *18*(1), 49–65.

Holley, S. R., Sturm, V. E., & Levenson, R. W. (2010). Exploring the basis for gender differences in the demand-withdraw pattern. *Journal of Homosexuality*, *57*(5), 666–684.

Holmberg, D., Blair, K. L., Phillips, M. (2010). Women's sexual satisfaction as a predictor of well-being in same-sex versus mixed-sex relationships. *Journal of Sex Research*, *47*(1), 1–11.

Howe, C. J., & McWilliam, D. (2006). Opposition in social interaction amongst children: Why intellectual benefits do not mean social costs. *Social Development*, *15*(2), 205–231.

Kilmann, P. R., & Vendemia, M. C. (2013). Partner discrepancies in distressed marriages. *The Journal of Social Psychology*, *153*(2), 196–211.

Kurdek, L. A. (1993). Predicting marital dissolution: A 5-year prospective longitudinal study of newlywed couples. *Journal of Personal and Social Relationships*, *64*(2), 221–242.

Laursen, B., & Hafen, C. A. (2010). Future directions in the study of close relationships: Conflict is bad (except when it's not). *Social Development*, *19*(4), 858–872.

Lewis, J. M., & Kreider, R. M. (2015). *Remarriage in the United States: American community survey reports*. Census.gov. Accessed 13 January 2017.

McKinney, C. M., Caetano, R., Rodriguez, L. A., & Okoro, N. (2010). Does alcohol involvement increase the severity of intimate partner violence? *Alcoholism: Clinical and Experimental Research*, *34*(4), 655–658.

Mohr, J. J., Selterman, D., & Fassinger, R. E. (2013). Romantic attachment and relationship functioning in same-sex couples. *Journal of Counseling Psychology*, *60*(1), 72–82.

O'Neil, J. M. (2008). Summarizing 25 years of research on men's gender role conflict using the gender role conflict scale: New research paradigms and clinical implications. *The Counseling Psychologist*, *36*(3), 358–445.

Ogolsky, B. G., & Bowers, J. R. (2013). A meta-analytic review of relationship maintenance and its correlates. *Journal of Social and Personal Relationships*, *30*(3), 343–367.

Ogolsky, B. G., & Gray, C. R. (2016). Conflict, negative emotion, and reports of partners' relationship maintenance in same-sex couples. *Journal of Family Psychology*, *30*(2), 171–180.

Olson, L. N., Baiocchi-Wagner, E. A., Kratzer, J. M. W., & Symonds, S. E. (2012). *The dark side of family communication*. Cambridge: Polity Press.

Podshadley, S., & Docan, T. (2005–2006). *Issues of infidelity: Physical, emotional, and communicative acts of cheating in romantic relationships*. Western States Communication Association Conference, San Francisco.

Prager, K. J., Shirvani, F., Poucher, J., Cavallin, G., Truong, M., & Garcia, J. J. (2015) Recovery from conflict and revival of intimacy in cohabiting couples. *Personal Relationships*, *22*(2), 308–334.

Reczek, C., (2016). Ambivalence in gay and lesbian family relationships. *Journal of Marriage and Family*, *78*, 644–659.

Ruggles, S. (2016). Marriage, family systems, and economic opportunity in the USA since 1850. In S. M. McHale, V. King, J. Van Hook, & A. Booth (Eds.), *Gender and couple relationships* (pp. 3–41). Switzerland: Springer International Publishing.

Scott, W. (2008). Communication strategies in early adolescent conflicts: An attribution approach. *Conflict Resolution Quarterly*, *25*(3), 375–400.

Stafford, L., & Canary, D. J. (1991). Maintenance strategies and romantic relationship type, gender, and relational characteristics. *Journal of Social and Personal Relationships*, *8*, 217–242.

Stanley, S. M., Markman, H. J., & Whitton, S. W. (2002). Communication, conflict, and commitment: Insights on the foundations of relationship success from a national survey. *Family Process*, *41*(4), 659–675.

Toubia, B. (2014). Gender role conflict, role division, and the gay relational experience. *Journal of Systemic Therapies*, *33*(4), 15–23.

Vater, A., & Schröder-Abé, M. (2015). Explaining the link between personality and relationship satisfaction: Emotion regulation and interpersonal behaviour in conflict discussions. *European Journal of Personality*, *29*(2), 201–215.

Volpe, E. M., Morales-Aleman, M. M., & Teitelman, A. M. (2014). Urban adolescent girls' perspectives on romantic relationships: Initiation, involvement, negotiation, and conflict. *Issues in Mental Health Nursing, 35*(10), 776–790.

Walsh, F. (2012). The new normal: Diversity and complexity in 21st-century families. In F. Walsh (Ed.), *Normal family processes: Growing diversity and complexity, 4th ed.* (pp. 3–27). New York: Guilford Press.

Williams, S. L., & Frieze, I. H. (2005). Courtship behaviors, relationship violence, and breakup persistence in college men and women. *Psychology of Women Quarterly, 29*(3), 248–257.

Winstok, Z. (2012). *Partner violence: A new paradigm for understanding conflict escalation.* New York: Springer.

Chapter 16

Conflict at the Workplace

Vocabulary

Chain of command	Norms
Conflict coaching	Open door policies
Conflict management system	Organizational chart
Dysfunctional role	Organizational culture
Echo technique	Organizational misbehavior
Emotional dissonance	Personal conflict coaching
Emotional labor	Quality control circle
Employee assistance programs	Role
Flat organizational hierarchy	Role emergence
Group	Silo mentality
Groupthink	Storming
Hierarchy of authority	Task role
Leadership	Teamwork
Maintenance role	XYZ-type feedback
Mentoring	

Objectives

After reading this chapter, you should be able to:

1. Explain how communication in an organizational setting is similar to and different from communication in other settings
2. Understand the dynamics of new employee socialization
3. Explain how leaders can prevent some conflicts and manage conflicts that do occur
4. Recognize how roles emerge and function in organizations

The Workplace Is a Unique Context

Most people spend a significant amount of their time at work—typically more than with family or socializing with friends. Because the work environment is specialized and professional, some erroneously believe there should be little conflict at work. These same optimists believe the rare conflicts in the work setting will be about work issues. The truth is the work environment neither is immune to conflict nor limited in the types of disagreements that occur. Conflict is just as likely to emerge at work as in other places we inhabit. Like other contexts, how conflicts are managed affects each individual in that situation.

CASE 16.1

You Are Not My Boss

Jon and Marc work in the repair shop at an outdoor recreation dealership. It's spring, and everybody brought their jet skis in for tune-ups and repairs. The shop is full of equipment, and the schedule has been falling steadily behind. Marc has worked in the shop for years; Jon has been there for about a year. A third employee, Heidi, works in the sales area and comes back to talk to Marc from time to time. It is 8:30 in the morning. Jon is working on a machine that is due for pickup in the morning, while Marc and Heidi talk over by the break room. The supervisor is out of town.

Jon:	"Hey, Marc, I can't get this cover off. The bolt is rusted shut. Can you come over and give me a hand for a second?" (Marc looks up and nods but keeps talking to Heidi. They both are laughing about something).
Jon:	"Hey, Marc, can you come over here for a minute?"
Marc:	"Just a second." (Jon waits a minute, then walks over to Marc).
Jon:	"What's the hold up? Can you come help me now?"
Marc:	"Don't be so impatient. I'm talking to Heidi about some important stuff."
Jon:	"That's great, but can't you two talk on break or something? We're wasting time here."
Marc:	"I don't care what you think. You are not my boss. We're just working half a day today, anyway, so why get all lathered up?"
Jon:	"We've got 10 people showing up at 6 A.M. tomorrow expecting to go to the lake with their waveriders. Are you going to be there to tell them you couldn't be bothered to fix their machines?"
Marc:	"Whatever. You're such a boy scout." (He and Heidi walk off, laughing).

Conflict at work is different from general interpersonal conflict in at least three significant ways. First, workplace conflicts are inextricably tied to one's work identity. Relationship goals may be more important for some people at home or with friends than with coworkers. For others who deeply identify with their careers and "live to work," face and power goals may be paramount. The stakes are different at work than in other contexts, but they are not different in the same ways for each individual.

A second reason conflict in the workplace is different from general interpersonal conflict is the group effort required to accomplish many tasks. The word **teamwork** captures how employees are expected to interconnect to accomplish tasks or provide services. Working in a group requires leadership—formal leadership from a supervisor and/or informal leadership from colleagues. When groups interact, members may see the task differently, vie for power, or offend each other's sensibilities in a number of ways, giving rise to conflict. The workplace offers numerous opportunities for coalition building, personal agendas, and power seeking. Groups can take on differentiated roles, norms, or create a unique culture all their own. Workgroups use conflict in a variety of ways, including as a means to spur innovation, to inspire increased performance, to manipulate the system, or to pursue personal goals.

A third way that conflict differs in the work context lies in the nature of organizations. Organizations have rules, structures, hierarchies, unique cultures, and numerous channels of communication across and among levels. Organizational units may come into conflict, or employees may vie for power within the organization. The organization may or may not provide structural outlets for productive conflict management and may or may not meet their obligations to protect individual workers from excess conflict, bullying, harassment, or retaliation.

This chapter examines conflict in the work context by starting with the larger entity, the organization, and then moving to the building-block level of organizations, the workgroup. We identify what is known about common conflict patterns in the workplace. We then examine conflict within workgroups.

Chain of Command: Who's In and Who's Out

Consider the organizational chain of command in a typical university. The university president (or sometimes a provost) sits atop the formal university hierarchy, even though the president may report to a state board of education or a board of governors. Reporting to the president are several vice presidents, each having "command" in his or her area—the VP of finance supervises all the employees in that area and controls the financial operations of the university, as directed by the president. The VP of student affairs controls matters that govern student life—residential complexes, student union staff, student clubs, student grievance procedures, recruitment, and retention—as directed by the president. The VP of academic affairs governs faculty, academic units, and curriculum matters. Each of the VPs have rules and internal operating processes that constrain their actions. For example, the VP of academic affairs controls the purse that funds academic programs, but the faculty have control over what the content of the academic programs will be (under a concept called faculty governance). That explains why a change in a student's program of study typically goes up the chain of command on the academic side and not to the VP of student affairs.

One factor that helps determine the chain of command is to look at who has decision-making authority or who fills in when someone is gone. If the president is away, the person who knows the most about the president's schedule is the executive assistant. The executive assistant controls the president's schedule and probably is the person most familiar with the president's thoughts on many matters. However, an executive assistant is not in the line of decision-making authority. If the president is away, decision-making authority is delegated (often by policy) to one of the VPs.

Workplace Communication

Although we obviously cannot give a comprehensive view of how communication is different in organizations than in interpersonal relationships, we can provide a glimpse into the worlds of group and organizational communication. To some extent, interpersonal conflict is the same wherever it occurs. But just as conflict in a family may evolve differently if the desire to remain bonded is seen as more important than the substantive issues, the nature of the workplace itself may transform how interpersonal conflict is played out.

Organizations have a **hierarchy of authority** that shapes communication from managers to workers and vice versa. In traditional management theory, the hierarchy of authority is called the **chain of command** (a military metaphor). The hierarchy of an organization is represented in an **organizational chart** that indicates who reports to whom.

In traditional organizations, the hierarchy is vertical, power is invested in top management, and messages trickle from the top of the organization down to those who create the products or do the services (workers). A **flat organizational hierarchy** has fewer layers between top management and workers and, theoretically, more communication flows up and down the hierarchy. To counteract the tendency of employees to communicate only with those in their unit, sometimes called a **silo mentality**, organizations may use tactics like quality control circles or open door policies.

In a **quality control circle**, a small group of workers from different areas of the organization meet to discuss problems and suggest solutions. When a company wanted to decrease damage during shipping of product, they started with a quality control circle comprised of someone in the shipping department, someone from the packing department, and a supervisor in the manufacturing unit. The group later invited a customer to sit in on the discussion. Because each participant brought different ideas to the problem, the group was able to come up with a series of suggestions resulting in reduced shipping damage.

Open door policies encourage employees to bring problems or creative ideas to their supervisor. The challenge is whether the supervisor sees employee comments as helpful or as a threat. Employees who want to express disagreement with how the organization is operating have the most success if the ideas are presented rationally and linked to the interests of the supervisor and the organization (Garner, 2016). Organizations with a mismatch between policy (the company has an open door policy) and practice (supervisors reject new ideas and retaliate against employees) create an environment where conflict is not managed successfully.

Good-Natured Banter

An interesting aspect of communication in some workplace groups is called *good-natured banter*. Banter is a form of teasing. Good-natured banter is intended to be witty and a sign of inclusion in a group or friendship circle. Hurtful banter is exclusionary and intended to make someone feel bad.

If a newcomer hears coworkers jokingly calling each other names or making fun of each other's foibles, then similar remarks addressed to the newcomer may be good-natured banter. For example, if the newcomer showed up with a very pink shirt, someone might say to her. "Wow! Couldn't you find something louder to wear?" Good-natured banter of a newcomer is a test. To pass the test, one must accept the banter and respond in kind with a smile: "Hey, somebody has to class this place up." Defensive remarks confirm that the newcomer is an alien who won't fit in with the group. Saying, "You don't have any right to talk about my shirt!" fails the good-natured banter test and creates a feeling that the newcomer deserves to be excluded.

A caution about good-natured banter is prudent. Newcomers must wait for the banter and not initiate banter with the old-timers, which could be perceived as pushy or disrespectful. Participating in banter requires a firm understanding of the norms of the group and the relationships of the parties. A good rule is to observe how the norm of banter works, and with whom, before initiating it yourself.

Organizations have internal sets of assumptions called **organizational culture**. Part of every new employee's unwritten job is to learn the organization's culture and to discover how to fit in. Some firms have a formal **mentoring** process where an established employee teaches the new hire how things work. Whether there is formal mentoring or not, during the first few weeks of an employee's time with the organization, socialization occurs that either integrates a new hire into the work team and its unique culture or results in a semi-permanent "outsider" status. For example, if the culture of a particular workgroup is that everyone goes out to lunch together on Friday and a new employee continues to go to lunch with old friends in another department, then crucial socialization time is missed and the new hire may be perceived as snobbish. Ideally, potential employees are aware of an organization's culture before making an application to avoid accepting employment in an organization with a culture that is a bad fit. For example, two high-tech firms may each be producing new-generation microchips, but that does not mean both have modern, employee-friendly cultures.

Part of the negotiation process for employment can include training and mentoring: Who specifically will train the new employee? What type of training will be offered? How many days or weeks will the trainer be available for consultation? Table 16.1 suggests a variety of methods to discover an organization's culture. Overt questions may be effective immediately after joining a company when more latitude is given to the newcomer. For example, during the first week, one might ask outright if the manager likes regular reports. Later on, a less direct strategy might be more effective, for example, asking how the manager would prefer to be kept up to date. If talking to the manager or supervisor directly seems unworkable, information can be sought from coworkers, managers in other units, or others knowledgeable about the organization. These moves must be carefully calculated. If they are perceived by one's immediate supervisor as circumventing his or her authority, conflict may ensue. Testing limits, or pushing beyond the range of what one thinks the

TABLE 16.1 Detecting Corporate Culture

- Read between the lines in the organization's policy manuals. What is emphasized and what is missing?
- Examine the generation, age, and ethnicity in each layer of the organization.
- Ask informants about the organization's culture and workplace climate during interviews.
- Seek training and a mentor.
- Ask questions.
- Test limits cautiously.
- Observe other employees.
- Listen to stories about the company.

corporate culture will allow, is risky. Observing what other workers do and how they communicate with each other and with supervisors can be very revealing.

DISCUSSION QUESTION • 16.1

Think about the place where you work or have worked in the past. Were you mentored when you first started your job? How were you socialized into that workplace culture? What would you tell new employees to help in their socialization?

Looking at the company's demographic profile is another way of inferring what it will be like to work there. Are most workers men or women? Does the population of ethnic and racial groups in the organization parallel those of the geographic area? For example, a company in Baton Rouge whose workers all are white men would not reflect the diversity of the area. Examining the generations (see Chapter 5) represented in management may be informative. For example, if all the managers are Boomers, a Boomer culture may exist in the company. By 2020 and for the first time in history, a workplace could contain five different generations—creating ample opportunity for generational conflict.

One way an organization's culture can be detected is how people talk about the organization. When employees at a marketing and public relations firm refer to their workplace as "the factory," going to work as "punching in at the time clock," and their supervisors as "the suits," they paint a picture of work as drudgery done only for a paycheck in an uncaring vertical hierarchy. In contrast, workers who describe going to work as "fun," the workplace as "the playground," and refer to their managers by their first names describe a warmer and more vibrant work culture.

DISCUSSION QUESTION • 16.2

What is the implication if people at the university are referred to by their role: "the dean" or "the department chair" or "the provost"? In some universities, people are referred to by their first names (Melanie) and in others by their full titles (Dr. Reese). In parts of the country, it is respectful to use a title and first name (Dr. Melanie). What implications might you draw about the organizational culture of these units based on how titles are used?

Organizational culture is dynamic and changing. For example, sexual and racial harassment that was common in the workplace of a few decades ago now is illegal. The popular series *Mad Men*, or a viewing of many movies depicting a workplace from before 1980, includes scenes of sexual harassment of female secretaries as a prerogative of management and ethnic/racial slurs from coworkers as an endemic reality. To escape the legal exposure from these behaviors when anti-harassment laws were passed, corporations wrote new policies, required training about illegal sexual and racial harassment, and coined terms like "respectful workplaces" or "diversity-friendly" employment. Behaviors, however, often lag behind policy.

Allen (2000) commented, "Black women frequently enter workplace roles where they previously have not been welcome and where governing ideologies generally have ignored their existence or have viewed them pejoratively" (p. 183). The film, *Hidden Figures*, chronicles the experience of three African-American women who worked at NASA during the 1960s. Acceptance into the culture as valued contributors was often slow and at times filled with challenge for an organization that consisted of mostly white men. When one of the women attempting to sit in at a meeting, she was told by one of the men, "There's no protocol for women attending." She smartly replied, "There's no protocol for a man circling Earth either, sir." Experiences of being dismissed or blocked persist among many groups who historically were excluded from desirable jobs and the upper ranks of corporate America.

Throughout time, more distinct groups join the ranks of those who face active discrimination (homosexuals, transgendered) or are stereotyped (Muslims). Bias and stereotyping affects the socialization process and creates a challenge for the organization that is not prepared to confront the prejudices of individual employees. For example, when someone breaks an employment barrier (i.e., is the first disabled, woman, openly gay, or foreign employee in a workgroup), rumors may reinforce perceptions that someone was hired for his or her token status rather than for superior qualifications. Changes in the world of politics, such as terrorism, may invoke prejudice and stereotyping of employees who shares any resemblance to the terrorists, such as coworkers who embrace the Muslim faith or wear a hijab.

The Nature of Groups

The group is a basic building block of an organization. A **group** includes three to twelve people—large enough that dynamics kick in that are different from dyadic communication, yet small enough that all individuals can interact meaningfully with each other. Several features make a group different from the two-person interpersonal context. Although a comprehensive discussion of group dynamics is beyond the scope of this chapter, three key areas are worthy of mention: norms, roles, and leadership.

Norms

Groups develop norms that characterize their combined identity. A **norm** is an unwritten rule of behavior. For example, even though it is not written down or discussed, everyone in a group may know that it is permissible to take an extra half hour for lunch on Friday and that the boss doesn't like anyone eating at a workstation. Because norms are informal, they can be difficult to learn. It is incumbent upon the new employee to watch and learn what is "normal." Examples can include what topics one can/can't talk about, if communication is face-to-face or via e-mail, what kind of jokes are acceptable. Norms might determine if people are on-time to meetings and even what nonverbal communication is accepted. Darien worked in a convenience store where she had to wear a smock. The smock had large pockets in the front, and Darien had a habit of putting her hands in the pockets. Although she always got her work done, the boss thought that the behavior looked sloppy and told her, "Look around. Do you see anyone else standing around with hands shoved in their pockets?" Darien had violated a norm without even being aware that it existed.

Roles

Groups develop formal and informal roles. A **role** is a function performed by an individual. In the social sciences, roles commonly are classified as maintenance, task, or destructive. **Maintenance roles** are functions necessary to keep a group together—to form enough cohesion that the group can perform their jobs and see the benefit of a common identity. Table 16.2 lists maintenance roles. For example, someone needs to encourage others and moderate conflict. Another example of a maintenance role is building cohesion. Someone in an office may have appointed himself or herself as the keeper of birthdays and buys a card for everyone to sign when a birthday approaches. As units become larger and birthdays more frequent, celebrating birthdays may be turned into a task. A staff person is "tasked" to keep track of birthdays and to send an e-mail card from "the group" on each birthday.

TABLE 16.2 Maintenance Roles

Encourager	Listening to others and praising their good work. "That was a great job, Jamal."
Harmonizer	Moderating differences and conflict among individuals. "We all want to get this job done, so let's try to keep focused on the best solution for the company."
Compromiser	Offering ideas to break deadlocks. "The ideas suggested really aren't all that different. What about using some components of both to see if a combination will work?"
Tension releaser	Breaking the tension, using humor to counteract high emotion. "Wow. That's quite an assignment. Let's all get our superhero suits on before we start!"
Gatekeeper	Ensuring that everyone has a chance to participate. "Ed, you haven't commented lately. What are your thoughts about the project so far?"
Observer	Attending to individual nonverbal communication or comments to help stop misinterpretations. "Sharon, you're looking like you have some reservations."
Follower	Supporting the leader(s) rather than contesting for leadership. "Devon, you're the boss. I'm behind you all the way."
Feeling expresser	Making comments about the emotional tone of the group. "I think everybody is really tired. Can we take a break?"
Standard setter	Calling for a discussion of how the group is working together. "Can we talk about how we are treating each other? I'd like us to have some standards to help us work together better."

Note: Most group dynamics textbooks discuss task, maintenance, and dysfunctional roles

Task roles are necessary to get the work done. Task roles may be performed by designated individuals, by management, or someone may take the role through personal initiative. The delegation of tasks and task roles requires leadership skills. A manager may be effective at encouraging workers to perform tasks, or a manager may dump a project on a group and then scurry back to a corner office. Understanding and practicing leadership and the various task roles that need to be performed in groups is crucial for career advancement and for the health of an organization's culture. Special projects are a good place to build competence in a variety of task and maintenance roles.

Table 16.3 lists typical task roles. For example, when you are assigned to a class group project, the instructor rarely determines who will lead the group, who will keep its records, and who will provide information. These essential roles emerge from the group (or sometimes don't and the work effort suffers from disorganization). In the work setting, everyone has tasks to accomplish for the product to be manufactured or the service completed. If no one in the group formally is assigned the task of making sure everyone knows how to use the software, one person usually steps up to do that part of the job (**role emergence**). If the supervisor is not present physically on the job site or chooses not to take an active role, people generally will volunteer themselves as leaders or try to take control.

Dysfunctional roles are adopted purely for personal reasons and detract from work performance (Table 16.4). For example, one person may make light of every situation (the group clown), tell inappropriately sexual jokes (the playboy/girl), or continually complain (the cynic). If these behaviors distract the group from accomplishing its goals, the behaviors are dysfunctional. Quality leadership, as well as the task and maintenance roles, is needed to curtail the damage that dysfunctional role behaviors can cause.

TABLE 16.3 Task Roles

Initiator	Making suggestions. "Let's talk about our goals and criteria for success before kicking around specific project ideas."
Information seeker	Asking for facts and ideas. "How do we know that the trend is increasing?"
Information giver	Sharing data relevant to the task. "The report from marketing estimates a 10 percent increase in the overseas market next year."
Opinion seeker	Asking for other ideas. "Darnell, you're the finance expert. What do you think about these projections?"
Clarifier/Summarizer	Summing up group consensus or progress. "It sounds like everyone agrees that we should shoot for a May opening date?"
Evaluator/Devil's advocate	Bringing critical thinking to the topic. "Are we forgetting that we can't control what will happen in the press or on the Internet?"
Procedural technician	Preparing for meetings: agenda, room arrangement, etc. "We'll need a projector and a laptop. I'll contact facilities."
Recorder	Keeping minutes/notes. "Here is a copy of last week's minutes and our agenda of what we wanted to cover today."

Note: Most group dynamics textbooks discuss task, maintenance, and dysfunctional roles

TABLE 16.4 Dysfunctional Roles

Aggressor	Using sarcasm and verbal aggression to push a personal agenda. "Sure, Jenny, we can hit that deadline. And next week, you'll win the lottery."
Blocker	Resisting others' ideas and group progress. "We've never needed to do that before, and we don't need to do that now."
Dominator/Stage hog	Monopolizing the discussion. "That reminds me of when I made that sale to our competitor . . ."
Clown	Inappropriately joking and goofing off. "Hey, look everyone—this is my favorite *South Park* clip on YouTube."
Deserter	Withdrawing active participation from the group or not showing up. "Sorry I'm late, and I can't stay but a few minutes."
Confessor/Help seeker	Inappropriately and continuously shares personal feelings that detract from task progress. "You won't believe what my husband said to me this morning!"
Special interest pleader	Advocating for the cause of an outside group or a pet idea to the detriment of the group's interests. "If we fly on British Airways, I can get double mileage points."
Cynic	Focusing on negatives and faultfinding. "We tried that once; it didn't work."
Playboy/Playgirl	Uses the group as a personal dating service. (After removing a chair from the room.) "Oh, too bad, Darla, you'll just have to sit on my lap during the meeting."

Note: Most group dynamics textbooks discuss task, maintenance, and dysfunctional roles

Managers who are focused on just the maintenance level may exacerbate conflict. A leader who is totally maintenance-focused is fun and caring, but the work may not get done. In contrast, a leader who is overly focused on the task tries to be efficient, but the group may fall apart because relational dynamics are not seen as relevant to completing the job. Maintenance-based conflicts occur when nobody in the group diffuses tensions, builds cohesion, or pays attention to this half of group life. When conflict is not managed well in groups, trust decreases, more time is spent in disagreement that does not advance the task, efficiency decreases, emotional exhaustion increases, and individuals begin to drop out physically or mentally (Giebels & Janssen, 2005).

Getting managers to pay attention to the maintenance part of group life, and thereby decrease conflict and increase efficiency, is one aspect of the corporate world's interest in style and emotional intelligence training. When entire organizations examine individual styles and/or emotional intelligence abilities, a new vocabulary is developed to talk about issues. All types of organizations, but particularly more traditionally "task" fields such as engineering, information technology, and computer programming, are discovering that productivity is increased when the workplace culture engages the entire human being—not just the task dimension.

Leadership

Leadership is necessary to keep a workgroup moving toward its goal and the accomplishment of the work objective. As mentioned earlier, leadership often is provided by management, although a boss who has the title but provides no direction is not uncommon. Likewise, it is not unusual for a subordinate to think and act like he or she knows more than the boss or the designated leader, whether true or not. The power to lead and struggles over leadership are frequent flashpoints for conflict in the work setting. For example, a boss may misuse the leadership role, subordinates may try to wrestle leadership control away from the boss, and subordinates may vie to establish ascendancy. The role of the leader in managing workplace conflict is very important and discussed in depth later in this chapter.

KEY 16.1

It is not enough to be a competent leader—one must nurture competence in others.

DISCUSSION QUESTION • 16.3

Which do you think is the best approach in a group: to assign a leader or let a leader emerge? What are the advantages and disadvantages of each approach?

Conflict in the Work Setting

Causes of Workplace Conflict

Causes of workplace conflict run the gamut of incidents previously discussed for general interpersonal conflict, plus additional work-related causes. For example, even though workforce training manuals have long extolled the value of telling the employee about a new task, showing the employee how to do a new task, and observing the employee trying the task several times to gain proficiency (Graupp & Wrona, 2015), some supervisors still casually toss out new jobs with only vague verbal instructions—resulting in failure, inefficiency, frustration, and conflict.

Some causes of workplace conflict bubble up from personal stress and tension, some are the result of poor communication with coworkers or bosses, and some conflicts center around job tasks or goals. The uncertainty that abounds in conflict, combined with goal interference and self-esteem threats, may make conflict at work the most significant of all work stress factors (Giebels & Janssen, 2005). Conflict at work threatens not only one's general well-being; it also threatens one's livelihood.

The concept of **emotional labor** was coined to describe the "work" of displaying emotion on the job. Service employees are expected to be happy and cheerful; collection agents may be required to be stern and demanding. When there is a mismatch between felt emotion (service employees do not feel cheerful when clients are obnoxious and grumpy), **emotional dissonance** results (Ashkanasy, Zerbe, & Hartel, 2002a; Eschenfelder, 2012). The greater the emotional labor and emotional dissonance, the more there is overall stress and the higher the necessity for an outlet. Lacking an appropriate outlet, interpersonally insensitive encounters may occur, leading to conflicts. Those conflicts also can spread. Unlike catchy advertisements that imply bad behavior on vacation is fine because "What happens in Vegas, stays in Vegas," what happens at work does not stay at work. Conflict from work migrates from office to office and from work to home.

> I was like a flea carrying the plague. Every person I touched was likely to be infected by the conflict I was bringing home from work.
> —Authors Runde & Flanagan, 2007, p. 7

Landau, Landau, and Landau (2001) classified workplace conflict into two causal groups: diversity within an organization and interdependence (see Table 16.5). Diversity in thought, style, or information arises from individual differences, professional differences, unclear vision, conflicting responsibilities, unclear responsibilities, and conflicting information. Conflicts arising from interdependence are related to scarce resources, power struggles, organizational structure, procedures, time pressures, job insecurity, and constant change. (Sandy & Cochran, 2000). It is important to note that a homogeneous workgroup is no protection from conflict. Whether coworkers are similar or diverse, conflict can and will emerge. Not surprisingly, conflict management skills are positively related to success in the workplace

Vardi and Weitz (2016) labeled one type of workplace conflict stemming from intentional rule or norm violations as **organizational misbehavior** (Table 16.6). Misbehavior may be intrapersonal, such as substance abuse, or interpersonal, such as incivility, insults, or bullying. For example, an employee who has been fired might delete all files on his workstation or intentionally misfile important documents.

TABLE 16.5 Diversity and Interdependence Conflict

Diversity-Based Conflict	Interdependence-Based Conflict
Individual differences	Scarce resources
Professional differences	Power struggles
Unclear vision	Organizational structure
Conflicting responsibilities	Procedures
Unclear responsibilities	Time pressures
Conflicting information	Job insecurity
	Constant change

Source: Landau, Landau, & Landau (2001)

TABLE 16.6 Organizational Misbehavior to Benefit the Self

Distorting data about work or one's performance
Theft
Overcharging, mistreating, or arguing with customers
Misusing facilities
Conducting private business on work time
Bullying, physical threats, or inappropriate sexual advances
Advancing one's career at the cost of the organization or coworkers

---

Source: Vardi and Weitz (2016)

Negative communicative behaviors exacerbate conflict. Sarcasm is just as unproductive at work as it is in personal relationships. Calabrese (2000) argues that sarcasm is an expression of anger that is pervasive in the U.S. workplace. He theorizes that managers who use aggressive verbal communication or passive-aggressive tactics set in motion a series of defense responses among employees that result in consequences like an "us" versus "them" mentality, antisocial behaviors, or violence. He argues that hostility (e.g., verbal aggressiveness) is a socially acceptable way of displaying anger. Thus it prospers in the workplace: Companies tolerate sarcasm and anger to avoid physical violence and yelling. Expressions of anger and sarcasm may be disguised as humor. For example, a biting remark is made and a speaker then claims to be "just kidding." This is not to say that all humor or all sarcasm is inherently negative. However, intending to put someone in their place, belittling through sarcasm, or using humor that is destructive to others runs counter to building healthy work environments.

For years, Suzanne has opened conflict workshops for business groups by asking participants these questions: What are common conflicts in your workplace? What are the consequences if these conflicts are not managed well? Although not scientific, the answers to these questions are remarkably similar across types of businesses and correlate well to the causes of business conflict identified by other authors. Conflicts arise about issues like change, personality/style differences, workload, and work assignments (see Table 16.7).

TABLE 16.7 Common Workplace Conflicts

Personality/Style Differences
One person is chatty and another needs quiet to work.

Power
One person pushes to get his or her way on new ideas and sulks when somebody else's idea is used.

Workload
One person thinks (accurately or not) her or his workload is harder than someone else's workload. "I do all the work around here!"

Work Assignments
One person perceives (accurately or not) his or her work assignments are a punishment or that others get more favorable assignments.

Time
Someone sees the workload (accurately or not) as more work than any one person can possibly do.

Arrogance
Some people think (accurately or not) that they know more and are better than others.

Communication
Someone cannot or will not verbally talk with coworkers.

A final perspective on the causes of workplace conflict can be derived from a study of troublesome people at work. Harden-Fritz (2002) itemized troublesome bosses as *the defensive tyrant* (incompetent, unethical, and fearful that others are after his or her job), *the taskmaster* (work and non-work excessive demands), *the different boss* (exhibits a style dramatically different from those of the employees), *sand in the gears* (a backstabbing boss who brings personal problems to work), and *the extreme unprofessional* (harasses, badmouths, and over-criticizes).

> Walk the talk. Leaders who talk a good game but do not lead by example will not be respected. Leaders must live by the traits they espouse. Anytime there is a gap between what a leader says and what that leader does, the credibility of that individual will suffer, and sometimes the cost will be too much for the leader (and the organization) to bear.
>
> —General Colin Powell, summarized by Harari, 2002, p. 213

Troublesome coworkers include the *independent other* (has a different style), the *soap opera star* (focuses on personal problems rather than work tasks), *the adolescent* (acts unprofessionally by yelling, demanding, or having tantrums), *the bully* (controlling, takes credit for other's work, intimidates), *self-protector* (shows concern only for one's own job and security), *the rebellious playboy/girl* (ignores legitimate authority, wants to be the center of attention, and sometimes sexually harasses others), the *abrasive and incompetent harasser* (peer who is bossy, sexually harasses, and doesn't do his or her job).

Troublesome subordinates are listed as *the intrusive unprofessional* (butts into others' business), *the backstabbing self-promoter* (advances herself or himself over the bodies of coworkers), *the harmless busybody* (is overly chatty), *the incompetent renegade* (resists orders and distracts others from work), or *the abrasive harasser* (incompetent worker who harasses).

Managing conflict with each of the different personalities requires a broad spectrum of conflict management tools. Sometimes avoidance is the best approach, especially if individual and organizational goals can be met without engaging the source of the conflict. Occasionally, accommodation is appropriate, if only temporarily, to achieve a more important goal. For example, a boss who yells or is demanding may be accommodated because fighting back means possible forfeiture of the goal of being employed. However, a decision to put up with problem behavior must be weighed in light of the long-term consequences to one's health and well-being. One should aim to fill a toolbox with a variety of conflict management skills to use in a variety of workplace situations.

Effects of Conflict in the Workplace

The consequences if conflict is not managed are similar across groups. Table 16.8 shows how effects of conflict at work can be grouped into consequences for employees, supervisors, and the company. Unmanaged conflict brings about stress. When stress goes up, productivity goes down, often resulting in people leaving or being fired.

The importance of good work relationships and conflict management among team members is important in all settings, but critical in the medical context. Research now recognizes that poorly managed conflict can have serious impacts on patients, as well as on the health of medical personnel (Johansen & Cadmus, 2016). For example, emergency room teams have individuals from different specialization areas (radiology, surgery, anesthesiology) and levels of traditional power, e.g., doctors with more status and power than nurses and technicians. Teams often are created from who is on-shift at the moment of an emergency. Their effectiveness requires good communication. How communication occurs depends on the individual's perception of power, status, and appropriate team behaviors. For example, an inexperienced doctor (who has traditional hierarchical power)

TABLE 16.8 Consequences of Unproductive Conflict in the Workplace

---

To Employees
- Increased stress
- Increased physical illness
- More time talking/worrying about the conflict
- Increased sick leave (real illness and because people don't want to go near the conflict)

To Supervisors
- More time and energy is spent on the conflict or avoiding the conflict
- Employees lose respect for supervisors
- Upper management notices the productivity loss
- Supervisor gets a bad evaluation or is fired
- Time is taken to hire new employees
- It gets harder to hire new employees

To the Business
- Profits decrease or services suffer
- It gets harder to hire good people
- The company gets a bad reputation
- Productivity goes down
- The good people leave
- New people have to be trained

---

may not ask for help or refuse to defer to more experienced nurses and technicians. Technicians and nurses who perceive a doctor to have a bullying style may not voice concerns (Janss, Rispens, Segers, & Jehn, 2012). The challenge in this highly charged context is to develop a procedure to balance the need for teamwork and communication with the sometimes chaotic context of emergency medicine (Boehler & Schwind, 2012).

De Dreu and Weingart (2003) conducted a meta-analysis on how conflict in groups affects team efficiency and satisfaction. (Meta-analyses use methodologies that mine the results of past studies to find important research trends.) They found that both task and relationship conflicts negatively affect team performance. Although some conflict is viewed as productive and a spur for creativity, the weight of psychological studies indicates the mere presence of conflict takes energy from task accomplishment. The negative effects can be mitigated when there is high trust, dissent is not viewed as a personal attack, team members feel safe, collaborative communication is more present than contentious communication, and the environment is tolerant of diverse viewpoints.

What do these studies imply for employees in today's multicultural and diverse workplace? As we discussed in Chapter 8, conflict style preferences vary across cultures. Therefore, workers cannot assume actions that would feel appropriate among a group from one's root culture are appropriate in a multicultural workplace. Likewise, attributions about intentionality during a conflict must be questioned.

Preventing and Managing Conflict at Work

Emotional Intelligence and Privacy Management

Conflict experts agree that preventing all work conflicts neither is possible nor desirable. However, preventing misunderstandings and dysfunctional conflict is essential to the health of the organization and to individual workers.

Emotional intelligence (Chapter 8) and social sensitivity in the workplace are beginning to be linked by researchers to four key areas: exhibiting transformational leadership, team effectiveness, interviews, and as a moderator of job insecurity (Ashkansy, Zerbe, & Hartel, 2002b). Those who lead employees toward a clear vision and mission are better able to motivate workers if they are sensitive to social cues and feedback. Teams have less conflict if members are aware of emotional reactions within the group. Socially sensitive interviewers can detect more about applicants (and vice versa) than those who rely mostly on objective data. For example, experts who conduct job interviews are trained to look for applicants who avert their gaze when answering questions or become very agitated when asked about reliability. Individuals who score higher in emotional intelligence, and who feel their job is insecure, are more likely to "ride" that pressure to success than employees with lower emotional intelligence, who are more likely to falter under the stress. Just as self-awareness enhances personal conflict management, emotional intelligence bolsters workplace conflict management.

Determining what individuals perceive to be invasions of privacy and how they respond to perceived privacy violations is helpful to prevent and to manage conflict in many contexts, including the workplace. For example, Jana worked in a physician's office with several other women. The staff shared information with each other about families, boyfriends, husbands, and children. Jana didn't engage in these conversations because she wanted to keep her personal life private. At her first performance evaluation, she was marked down for not being a "team player" and was told that the other employees thought she was standoffish. Jana's boundary management strategy created a conflict in the office.

Surveillance in the workplace is an emerging practice in which employees and employers may differ over who controls information boundaries. What employees think is private communication via e-mail or phone may be overtly or covertly recorded, studied, and appear in reports given to management. Allen, Coopman, Hart, and Walker (2007) explored how employees perceive boundary management at work and the effort made to avoid inadvertent disclosure of so-called private information. Surveillance at work can be harmful or helpful. One workplace secretly investigating if a boss harassed employees in the workroom inadvertently discovered something about one of its employees. One employee, who the rest of the group thought of as an angry outsider always came in early to make coffee for the group. They thought kindly of this action as his way of trying to fit in. In reality, he urinated in the coffee urn every morning while making the beverage.

Conflict Management From the Supervisor/Leader's Viewpoint

The very title of this section indicates what Nicotera and Dorsey (2006) identify as the primary bias of research in organizational conflict: It looks at conflict from the manager's perspective and from the top of the organization's hierarchy, while ignoring the employee's viewpoint. We summarize some of the useful insights and research about how managers deal with conflict.

Although the demands of each workgroup are different, mutual gains approaches generally better moderate workplace conflict in the long term than traditional power-over methods. For example, when an employee requests a shift change, the boss has the power just to say "No." Likewise, an aggressive boss who sees coworkers having a conflict probably either tells employees what to do or to "get over it" (see Table 16.9). A detached boss may say "No, it's out of my hands" without giving any explanation and then avoid the person for a week. Although these strategies successfully avoid the immediate issue, there frequently are unintended consequences to using power, aggression, or avoidance as the route to moderate conflict. The employee may call in sick, subvert the boss, or take other anti-boss actions while the conflict goes on.

TABLE 16.9 Top Ten Behaviors of Aggressive Managers

1. They are poor listeners—they "tell" but they don't listen.
2. They are adversarial—they attack and humiliate subordinates.
3. They lack people skills—they don't show compassion.
4. They use adversarial styles—they bully.
5. They get angry and are impulsive—they lose their temper or swear.
6. They are controlling and don't delegate—they show no confidence in subordinates' abilities.
7. They are autocratic—they make all the decisions and don't seek input.
8. They are arrogant—they can't accept the possibility of being wrong.
9. They are power seeking and exploitative—they steal credit for other people's work on their way to a bonus or a promotion.
10. They blame employees and are critical—they don't give positive feedback.

Source: Excerpted from Elbing and Elbing (1994)

DISCUSSION QUESTION • 16.4

Which of the aggressive management behaviors in Table 16.9 have you observed? How did these behaviors affect productivity? How did the behaviors affect the general culture of the workplace?

Unmanaged employee conflict is the largest reducible cost in organizations; it also is the least often realized (Dana, 2005; Slaikeu & Hasson, 1998). However, there are alternatives to aggressive or avoidant management responses. In conflict, the mutual gains boss would ask questions to determine the employee's interests in the situation, then educate the employee about policies, negotiate, or even agree that a change is better for everyone (Table 16.10).

Managers spend at least 20 percent of their time working on employee "personality" conflicts (Masters & Albright, 2002). The manager's job during conflict is inextricably intertwined with goals for productivity. Masters and Albright (2002) itemize the goals for workplace conflict as preventing escalation, solving the real problem, depersonalizing the issues, inventing solutions, building relationships, and achieving workplace goals.

Thus far, we have discussed options from the manager or supervisor's perspective. Some managers just do the minimal paperwork and requirements to monitor that work gets done. Others go beyond the minimal requirements of a job and act as true leaders. Leaders, in some ways, inspire workers rather than just require that work be done. In the work setting, persuading employees to

---

TABLE 16.10 Mutual Gains Strategies for Supervisors

Reframe the conflict into a problem.
Develop trust.
Ensure that more than one person comes up with ideas for a potential solution.
Focus on interests rather than positions.
Use a structured process to examine problems.
Brainstorm.
Evaluate solutions using objective criteria.
Use the Best Alternative to No Agreement (**BATNA**) to promote new ideas.

Source: Landau, Landau, and Landau (2001)

TABLE 16.11 Constructive and Destructive Conflict Behaviors of Leaders

Constructive	Destructive
Perspective taking	Winning at all costs
Creating solutions	Displaying anger
Expressing emotions	Demeaning others
Reaching out	Retaliating
Reflective thinking	Avoiding
Delay responding	Yielding
Adapting	Hiding emotions

Source: Runde and Flanagan (2007)

adopt better conflict management behaviors requires leadership rather than just a new rule being posted by management (see, for example, Liu, Inlow, & Feng, 2014).

Runde and Flanagan (2007) argue there are four primary competencies for leaders to be "conflict competent": understanding the dynamics of conflict, knowing one's personal reactions to conflict, working toward more constructive and less destructive responses to conflict, and carrying the vision of productive conflict throughout the unit. In other words, for true leadership, it is not enough to be competent. One must nurture competence in others and change the organization's culture if necessary. Table 16.11 lists seven constructive behaviors for leaders that help manage conflict and seven destructive behaviors that may cause conflict (Runde & Flanagan, 2007).

Contrary to popular thought, doing nothing can be constructive (if delaying a response) or destructive (if avoiding or yielding). Expressing emotions can be constructive (when telling others how their behavior affects you) or destructive (if lashing out in anger). As discussed earlier, sarcastic remarks at the expense of others may be one of the most common workplace behaviors that pierce the fabric of working relationships. The speaker may consider it "good fun," but the recipient can feel disrespected and put down.

Managers and employees can benefit from thinking creatively about all of the available power currencies (see Table 16.12). For example, a manager may not be able to change a person's hours

TABLE 16.12 Workplace Power Currencies

Titles
Knowing who to contact in upper management
Technical resources
Authority to order perks (like a new chair)
Ability to alter employee assignments
Having an expensive desk
Ability to allow/take flextime
Ability to allow casual days
Authority to permit personal furnishings in the office
Influence with other employees
Where one sits at meetings
Taking/giving time off
Sending employees to training
People management skills
Speaking skills
Years in the workplace

TABLE 16.13 Asking for Trouble

Here are some basic ways supervisor/managers inadvertently create conflict.

- **Set policies that can't be met.** Result: the policy inevitably is broken.
- **Hire the wrong people.** Result: someone is incompetent who has the wrong skill set.
- **Don't give employees enough orientation/training.** Result: other employees train the newcomer the wrong way or the newcomer pulls the unit down because he or she can't do the job yet.
- **Allow employees to use work computers and social media without oversight.** Result: a computer is full of pornography or employees spend their work time shopping.
- **Ask for employee input when you've already made up your mind on what to do.** Result: employees are resentful about the decisions you make when they unanimously suggested something else.
- **Avoid the conflicts that emerge in your workgroup.** Result: good employees start to leave or productivity goes down.

but might be able to change the work assignment or offer perks as a reward for long-standing service. If power is perceived only as control of the budget, other options will be missed. With a broader view of the power available to a manager, better outcomes are possible.

DISCUSSION QUESTION • 16.5

Discuss the subtle, and maybe not so subtle, nonverbal communication workers may use to display their displeasure or disapproval of others at work.

A manager who is evaluating someone's work must consider the most important question to ask about problematic behavior: Is the behavior affecting productivity? Just because an employee has a messy workstation doesn't mean that what a manager perceives as a "mess" isn't an efficient way of working. Numerous behaviors may annoy supervisors, but the behaviors may not affect productivity. In general, behaviors that do not affect productivity do not require supervisor intervention. In fact, some industries that altered traditional rules found either no change or an increase in productivity after relaxing the rules (e.g., rules that did not allow family pictures, outlawed plants in the office, or required rigid dress codes).

In some types of work, what one wears matters—for example, uniforms for nurses to identify them as health professionals, business attire for upscale salespeople to build credibility, or reflective safety clothing for road construction workers. For people working a phone bank where the public never visits, a uniform may be unnecessary. Managers must sort through what is bothersome because it affects productivity and what is bothersome for personal preference reasons. Table 16.13 lists some of the decisions managers make that cause conflict.

Conflict Management From the Employee's Viewpoint

When there is trouble at work, sometimes talking with coworkers can help. If that talk is negative, however, stress might be enhanced (Boren, 2014). It is best to think about workplace problems strategically rather than just as a topic to complain about.

How conflict management skills apply in the work setting depends on an analysis of one's role and place in the organization, as well as the role and place of the other person in the conflict. The situation can be among coworkers who are equals, among coworkers of different experience/status levels, with bosses, or with subordinates. Although it always is better to take the interests of the other party into account, it is crucial when talking to a boss. For example, if employees are having difficulties that they have not been able to resolve, it is better to analyze the supervisor's interest in the situation and plan an approach than to demand that the boss fix the situation or to start complaining about the coworker. The boss's interests probably include having a productive workgroup that doesn't bother him or her with petty difficulties. It is strategically wise to approach the boss by explaining how the difficulty affects productivity, summarizing your attempts to resolve the issue, and then asking the boss to assist you and the other person in working out the problem. Several techniques useful to employees are discussed next.

The **echo technique** repeats words or startling statements back to the boss or coworker who made the comment, then pausing. Elbing and Elbing (1994) recommend the echo be made in a nonjudgmental tone. The echo helps the other person hear what she or he just said, and the pause gives that person an opportunity to rephrase the comment. For example, if the manager says, "You are a disaster!" the echo would be (said neutrally) "Disaster." The manager might change the word or might react negatively. When the latter response occurs, this is not a good technique for that person. Delicately validating the boss is a good strategy to move the conversation into safer waters. For example, "*Disaster* is a strong word so you must be really upset with what is occurring. I get it."

Delayed XYZ-type feedback is a variation of the XYZ technique used in personal relationships (When you do X, in situation Y, I feel Z). If an uncomfortable situation occurs in the workplace, a conversation about the potential conflict can be engaged at a later time when tempers have cooled. The formula is "When you say *A* in situation *B*, I feel my work is affected in *C* way. Because we both want goal *D*, can we try *E*?" Any feedback should be delivered privately and respectfully. For example, in a private area outside of others' hearing, an employee might say, "When you call me stupid in front of the other employees, my work is affected because I have a big reaction. Because we both need to get the job done, can we try to work together as a team without calling each other names?"

Offering multiple solutions tied to the boss' interests recognizes that modern managers may be trained to kick problems back to employees. In addition, some bosses are prone to attribute suggestions from employees as a threat to their authority. These two boss perspectives make asking the boss to solve your problem or offering just one solution problematic. Instead of presenting one suggestion ("Here is what we should do to fix that problem . . ."), give the boss multiple ideas. For example, if there is a conflict with another employee about how to complete a project that the two of you can't resolve, approach the boss and say, "I don't know if you've noticed, but Lana and I can't agree on how to proceed with the Buchanan project. We're at the point where we have to have a decision. Maybe we could both give you our ideas on what to do, or maybe you have something in mind that would settle the problem, or maybe we could get somebody else to come in and help us decide how to proceed. What do you think?" Giving the boss multiple ideas informs her or him about the issue without blaming anyone, presents a menu of possible outcomes, then places the decision making with the boss.

The *style adaptation technique* recognizes bosses and employees frequently have different work styles and those differences can cause conflict. For example, a boss who does one thing at a time may see an employee who works on several projects simultaneously as disorganized. Cleaning up one's work area at the end of every day would do much to allay the boss's misperception. If a coworker is thoughtful and rarely responds quickly to a new idea, the style adaptation of waiting for that person to respond rather than continuing to talk will foster better communication.

Consciously *questioning assumptions* also helps. Attribution errors based on cultural assumptions are common in the work world. For example, Shuter and Turner (1997) documented that European-American and African-American women see each other's behaviors in the workplace differently. Some African-American women prefer a direct communication style to reduce conflict, and see these those who are not direct as wishy-washy. In turn, directness was misinterpreted as pushy by European-American women, who were more avoidant. Realizing someone uses a different communication style can offset a "feeling" that the other is behaving inappropriately.

In general, assuming other people communicate the same way you do is not a winning strategy. Studying the boss to determine his or her conflict management and communication style not only helps the employee interpret the boss's messages, it also helps strategize how to respond to conflict with the boss. If the boss is direct, indirect messages from employees probably will not be noticed. For instance, if a boss routinely gives directives like, "I need this report by noon," hinting there is a problem with that demand probably will not be effective (Hint: "Gee, Mrs. Washington just gave me some work to do too"). If the boss is indirect, direct messages may be poorly received. If the boss avoids all emotional-level discussions and runs away from conflict, asking the boss to intervene in a coworker conflict may be futile. Instead, ask the boss to find a mediator from the outside.

In general, employees need to have excellent people skills in addition to the technical skills of their chosen vocation. A Forbes article based on interviews of over 100 Human Resource Managers and CEOs concluded businesses want technical skills, but value soft skills more in applicants. Soft skills include leadership, communication abilities, collaboration, the ability to concentrate and follow-through, the adaptability and the ability to learn new things, and humility (Beaton, 2017).

Groupthink

Groupthink, first postulated by Irving Janis (Janis, 1972), occurs when a highly cohesive set of individuals make a series of thinking errors that lead to bad decisions, typically around taking excessive risks. As the symptoms in Table 16.14 show, part of groupthink involves protecting members from outside information, even demonizing those who disagree with the group's supposedly "superior" decisions. Outsiders are viewed suspiciously through stereotypical lenses. At the national level, groupthink is believed to have contributed to the poor decisions that led to the U.S. entry into wars with Korea, Vietnam, and Iraq, the Bay of Pigs invasion, the Watergate burglary, and the space shuttle *Challenger* explosion. Innumerable bad business choices are made because decision makers who only talk to their colleagues become convinced, against all evidence to the contrary, that a product or venture could not fail.

Groupthink is not inevitable, and informed leaders can prevent it. Leaders counteract groupthink by allowing, even encouraging, dissenting opinions—coordinating differences through productive conflict management and encouraging participation. Specifically, leaders can (1) assign the role of critical evaluator if individuals are reluctant to express their reservations; (2) refrain from expressing preferences at the outset of meetings, so group members don't feel pressured to agree with what the leader/boss wants; (3) bring in outsiders to examine decisions; and (4) always analyze solutions for possible downsides and unintended consequences.

TABLE 16.14 Groupthink Symptoms

- The group feels invulnerable and that it can't make a wrong decision.
- The group rationalizes away warnings.
- The group ignores ethical or moral considerations and sees whatever it does as moral.
- The group stereotypes opponents as weak or stupid.
- Group members hide their doubts because they don't want to break from the consensus.
- Any individual group member who dissents is pressured to conform.
- Each thinks he or she is the only one with doubts, creating an illusion of unanimity.
- Members shield each other from dissenting views and opinions.

Source: Janis (1972)

Group Conflict

In addition to individual conflict among employees or between employees and bosses, workgroups also experience conflict with other groups. Furthermore, the amount of conflict seems to make little difference whether a group works face to face or if they meet only online. Technology to assist groups does not positively change group conflict: Computer-mediated groups have no less conflict than face-to-face groups; their conflicts just take longer to emerge (Hobman, Bordia, Irmer, & Chang, 2002).

At least two themes of research examine conflict in groups: instrumental and developmental (Poole & Garner, 2006). The *instrumental theme* examines group conflict as an extension of interpersonal conflict that can be productive or destructive. This does not mean that groups cause conflict; rather the group is a location where interpersonal conflicts occur.

Group process scholars also identified *group development* itself as a cause of conflict. They observe that almost all new groups go through a conflict stage as they work out roles, responsibilities, power, and leadership duties. The conflict phase in groups sometimes is termed **storming** (Poole & Garner, 2006; Tuckman, 2001). Like other places where conflict occurs, group conflict has the potential for negative or positive outcomes. In groups, the positive outcome might be greater bonding, cooperation, or clarity about roles and power structures within the group.

The basic cause of conflict during the group development phase are similar to the interpersonal conflict realm—perceived or actual goal interference. Group communication scholars list conflict topics such as who has power in the group, who is the leader of the group, what roles are appropriate among group members, how the group should communicate among its members, what tasks the group should accomplish, how decisions are made, and who has responsibility for which tasks. Group conflicts emerge around three basic clusters: perceived scarce resources that members compete to acquire, diverse backgrounds that carry divergent expectations about communication, and varying views about task accomplishments.

Conflict Management Systems

The link between conflict and turnover has motivated corporations to examine their rules and processes because replacing and training employees is expensive. Corporations and government agencies want to reduce the costs of conflict. For example, litigation from conflicts that are mismanaged and turnover are large cost centers in some organization. The cost of turnover—including advertising, interviewing, hiring, and training—is pegged at 150 percent of the position's previous salary. Although challenges remain in measuring the success of conflict management systems, over 30 percent of Fortune 1000 corporations have a conflict management system (Lipsky, 2015).

The idea of approaching conflict systematically in organizations is beginning to gain momentum. Companies accept that it might be challenging for all new supervisors to be equally skilled at managing conflict, but think it is too expensive to rely solely on formal grievance procedures to settle conflicts. Instead, conflict management tools are placed throughout the organization to create a **conflict management system**. A conflict management system separates regular conflict management from formal grievance or legal options. They include some combination of five elements, summarized in Table 16.15.

A conflict management system is comprehensive. It can process personnel conflicts, stretch across different departments, negotiate work condition issues, or address any type of dispute related to work productivity. In order for it to be effective, management at all levels must support the use of the conflict management system. The system includes the formal grievance processes and creates new access points for employees to seek assistance in resolving difficulties, including problems that would never qualify in the formal grievance procedure. For example, a chatty coworker who annoys a colleague probably would not qualify in a formal grievance process because the behavior is not technically against policy. But, the two employees still need help so productivity is

TABLE 16.15 Five Elements of an Organization's Conflict Management System

1. *Wide scope* of application to all types of conflicts and disputes
2. *Cultural acceptance* of conflict as inevitable and often productive when well-managed
3. *Multiple access points* to conflict management assistance
4. *Multiple options* for assistance
5. *Support structures* for all employees

Source: Lipsky and Seeber (2006)

not affected, perhaps through mediation or coaching. The final component in a conflict management system is the presence of support systems. **Employee assistance programs** (EAPs) are offered so employees can seek private counseling for personal problems of any type—from stress, quitting smoking, family issues, coping with divorce, or even alcohol/drug counseling. Training opportunities may be offered in negotiation, life skills, communication, and other conflict management tools.

Conflict coaching, sometimes called communication coaching, is an option within conflict management systems. Previously, personal coaching to improve communication and conflict skills only was available to top management. Corporations realized coaching an employee is more cost effective than letting conflict stew or firing and retraining a new person. The coach typically has a background in mediation and other conflict management approaches (Blessing, 2006). In general, the coach listens to determine the employee's goals and discovers what is preventing that individual from moving forward. Then coaching expands the perception of how communication and conflict might be managed and improves skills in needed areas. Coaching can occur before or after mediation with a coworker or as an independent activity (Brubaker, Noble, Fincher, Park, & Press, 2014).

Summary

Communication and conflict at work occur in a context that is different from interpersonal communication in at least three ways: (1) Work goals alter the valuing of personal relationships, (2) teaming in groups is required to accomplish many work tasks, and (3) organizations contain hierarchies, multiple channels of communication, and unique rules and roles.

The hierarchy of authority in an organization is diagrammed in an organizational chart that may delineate a chain of command. A flat organizational hierarchy implies fewer layers of management and easier communication between workers and upper management. Organizations develop unique cultures that are conveyed to new employees during a formal or informal socialization process. Organizational culture is a dynamic feature that changes over time, and an astute employee should learn to recognize norms and rules in order to be personally effective and fit in. Organizations may attempt to overcome silos by instituting quality control circles. Encouraging communication, particularly with supervisors, can be accomplished with effective open door policies.

Groups are the basic building blocks of an organization. A group can be defined as three to twelve people. Group dynamics include norms, roles, and leadership. A norm is an unwritten rule that governs group behavior. Roles are task, maintenance, or dysfunctional behaviors adopted by group members. Task roles move the group toward accomplishing a work goal. Maintenance roles keep the individuals bonded together sufficiently to accomplish its goals. Dysfunctional roles deter the group from task accomplishment. Leadership roles can be designated or emerge as needed from the group. Many conflicts are about who has leadership in the group.

Workplace conflict arises from an array of topics, many of which are similar to the interpersonal context. Unique sources of workplace conflict include topics such as leadership struggles, emotional labor stress, and differences on how to accomplish tasks. The effects of workplace conflict include a loss of trust in coworkers or management, stress, and productivity decreases. Effects can be categorized as consequences for employees, for managers, and for the company.

Preventing and managing conflict requires a combination of self-awareness, cultural/style sensitivity, and skill development from bosses and employees. Aggressive bosses use a variety of tactics that are conflict producing. Supervisors are estimated to spend at least 20 percent of their time managing employee conflicts. In contrast, numerous creative methods exist to help the conflict competent manager.

Workers need to analyze who a conflict is with to determine which interpersonal conflict skills are appropriate. The echo technique, the delayed feedback technique, and style adaptation are positive responses to conflict producing situations.

Research into group conflict views it as instrumental (stemming from goal differences) or developmental (a unique phase that groups go through as they begin to grow and bond together). Groupthink is a danger to any highly cohesive workgroup. Strong leadership is necessary to prevent groupthink, including welcoming critical evaluation, refraining from expressing the leader's opinion first, and bringing in outsiders.

Many organizations are adopting a conflict system approach. Conflict management systems combine formal grievance procedures with employee coaching, training, mediation, and other skill development methods.

Chapter Resources

Exercises

1. As a group, view a pre-1980 film or television show set in the workplace, such as *Adam's Rib* (Spencer Tracy and Katharine Hepburn, 1949) or *Mad Men*. What work culture is present in that time and place? What might you infer about the workplace from its demographics? What are the sources of conflict in that workplace? How is the workplace different from one you might see today? What behaviors do you spot in the film that are illegal workplace behaviors today?
2. View a film or television program set in the workplace, such as *The Devil Wears Prada*, *The Office*, or *Ugly Betty*. What norms and roles are present in the workplace? What sources of conflict are depicted in that workplace?
3. Make a list of power currencies that employees or managers have at your workplace.
4. Find an organizational chart for a local company. What does the organizational chart imply about how communication is channeled in the company?
5. Identify a conflict you experienced or witnessed at work. How did the conflict affect productivity?
6. Discuss the list of rules for appropriate e-mail use at work.
7. If your workplace allows texting for business purposes, what rules would you recommend to make sure texting is appropriate and effective?

Journal/Essay Topics

1. Describe and analyze a workplace conflict you personally experienced. Explore the types of norms, roles, and leadership that were present.
2. Write an essay about a personal experience that illustrates one of the types of office incivility identified in a survey of business practices (see, "Manners," 2006). Do you agree that these behaviors are not civil: use of profanity, using a snotty tone, public reprimands by the boss,

talking too loudly, cell phones ringing during meetings, speakerphones used during meetings, talking about personal matters in meetings, micromanaging, and using PDAs during a meeting?

3. Describe the responses to conflict present in organizations you have worked in. Was there a conflict management system approach or just rules and grievance procedures? If you were running a company, what formal or informal systems would you put into place?

Research Topics

1. Review the published literature on work metaphors, beginning with Smith, R. C., & Eisenberg, E. M. (1987). Conflict at Disneyland: A root-metaphor analysis. *Communication Monographs*, 54(4): 367–380. After analyzing several studies, draw conclusions about the impact of metaphor and language on corporate culture.
2. Examine the published research literature on groupthink for the past five years. Do these studies mention electronic communication and access to information through the Internet? If so, how? Draw conclusions about whether the Internet, chat rooms, or other electronic communication options can help alleviate groupthink or are making it worse.
3. Who is in the chain of command at your college? Is it like the chain of command described on page 281 or different? When might it be important to understand the chain of command in your major department? For example, where would you go to make a change in the requirements for your major?

Mastery Cases

Which ideas from the chapter shed light on the cases?

Case 16A: We Missed Your Blue Shirt

A newer employee was out on sick leave for an extended period. The rest of the employees were joking about him while he was gone and then felt bad about it, so they made a poster for him on his door with their good intended humor about him as a way of welcoming him back. Their top ten reasons we missed you included, "We miss your blue shirt every day," "We missed hearing about football every day." While this type of ambiguous humor can be taken defensively, the returning employee interpreted it as a welcoming attempt and commented: "That was a really cool day for me. That was the first day I felt a part of the office. . . . I was really part of the group" (adapted from the research of Heiss & Carmack, 2012).

Case 16B: Don't Mess With My Commission

Lily and Mac work on commission at a sports retail store. The norm is to take turns as customers come in. Lily's first customer was a big spender, outfitting a cabin for a big family reunion—the commissions were going to be huge. Meanwhile, Mac worked with four customers, and made small commissions during that same time. By noon, Lily was out-earning Mac by a considerable amount, and Mac noticed. Lily usually worked the noon hour, but Mac wanted the store to himself to make up his lagging commissions. Mac said, "Lil, you go ahead and take your lunch today. My plans fell through and I'd rather just work." Lily replied, "No, thanks. I wasn't planning anything and am not hungry. I'd rather just keep at it." A customer came in, and as it was her turn, she walked toward him. But Mac made eye contact with the customer first and said, "How can I help you?" Lily just lost what she believed was her customer. Irritated, Lily leaves the store and takes a walk for her lunch. Mac notices she didn't clock out or say goodbye as usual.

References

Allen, B. J. (2000). "Learning the ropes": A black feminist standpoint analysis. In P. M. Buzzanell (Ed.), *Rethinking organizational & managerial communication from feminist perspectives* (pp. 177–208). Thousand Oaks, CA: Sage.

Allen, M. W., Coopman, S. J., Hart, J. L., & Walker, K. L. (2007). Workplace surveillance and managing privacy boundaries. *Management Communication Quarterly, 21*(1), 172–200.

Ashkanasy, N. M., Zerbe, W. J., & Hartel, C. E. J. (2002a). Managing emotions in a changing workplace. In N. M. Ashkanasy, W. J. Zerbe, & C. E. J. Hartel (Eds.), *Managing emotions in the workplace* (pp. 3–22). Armonk, NY: M.E. Sharpe.

Ashkanasy, N. M., Zerbe, W. J., & Hartel, C. E. J. (2002b). What are the management tools that come out of this? In N. M. Ashkanasy, W. J. Zerbe, & C. E. J. Hartel (Eds.), *Managing emotions in the workplace* (pp. 285–297). Armonk, NY: M.E. Sharpe.

Beaton, C. (2017). *Top employers say millennials need these 4 skills in 2017*. Forbes.com. Accessed 12 March 2017.

Blessing, K. (2006). *Communication coaching*. Mediate.com. Accessed 13 March 2017.

Boehler, M., & Schwind, C. (2012). Power and conflict and the performance of medical action teams: A commentary. *Medical Education, 46*, 830–837.

Boren, J. P. (2014). The relationships between co-rumination, social support, stress, and burnout among working adults. *Management Communication Quarterly, 28*(1), 3–25.

Brubaker, D., Noble, C., Fincher, R, Park, S., & Press, S. (2014). Conflict resolution in the workplace: What will the future bring? *Conflict Resolution Quarterly, 31*(4), 357–386.

Calabrese, K. R. (2000). Interpersonal conflict and sarcasm in the workplace. *Genetic, Social, and General Psychology Monographs, 126*(4), 459–494.

Dana, D. (2005). *Managing differences: How to build better relationships at work and home*. Prairie Village, KS: MTI Publications.

De Dreu, C. K. W., & Weingart, L. R. (2003). Task versus relationship conflict, team performance, and team member satisfaction: A meta-analysis. *Journal of Applied Psychology, 88*(4), 741–749.

Elbing, C., & Elbing, A. (1994). *Militant managers*. New York: Irwin Professional Publishing.

Eschenfelder, B. (2012). Exploring the nature of nonprofit work through emotional labor. *Management Communication Quarterly, 26*(1), 173–178.

Garner, J. T. (2016). Open doors and iron cages: Supervisors' responses to employee dissent. *International Journal of Business Communication, 53*(1), 27–54.

Giebels, E., & Janssen, O. (2005). Conflict stress and reduced well-being at work: The buffering effect of third-party help. *European Journal of Work and Organizational Psychology, 14*(2), 137–155.

Graupp, P., & Wrona, R. J. (2015). *The TWI workbook: Essential skills for supervisors*. Boca Raton, FL: CRC Press.

Harari, O. (2002). *The leadership secrets of Colin Powell*. New York: McGraw-Hill.

Harden-Fritz, J. M. (2002). How do I dislike thee? Let me count the ways. *Management Communication Quarterly, 15*(3), 410–438.

Heiss, S. N., & Carmack, H. J. (2012). Knock, knock; Who's there? Making sense of organizational entrance through humor. *Management Communication Quarterly, 26*(1), 106–132.

Hobman, E. V., Bordia, P., Irmer, B., & Chang, A. (2002). The expression of conflict in computer-mediated and face-to-face groups. *Small Group Research, 33*(4), 439–465.

Janis, I. L. (1972). *Victims of groupthink: A psychological study of foreign-policy decisions and fiascoes.* Boston: Houghton Mifflin.

Janss, R., Rispens, S., Segers, M., & Jehn, K. A. (2012). What is happening under the surface? Power, conflict and the performance of medical teams. *Medical Education, 46,* 838–849.

Johansen, M. L., & Cadmus, E. (2016). Conflict management style, supportive work environments and the experience of work stress in emergency nurses. *Journal of Nursing Management, 24,* 211–218.

Landau, S., Landau, B., & Landau, D. (2001). *From conflicts to creativity: How resolving workplace disagreements can inspire innovation and productivity.* San Francisco: Jossey-Bass.

Lipsky, D. B. (2015). The future of conflict management systems. *Conflict Resolution Quarterly, 33*(1), S27–S34.

Lipsky, D. B., & Seeber, R. L. (2006). Managing organizational conflicts. In J. G. Oetzel & S. Ting-Toomey (Eds.), *Handbook of conflict communication: Integrating theory, research, and practice* (pp. 359-389). Thousand Oaks: SAGE.

Liu, L. A., Inlow, L., & Feng, J. B. (2014). Institutionalizing sustainable conflict management in organizations: Leaders, networks, and sensemaking. *Conflict Resolution Quarterly, 32*(2), 155–176.

Manners a top priority at work: Incivility can disrupt productivity. (2006, March 15). *Washington Times.*

Masters, M. F., & Albright, R. R. (2002). *The complete guide to conflict resolution in the workplace.* New York: American Management Association.

Nicotera, A. M., & Dorsey, L. K. (2006). Individual and interactive processes in organizational conflict. In J. G. Oetzel & S. Ting-Toomey (Eds.), *Handbook of conflict communication: Integrating theory, research, and practice* (pp. 293–326). Thousand Oaks, CA: Sage.

Poole, M. S., & Garner, J. T. (2006). Perspectives on work-group conflict and communication. In J. G. Oetzel & S. Ting-Toomey (Eds.), *Handbook of conflict communication: Integrating theory, research, and practice* (pp. 267–292). Thousand Oaks, CA: Sage.

Runde, C. E., & Flanagan, T. A. (2007). *Becoming a conflict competent leader.* San Francisco: Wiley.

Russell, B. (1938). *Power: A new social analysis.* New York: Norton.

Sandy, S. V., & Cochran, K. M. (2000). The development of conflict resolution skills in children: Preschool to adolescence. In M. Deutsch & P. T. Coleman (Eds.), *The handbook of conflict resolution: Theory and practice* (pp. 316–342). San Francisco: Jossey-Bass.

Shuter, R., & Turner, L. H. (1997). African American and European American women in the workplace: Perceptions of conflict communication. *Management Communication Quarterly, 11*(1), 74–96.

Slaikeu, K. A., & Hasson, R. H. (1998). *Controlling the costs of conflict: How to design a system for your organization.* San Francisco: Jossey-Bass.

Tuckman, B. (2001, Spring). Developmental Sequence in Small Groups (PDF). *Group Facilitation: A Research and Applications Journal,* 71–72. Accessed 7 March 2017.

Vardi, Y., & Weitz, E. (2016). *Misbehavior in organizations: A dynamic approach* (2nd ed.). New York: Routledge.

Chapter 17

Conflict and Social Media

Vocabulary

Audience	Flaming
Autonomy	Lowest common denominator of acceptability
Competence	Netiquette
Context collapse	Presentation of self theory
Curator	Relatedness
Cyberbullying	Selective exposure
Drama	Self-determination theory (SDT)
E-bile	Spiral of Silence theory
Face-to-face (FtF) communication	

Objectives

After reading the chapter, you should be able to:

1. Identify leading theories of online behavior
2. Explain online impression management activities
3. Explore how the role of audience impacts behaviors online
4. Recognize cyberbullying

The World of Social Media

Globally it is estimated that more than 3.5 billion people use the internet (Internet Livestats, 2017). Founded in 2004, Facebook alone boasts almost two billion active users worldwide per month ("Number of monthly Facebook," 2017). Given the popularity of social networking sites as a means to connect to others, express opinions, and maintain relationships, it is not surprising that interpersonal conflict is played out through social media. Hertlein (2012) reports, "One functional result of having a permanent connection to the electronic world is an increased opportunity for violence in online interactions" (p. 379). Personal conflict via social media has become a substantial area for research (Friedman & Currall, 2016; Ging & Norman, 2016; Jane, 2015; Kim & Ahn, 2013; Lee, 2005; Marwick & Boyd, 2014; Turnage, 2008).

Millennials are adept at social media and tend to use it to address conflict. One study of millennial college students in dorm roommate situations showed students had a lower tolerance for stress and tended to take concerns to social networks before taking the situation to a resident advisor or hall director (Molina, Heiselt, & Justice, 2015). Those attempts at managing the conflict with social media often included negative strategies such as rumor or revenge seeking.

With the popularity of social networking, the pervasiveness of cyberbullying has risen to a national level concern (Mehta, 2016) and concepts such as "flaming" and "trolling" are part of the lexicon describing extreme conflict and baiting techniques. This chapter explores the nature and impact of conflict in online interactions, and provides strategies for increasing civility and satisfaction when using social media.

Theories of Online Behavior

What motivates individuals to participate in social networking and online communications? **Self-determination theory** (SDT) addresses an individual's motivations, as influenced by both environmental factors and internal states (Ferguson, Gutberg, Schattke, Paulin, & Jost, 2015). SDT explains how motivation is related to need satisfaction, particularly the satisfaction of autonomy, competence, and relatedness. If we feel that we have control over ourselves (**autonomy**), that we are capable to act (**competence**), and that we have meaningful relationships with others (**relatedness**), we have greater satisfaction (Deci & Ryan, 2000). According to SDT, online interactions feed our sense of well-being because they feed our desire for self-determination.

SDT theory helps explain how specific individuals use social media. For example, Andrea is a single parent of three and has one son with a severe disability. Navigating her life in a city apart from extended family requires knowing the resources available to her. She found a chat room for single parents of children with special needs and has made friends with parents like her in cities across the nation. She finds validation and support but also helpful information about social services and working with Medicaid. After a year on the site, she now is offering sage advice and support to new chatroom members. Self-determination theory explains Andrea's use of social media by explaining how Andrea found her own power to control her circumstances via the chat room. She was further empowered with information from the web and support of her online friends (autonomy). The knowledge gained increased her confidence in knowing the system and how to get her needs met (competency), and she now offers value to others in the group (relatedness).

DISCUSSION QUESTION • 17.1

In what ways have your online activities fulfilled your needs for autonomy, competence, and/or relatedness?

Another theory, **presentation of self**, which uses theater imagery to explain how and why humans interact, has gained popularity in explaining online behavior. Individuals, like actors in a play, try to guide the impressions the audience has of their actions, and at the same time work to avoid being embarrassed or embarrassing the audience. In the land of the Internet, people prepare for their performances by choosing behaviors and costuming (through an avatar). Goffman, who created the theory in the late 1950s, probably would be amazed that his ideas still are relevant to the technological world of today.

Hogan (2010), utilizing Goffman's drama metaphor, argued that in many online interactions, we are performing as actors on stage. Our performances are made up of *exhibitions* (such as status updates on Facebook) and *activities* (such as chatting or messaging). Because technology stands between the individuals interacting in chat rooms, interactive games, and other web contexts, presentation of self has innumerable opportunities for manipulation. An apt description of this manipulation is illustrated in a classic *New Yorker* comic where Peter Steiner depicts a dog surfing the web, presumably chatting with humans online, telling his dog buddy, "On the Internet, nobody knows you're a dog."

We live in an online world where the interaction often is managed by a virtual curator—someone outside the self who manages the *staging* (or digital content). Prior to 2014, Facebook subscribers could have their accounts closed for showing a bare breast in photos. The curator in this case, the moderators at Facebook, had a policy forbidding the display of breasts—the nipple, specifically. This policy was protested by many, but in particular breastfeeding mothers. A campaign to "free the nipple" ultimately prompted Facebook to change their policy (Lu, 2014; Nelson, 2014). The presentation of self for these nursing mothers was inextricably tied to their ability to provide artifacts (pictures). The **curator**, "a key role generally absent from everyday life situations," (Hogan, 2010, p. 378) is ever-present in online impression management activities.

Individuals moderate their online persona in relationship to their audience, both online and in person. Lily, an avid Bernie Sanders supporter in the 2016 presidential primaries, comes from a family of staunch Republicans who she preferred not to engage with on politics. Lily opened a Twitter account and felt free to rail against politicians and proposed policies that were anathemas to her. She gained many followers who appreciated her snarky humor and pithy remarks. Then she noticed she had a new follower, her brother. As she valued peace in her family more than her online rants, she deleted her Twitter account. The interface of her online communication with her newest audience member, her brother, caused her to modify her messaging.

The **audience** component of the dramaturgical theory comprises those who observe the presentation. As Hogan (2010) describes the performance:

> More succinctly, these are those for whom one "puts on a front." This front consists of the selective details that one presents in order to foster the desired impression alongside the unintentional details that are given off as part of the performance.
>
> (p. 378)

A primary avenue for millions of daily performances is Facebook, where the audience is made up of "friends."

Facebook "friends" are defined differently than **face-to-face** (FtF) friends, although they may fill both roles. Melanie has been out of high school for several decades, and had lost contact with many individuals she grew up with in a small town. After a 30-year class reunion, many of these long forgotten peers are now part of her Facebook friendship circle. Where those long ago classmates previously occupied no space in her adult world, she now knows the names (or at least sees regular pictures) of their grandchildren and could tell you where some ate dinner earlier this week. The recent U.S. presidential election brought postings of diverse and polarized memes, many offensive to her. Marked as a Facebook "friend" now meant she was an audience in many performances and had to make a choice of participating or walking out (de-friending or unfollowing in Facebook parlance), or staging her own performance in response to those actors. Furthermore, employed in state government, she had to be aware that her performances online may be seen as offensive to others. Impression management, or self-presentation, requires constant vigilance to how our presentations will be perceived by audiences, even unintended audiences.

Hogan (2010) notes that the notion of "friends" is now a blurred line of "family members, coworkers, actual friends, neighbors, acquaintances, high school friends, people from online hobby groups or gaming sites, one-night stands, distant friends of friends, students past or present, and generally any other potentially personal relationship" (p. 383). Individuals may have more than one site where they share different artifacts to different audiences, so they end up managing more than one presentation of self.

Posting artifacts designed for one audience that may be accessed by an unintended audience requires us to define what Hogan calls the **lowest common denominator** of what is acceptable. **Context collapse** (Marwick & Boyd, 2011) explains that what was once kept as unique audiences where we managed our presentation of self separately has now melded together into one audience. We disclose to the lowest common denominator of what is acceptable to all audiences. For example, 27-year-old Grace never wants to get married nor does she have any intentions of being with only one partner. She considers herself to be a "serial monogamist" with her longest relationship lasting only one year. She is honest with her relationship partners, and her friends are aware of her commitment to being unattached. However, some members of her conservative and fundamentally religious family would be appalled by Grace's life choices. Subsequently, her lowest common denominator of self-disclosure due to the context collapse of having friends and family on Facebook means she only shares photos of her pets online and never discusses any current romantic interest.

DISCUSSION QUESTION • 17.2

Have you experienced context collapse in your online social networks? How has this led to filtering down information to the lowest common denominator of acceptability?

However, Grace may have more than one online social network. On Facebook, her parents and a first grade teacher are listed as friends. There Grace posts pictures of a recent trip to the Grand Canyon and selfies with her new puppy. Where Facebook friends may see the "clean" profile, the family may be astonished to find what the lowest common denominator would be on a different site where she discloses her more controversial information. As Hogan (2010) offers, "one may be sexually ambiguous or even deceptive on Facebook or one's Twitter account, but still have an openly gay profile on Gaydar.co.uk, Gay.com, Manhunt.com, and so on" (pp. 382–383). Each site has a different lowest common denominator, where presentation of self may be in stark contrast in another context.

A third theory also has emerged to explain some aspects of internet communication. The **Spiral of Silence theory** juxtaposes how one sees public opinion and how that affects the expression of ideas (Gearhart & Zhang, 2015). The vast frontier of the Internet holds something for everyone, and many varied opportunities to express opinions on any matter. However, the Spiral of Silence theory explains that as public opinion gains traction, those in opposition lessen their input. Gearhart and Zhang (2015) supported this theory with their research, noting that the stronger negative reaction is to an opinion, the more self-censorship a person engages in while in a communication event. Additionally, the likelihood of seeking out communication that affirms an already held opinion is more likely after having one's contrary opinion critiqued. Gearhart and Zhang caution that this pattern may lead to increased extremism due to self-selection of information.

DISCUSSION QUESTION • 17.3

Provide an example of how an individual's ideas and comments may become more extreme due to self-selection of information online. Are there ways to temper this cycle of radicalization?

Facebook and Conflict

What makes Facebook different from many other social network sites is its lack of anonymity; Facebook generally is tied to a real person using a real name. In Kim and Ahn's (2013) study, those interviewed described Facebook as not as contentious, in their own experiences, as other sites where people could use pseudonyms more readily. As actors make presentations on Facebook, they are aware of the personal relationships that make up their network, and conflict is often seen as an unnecessary risk. Kim and Ahn examined two questions through interviews of Facebook users who had identified a conflict in their Facebook newsfeeds. They asked: "When do people experience conflict on Facebook?" and "What were the participants' thought processes in perceiving and dealing with conflicts?" Participants described the purpose of Facebook as a tool to keep connected to others; conflicts over politics and religion emerged as common triggers. Conflict seemed to escalate when a perceived social norm of civility was broken. Three types of actors emerged in Kim and Ahn's research: the brave, the careful, and the inconsistent. Those categorized as the brave posted without worrying about what others thought of their presentations. The brave talked of playing the devil's advocate on polarizing issues or just looking for responses. While conflicts might arise, the risk was calculated.

Unlike the brave, the careful looked at Facebook as a means to stay connected to others and build relationships. The careful took full advantage of privacy settings to filter out unintended audience members, although they may not always trust it. The inconsistent were just as the label implies; they sometimes acted as the brave or as the careful, depending upon the circumstances. One interviewee didn't post messages online often, but when he did, he felt others took notice and his audience was impacted more strongly. For others, being the brave came with ramifications that turned them into more guarded participants, like the careful.

Kim and Ahn (2013) found interviewees further modified their responses depending upon the level of personal relationship they had with their "friends." Acquaintances may warrant a perfunctory, "that's cool," as a response, whereas a close friend may elicit a reply with personal attitudes about the topic. Some participants shared frustration about learning something through a controversial post. A comment on a post can open the door to escalation of a conflict as "friends of friends" have access to the conflict playing out online. An individual disagreement, perhaps starting as a means to seek more clarity on someone's opinion, can spiral into conflict with a larger group. Some, in this scenario, resorted to "backstage" tactics to reconcile a conflict—seeking to "private message" someone rather than have the conflict further play out on the front stage in front of a larger audience.

Beyond conflict with friends, researchers have examined the effect of Facebook on intimate relationships (Clayton, Nagurney, & Smith, 2013; Marshall, 2012). Access to personal information and regular status updates can lead to obsessive behaviors, particularly with respect to ex-partners. There has been some support for the claim that Facebook and other social networking sites have increased and made stalking easier, both online and in person (Chaulk & Jones, 2011). On Facebook, although seen by many as a positive relationship-building and maintenance site where parties can share and access details about others, there appears to be a darker side of the phenomenon.

Clayton, et al., (2013) sought to investigate whether increased use of Facebook had negative outcomes on intimate relationships (i.e., physical cheating, emotional cheating, breakup, and divorce). High use of Facebook included self-reporting by participants of daily or hourly use. Additionally, participants were surveyed about their past and current relationship status, as well as patterns of conflict with respect to Facebook. For example, respondents were asked if they ever had a conflict with their significant other over viewing friends' Facebook profiles. A third area of questions concerned the impact of conflict over Facebook. Questions such as, "Have you physically cheated on your significant other with someone you have connected or reconnected with on Facebook?"

High Facebook use was correlated with negative relational outcomes, mitigated by the length of the relationship. The length of time a relationship has been in effect (noted as three years or more) does seem to reduce the negative impact of high Facebook use on intimates. The more vulnerable a relationship, the more likely high Facebook activity will have negative effects. According to Clayton, et al., "High levels of Facebook use may also serve as an indirect temptation for physical and/or emotional cheating" (2013, p. 719). The researchers also noted jealously and conflict increases as a partner "friends" an old acquaintance or past partner. Hertlein (2012) also found increased resentment among partners who sacrifice face-to-face time to be online, leading to increased dissatisfaction with the relationship.

Cyberbullying and Drama

The 2016 U.S. presidential election has been deemed by many as the nastiest election cycle in the modern era. Candidates and surrogates made frequent use of social media, particularly Twitter, and attacks against political rivals often turned into personal attacks. Social media also was used extensively to disseminate fake news (factually untrue information packaged as objective news) from domestic political sources and foreigners using sensationalism to make money (Kirby, 2016; Read, 2016). Name-calling, belittling, and general meanness was a hallmark of political speech in 2016.

When does meanness online become **cyberbullying**—persistent intimidation or threats via the Internet? There are differing views (Arntfield, 2015). Bullying, in the traditional sense, is a power-based act resulting in ongoing physical and/or emotional victimization. The research on bullying has in recent years moved out of the context of the school-yard bully and into adult contexts such as the workplace (Samnani & Singh, 2012).

According to the Pew Research Center, 92 percent of American teenagers use the Internet every day, with 24 percent using smartphones to stay online "almost constantly" (Lenhart, 2015). Children and teens also are identified as the most frequent targets of cyberbullying (Arntfield, 2015), and most cyberbullies simultaneously have a FtF presence in the victim's world (such as school or neighborhoods). Lenhart et al. (2011) report that within the previous year, 19 percent of teens report being bullied, and 88 percent witnessed mean or cruel behavior on social network sites. Many teens refer to this meanness as "drama" and not necessarily as "bullying" (Marwick & Boyd, 2014).

Interviews of a socially and racially diverse population of 166 youth (age 13–19) in 17 states were conducted, with the first set of interviews focusing on general use of social media, and follow up interviews delving into bullying and privacy (Marwick & Boyd, 2014). Defining "drama" proved to be a difficult task. Marwick and Boyd report, "Defining drama is not easy, as its conceptual slipperiness is part of its appeal. To the teens we talked with, drama was like Justice Potter Steward's definition of obscenity: you know it when you see it" (p. 1190). The teens in the study were forthcoming with examples of drama in their interviews. The researchers operationalized **drama** as "performative, interpersonal conflict that takes place in front of an active, engaged audience, often on social media" (p. 1191). This definition highlights the relational nature of the conflict, and the performance of acting out the drama in front of an audience. Drama appears to be a different phenomenon from bullying, in that there is conflict and excessive emotionality, involving considerable time. However, bullying may be a part of the drama, as can gossip and relational aggression (for example, posting embarrassing photos of the bullying target). Generally, teens conceptualized drama as bidirectional (as opposed to bullying, which was directed from the bully toward a specific target).

DISCUSSION QUESTION • 17.4

What kinds of Internet drama have you experienced?

In a disturbing trend, suicides related to cyberbullying are reported with increased frequency. In December 2016, 18-year-old Brandy Vela shot herself in front of her family after she received numerous abusive texts for months, and a fake Facebook page of her was created (CBS/AP, December 2016). Most of the comments focused on Brandy's weight, although her image was fraudulently posted on dating sites with promises of easy sex. Unfortunately, Brandy's experience is typical of cyberbullying among girls. Ging and Norman (2016) explain the dynamics of conflict in social media, and note that gender differences are evident, for example: "The insults that the girls reported were always related to physical appearance (fat, ugly, ginger), sexual morals (slut, whore, slapper), or self-harm ('everybody hates you,' 'go and kill yourself,' 'go and cut yourself with glass')" (p. 815). Boys were attacked more on their appearance, perceived sexual orientation, or their physical abilities. The participants did not discuss these incidents as example of bullying, instead employing words like "messing," "slagging," or "b****" fights.

Marwick and Boyd (2014) note that most teens Facebook "friended" almost all students in their class or school. This widespread friending creates a massive audience for performances, reaching into individual students' non-virtual social and peer networks. Interviewees did note that when drama occurs, the presence of a large audience spurs some into defending the victim and others into joining the fray. The importance of looking at how the teens themselves define their reality by referring to the social media conflicts in terms such as drama instead of bullying connotes an important part of their lived experience. The effect of the drama may be as devastating as being bullied, but in an effort to save face, students may choose to not paint themselves into the victim role.

Another interesting point of Marwick and Boyd's research is that drama is seen as gendered—it's a "girl thing" (p. 1199). This reduction of the drama to a girl thing stereotypes negative behaviors as silly or frivolous, and thus not serious. In a different study, Ging and Norman (2016) reported girls' experiences were self-conceptualized as "just messing" instead of bullying. They state, "Where online scapegoating stops and cyberbullying begins is not always clear" (p. 809). Cyberbullying was downplayed by those in the study, with a theme that "cyberbullying happens to other people" (p. 815).

Marwick and Boyd (2014) note, "While teen conflict will never disappear, social media has changed how it operates. 'Drama' is a messy process, full of contradictions and blurred boundaries" (p. 1201). Understanding how teens conceptualize drama and recognize their own language for the experience provides opportunity to help them navigate conflict more effectively.

DISCUSSION QUESTION • 17.5

What is the potential impact of having an historical record of one's life available to a wide audience on the web? Is being a teen more difficult than for previous generations?

Incivility

Wired online magazine writer Klint Finley (2015) addressed a trend where publishers remove the comment sections from their webpages. He writes:

For years, comment boxes have been a staple of the online experience. You'll find them everywhere, from *The New York Times* to Fox News to *The Economist*. But as online audiences have grown, the pain of moderating conversations on the web has grown, too. . . . So many media companies are giving up on comments, at least for now.

In other words, many responses were so uncivil and vitriolic, that it was deemed better to take everyone's opportunity to comment away, since the more thoughtful comments were buried in a morass of mostly unsubstantiated negativity.

KEY 17.1

Never send e-mail, texts, or other social media messages when you are really angry.

Kenski, Coe, and Rains (2012), in a study on the appearance of incivility in the comments to articles in an online newspaper, identified seven categories of incivility reported in Table 17.1. They note:

> American political debate has always had its share of incivility, and the current era is no different. What is different now, however, is that the 21st century's vast, interactive media environment (e.g., blogs, video-sharing websites, social network websites) has created broader opportunities for public debate and engagement, be it civil or uncivil.
>
> (p. 1)

In their study of over 6,400 comments to online news stories, over 20 percent of the comments contained incivility, with *ad hominem* attacks, or name-calling, making up over 14 percent of the incidences. The 2016 presidential campaign added fake news to the list of tactics.

Even communities where participants are brought together by a common interest can devolve into negativity. Aakhus and Rumsey (2010) analyzed a conflict that occurred in an online cancer support group. The researchers aimed to understand how the conflict in this group stemmed from the participants' differing understandings of the purpose of the group. The conflict in their study concerned a parent (Sue), frustrated by what she felt was poor resource management at a hospital treating her child's cancer. In the online group, Sue criticizes the hospital's allotting space to girls with anorexia who are "up there painting there [sic] nails" with nurses while the "cancer kids are up there puking there [sic] brains out & waiting for help." The response to Sue's criticism set off a conflict in the group over Sue's right to vent and criticize the caregivers, while others in the group attempted to explain Sue's complaint as expressing frustration and being emotionally driven.

TABLE 17.1 The Many Types of Incivility

Type	Definition	Example
Name-calling	Attack on the person	"Libtard," "right-wing crackpot," "moron," "idiot"
Aspersion	Attack on idea	"Ridiculous argument," "uneducated assertion"
Lying	Being dishonest or accusing others of dishonesty	"Cherry-picking facts," "untrustworthy sources"
Vulgarity	Use of expletives/profanity	"Quit b****ing," "F*** off!"
Pejorative speech	Attack the manner of communication	"You should learn to spell/write," "third-grade vocabulary"
Hyperbole	Extreme exaggeration	"There is no money for education in this state," "She always lies"
Noncooperation	Communicating impasse	"Bipartisanism is dead," "I give up talking to you"

A common assumption about those who engage in online communities is that individuals will seek out those who think as they do, and this **selective exposure** will lead to greater polarization (Stroud, 2008; Sunstein, 2001). Lee, Choi, Kim, and Kim (2014) however found that those who engage more in online social networks are actually faced with greater differences, or heterogeneity, on social media. The activities people participate in (getting information, posting information, and discussing politics) actually increases exposure to ideas contrary to their own. They did find that as individuals engaged in more political discussions, however, the amount of engagement was positively associated with more polarized opinions. In other words, as individuals were exposed to diverse opinions, they did not develop a more open viewpoint.

Jane (2015) coined the term **e-bile** to describe the increase in hostile communication online, marked by vulgarity, hostility, or misogyny—noting that "contemporary netiquette not only tolerates—but often *expects*—internet interlocutors to reach for a hyperbolic rape, torture, or death threat the moment they disagree or disapprove" (p. 65). **Flaming** is the presentation of a message "showing the attributes such as hostility, aggression, intimidation, insults, offensiveness, unfriendly tone, uninhibited language, and sarcasm" (Turnage, 2008, p. 44). Style choices such as the type of font, use of excessive punctuation, or typing in all capital letters may be deemed as flaming. For example, accounting sends this flaming e-mail to a department head, "WOULD YOU PLEASE HAVE YOUR PEOPLE F***ING PROOFREAD??????!!!!!!!!! WE ARE SICK AND TIRED OF CLEANING UP THEIR MISTAKES!!!!!" Flaming is a metaphorical lighting on fire of a person or idea.

Leslie Jones, a cast member of "Saturday Night Live" and co-star of the 2016 reboot of the *Ghostbusters* franchise, was the victim of flaming on Twitter. She was "compared to primates, sent pornography, called racial slurs and accused of baiting the troll's ire just by having starred in the film. A fake Twitter account even emerged that posed as Jones to post racially insensitive hate speech" (Garofalo, 2016). Ms. Jones chose to leave the online social media network, stating: "I leave Twitter tonight with tears and a very sad heart. All this cause I did a movie. You can hate the movie but the s*** I got today . . . wrong" (July 18, 2016). While writing before the Jones attack, Jane (2015) notes, "Such e-mob 'lynchings' have become an escalating problem for girls and women whose public profiles does not extend beyond a low-key blog or occasional tweet" (p. 77).

De-Flaming at Work

Professional conflict consultants have a saying about e-mail and texting: "It's making us a lot of money." When an e-mail arrives at a worker's inbox, it lacks context. Despite the occasional happy emoticon, e-mail and texts have little of the nonverbal and vocal nuances to help a recipient interpret a message as it was intended. Frequently, business e-mails are written in a hurry, and, consequently, the sender's intention can be misunderstood. When people are upset, messages may seem angry and negative, a type of message awarded the searing moniker **flaming**. At worst, e-mail messages might contain diatribes that one later regrets, particularly because the message was written in a format easily forwarded to others (not to mention that corporations and state agencies often keep copies of all e-mails in permanent storage). A hasty e-mail can provide a kind of fame and immortality, but it's probably not the fame anybody really wants.

E-mail may begin an escalatory conflict spiral if it (1) uses aggressive tactics, (2) is so ambiguous that it is open to negative interpretation, (3) weakens
interpersonal bonds, and/or (4) is inappropriate for the problem to be solved
(Friedman & Currall, 2003). The last item primarily refers to the asynchronous
nature of e-mail, which makes it inappropriate for problems requiring immediate attention or creative responses.

Flaming can occur in a variety of contexts, including organizations. Turnage (2008) highlights factors that lead to flaming e-mails in the workplace including the immediacy of the communication,
informal norms in place about communication, lack of nonverbal channels to mitigate emotions
and misunderstandings, the solitary activity of writing a response without social buffering, and
allowing depersonalizing of the recipient. Once an inflammatory e-mail is received, the emotion is
easily reciprocated and often escalated.

Lee (2005), in his analysis of an online newsgroup, identified three types of conflict behavioral
strategies: competitive-dominating, cooperative-integrating, and avoiding (Table 17.2). Lee finds
that "group members develop various behavioral strategies to deal with the potentially disruptive
effects of flaming upon interpersonal relationships" (p. 401). When regulars in the newsgroup are
faced with outright aggression ("That's the stupidest comment ever and someone should knock
you around to see if you can get that head on straight"), flaming ("Nazis like you are ruining this
country"), or other competitive/dominating tactics, efforts to bring the conversation to civility
are offered in the form of cooperative/integrative strategies. Examples of cooperative/integrative
strategies may include apologizing ("Maybe I wasn't clear before, I'm sorry"), showing solidar-
ity ("We're all in this together and hopefully we can find common ground"), and normalizing
("Obviously we are very passionate about this topic"). The online strategies were very similar to
face-to-face conflict behaviors.

Within a closed system, like an organization or a closed LISTSERV, efforts to improve online
tone can be implemented through the establishment of explicit norms, or **netiquette** (Baruch,
2005). Examples might include a policy against profanity, all capital letters, or excessive punctuation (Turnage, 2008). In a work environment, handling conflict issues in person or by phone
may lessen the likelihood of misunderstandings and heightened emotions. Trainings on managing
stress and learning de-escalation strategies, such as taking a walk before hitting the send button,
may be prudent.

TABLE 17.2 Three Online Conflict Behavior Strategies

Competitive/Dominating	Cooperative/Integrative	Withdrawing
flaming	apologize	disregard the issue
denouncing	mediate	avoid the issue and person
aggression	joke to break ice	pretend
withdrawing	show solidarity	give in
defending self	ritualize	involve a third party
threatening	normalize	joke to deflect
requesting compliance	compromise/offer concessions	be silent
persuading	consider others	hide disagreements
joke at expense of other	talk about the problem	

TOOLBOX 17.1   Rules for Interactive Messaging

To use e-mail and interactive messaging more professionally and with less probability of starting or sustaining a conflict, follow these guidelines:

1. Never write an e-mail or text when you are consumed by emotion.
2. The more important the message, the more you should provide background context.
3. Always read your message before sending and think about how it could be misinterpreted.
4. Imagine the effect on you if anyone other than the intended recipient saw the message—other coworkers, your boss, everyone in the community, your mother.
5. Avoid sending jokes, cartoons, and non-business e-mails. They clutter up the inbox, and everyone doesn't have the same sense of humor.
6. If you've had e-mail misunderstandings in the past with a specific person, try to talk to that person face-to-face instead of sending the e-mail.
7. No flaming, no matter how tempting.
8. Put the person's name at the top of the e-mail to make it more personal and sign your name or initials at the end.

Summary

The increase in the use of social media and online communications warrants attention from researchers to address the unique challenges these forums pose. Several theories have been applied to the online social networking context. Self-determination theory (SDT) addresses how motivation to act is affected by both internal states and situational factors. The underlying motivation concerns how individuals get their needs of autonomy, competence, and relatedness met through social media.

Impression management theories, like Goffman's dramaturgical metaphor, explain how actors use performances to create a perception of themselves online. While Goffman's original theory was born in the 1950s, social networking sites offer a means to analyze the complex process. One primary difference in online impression management and the traditional approaches is how online spaces are moderated by curators. The curators set boundaries limiting actors' choices.

The Facebook and other social networks are deserving of attention given the immense growth and ubiquity of the platforms in everyday life. Facebook has redefined what "friends" are and require that we consider an expanded audience as we navigate the presentation of self. The concept of the lowest common denominator is one means by which we gauge appropriateness of what to disclose online. Three types of actors (the brave, the careful, and the inconsistent) approach self-disclosure differently as they consider the impact on select audiences.

Research into cyberbullying, particularly with regards to youth, is limited given the language differences in describing the events in question. Youth are more likely to categorize bullying as a physical engagement; they label online bullying as a drama or "just messing."

The rise of flaming and other dysfunctional behaviors in all contexts, including business, are disruptive and hurtful, no matter what it is called. In efforts to recognize the impact of incivility, suggestions for improving online communication behaviors were offered. Creating norms for respect and having options for addressing frustrations prior to responding were offered as mitigating activities for healthier online interactions.

Chapter Resources

Exercises

1. Watch the Netflix series *Black Mirror*, episode "Nosedive." What message does the program contain about social media? Are there aspects of social media in real life that resemble the program?
2. As a group, self-identify yourselves as high users of social media or those who use social media little to none at all. Discuss the benefits and costs of high or low social media usage.
3. As a group, discuss the styles of the brave, the careful, and the inconsistent person online. How are each perceived by members in your group in terms of their effectiveness as communicators?
4. As a group, discuss what rules could create a more civil discussion board for controversial topics?

Journal/Essay Topics

1. How do you manage your online image? Do you have different personas for different networks?
2. Have you experienced a negative impact on a relationship due to online activities? Analyze why this may have occurred according to a theory in the chapter.
3. What are some practical ways in which one person can combat online bullying?

Research Topics

1. Identify and join an interest group where individuals are part of an online community. Identify the elements that makes this a community. What needs are being met by the participants in the group? Are there rules or norms for communication among the group?
2. Do a review of an online comment section for a controversial news story. Identify categories of incivility (Table 17.1) that you find in the articles.

Mastery Case

Which ideas from the chapter shed light on Mastery Case 17A?

Anti-Social Media

Williams Market and Deli is a locally owned neighborhood grocery store in the suburbs of a large city. Grandpa Pappy Williams started the grocery in the 1950s, and his son Paul now manages the store. Paul's daughter, Kendra, moved back after college and is now Paul's Assistant Manager.

Kendra sees it as her job to utilize social media to better market the grocery and deli, particularly the little eatery she started where customers can get a sandwich and soup. There is a Williams Market and Deli Facebook page with 5,200 followers. There Kendra does "give-aways" and various contests to keep people engaged in the site. She personally responds to reviews on Yelp and Urban Spoon. These and other activities have really paid off by bringing in new customers.

However, they may have grown too fast. Some of the comments on Yelp and Facebook have addressed the slow service at the deli and the grumpiness of a couple of workers. Paul rarely has had to coach his people on customer service—things have always just worked. Daily now it seems that Kendra comes to him with yet another complaint about an interaction or the service. Some are legitimate, but most, according to Paul, are mean and unnecessary.

On Facebook, a few posters have created nicknames for the different workers. "Grumpy Gus" is the name for the sandwich maker, "Pimply" is the nickname for the teenage courtesy clerk, "Smilin' Dave" is the 20-something cashier, "Fluffy" is an older female cashier with a large hairstyle, and other names are even more mean-spirited. The staff are very uncomfortable with the nicknames. Kendra has tried to quell this trend, but it's caught on.

One day someone posted an anonymous Yelp comment about Smilin' Dave and said he now needs to be called "Sleazeball Dave" because he won't quit coming on to her when she comes to the store. Another Yelp reviewer agreed. Paul asked Dave about the complaints, which Dave denied, and Paul believed him. The conversations on Facebook turned to discussing whether Dave was a "sleaze" or just friendly. This escalated into graffiti on the market wall that claimed, "Watch out for Sleazy Dave!" Dave became so embarrassed that he told Paul he wanted to quit. Paul told Kendra to "Get rid of all of our social media. We don't need it." Paul doesn't understand that Kendra doesn't control anything but Facebook, and she doesn't want to lose this beneficial marketing tool.

References

Aakhus, M., & Rumsey, E. (2010). Crafting supportive communication online: A communication design analysis of conflict in an online support group. *Journal of Applied Communication Research, 38*(1), 65–84.

Arntfield, M. (2015). Toward a cybervictimology: Cyberbullying, routine activities theory, and the anti-sociality of social media. *Canadian Journal of Communication, 40*, 371–388.

Baruch, Y. (2005). Bullying on the net: Adverse behavior on e-mail and its impact. *Information and Management, 42*, 361–371.

CBS/AP. (2016, December 2). *Cyberbullying pushed Texas teen to commit suicide, family says.* Cbsnews.com/news/cyberbullying-pushed-texas-teen-commit-suicide-family/. Accessed 12 December 2016.

Chaulk, K., & Jones, T. (2011). Online obsessive relational intrusion: Further concerns about Facebook. *Journal of Family Violence, 26*, 245–254.

Clayton, R. B., Nagurney, A., & Smith, J. R. (2013). Cheating, breakup, and divorce: Is Facebook use to blame? *CyberPsychology, Behavior and Social Networking, 16*(10), 717–720.

Deci, E. L., & Ryan, R. M. (2000). The "what" and "why" of goal pursuits: Human needs and the self-determination theory. *Psychological Inquiry, 11*(4), 227–268.

Ferguson, R., Gutberg, J., Schattke, K., Paulin, M., & Jost, N. (2015). Self-determination theory, social media and charitable causes: An in-depth analysis of autonomous motivation. *European Journal of Social Psychology, 45*, 298–307.

Finley, K. (2015, October 8). A brief history of the end of the comments. *Wired.* Wired. com/2015/10/brief-history-of-the-demise-of-the-comments-timeline/. Accessed 30 September 2016.

Friedman, R. A., & Currall, S. C. (2003). Conflict escalation: Dispute exacerbating elements of e-mail communication. *Human Relations*, *56*(11), 1325–1347.

Garofalo, A. (2016, July 19). Why is Leslie Jones being attacked on Twitter? Celebrities react to the Ghostbusters' star's troll controversy. *International Business Times*. Ibtimes.com/why-leslie-jones-being-attacked-twitter-celebs-react-ghostbusters-stars-troll-2392946. Accessed 30 September 2016.

Gearhart, S., & Zhang, W. (2015). "Was it something I said?" "No, it was something you posted!" A study of the spiral of silence theory in social media contexts. *CyberPsychology, Behavior, and Social Networking*, *18*, 208–213.

Ging, D., & Norman, J. O. (2016). Cyberbullying, conflict management or just messing? Teenage girls' understandings and experiences of gender, friendship, and conflict on Facebook in an Irish second-level school. *Feminist Media Studies*, *16*(5), 805–821.

Goffman, E. (1959). *The presentation of self in everyday life*. New York: Anchor Books.

Hertlein, K. M. (2012). Digital dwelling: Technology in couple and family relationships. *Family Relations*, *61*, 374–387.

Hogan, B. (2010). The presentation of self in the age of social media: Distinguishing performances and exhibitions online. *Bulletin of Science, Technology Society*, *30*(6), 377–386.

Internet livestats. Internetlivestats.com. Accessed 25 January 2017.

Jane, E. A. (2015). Flaming? What Flaming? The pitfalls and potentials of researching online hostility. *Ethics and Information Technology*, *17*, 65–87.

Kenski, K., Coe, K., & Rains, S. (2012, October 13). *Patterns and determinants of civility in online discussions*. Final Report to the National Institute for Civil Discourse. University of Arizona. Nicd.arizona.edu/research-report/patterns-and-determinants-civility. Accessed 8 September 2016.

Kim, J., & Ahn, J. (2013, November 1–5). *The show must go on: The presentation of self during interpersonal conflict on Facebook*. Proceedings of the 76th ASIS&T Annual Meeting: Beyond the Cloud: Rethinking Information Boundaries, 1–10, Montreal, Quebec.

Kirby, E. J. (2016, Dec 5). The city getting rich from fake news. *BBC News*. BBC.com. Accessed 16 December 2016.

Lee, H. (2005). Behavioral strategies for dealing with flaming in an online forum. *The Sociological Quarterly*, *46*, 385–403.

Lee, J. K., Choi, J., Kim, C., & Kim, Y. (2014). Social media, network heterogeneity, and opinion polarization. *Journal of Communication*, *64*, 702–722.

Lenhart, A. (2015, April 9). *Teens, social media, and technology: Overview 2015*. Washington, DC: Pew Internet American Life Project. Pewinternet.org/2015/04/09/teens-social-media-technology-2015/. Accessed 11 November 2016.

Lenhart, A., Madden, M., Smith, A., Purcell, K., Zickuhr, K., & Rainie, L. (2011, November 9). *Teens, kindness and cruelty on social network sites*. Washington, DC: Pew Internet American Life Project. www.pewinternet.org/2011/11/09/teens-kindness-and-cruelty-on-social-network-sites/ AccessedPewinternet.org. Accessed 12 November 2016.

Lu, A. (2014, July 13). Facebook scraps ban on nipple photos because it's high time to "free the nipple." *Bustle*. Bustle.com/articles/28056-facebook-scraps-ban-on-nipple-photos-because-its-high-time-to-free-the-nipple. Accessed 28 September 2016.

Marshall, T. (2012). Facebook surveillance of former romantic partners: Associations with postbreakup recovery and personal growth. *CyberPsychology, Behavior and Social Networking*, *15*, 521–526.

Marwick, A. E., & Boyd, D. (2011). I tweet honestly, I tweet passionately: Twitter users, context collapse, and the imagined audience. *New Media & Society*, *13*, 114–133.

Marwick, A. E., & Boyd, D. (2014). 'It's just drama': teen perspectives on conflict and aggression in a networked era. *Journal of Youth Studies*, *17*(9), 1187–1204.

Mehta, S. (2016, November 3). Melania Trump lamented cyberbullying, and the Internet went crazy. *Los Angeles Times*. Latimes.com/la-na-trailguide-updates-melania-trump-lamented-cyberbullying-1478211766-htmlstory.html. Accessed 3 November 2016.

Molina, D. K., Heiselt, A., & Justice, C. (2015). From matchmaker to mediator: Shifting trends in roommate relationships in an era of individualism, diversity, conflict and social media. *The Journal of College and University Student Housing, 41*(2), 104–117.

Nelson, S. C. (2014, June 12). Facebook breastfeeding photo ban lifted after #FreeTheNipple Campaign. *The Huffington Post*. Huffingtonpost.co.uk/2014/06/11/facebook-breastfeeding-photo-ban-lifted-freethenipple-campaign-pictures_n_5484788.html. Accessed 14 January 2017.

Number of monthly active Facebook users worldwide as of 1st quarter 2017. (2017). *Statista*. Statista.com. Accessed 9 July 2017.

Read, M. (2016, November 9). Donald Trump won because of Facebook. *New York Magazine*. Nymag.com. Accessed 16 December 2016.

Samnani, A., & Singh, P. (2012). 20 years of workplace bullying research: A review of the antecedents and consequences of bullying in the workplace. *Aggression and Violent Behavior, 17*(6), 581–589.

Stroud, N. J. (2008). Media use and political predispositions: Revisiting the concept of selective exposure. *Political Behavior, 30*, 341–366.

Sunstein, C. (2001). *Republic.com*. Princeton: Princeton University Press.

Turnage, A. K. (2008). Email flaming behaviors and organizational conflict. *Journal of Computer-Mediated Communication, 13*, 43–59.

Appendix

Sample Mediation Case: Discontented Roommates

Note: Do not read this appendix unless told to do so by your instructor.

Mediator Case Notes

Mediator Instructions

Using the information in Chapter 12 on how to conduct a mediation, act as the impartial and neutral third party to mediate the following case. Read only the instructions and information on this page. Do not read the confidential information for Marty or Charlie on the next pages.

Case Information

The two parties (Marty and Charlie) approached the student mediation center to help them with their roommate dispute.

You received these pre-mediation notes from your case developer:

- The two disputants live in an apartment off campus.
- They both are juniors and have one year remaining.
- Each person has a private room.
- The individuals are not and have never been romantically involved with each other.
- They share the rest of the apartment.

Your goal as the mediator is to help the parties resolve their differences without making suggestions or intruding into "their" solution. Before beginning the mediation, think for a moment about open-ended questions or background that might be useful to ask to get the specifics of their conflict out on the table, such as these:

- How long have you been living in this apartment?
- What are your concerns about the living situation?
- What are your views of what it means to be a good roommate?
- What are your views on appropriate behavior? [insert a concern they raise. For example, roommates are often concerned about cleanliness or noise.]
- How long has [this issue] been a problem for you?
- What is your daily schedule like?
- When do you do your studying?

Confidential Information for Marty

Note: Read this page only if you are assigned the role of Marty

Instructions

Your task is to play the role of Marty. Read only the instructions and the confidential case information here. Do not read the confidential information for Charlie on the following pages. The case information may not include every detail that will come up during the role-play. For example, the mediator may ask you what kind of music you like or other details that are not specifically discussed in the case information. When that happens, draw on your life experience and make up an answer. Try not to make up answers that are too exotic or bizarre. For example, if the mediator asks what your concerns are, don't make up a boa constrictor snake that gets loose in the apartment.

Case Information

- You are a junior and this is your first experience living off campus.
- You are from a small farm town in a rural part of the state. You have three brothers and two sisters.
- In your family, everybody was always in everybody else's business. Wanting to know every detail of their lives was the basis of daily conversation. You assume that everyone is the same and that borrowing from your roommate is just like borrowing things in your family, i.e., "what's yours is mine."
- You also share all sorts of information with your roommate, who has said several times that you were giving "too much information."
- Classes always were pretty easy for you in high school and you got good grades. However, your grades have declined considerably this semester, probably because you've been having a good time.
- You like to have your friends over on weekends to watch cable, and sometimes during the week. You have really good parties, although they sometimes leave the place full of pizza boxes and other trash.
- Lately Charlie has been giving you dirty looks and making snide comments about the place "smelling like Marty's family pig sty." You don't like insults about your family, so you've been rude back. Your room might be a little smelly, but you'll take your laundry home in a couple of weeks for your mom to wash.
- When your roommate threatened to move out and leave you with the lease, you decided to go to mediation to work things out. You can't afford the apartment by yourself.

Your Interests

- You want to stay in the apartment.
- You want Charlie to stop making rude comments.
- You want to get good enough grades to stay in college.
- You want your friends to be able to visit you.

Confidential Information for Charlie

Note: Read this page only if you have been assigned to play the role of Charlie.

Instructions

Your task is to play the role of Charlie. Read only the instructions and the confidential case information here. Do not read the confidential information for Marty. The case information may not include every detail that will come up during the role play. For example, the mediator may ask you what kind of music you like or other details that are not specifically discussed in the case information. When that happens, draw on your life experience and make up an answer. Try not to make up answers that are too exotic or bizarre. For example, if the mediator asks what your concerns are, don't make up a boa constrictor snake that gets loose in the apartment.

Case Information

- You are a junior and this is your first experience living off campus.
- You are from the biggest city in the state and grew up with your single mom.
- Your mom worked long hours to keep the two of you housed and to save for your college tuition and expenses, so you take the responsibility to do well in college very seriously.
- Because you know how hard your mom worked to get you to college, you are determined to succeed. You like to have fun on weekends, but getting good grades is your first priority. You study every night.
- You like Marty and thought that rooming together would be easy. It isn't. Marty parties until three in the morning at least one school night every week—so it is hard for you to study or to get to sleep for your morning classes. Maybe Marty doesn't care about flunking out, but you do!
- You have noticed occasionally that Marty is wearing a shirt or jacket of yours without asking. You would let Marty borrow it if asked, but are bothered at how inconsiderate this behavior is—especially when items come back dirty.
- Marty also has turned out to be a pig. Marty's room really is smelly from the dirty laundry that has piled up, and you're pretty sure that Marty never does any cleaning. You're sick of it.
- You have hinted around several times that Marty should help out cleaning the apartment, and specifically asked Marty to clean the bathroom once in a while or pick up immediately after a party, and you just got these blank looks back. The fact that Marty ignores you really ticks you off, and you have taken to making a few snide comments about "farm kids and their pig sty houses coming to the big city." You feel a little bad about the comments, but think Marty had it coming—and at least you are getting some reaction.
- You told your roommate that if things don't change immediately you will move out.

Your Interests

- You have to be able to study and get good grades.
- You want to be asked before someone borrows your things, and you want them returned in the same condition they were in before being borrowed.
- You need to be able to get to sleep at a decent hour on school nights.
- You want to live in a place that doesn't stink.
- You want Marty to share in the cleaning responsibilities.

Glossary

The glossary gives general definitions for common terms used in conflict management studies. Particular theories or techniques may use a variation on the common meaning of a term.

A

Abstract: Ideas that are not specific or are vague.

Accommodation cultural style: A style or tactic of response to conflict by complying with the other's wishes.

Active listening: The process of purposefully attending to the speaker's expressed and unexpressed messages (see mindfulness).

Adjudication: Litigation or legal processes.

Affect/Affective event: Anything that causes an emotional response.

Alternative dispute resolution (ADR): Conflict resolution processes that provide alternatives to legal actions, such as mediation or arbitration.

Anchor point: In negotiation over fixed items, the first offer that sets one end of the negotiation range.

Anger: A secondary emotion where one is irritated, annoyed, upset, or enraged by a stimulus that, on deeper analysis, was rooted in fear, hurt, or some other primary emotion.

Appreciative listening: Attending to the artfulness of a message.

Approach-approach conflict: The choice between two equally attractive options.

Approach-avoid conflict: The choice between two opposing options, one negative and one positive.

Arbitrator: A third party who investigates and makes a decision for the parties in a conflict (see binding arbitration).

Argument: Providing reasons to support an assertion or claim.

Argumentativeness: A tendency to defend one's position from a competitive stance.

Assertiveness: The ability to advance one's thoughts or goals without aggression.

Assurances: Communicating to a partner the expectation of a future together.

Attitude: A relatively stable predisposition to act or believe in specific ways.

Attribution error: In attribution theory, where one ascribes motivations for another's behavior to a personality or character trait when it actually results from a situational influence, or vice versa.

Attribution theory: The concept that people consistently make sense of the world by assigning meaning and motives to others' behaviors.

Autonomy: A state of independence from the influence of others.

Avoidance: A style or tactic in response to conflict not to engage directly in conflict.

Avoid-avoid conflict: The choice between two equally unattractive options.

B

Balanced Model of Mediation: A mediation model that considers conciliation and problem-solving approaches equally valuable depending on the circumstances.

Bargaining: Interactions between parties for the purpose of individual and/or joint goal attainment (also called negotiation).

Bargaining range: The areas of overlap in the parties' goals where a beneficial outcome might be reached.

Barnlund's six views: A theory that each person in a conversation has three views: my view of myself, my view of you, and my view of how you view me.

BATNA: Best alternative to no agreement.

Biased punctuation: A tendency of individuals to see the cause of a conflict as starting from the other person's actions.

Binding arbitration: A third party (arbitrator) who makes a decision where the parties have agreed that they will implement the arbitrator's decision.

Boulwarism/Boulware strategy: In negotiation, making a reasonable first offer on a take-it-or-leave-it basis without further bargaining.

Boundary management theory/Communication privacy management theory: An explanation of how individuals set limits around their personal interactions or relationships.

Brainstorming: A communication technique to spur creativity and quantity of ideas in problem solving.

Bullying: Frequent harassment over time that harms the intended recipient (also called mobbing and psychological terror).

C

Cascade model: Gottman's theory that four behaviors (criticism, contempt, defensiveness, and stone-walling) create a spiral of isolation and loneliness leading to relational dissatisfaction and dissolution.

Chain of command: A formal or informal hierarchical ranking system where each rank has decision-making authority over those of lower rank (see also hierarchy of authority and organizational chart).

Channel/Communication channel: The medium through which a message is conveyed.

Choice point: A critical moment during an interaction when one choice of how to respond will set the tone for future interaction and possibly change the direction of a relationship.

Civility: Showing respect for others.

Close-ended questions: Questions answerable with limited options, such as "yes" or "no," or other forced choice answers; opposite of open-ended questions.

Closure: The final phase in the Balanced Mediation Model where the agreement is summarized or parties told the next steps if the mediation participants fail to reach agreement.

Coalition: A group that unites on a particular issue to advance mutual goals.

Codependence: A pathological condition characterized by a person's overreliance on another to satisfy his or her needs, often demonstrated by the manipulation of one person by another.

Coercion/Coercive power: Forcing others to comply (also called power-over).

Collaboration: A style of conflict management where parties work until all agree that the chosen solution is the best possible solution available for all parties.

Collectivist culture: A society that values the group above the individual.

Commonality: Any issue, circumstance, or goal shared by all parties.

Communication infidelity: Being unfaithful to a partner through verbal or simulated intimacy with another person without physical sexual contact.

Compensational forgiveness: Giving forgiveness only after receiving some value to compensate for your loss (also called restitutional forgiveness).

Competition: Seeking to advance one's personal goals without consideration of others' goals.

Competitive worldview: A social construct in which the way humans interact is based on the assumption that the only choices are win, lose, or tie (also called distributive).

Comprehensive Conflict Checklist: An analysis tool that asks a series of wide-ranging and thorough questions to examine a conflict.

Comprehensive listening: Attending to acquire the overall meaning of a message (see also content paraphrasing).

Compromise: A style or tactic in response to conflict where each party gives up some part of goal achievement in order to reach agreement.

Concession: Something given to the other party in a negotiation.

Conciliation: The process of overcoming past difficulties or to reconcile a relationship.

Concrete/Concreteness: Very specific ideas or behaviors.

Confidentiality: A promise during mediation that information will be not be shared with others, unless required by law.

Conflict assessment: Formal analysis of a conflict using an assessment tool.

Conflict coaching: Part of a systematic response to conflict in organizations where individuals are provided with private coaching to improve their conflict and communication skills.

Conflict management style: An individual's preferred or habitual responses to conflict situations.

Conflict management system: An organization's systematic response to conflict by providing multiple formal and informal access points for the resolution of conflicts.

Conflict Road Map: An assessment tool based on Wehr's large group conflict and adapted to the interpersonal conflict context.

Connotative meaning: An individualized reaction to a word derived from one's personal association or experience with it.

Consensus: A decision-making method where, after all parties have weighed in on the issue, a decision emerges that all parties agree to support.

Constructive conflict: Conflict that moves toward positive outcomes.

Constructivism: An interaction theory advanced by Delia and others, that holds individuals create meaning and interpret reality through a series of personal constructs or schemas.

Content paraphrasing: A communication technique to summarize the denotative message of the speaker.

Context collapse: A phenomenon of information being equally available to one's friends, family, work, and other persons because of the ubiquitous nature of the Internet.

Contingency Agreement: A tentative agreement that is open to renegotiation depending on how the remaining negotiation items are settled, the acquisition of new information, or the outcome of benchmarks for future performance.

Conversational style: Speech habits, vocal patterns, and preferred means of expression.

Cool posing: Socially appropriate behaviors adopted when one is angry and expression of anger could have severe consequences.

Cooperative worldview: The view that with work and creativity, the needs of all people can be met (also called mutual gains, interest-based, or win-win).

Creating value: Using the decision-making process to create outcomes that add benefit to the individuals involved.

Culture: Common assumptions, tendencies, and experiences shared by a group.

Currency/Power currency: A social exchange theory concept that controlling assets, abilities, traits, and so on, valued by others creates power.

Cyberbullying: Bullying through the Internet, text messaging, or other electronic media.

D

Defense-provoking: Types of communicative behaviors posited by Gibb to provoke protective or negative reactions.

Deficit language: Framing things negatively or as a deficiency.

Demand-withdrawal pattern: Where one partner pursues a conflict, causing the other to avoid, thereby increasing the efforts of the first partner to pursue, in an escalating spiral.

Denotative meaning: The literal dictionary definition of a word.

Descriptive language/descriptive statements: Communicating direct observations about behaviors without adding evaluation or interpretation.

Destructive conflict: Conflict that moves toward destructive outcomes.

Deviance: In social science research, any variation from the norm.

Dialectical tension: A pull between opposing forces.

Dialogic (relational) listening: Taking turns speaking and listening for the purpose of mutual understanding.

Directiveness: In mediation, how tightly the mediator controls the process and communication during a mediation session.

Directness: How open and clear an individual is about thoughts, goals, or interests.

Disclosiveness: The level of personal information an individual reveals to others.

Discriminative listening: Attending to particular signals; isolating particular words or sounds from the mass of background sound.

Discussant cultural style: An intercultural conflict style that is low in emotional expressiveness and high in direct communication.

Disputants: The individuals invested in the outcome of a conflict or a mediation.

Dissonance: A state where an individual holds conflicting attitudes, beliefs, or values; the presence of an attitude, value, or belief that is in direct conflict with one's behavior.

Distressful ideals hypothesis: When expectations for relationship communication do not match reality, relationship satisfaction decreases.

Distributive conflict/Distributive negotiation: A competitive view that conflicts are win-lose where what is at stake will be divided among those in the conflict.

Dyad/Dyadic communication: Communication between two people.

Dynamic cultural style: An intercultural conflict style that is high in emotional expressiveness and low in directiveness.

Dysfunctional family: Families that create or exist in a toxic environment or that do not provide emotional or social support to its members.

Dysfunctional roles: Roles assumed for personal reasons that detract from relationship maintenance or task accomplishment.

E

E-bile: Hostile, vulgar, misogynistic, racist, or other negative online communication.

Echo technique: Repeating a comment back to the speaker.

Egocentrism: Singular focus on one's personal needs and desires.

Emotional disengagement: The ability to remove one's emotions from a highly emotional situation or interaction—can be a positive skill allowing for one to remain calm, but can also be a means to avoid intimacy.

Emotional intelligence/EQ or EI: A counterpart to intellectual intelligence (IQ) that holds that individuals possess measurable levels of self-awareness, emotion management, self-motivation, awareness of others, and relationship management.

Emotional labor: The work of displaying or containing certain psychological or physical reactions to situations on the job.

Emotional paraphrase: A listening technique to show empathy and validate the feelings of others, often to the effect of decreasing the emotional affect in others.

Emotional dissonance: The conflict experienced between the emotion one feels and the emotion one displays to conform with workplace norms and rules.

Empathetic listening: Attending to a message in order to understand another person's perspective without evaluation or criticism.

Empathy: The ability to understand, but not necessarily share or agree with, another person's view or emotional state.

Employee assistance program: A workplace intervention program to assist employees and their families in managing personal issues.

Empowerment: Identifying and making apparent power resources for the purpose of increasing an individual's independence and self-determination (also called power-to).

Enculturation: The informal process through which individuals learn social or group rules, customs, and appropriate behaviors.

Engagement cultural style: An intercultural conflict style that is high in expressiveness of emotions and high in directness of expression.

Entitlement: A view that one is owed privileges or special treatment.

Escalation: A communication behavior where a response is designed to expand the size, scope, or intensity of the conflict.

Essentializing/Essentialists' approach: Assuming that all persons in a gender, social, racial, or ethnic group think essentially the same way or have the same experiences.

Ethnocentric errors: Thinking errors caused by cultural stereotyping or essentializing.

Evaluative (critical) listening: Attending to a message in order to judge it.

Evaluative language: Communicating to the other an attribution of his or her motivation or to interpret behavior as having purposeful intent (generally negative).

Expectation management: Communication to bring the perceptions and expectations held by different people closer together.

Exchange theory: The idea that people make life choices based on a cost-benefit analysis of what better meets personal goals.

Expectancy violation: A mismatch between what is expected and what occurs.

Expectational forgiveness: Forgiving because of social pressure or a belief that it is the right thing to do. In lawful expectational forgiveness, you are required by rule or law to demonstrate surface forgiveness.

Expert power: Power derived from having knowledge or skills valued by others.

Extended family: Individuals related but not a part of the immediate familial structure; those outside of the nuclear family—typically referring to multigenerational families.

External attribution: Assigning motive to factors external to the individual, such as the environment or outside circumstances.

Externalizations: External attributions.

Extrovert: A personality type that gains personal energy by socializing and being with other people; a personality trait where one is comfortable with personal expression.

F

Face: The public or private image one holds about oneself (also called self-face).

Face goals: Goals regarding the expression of self-worth, pride, or self-respect.

Face-to-face (FtF) communication: Communication occurring in the same physical space.

Facework: Active attempts to moderate or manage one's self-image or image presented to others; can also apply to attempts to modify the self-image of another person.

Fake apologies: Verbalizations of insincere apology.

Family: A self-defined group of intimates who create and maintain an identity among themselves and with others (see also nuclear family extended family, gay/lesbian family, nontraditional family, family of origin).

Family boundaries: Determinations of who is included in the family group and who is intentionally excluded by social or legal action.

Family communication: The quantity and quality of interactions among family members that create their unique rules, customs, style, and functionality.

Family meeting/Family home night: A ritualized time and format for a family to gather together to work on their relationship, to engage in a joint activity, or to discuss family issues.

Family of choice: A group that forms a long-term association and/or residence (also called voluntary families).

Family of origin: The family into which one was born and/or raised.

Family ritual: Customary events or repeated patterns of interaction specific to a family.

Family stories: Narratives repeatedly told about family members or family events that serve to sustain rules, customs, or teach lessons.

Fear: A primary emotion rooted in a psychological belief that harm will result if a stimulus occurs.

Feeling paraphrase: A listening technique to show empathy and validate the emotions of others, often to the effect of decreasing the emotional affect in others.

Field theory: Developed by Lewin and others; the theory suggests there are types of forces that drive conflict and forces that restrain conflict.

Flaming: Attacks on others via electronic media, such as e-mail, chat rooms, blogs, or text messaging.

Flashpoint: The event that precipitates a conflict episode (also called triggering events).

Flat organizational hierarchy: An organization with fewer layers of management between workers and upper management.

Fogging: A technique of admitting to accusations that are true but not relevant to the issue in discussion.

Forgiveness: Accepting an apology for hurt caused by another person or group or giving up active mulling about the offense.

Fractionation/Fractionator: A style or tactic of conflict to respond to issues by breaking them down into smaller parts for problem solving. A fractionator is someone who uses fractionation.

Frame: How an idea is defined.

Future focus: A conflict management technique that requires disputants to attend to the changes to be made in the existing circumstances instead of focusing on past events, previous problems, or root causes.

G

Game theory: A theory that models the outcomes of conflict based on choices made by players through a rational process.

Gaslighting: Achieving personal goals by inducing the others to question their sanity.

Gay/lesbian family: A same-sex couple and their children.

Genderlect: A hypothesis that differences in women and men's speech are caused by socialization.

Generational cohort: An age group influenced by similar events or experiences.

Genuine forgiveness: Forgiveness that is sincere and intentional.

Goal: The end or desired condition.

Gregorc styles model: A personal style classification based on whether individuals are abstract or concrete and sequential or random.

Grievance story: The portrayal of oneself in conversations to others as a victim.

Group: A small group typically includes three to twelve people who interact meaningfully with each other long enough to form norms and other group dynamic features.

Group forgiveness: The giving or asking of one group to forgive another for past injustices.

Groupthink: A phenomenon posited by Janis that explains how highly cohesive groups function to make bad decisions.

Gunnysacking: Holding complaints or issues (as if collecting them in a sack) until one cannot bear any more. Then the entire sack of issues is dumped on the other person.

H

Hearing: An automatic physiological process of receiving sounds.

Heteronormativity: Assuming all people are heterosexual in research and policy.

Hierarchy of authority: A formal or informal ranking of who has designated decision-making power in a family, group, or organization (see also chain of command, organizational chart).

High-context culture: A concept developed by Hall that some cultures interpret most of the meaning in a message from the general social and physical environment where the message occurs.

High-rights: A view that one's personal goals should receive precedence.

Hollow forgiveness: Accepting an apology without giving up the inner hurt.

Hypothetical offer: A negotiation tactic to make an offer without actually putting the offer on the table.

I

Illusion of transparency: The assumption that one's motives and emotional states have been expressed enough that others should understand (even when no direct conversation has occurred on that topic).

Imagined interaction: An analysis tool to rehearse mentally different conflict tactics and strategies.

Impartiality: In negotiations, a person (usually a third party) who has no stake in the outcome of a dispute; the state of being divested in the outcome.

Impasse: In negotiation, a state where the parties are stuck and can make no progress toward resolution.

Impulse control: The ability to moderate emotional and spontaneous reactions.

Incompatibility: Goals or other actions that do not fit well together.

Individualistic culture: A society that values the individual over the group.

Initial goals: Goals held by individuals at the beginning of a conflict.

In-group: The small group with which an individual most identifies.

In-process goals: Goals that evolve and change as a conflict episode progresses.

Integrative engagement model/style: A conflict management style that is cooperative and seeks mutually beneficial outcomes for all parties.

Integrative power: The concept that the ability to influence is based on the connections between individuals.

Interaction theories: Explanations that focus on the communication that occurs between people in conflict rather than on an individual or internal processes.

Interactive conflict analysis: An assessment tool for disputants to work through past, present, and future views of an issue.

Intercultural Conflict Style Inventory: An intercultural conflict style diagnostic test that measures how directly issues and emotion are expressed.

Interdependent/Interdependence: A state where one thing or person requires another thing or person to meet goals.

Interest: A need that drives a goal.

Interest-based bargaining: Negotiating or working through conflict by discovering each person's underlying needs.

Internal attributions: Assuming a behavior was caused by factors inherent to the person, such as personality, values, or characteristics, and not some external situation.

Internal rationalizing process: The reasoning within oneself justifying one's own beliefs or actions.

Interpersonal conflict: A struggle among a small number of interdependent people (usually two) arising from perceived interference with goal achievement.

Interpersonal forgiveness: Forgiveness given or received in an interpersonal context.

Interpersonal reconciliation: Reconciliation that is experienced in an interpersonal context.

Intrapersonal communication: Communication within oneself; self-dialogue.

Intrapersonal conflict: An internal struggle with competing personal goals.

Introvert: A personality type that gains personal energy by solitude or intimate interactions; a personality trait where one may be uncomfortable expressing oneself.

Intrusiveness: In the context of mediation, a mediator who makes suggestions to the parties on what the solution could or should be.

Issue: In conflict, that which must be resolved.

"I" statement: A statement taking responsibility for one's personal feelings or thoughts.

L

Latent conflict: Issues that have potential for conflict that the parties do not yet perceive to be a problem.

Lawful expectational forgiveness: Forgiving because of social pressure or a belief that it is the right thing to do. In lawful expectational forgiveness, you are required by rule or law to demonstrate surface forgiveness.

Leadership: A role assumed to channel the resources and energy of a group toward accomplishing its goal.

Legitimate power: Institutional influence derived from titles, offices held, or rightful authority within a structure.

Listening: The physical and psychological processing of aural stimuli (see active listening, appreciative listening, comprehensive listening, content paraphrase, discriminative listening, emotional paraphrase, empathic listening, evaluative listening, and feeling paraphrase).

Lose/lose: A resolution of conflict where both parties sacrifice some needs in order to reach agreement; the actual outcome of many win/lose negotiations where the loser makes sure the winner is not able to benefit from the victory.

Low-context culture: A concept developed by Hall that certain cultures gain most of the meaning in messages in the words and symbols that are used apart from the environment in which they were expressed.

Lowest common denominator of acceptability: Determining the level of risk in communicating information or opinions online given the diversity of the audience who may attend (then speaking at a level that offends no one).

M

Maintenance role: A role assumed to foster the relationship health among individuals in a dyad or a group.

Mapping: Diagramming conflict factors in order to determine primary issues and best strategies for managing negotiations; an assessment tool based on the Australian Conflict Resolution Network Needs and Fears Worksheet.

Maslow's hierarchy of needs: A theory that individuals focus on their unmet needs in a specific order and will only go on to the next set of needs when the prior are met. The first three levels are the most basic needs. (1) Physiological (enough food, water, sleep, sex), (2) Safety (personal and economic security), (3) Love/Belonging (friendship, family, intimacy), (4) Self-esteem (confidence, achievement, respect), (5) Self-actualization (development of morality, creativity, acceptance of others and factual reality).

Mechanical model: The mistaken idea that communication processes work like machines where one component can be removed and understood apart from the system in which it occurs.

Mediation: The assistance of a neutral and impartial third party who facilitates the parties in creating their own mutually agreeable outcome.

Mediator monologue: A presentation of the opening statement by the mediator (also called mediator opening statement).

Meeting management: Leadership activities to coordinate group interactions and make them effective.

Mentoring: The guidance by an experienced employee given to newcomers on how to behave in an organization, how to perform a job, and/or how to achieve professional goals.

Meta-analysis: A research methodology that mines past studies to discover trends.

Metacommunication: Focusing discussion on the interaction process; communication about communication.

Mindfulness: A personal commitment and mental state to attend fully to someone without distraction (see active listening).

Mirroring: Reflecting back the same tactics or communication behaviors that another person uses.

Mixed motive: Situations where an individual's goals are somewhat cooperative and somewhat competitive.

Mulling: Reliving or obsessively replaying a past interaction.

Multitasking: Doing one thing while mentally or physically engaging in another thing.

Mutual gains: The view that through interest-based negotiations the needs of all parties can be met to some extent (also called cooperative, integrative, win-win, interest-based bargaining).

Myers-Briggs Type Indicator: A personality style test based on the Jungian theory of psychological types that assesses preferences in four dichotomous areas: extroversion/introversion, intuition/ sensing, feeling/thinking, and perception/judging.

N

Nature: A theory that holds one's personality and behavior are influenced by biological development rather than social development.

Negative interdependence: A state where if one person achieves a goal, the other person will not.

Negative settlement range: In bargaining, a gap between the bargaining ranges of the individuals where there is no overlap in their preferred outcomes.

Negotiation: Interactions between parties for the purpose of individual and/or joint goal attainment (also called bargaining).

Neutral/Neutrality: In negotiations, a person (usually a third party) who has no relationship to the parties in a dispute or no preference for either party.

Netiquette: Explicit norms for online behavior.

Nontraditional family: A family unit that is structurally different than the normative expectation of a mother, father, and their biological children.

Norm: An unwritten rule that governs how people behave.

Nuclear family: A Western conceptualization of a family group consisting of parents (generally a mother and father) and their children; the core family unit as compared to the extended family.

Nurture: A theory that holds one's personality and behavior are influenced by social development as opposed to biological development.

O

Open door policy: A supervisor's willingness to explore ideas and hold conversations with employees at any time.

Open-ended questions: Questions designed to elicit answers that demonstrate the speaker's opinions, perceptions, and personal experiences; opposite of close-ended questions.

Opening statement: The first phase in the mediation process where the mediator outlines the mediation process and the guidelines governing roles and expectations to be followed (also called mediator monologue).

Openness: A measure of how much information is shared with others.

Organizational chart: A diagram listing the formal hierarchy of authority in an organization and who reports to whom (see also hierarchy of authority and chain of command).

Organizational culture: The formal or informal norms, rules, and assumptions of how to behave and what it means to be a member of that organization; the expressed values of an organization and its members.

Organizational misbehavior: Any action that violates the organization's formal or informal rules, culture, or policies.

P

Parties: The individuals in a conflict.

Pause gap: The pause between the end of one person's utterance and the beginning of the next.

Perception: The process through which stimuli are attended to, interpreted, and evaluated.

Perceptual filters: Biases, values, experiences, attitudes, and other factors that affect how stimuli are interpreted and evaluated.

Personal conflict coaching: See conflict coaching.

Personality style: A relatively stable pattern of thinking and processing information that impacts behavior.

Position: A demand, proposed solution, or fixed outcome statement.

Positive intentions: The general benefit one hoped for when beginning something new or a new relationship.

Positive interdependence: A state where one person will achieve a personal goal when the other person achieves a personal goal.

Positive settlement range: The overlap in bargaining positions in which a settlement may be created.

Positivity: The demeanor a couple projects about how happy they are together.

Postponement: A tactic of deferring discussion of the conflict to a specific time.

Power: The ability to influence others or to bring about desired outcomes.

Power currency: Any possession, trait, or action that is valued by someone else that can be used to gain influence with that person.

Power management: The concept that power may need to be increased or decreased when differences are too great before meaningful conflict management or negotiation can occur (formerly called power balancing).

Power differences approach: A view explaining differences in how men and women communicate based more on situational than biological factors.

Presentation of self theory: Individuals act out behaviors to manage their self-image and how others perceive them.

Prisoner's Dilemma: A classic game theory example using two criminals pitted against each other during police interrogation.

Privilege: The taking of an advantage—whether earned or unearned; the existence of an advantage.

Probing questions: Questions aimed to uncover additional details.

Problem-solving mediation: A philosophical approach to mediation that is issue-centered and focused more on problems than on the disputant's emotions.

Process goal: In negotiation, a party's desired means of how an event should happen or a negotiation should proceed.

Promise: A tactic of stating a positive reward will occur if the other party complies with certain conditions.

Provisionalness/Provisionalism: The ability to withhold judgment or offering solutions until all information is on the table; the state of being open-minded to ideas and beliefs that are not personally held.

Pseudo-conflict: Conflicts caused by misinterpretations and misinformation.

Psychodynamic theory: Freud's psychological theory that behavior is motivated by both the conscious and subconscious mind where the id, ego, and superego are all vying for control.

Q

Quality control circle: A strategy adopted from Japanese management theory where individuals from different parts of the organization work together to resolve problems and make suggestions for improvement.

Quid pro quo: A negotiation strategy of offering something for something.

R

Rapport talk: Tannen's description of a cooperative conversational style engaged in for the purpose of building a relationship or affirming the connection between the parties.

Reality testing: Comparing decisions to feasibility and workability criteria.

Reconciliation: The rebuilding of a relationship broken or tarnished in conflict.

Referent power: Individual power derived from association with power sources or personality traits that others value.

Reformed sinner: A negotiation tactic of admitting a past mistake while changing negotiation tactics.

Reframing: A technique to move an issue or topic from a narrow interest or negative frame into a larger or neutral frame where defensiveness is decreased and productive negotiation is encouraged.

Relational framing: Making a statement of commitment to the relationship before raising a potentially conflictual topic.

Relationship goal: A party's preference for the depth or type of connection to another person.

Relationship maintenance: The mindset and behaviors necessary to keep relationships healthy, stable, and trending in the desired direction.

Repair work: Intentional behaviors and communication intended to mitigate the negative effects of conflict or disagreement.

Report talk: Tannen's description of a competitive conversational style engaged in for the purpose of convincing the other, presenting definitive information, or otherwise gaining a competitive advantage in the interaction.

Responsiveness: The level of emotion displayed or information given.

Restitutional forgiveness: Forgiving after being compensated for your loss (also called compensational forgiveness).

Restorative justice: A view that fairness is better served by bringing balance to a community or a victim by requiring reparations and/or acknowledgments by the offender in addition to or in lieu of punishment by the system.

Retrospective goals: What one says one's goals were after a conflict episode ends.

Revengeful forgiveness: Forgiving only after one has hurt the one who hurt you.

Reward power: Power derived from one's ability to provide benefits to others.

Rights-based: Decision-making or resolution criteria based on legal or other institutionalized rights (see adjudication).

Role: A function performed by an individual.

Role emergence: The process in relationships or groups where individuals choose to adopt particular task or maintenance roles.

Root culture: The cultural group a person was born into or received the most influence from as a child.

S

Scarce resources: Anything perceived to be in short supply.

Schema: A personally constructed attitudinal pattern or frame that affects how one selects and interprets stimuli.

Selective attention: Focusing only on those things that one expects to see or hear; consciously or subconsciously attending to particular stimuli and forgoing other stimuli.

Selective exposure: Focusing on or actively seeking sources of information or input while simultaneously limiting or eschewing other sources of information, usually with the result of reinforcing previously held opinions.

Selective perception: The process of filtering out input during the perception process or focusing only on what one expects to see.

Self-actualization: From Maslow's hierarchy of needs, the drive an individual has to reach or actualize one's potential.

Self-concept: A relatively stable set of perceptions, values, attitudes, and beliefs an individual holds about oneself.

Self-construal: A view of oneself; how people construct their personal cultural identities.

Self-determination theory (SDT): Examines how motivation, as influenced by both environment and one's internal state, is related to need satisfaction.

Self-identity: One's view of oneself.

Self-serving bias: In attribution theory, where one ascribes motivations for personal behavior to a personal character trait when it is most flattering and to situation constraints to diminish personal responsibility (the precise opposite of how motivations are attributed to others).

Semi-apologies: A statement that has the form of an apology without taking responsibility for the action that caused the offense.

Sense-making: The process by which individuals weave together facts, feelings, and inferences to explain the world.

Settlement range: The area of overlap between negotiators' offers.

Silent forgiveness: Forgiving another individual but not telling that person.

Silo mentality: Only talking to or seeing the perspective of one's own workgroup.

Sincere apologies: Apologies that are truthful and well-intended.

Social exchange theory: A relational theory suggesting individuals make choices about relationships by evaluating the personal rewards, costs, and expected profits/benefits involved in maintaining that relationship.

Social harmony forgiveness: Forgiving because one believes peace is better than conflict or forgiving to maintain good social relationships.

Socialization/Cultural socialization: Theories that explain differences in behavioral patterns, such as gendered behaviors, as learned through cultural and societal influences.

Social learning theory: A behavioral theory that holds that individuals learn what attitudes and behaviors are appropriate through observation and social interaction.

Social networks: Relationships with others outside of a primary relationship.

Social styles model: Interpersonal styles identified by trained observers along assertiveness and responsiveness dimensions.

Spiral of silence theory: As one opinion gains public traction, those in opposition lessen their input.

Splitting the difference: A negotiation tactic to compromise and settle at the midpoint between two offers.

Spousal discrepancy theory: Theorizes that couples with vastly different personalities have more distress than couples whose personalities are more alike.

State anger: Anger caused by a momentary state of mind or a situation that will abate (the opposite of trait anger).

State forgiveness: Forgiveness based on a specific situation (see also trait forgiveness).

Stereotype: A generalization that ascribes the same characteristics to all members of a group.

Stereotype confirmation: Individual evidence of observed behaviors that seem to prove a stereotype correct.

Stonewalling: Refusing to discuss a topic to protect oneself from disclosing disadvantageous information or facing negative consequences.

Storming: The conflict phase of group development.

Structure: The external framework, rules, setting, and processes in which a conflict occurs.

Style: A person's habitual and/or preferred way of operating in the world (see conversational style and personality style).

Substantive goals: Goals around tangible resources.

Summarizing: A short recap of the main points in a conversation.

Symbol: A word, gesture, or picture than stands for something else.

Systems theory: A theory that highlights the complex nature of life and holds that the interdependency of all the relationships among individuals in a system, as well as the surrounding environment, must be considered to understand the whole.

T

Taboo: A forbidden behavior or topic.

Tag question: A powerless form of speech that ends a statement with a question (e.g., "doesn't it?").

Taking value: Claiming resources or credit for solutions; depleting value that previously existed.

Task role: A role assumed to promote movement toward accomplishment of a task goal.

Theories: Tentative explanations for observed behaviors.

Third party: In conflict, a person who is not a party to the conflict who assists the conflicting parties to reach a settlement (see arbitration and mediation).

Threat: A tactic promising negative sanctions will occur if the other party does not comply (see coercion).

Tit for tat: A negotiation strategy of doing to the other party what they do to you.

Topic: The general conversational area in which a conflict issue may be embedded.

Toxic secrets: Family secrets that conceal information destructive to one or more family members.

Trait anger: A relatively stable personality style that responds to many situations with anger (the opposite of state anger).

Trait forgiveness: A relatively stable predisposition to forgive (see also state forgiveness).

Transactional model: The idea that communication occurs as a simultaneous, complex process.

Transactional process: A simultaneous, ever-changing, interactive flow of communication.

Transformation: Moving from one state or condition to another; changing a key element that sustains a conflict.

Transformational leadership: Leadership at the vision and overall goal level of the organization (as opposed to transactional leadership, which focuses on the accomplishment of goals).

Trust: The belief that another person is dependable, consistent, and will do what is promised.

Truth and reconciliation process: Typically, a large group effort to admit facts about past harms to a group, accept responsibility, and begin a reconciliation process.

U

Unearned privilege: The taking of a social or other advantage on the basis of social ranking.

Unforgiveness: The active state of recalling and reliving a past hurtful event.

Universal team approach: A strategy to move competitive situations to cooperative situations by putting everyone on the same team rather than on opposing teams.

Unmet ideals hypothesis: Satisfaction decreases when communication does not match one's ideals for what communication should be.

V

Validating/Validation: Recognizing the other person's thoughts or feelings without agreement or criticism (see empathic listening, emotional paraphrase, and feeling paraphrase).

Values: Deeply seated beliefs and core ideas about right and wrong.

Variable: A specific trait, behavior, factor, or pattern isolated for investigation.

Verbal aggressiveness: Ultra argumentativeness using personal attacks, name-calling, and other aggressive tactics.

W–Z

Whiteness: A concept surrounding unearned social and other privileges taken on the basis of race.

Winner's curse: Being victorious in a negotiation, but paying too much or not really wanting the outcome.

Withdraw-complain cycle: A pattern where one party avoids contact with the other person involved in the conflict, but talks about the conflict or complains about it to other people.

Worldview: An overarching set of beliefs about how the world works and one's place in it.

XYZ-type feedback: A feedback technique using the formula "When you do X, in Situation Y, I feel Z." Specific and concrete behavioral descriptions are inserted for X and Y.

Zero-sum: A distributive view that resources are limited. As they are allocated, the amount of resources left ultimately will reach zero.

Index

Note: Page numbers in bold tables.